Company Men

Company Men

*The Invention of Shareholder Value and the
Splintering of the American Economy*

SEAN DELEHANTY

THE UNIVERSITY OF CHICAGO PRESS   CHICAGO AND LONDON

The University of Chicago Press, Chicago 60637
The University of Chicago Press, Ltd., London
© 2025 by Sean Delehanty
All rights reserved. No part of this book may be used or reproduced in any manner whatsoever without written permission, except in the case of brief quotations in critical articles and reviews. For more information, contact the University of Chicago Press, 1427 E. 60th St., Chicago, IL 60637.
Published 2025

34 33 32 31 30 29 28 27 26 25   1 2 3 4 5

ISBN-13: 978-0-226-82718-6 (cloth)
ISBN-13: 978-0-226-84370-4 (ebook)
DOI: https://doi.org/10.7208/chicago/9780226843704.001.0001

This book was prepared by Sean Delehanty in his personal capacity. All opinions are the author's own and do not reflect official positions or statements of the US government.

Library of Congress Cataloging-in-Publication Data

Names: Delehanty, Sean Thomas, author.
Title: Company men : the invention of shareholder value and the splintering of the American economy / Sean Thomas Delehanty.
Description: Chicago : The University of Chicago Press, 2025. | Includes bibliographical references and index.
Identifiers: LCCN 2024061810 | ISBN 9780226827186 (cloth) | ISBN 9780226843704 (ebook)
Subjects: LCSH: Corporations—Investor relations—United States. | Stockholder wealth—United States. | Corporate governance—United States. | Corporate profits—United States.
Classification: LCC HD2795 .D44 2025 | DDC 338.50973—dc23/eng/20250217
LC record available at https://lccn.loc.gov/2024061810

TO ALEX AND RILEY, MY TOUCHSTONES, ALWAYS AND FOREVER

Contents

Introduction: The Other Shock Therapy 1
CHAPTER 1.   The Conglomerates 17
CHAPTER 2.   Can the Corporation Survive? 39
CHAPTER 3.   The Fourth Merger Wave 62
CHAPTER 4.   The Reagan Revolution 81
CHAPTER 5.   The Eclipse of the Public Corporation 106
CHAPTER 6.   Give Stock a Chance 137
CONCLUSION: The End of Enron and the Last Man 171

Acknowledgments 187

Notes 191

Bibliography 233

Index 269

INTRODUCTION

The Other Shock Therapy

"The American dream is alive, but fraying."

In August 2019, Jamie Dimon, then the chief executive officer of JPMorgan Chase & Co., delivered remarks on behalf of the Business Roundtable, a lobby group and trade association of CEOs representing 181 of America's largest companies. Dimon was announcing that these major American corporations had agreed that businesses needed to recommit themselves to "continue to push for an economy that serves all Americans." To achieve these ends, the group was urging all American businesses to incorporate a "fundamental commitment to all of our stakeholders"—customers, employees, suppliers, communities, and shareholders—into their operations.[1] This commitment included such elements as compensating employees "fairly," providing them with "important benefits," and treating them with "inclusion, dignity, and respect."

Remarkably, the press release announcing the Business Roundtable's broader conception of corporate citizenship acknowledged that its earlier declaration on the matter, which argued that corporations existed to maximize the value of their shareholders' investments, was mistaken. "Since 1978, Business Roundtable has periodically issued Principles of Corporate Governance," the release read. "Each version of the document issued since 1997 has endorsed principles of shareholder primacy—that corporations exist principally to serve shareholders. With today's announcement, the new Statement supersedes previous statements and outlines a modern standard for corporate responsibility."[2]

The commitment was short-lived. Less than one year after the Business Roundtable renounced shareholder-value maximization, the onset of the COVID-19 pandemic provided an early test of business leaders' true commitment to building "an economy that serves all Americans"—and a total retreat ensued. In December 2020, as the United States stared down an especially grim winter marked by the profound economic and social devastation of the worst days of the pandemic, *The Washington Post* reported that forty-five of the fifty largest companies in the United States had enjoyed hefty profits since pandemic-related shutdowns began in March 2020. Despite commitments to a more inclusive capitalism (and even some firms' explicit promises not to fire workers), these companies redistributed billions of dollars in profits to shareholders in the form of stock buybacks and dividend payments, while laying off more than 100,000 workers.[3] Similarly, CEO pay in the US skyrocketed during 2020, and Americans who owned substantial blocks of stock saw their wealth levels surge, while those on the other side of the economic divide were forced to cope with furloughs, layoffs, or the extraordinary difficulties of living and potentially trying to raise a family while doing the dangerous labor of "essential jobs."[4]

Even when factoring in the effect of wage increases for some essential workers driven by the demand effects of the pandemic and a much-publicized wave of worker activism and organizing, the unequal distribution of wealth generated during the pandemic years was, in historical context, staggering. A 2022 report from the Brookings Institution examined the business decisions of twenty-two of America's largest companies across the retail, fast food, delivery, hotel, and entertainment sectors, which together employed more than seven million so-called "frontline" workers (most of them people of color).[5] Despite the clear hardships caused by the pandemic, twelve of the twenty-two companies in the Brookings report saw their profits grow by billions of dollars during the first twenty-two months of the pandemic, with an average stock price gain of 65 percent.[6] More stark was the report's finding that even companies that lost money during the pandemic and laid off tens of thousands of workers were still able to realize stock market gains. Despite the fact that six of the companies Brookings examined lost a combined total of $13.9 billion over the course of the first twenty-two months of the pandemic and laid off or furloughed at least 350,000 people, these firms were swept up in the bull market of the pandemic years and still experienced an average stock price gain of 31 percent.[7] In total, the twenty-two companies surveyed gained

$1.5 trillion in shareholder value over the course of the pandemic. These firms' workers (at least those who kept their jobs and survived the pandemic) *did* receive some pay raises, but the total value of workers' wage gains amounted to about $27 billion—a little more than half of the $49 billion these same companies paid to their shareholders in the form of share buybacks, and less than half of the $55 billion they issued in dividends.[8] While these wage gains were meaningful for workers, they were quickly eroded by inflation: in real (adjusted) terms, workers likely only experienced a 2 to 5 percent pay increase between January 2020 and October 2021. The continued levels of high inflation after October 2021 meant that these wage gains may have amounted to even less. Indeed, by October 2021, the Brookings report's authors estimated that at least two-thirds of the companies they surveyed did not pay even half of their employees a living wage, which would be the bare minimum needed to provide a dual-income household of four with the basic necessities of life: food, rent, transport, medical care, childcare, and taxes.[9]

The mismatch between corporate leaders' rather forceful denunciation of shareholder primacy as a threat to the "American dream" and their full-throttle pursuit of shareholder value maximization during the COVID-19 pandemic at the expense of the stakeholder groups executives had promised to prioritize only a year earlier underlines how important the issue of corporate purpose has been to understanding the recent political economy of the United States.* American business leaders, along with academics, politicians, and media commentators, have all identified the corporate pursuit of shareholder value maximization as a threat to prosperity, popular acceptance of capitalism, and even democracy itself.[10] Yet, as seen during the COVID-19 pandemic, shareholder value maximization remains a, if not the, core principle of American business.

This situation begs the question of why. Why would American companies so uniformly pursue a business agenda that those organizations' leaders identify as destructive? Or to put it more cynically, why would

---

*A note on terminology: I use the term "manager" to refer to the very highest level of decision-makers within a company, typically the small group of executive officers and their immediate subordinates. Both my sources and other writers use other terms such as "executive" interchangeably with "managers" to describe this small group of corporate leaders. Other authors and sources sometimes favor using a certain term when describing specific topics—i.e., writers uniformly choose to write about "*executive* compensation" as opposed to "*managerial* compensation." In this book, unless specifically noted, I use the terms "executive" and "manager" interchangeably, and choose to favor whatever term is used by my sources when discussing specific topics such as the theory of the firm or executive compensation.

corporate leaders even *bother* to denounce a goal that seems to make them so much money, and to which they clearly remain committed?

These questions are all the more puzzling because, as the Business Roundtable reminded Americans, the decision to formally embrace shareholder value maximization was a choice they made in front of everyone in 1997—as in, not that long ago in the grand history of American industry. Given that the commitment to shareholder value maximization was a relatively recent development in American political economy, why has it proven so powerful and so enduring?

This book provides the answers to these questions by telling the history of the idea that corporations exist to maximize the value of their shareholders' investments—where this idea came from, why corporations chose to adopt it, and what it has meant for Americans. The ascent of shareholder value maximization in the second half of the twentieth century, a process I refer to as the *shareholder value revolution*, fundamentally transformed one of the most important institutions in American life: the publicly traded corporation.[11] The management scholar Gerald Davis described this transformation as a "Copernican revolution," in the sense that one paradigm of understanding the corporation as a durable institution with obligations to society was discredited and supplanted by another centered around the promotion of shareholder value and stock prices.[12]

While it is true that the shareholder value revolution had an enormously transformative effect on American economic life, comparing it to a scientific revolution simplified the role of ideas in this story by overlooking the origins of shareholder value: an idea crafted by economists, then refashioned by corporate raiders, management consultants, and business leaders to serve those groups' respective purposes. A better point of comparison for the shareholder value revolution would be one of history's great political revolutions, like the French or Russian revolutions, in which an ailing *ancien régime* was toppled by a crisis it brought on itself. In the uncertainty that followed, a group of ideologues was able to seize the moment to advance their cause. Like the Jacobins in France or the Bolsheviks in Russia (either of which would loathe being included in this comparison), the finance scholars who formulated the theories behind the shareholder value revolution ultimately met with frustration as they reckoned with the unanticipated consequences of their own success. They watched as their revolutionary allies cut deals with each other, and even with remnants of the old regime, to ensconce themselves in power at the expense of some of the ideals that lay behind the revolution in the first place.

The frustrations these finance scholars faced were borne of the very same abstractions about the nature of the corporation that allowed their work to have such power in the first place. In the academic push to open the "black box" that was the modern business firm—how they work, why some succeed, why others fail—academic economists emptied the box by reinventing it.[13] Shareholder value theorists offered a vision of the corporation as fundamentally a vehicle for financial investment; this amounted to a legal fiction created and financed so that it could generate returns on shareholders' investments that exceeded what the broader marketplace could deliver. To hear these economists tell it, corporations no longer existed primarily to make things, provide jobs, grow internally, or even make profits; corporations existed to generate returns for investors. Offering jobs or making products and services were means to this end—to generating shareholder value.

Accordingly, the entire practice of corporate management could be reduced to figuring out how to organize and finance your company to ensure that it generated returns for your shareholders. Financial economists believed corporate management was all about aligning incentives—that is, designing the proper set of rewards and punishments to ensure that rationally self-interested individuals would work toward the maximization of shareholders' wealth. In turn, the theory held, all of society would prosper.

Economists even offered a new way to understand corporate success. Instead of measuring success by profit margins or sales figures, they could judge success by the movement of a company's stock price: if managers' actions made their firm's price rise, they were creating value for shareholders and on the right track; if the firm's price fell, managers were destroying value and harming their investors.[14]

While these abstract arguments were initially of limited use to the embattled corporate managers of the 1980s and early 1990s, they were tremendously useful to a cohort of upstart investors, consultants, and media figures looking to explain the troubles American firms experienced during these years. By elevating these theories, these same influential actors offered a new direction for American management—one that would in the process also make them incredibly rich. The allure of shareholder value theory to these figures was not found in its elegant mathematics or in the stacks of academic journal articles providing empirical evidence for some of its claims; rather, what made it useful was the ways in which it could seemingly explain the vexations of the 1980s, a bewildering time in American business when companies' stock prices were low, growth was slowing, and aggressive upstarts armed with seemingly unlimited amounts of money were able to threaten once rock-solid companies. With hindsight, historians and economists can now outline how the economic conditions of the 1980s stock market boom and takeover mania were fueled by more than a decade of stagflation brought about by overly expansionary American fiscal and monetary policy in the 1960s and early 1970s, mixed with ill-advised corporate growthsmanship that the US government eventually countered through the shock therapy of Paul Volcker's massive interest rate hikes. But that couldn't be known then. Instead, when Volcker's hikes finally wrung inflation out of the economy in the early 1980s, the pro-Wall Street tax and regulatory policy of the Reagan administration, along with a global liberalization of capital flows, unleashed a horde of newly empowered financiers to menace American firms whose stock prices had suffered through the preceding several years.[15]

Corporate executives and investors of the 1980s had neither the benefit of hindsight nor the patience to sift through the complexities of the past several decades of American political economy; they had other wolves at their door. For those who lived through the 1980s, the world seemed to be turning upside down, and they sought easy-to-understand reasons why and actionable ideas about how to respond. Shareholder value evangelists rose to meet this need, taking a set of abstract but pointed academic arguments and fashioning them into both a diagnosis of American businesses' woes and (conveniently) a potential cure.

Armed with their retelling of shareholder value theory, these figures could claim—with some (albeit limited) degree of truth—that the woes of American business in the 1970s and early 1980s were principally due to corporate managers hoarding money that belonged to shareholders. If this was the problem, then the solution was simple: break managers' hold over their companies and force them to do whatever it took to raise stock prices and give money back to shareholders. Thanks to the work of financial economists, activist investors led by larger-than-life "corporate raiders" such as T. Boone Pickens and Carl Icahn, who made fortunes attempting—rarely successfully—to take over some of the largest corporations in America, could claim that they were simply trying to restore shareholder value that had been destroyed by incompetent managers.[16] A new generation of consultants such as Joel Stern, a former banking executive who had learned the underpinnings of shareholder value theory at the University of Chicago's business school, sold nervous corporate managers on the idea of "restructuring" their businesses around the promotion of shareholder value, a process that often involved layoffs, divestitures, and generous share buybacks and dividend payments to reward investors. These restructuring programs of the 1980s and 1990s redefined success for executives and their subordinates around the promotion of shareholder value.[17] Instead of the celebration of stability and growth associated with American business in the 1950s and 1960s, the shareholder value revolution celebrated the firms that embraced financial risks, downsized, and outsourced nonessential functions in order to focus on "core competencies."[18]

Chief among the theorists who pioneered shareholder value maximization was Michael Jensen a University of Chicago-trained finance professor who, along with his colleague William Meckling, wrote the canonical articles in the field. Jensen split his time between teaching shareholder value maximization to the students of Harvard Business School and working as a consultant to help companies put his ideas into practice. All of this was cheered along by business press outlets such as *Fortune* and by columnists in *The Wall Street Journal*, which together raised the profiles of well-known figures like Pickens and Icahn as well as previously obscure academics like Jensen, making the ideas they were selling all the more appealing to frustrated investors (and, in turn, to corporate managers, who increasingly realized that they would need to find some way to accommodate restless investors).[19]

This process of accommodation between managers and investors cemented the primacy of shareholder value maximization in American business, then and now. Though it was the subject of bitter contestation throughout the 1980s and early 1990s, the maximization of shareholder value was the raison d'être for corporations by the time of the 1997 Business Roundtable declaration. In adopting and promoting this change, managers and investors reached an enormously lucrative accord that brought the shareholder value revolution to a close and smothered some of its most important reformist ideas.[20] Like activist investors and pro-shareholder intellectuals before them, corporate managers in the early 1990s discovered that, rather than being a threat, shareholder value maximization could bring them tremendous financial rewards. In an ironic twist of fate, these managers, with the help of so-called compensation consultants and scores of reformist investors and politicians looking to tie executive pay to corporate performance, were able to harness the energies behind the drive for managerial accountability that powered the shareholder value revolution and use them to help create a system of managerial compensation that provided managers with previously unthinkable amounts of money at very little risk. At the heart of this irony was the issue of executive compensation. As investors and political reformers cheered them on, corporate directors showered managers with ever-larger compensation packages made up of stock options that would supposedly tie managers' pay to the financial performance of their companies. While in theory shifting managers' pay into stock options would force those managers to risk their salaries on the performance of their companies, the simplistic form of options that directors gave to managers allowed those managers to make vast fortunes with very little risk.[21]

While the rise of stock option compensation did nothing to rein in executive pay and very little to meaningfully limit corporate managers' power, it did cement an alliance between corporate managers and their investors that remains to this day the central feature of American corporate life. In this way, the shareholder value revolution did not end with the victory of shareholders over managers, as some scholars have characterized it. Instead it ended with a truce between the two sides that was cemented by stock options. Shareholders agreed to allow managers to run their businesses with little interference, provided managers agreed to focus on keeping stock prices high. As long as managers pledged to focus on the price of their firms' stock, investors allowed them the autonomy to engage in the kind of corporate empire building and, sometimes, socially responsible corporate behavior that shareholder value maximization was crafted to reject. Indeed, the ability of managers to boost their own compensation through manipulation of their options contracts, and investors' willingness to support them, was deeply disheartening for the academic progenitors of the shareholder value revolution. By the early years of the twenty-first century, Michael Jensen himself expressed his disappointment with the outcome of the shareholder value revolution he helped to start, and he criticized corporate managers for paying too much attention to Wall Street.[22] But by this time, the managers and investors who had enriched themselves through their refashioning of the ideas behind shareholder value maximization no longer had any interest in what economics scholars had to say, and the economists' critiques fell on deaf ears.

Though it fell short of its intellectual founders' hopes, the shareholder value revolution was a transformational event in the history of American capitalism. What started as a pessimistic academic critique of mid-century American management and politics was later refashioned by a new generation of corporate managers—helped along by a legion of consultants, reformers, politicians, activist investors, and some entrepreneurial academics—into a political and economic doctrine that elevated the material gain of shareholders above all other reasons for corporate activity in the United States. The bifurcated economy that Americans have experienced in the twenty-first century is a direct result of the decisions taken by business leaders and the support of those decisions in the business press and business education. The gains from this revolution have not simply gone to a small club of corporate elites and wealthy investors; rather, they have benefited a larger group of professionals and workers fortunate or privileged enough to have survived the economic restructuring of the 1980s and 1990s with their careers and 401(k)s intact.[23] The shareholder value revolution has brought these millions of Americans who make up the upper strata of the country's workforce not only a greater amount of wealth, but also increased opportunities to work in creative and personally fulfilling fields.[24] However, for the majority of American workers, especially those already excluded from the benefits of the New Deal order, the shareholder value revolution has led to lower wages and even less job security.[25] While the American economy as a whole is more prone to disruptive shocks thanks to business leaders' decisions to embrace risk as part of their drive for greater financial profits, the beneficiaries of the shareholder value revolution have proven that they are far better equipped to handle the fallout from any economic downturn than those who were displaced by the rise of shareholder value maximization.[26]

The Separation of Ownership and Control

If the American corporation was the setting of the shareholder value revolution, then it is necessary to (at least to some degree) understand the history of its development through the first half of the twentieth century. Though corporations are structured as bureaucratic hierarchies, they typically operate along patrimonial lines, especially at managerial levels. The hierarchical structure of almost every large business in the United States ensures that decisions about corporate strategy are reserved for a very small group of people, namely the CEO and high-ranking executives in consultation with a firm's board of directors.[27] This means that the decisions to adopt shareholder value maximization were made by a very small group of elite managers, most of them White men who were often trained in a small group of elite educational institutions.[28] Thanks to the social and institutional organization of American corporations, these elites were also the primary audience for—i.e., implementers of—managerial decisions. As the sociologist Robert Jackall showed in his study of corporate managers, to move up in the corporate hierarchy an ambitious lower-level manager had to win the favor of an influential patron who could shepherd that manager up the corporate ladder.[29] As is often the case in patrimonial organizations, managers' status was highly contingent, regardless of their rank.[30] Any perceived failures or weaknesses on a rising manager's part could lead to a loss of favor, reassignment to a dead-end position, or even termination. Accordingly, a great deal of managerial work was performative in nature. Ambitious managers at every level had to project an image of hard work, loyalty, and success while also appealing to the specific interests and styles of those above them in the hierarchy, especially the CEO.[31]

Meanwhile, CEOs performed their leadership roles for an audience of their fellow chief executives, investment analysts, and media outlets.[32] CEOs perceived as successful leaders could often win appointments to corporate boards, more lucrative job offers from other firms, and, for a few superstars, even celebrity status.[33] Despite the intentions of some of its earliest champions, the shareholder value revolution did not change the fact that managers still exerted firm control over the nation's businesses. The rise of shareholder value maximization did force managers to perform for an expanded audience of powerful shareholders and investment analysts as well as their fellow executives, but in return for this increased attention to shareholders managers were allowed to retain much of the autonomy they had won over the past century.[34]

Because of the inherent elitism in American management, the attitudes of the general public—or any dissenting voice, for that matter—counted for relatively little to the champions of shareholder value maximization. The shareholder value revolution was not a battle for public opinion, at least not in any traditional sense. Champions of shareholder value had to convince high-level managers, and the media, legal, and financial figures who came into close contact with them, of the wisdom (or monetary value) of subscribing to their arguments. By contrast, these figures put little effort into convincing middle- or working-class Americans of the righteousness of their cause, because there was almost nothing those people—few of whom owned any meaningful share of ownership in large corporations—could do to affect the course of the shareholder value revolution. Insofar as broad public opinion mattered to the course of the shareholder value revolution, it operated as a sort of boundary-setting force. If executives and financiers pushed too far beyond the bounds of what the public felt was acceptable political or ethical behavior, they risked legal or political blowback in the form of either enhanced scrutiny from regulators or law enforcement, or legislative action that could rein in their behavior.

Despite the shareholder value revolution being mostly fought out in the rarefied world of corporate boardrooms and business school lecture halls, the specter of political action did hang over the heads of those involved. Nervous corporate executives needed only to look back to the 1930s, when the long-running worries about the rise of massive publicly traded corporations and uncertainties about managers' obligations to their shareholders and American society prompted massive political change. In 1932, Adolph Berle, a law professor at Columbia University and a member of President Franklin Roosevelt's brain trust, and Gardiner Means, an economist at Harvard University, published *The Modern Corporation and Private Property*, a landmark study of the legal challenges posed by the growth of large corporations. The work is widely considered to be the founding text of corporate legal studies.[35] When they were writing it, Berle and Means believed they were witnessing the end of three centuries of progressive corporate evolution, from the individual proprietorships of the seventeenth century to the massive widely owned corporations of their own moment.[36] In Berle and Mean's telling of corporate history, the driving force behind this evolutionary change was what they described as the "separation of ownership from control."[37] The authors defined owners as anyone who was "*in a position* both to manage an enterprise or delegate its management and to receive any profits or benefits which might accrue," while managers were those who "operated an enterprise, presumably in the interests of the owners."[38] By the time Berle and Means were writing, the nation's largest corporations each had hundreds of thousands, if not millions, of individual shareholders (owners), each of whom in turn might have owned stock in several different companies.[39] Since ownership was so fragmented, it was effectively impossible for shareholders to exercise any meaningful form of control over the corporations they nominally owned. Shareholders may still have elected corporate managers and occasionally voted on major decisions each year at a company's annual meeting, but individual shareholders lacked the information, voting power, and ability to coordinate among themselves that were needed to have any meaningful influence over corporate decisions. The separation of ownership from control, Berle and Means argued, was total and complete. Shareholders had the symbolic trappings of ownership (in the form of their stock certificates) and retained legal claims to the corporation's profits in the form of dividends, but almost all power over corporate decision-making and the responsibility for those decisions rested in the hands of the managers of the nation's large corporations, and those managers could use their power in whatever way they saw fit.[40]

The separation of ownership from control was truly revolutionary because it prompted corporate managers and intellectuals to rethink the position of the corporation in American society—as a social actor, like people and governments. The sheer size of the nation's largest corporations, and the resulting power they held over the nation's economic future and the lives of its citizens, prompted many Americans to think of these corporations not just as businesses, but as social institutions.[41] For those who adhered to it, the idea of modern corporations as social institutions meant that these businesses were no longer truly private enterprises that existed solely to make money; instead, they were durable pillars of the nation's social order, responsible for creating not only private wealth, but also public goods such as stable employment, labor peace, and investment in both communities and technological innovation.[42] This idea of businesses as social institutions also prompted a reexamination of the role of business managers. Here again, the issue of managerial accountability reared its head. With the visible hand of management directing the nation's economy by the 1930s, and with antitrust laws doing seemingly nothing to prevent the creation of giant corporations, business managers appeared to have amassed a tremendous amount of economic power.[43] In a nation with as deep a tradition of scorning excessive concentrations of economic or political power as the United States, this was especially problematic, given that corporate managers seemed to be accountable to no one.

To address this problem, legal theorists and some of the nation's leading corporate executives, including Owen Young of Radio Corporation of America and Gerald Swope of General Electric, refashioned older ideas of welfare capitalism into a doctrine of managerial social responsibility that would form the core of what would later be termed corporate social responsibility (CSR).[44] These early proponents of CSR claimed that corporate managers had the legal right to consider more than just their shareholders' interests when making corporate decisions, and that managers should use the broad authority they possessed to promote the social and economic well-being of the nation. Instead of focusing on the interests of shareholders alone, socially responsible managers would seek to balance the interests of shareholders with those of their employees, customers, and communities.[45] By embracing socially responsible behavior, managers would be able to alleviate the problems of democratic legitimacy posed by the rise of large corporations. Socially responsible managers would not be the kind of "economic autocrats" that people like Berle and Means warned about; instead, they would be a form of economic civil servants who earned the immense power they held over the lives of their fellow Americans by promoting the public good.[46]

These ideas—of the corporation as a social institution and of managerial social responsibility—were empowered by President Franklin Roosevelt's New Deal.[47] While many of the nation's business leaders were skeptical of, if not outright opposed to, the New Deal, all but a reactionary fraction of corporate leaders were forced to find ways to accommodate it thanks to Roosevelt's political popularity and the business community's own lack of popular support in the midst of the Depression.[48] As business leaders begrudgingly began to accept things like unions, they also embraced ideas of social responsibility, out of either a form of *noblesse oblige* or a more cynical desire to cut off momentum for further government regulation by voluntarily providing benefits to workers and communities.[49] This process of accommodation created an implicit bargain between government and business that formed the core of managerial capitalism.[50] The terms of this bargain allowed for corporate managers to maintain the bulk of their vast power over the nation's largest businesses, while imposing in return an expectation that managers would accept industry-wide regulation and pledge to balance the interests of workers and communities with the interests of their shareholders. The American participation in World War II gave business managers the opportunity to prove their commitment to socially responsible behavior, and business managers rose to the challenge by taking a leading role in organizing the nation's wartime production efforts. After the war, the nation's corporate giants were credited with helping to propel the Allied forces to victory, and business managers won newfound public esteem and government support for both their patriotism and their organizational prowess. In this new, more business-friendly political environment, managerial control over the nation's businesses became more acceptable to the public.[51] Managers themselves even began to be celebrated as one of the nation's most important strategic assets, especially since the nascent Cold War between the United States and the Soviet Union was likely to be fought as an economic contest as much as a political or military one.[52]

Managerial capitalism flourished under the postwar New Deal order, and it served as one of the most important pillars of the New Deal social contract. With political leaders willing to accept managerial control over the economy, and the public seemingly tolerant of big business's place in American society, corporate managers were able to embrace their new identity as socially responsible corporate statesmen. During the two decades after the end of the Second World War, business managers set about creating many of the most recognizable hallmarks of the New Deal order. In return for loyalty, corporate managers offered their workers the prospect of lifetime job security, predictable and steady wage increases, and fringe benefits for both workers and their families and communities.[53] Within communities themselves, corporate managers sponsored public goods such as educational and cultural institutions as well as civic organizations. In keeping with the nation's commitment to Keynesian macroeconomic orthodoxy, the dominant corporate goal in this period was growth, and managers often sought to maximize revenue or the overall size of their corporations, two metrics that ultimately had little connection to shareholders' return on investment.[54] Politically, managers sought to maintain labor peace within their own organizations, while also agreeing to serve on government commissions and offering their services as high-ranking civil servants when called upon by political leaders. For almost thirty years, corporate managers were able to do their part to ensure that Americans enjoyed rising standards of living and the fruits of what seemed like unprecedented technological advancement.[55] Despite these real successes, the postwar economy had no shortage of critics from both the Right (which claimed that regulation, strong unions, and a lack of competition were choking off innovation) and the Left (which decried the homogenizing aspects of corporate life and the antidemocratic nature of concentrated economic power). However, the economic growth of the 1950s and 1960s did much to paper over this dissent and produce an uneasy truce in which Americans expressed their contentedness with corporations' place in society.[56]

Underneath this façade of consensus, however, there were several serious problems with the New Deal order. By far the greatest failure of the New Deal order was that it was not accessible to most Americans. Like the New Deal itself, the postwar industrial social contract excluded women and people of color, especially Black Americans, while embracing and serving White men and their families.[57] The stable jobs marked by lifetime tenure, rising wages, and opportunities for advancement that were the bedrock of the New Deal order were only open to White men who possessed some minimal amount of education and either already lived in areas where large corporations were hiring or had the means to move to those locations. If large corporations did hire women or racial minorities at all, they almost always hired members of these groups as low-level clerical or support staff and refused to extend to them the same benefits and opportunities they gave to White male employees.[58] Even among this privileged class of White male workers the extent of workplace benefits in this time period can often be overstated, given the fact that the practice of replacing employees with temporary workers dated back to the 1950s and large companies were more than willing to relocate operations in an effort to break unions.[59] The managerial class itself was almost exclusively made up of White men, who, at their best, often only embraced cautious programs of racial integration or sexual equality in their workplaces.[60] In economic terms, the dazzling prosperity of the postwar years obscured the fact that, as European and East Asian nations rebuilt themselves from the devastation of the Second World War over the course of the 1950s and 1960s, American firms were increasingly being subjected to a degree of foreign competition that many had never experienced before.[61] While new forms of competition were a challenge in and of themselves for American businesses, the rise of global competition in the 1960s was especially problematic because such economic features of the New Deal order as lifetime employment relied on predictable and endless economic growth.[62] If American companies could not find ways to either keep growing or continuously improve the efficiency of their existing operations, the very foundation of both managerial capitalism and the New Deal order was in danger of falling away.

Despite the dangers posed by the rise of foreign competition and the questionable efficiency levels of large American businesses, managers did not abandon their quest for growth in the 1960s. Instead, they pushed the logic of postwar growthsmanship to its extremes. Having already exhausted opportunities to grow by expanding into new markets, American firms chose to grow by merging with each other.[63] Fueled by a stock market bubble and the expansionary fiscal and monetary policies of the Kennedy and Johnson presidencies, American businesses were swept up in what was to that point the largest wave of mergers and acquisitions in the nation's history.[64] The most visible products of this merger wave were the massive combinations of unrelated businesses known as conglomerates. These conglomerate firms were the apogee of managerial capitalism.

Conglomerate managers promised their investors that they, by virtue of their managerial expertise, could create a diversified and efficient collection of businesses that would deliver constant growth while being virtually immune from economic downturns like recessions. Many investors, media commentators, and academics believed these promises and predicted that the conglomerates represented the future of American business. Unfortunately, the conglomerates did not live up to these expectations. When an economic downturn arrived at the end of the 1960s and helped put an end to the decade's bull market, it revealed that most conglomerates were gravely inefficient and mismanaged. As these businesses began to collapse under their own weight and the full extent of their wasteful and even fraudulent behavior was revealed, investors, politicians, and the press turned on conglomerates and the people who ran them with a vengeance. Within the span of only a few short years, the conglomerates went from being seen as the future of managerial capitalism to being considered the symbol of everything that was wrong with it.[65] Their downfall discredited managerial capitalism, as it revealed that corporate managers were neither trustworthy protectors of their shareholders' investments nor the socially responsible stewards of the public good the nation could count on to steer it through economic difficulties. As the 1970s began, critics from both the Right and the Left identified the corporation as an institution in dire need of reform, and for the first time since the 1930s the place of the corporation in society became a deeply contested issue.

The New Deal order broke apart amid overlapping political, economic, and corporate crises in the late 1960s and 1970s. The shareholder-centric economy that emerged from its ruins, which persists to this day, was formed through a long and bitterly contested process that balanced the interests of financial economists, management consultants, activist investors, and (eventually) business managers. Given the harms shareholder value maximization has caused in the decades since, the Business Roundtable was right to identify it as a threat to the "American dream" of economic opportunity and social mobility, even if its members have done little to address this threat. The shareholder value revolution fundamentally reshaped one of the most important institutions in American life. Its story blends intellectual and business history to show how ideas about the corporation transformed American capitalism. To understand this transformation, this book begins with the spark that set off the shareholder value revolution: the conglomerates.

CHAPTER ONE

The Conglomerates

The shareholder value revolution began with a letter. On January 22, 1968, Litton Industries, one of the most well-respected members of a group of relatively new, highly diversified corporations known as conglomerates, sent an open letter to its shareholders announcing the first drop in quarterly earnings in the company's fourteen-year history.[1] This first sign of weakness in one of the nation's leading conglomerates helped to spark a massive crisis of confidence in the business community as investors began to express their doubts about the value of diversification.[2] Prior to Litton's announcement, many business leaders, investors, and economists believed that the conglomerates were the future of American business. The people who ran the conglomerates appeared to represent the best of postwar scientific management, and over the course of the 1960s they had assured investors that they could combine seemingly unrelated companies into a well-balanced and fully integrated corporate structure that would be impervious to the kinds of cyclical downturns and competitive pressures that bedeviled more traditional businesses. For their part, investors happily believed these assurances, and from 1965 to 1969 the nation's businesses were swept up in what was known as the Third Merger Wave, with both the conglomerates and their most established rivals engaging in a frenzy of mergers and acquisitions.[3] Litton's earnings drop proved to be the first sign that the conglomerate bubble was about to burst, and it was followed by two years of continuous bad news for the conglomerates, including government investigations, falling profits, and growing hostility from the general public. By the end of the decade, the conglomerate movement had fallen into a mess of inefficiency and waste that helped to turn public opinion against managers and business in general. In doing so, the fall of the conglomerates dealt a fatal blow to the credibility of managerial capitalism and helped to clear the way for shareholder value maximization's ascent.

Despite their importance to the American economy, the new breed of conglomerates associated with the Third Merger Wave have received little attention from business historians. Despite the sheer size of the Third Merger Wave—which in terms of number of merger transactions was larger than the takeover wave of the 1980s—historians have largely missed the historical significance of the relative handful of emerging conglomerates that briefly seemed to be at the forefront of managerial capitalism.[4] One difficulty in assessing the legacy of the conglomerates was that, for all of the public attention given to the conglomerates in the 1960s, defining what a conglomerate actually was proved a surprisingly difficult task, since most major American firms embraced diversification in the decades after the Second World War.[5] After the passage of the Celler-Kefauver Act of 1950, which essentially outlawed both horizontal and vertical mergers, growth-hungry American businesses were left with little choice but to seek out merger partners in unrelated industries in their quest for continual earnings growth.[6] By the 1960s, American firms were already locked in fierce competition in domestic markets—including growing competition from foreign rivals—and were quickly exhausting opportunities to expand profitably abroad as well. Though increasing competition was eroding corporate profit growth, most large American business were sitting atop massive reserves of retained earnings generated during the heyday of the postwar boom, and business managers were forced to seek out new ways to profitably invest this surplus.[7] As managers confronted the prospect of diminishing returns on investment in their existing lines of business, they increasingly began to focus on either acquiring rapidly growing firms in unrelated industries or funding internal expansion into unrelated business lines in order to keep generating earnings growth. The historian Alfred Chandler identified this moment as the first time in American history that business managers deliberately chose to diversify into industries in which they possessed no competitive advantage.[8] These diversification activities did provide American businesses with growth opportunities, at least in the short term, and by the end of the

1960s 90 percent of Fortune 500 companies were operating in several different lines of business.[9]

With almost every major American firm engaging in diversification, it was clear that diversification alone was not enough to qualify a company as a conglomerate in the minds of media commentators and investors. For example, General Motors made everything from refrigerators to cars, locomotives, jet engines, and missile guidance systems, yet it was rarely included among the lists of Third Merger Wave conglomerates such as Gulf & Western or Litton Industries.[10] What made the conglomerates distinct was who ran them and how they were put together. The managers of these conglomerates were noticeably younger than executives at more established firms, and many were graduates of the nation's elite MBA programs.[11] Though these young conglomerate builders often had little or no experience with the various businesses they acquired, they claimed that the knowledge of quantitative management techniques they gained in business school equipped them to run any business effectively.[12] These conglomerate builders also possessed a combination of individualistic ethos and grandiose ambition that differentiated them from the "organization man" stereotype prevalent in American business during the 1950s and 1960s.[13] This ambition manifested itself in the way conglomerate managers assembled their companies. Unlike diversified old-line companies like GM or General Electric or even contemporary emerging powerhouses like Xerox, which primarily grew internally sometimes over the course of years or even decades, the conglomerates grew via mergers.[14] Growth by merger allowed acquisitive conglomerates to assemble companies worth hundreds of millions and even billions of dollars in only a few short years by purchasing preexisting businesses. Instead of buying businesses based on their potential for long-term profitability, the conglomerates often chose to acquire businesses that would boost short-term earnings regardless of their long-term prospects. Conglomerate firms also tended to be based in the high-growth technology and defense sectors, which allowed them to take advantage of investors' fascination with technology companies and the federal government's generous military spending during a period of prolonged military buildup.[15] Focusing on mergers in these high-growth sectors allowed conglomerates to emerge seemingly out of nowhere to leap into the ranks of the very largest American companies in a remarkably short time, something that made them both awe-inspiring and threatening.

For all of the admiration and concern they inspired in the 1960s, the conglomerates have mostly been remembered as a fad, a manifestation of the kind of irrational exuberance that often overtakes executives and investors during stock market bubbles.[16] For their part, historians have largely written off the conglomerates simply as failures, something to be mentioned in passing but rarely examined in any great detail.[17] However, there is a great deal that business historians can learn from failures, both from the internal operations of failed businesses themselves and from the narratives contemporaries created to explain failures.[18] Indeed, one of the most important legacies of the conglomerates was how they were used as an example of everything wrong with American business. The historical memory of the conglomerates was largely shaped by the business community itself.[19] Beginning in the 1970s, management consultants, investment bankers, and financial economists, along with sympathetic writers in the business press, held up the conglomerates as an example of the dangers of large, unfocused corporations. The conglomerates were cited as proof that managers, no matter how sophisticated they were, could not tame the power of markets and that corporate efforts to diversify away risk and deliver constant growth by internalizing market functions were doomed to fail. The historian Louis Hyman has argued that the restructuring of American corporations in the final three decades of the twentieth century would not have been possible without the failure of the conglomerates to motivate reform-minded management consultants to offer corporate managers new strategies.[20] Even though many of these critics had supported the creation of the conglomerates during the 1960s, they succeeded in crafting a narrative of the conglomerate wave in which corporate managers took advantage of foolish investors during the 1960s to build inefficient companies to satisfy their own egos as much as anything else.[21] This narrative, in turn, helped to justify the work of investment bankers, management consultants, and activist investors to disassemble the conglomerates and force corporate managers to streamline their operations and focus on core competencies.[22]

Beyond prompting a reevaluation of corporate strategy, Hyman, as well as Neil Fligstein and a handful of other sociologists, have argued that the rise and fall of the conglomerates also spurred the financialization of American businesses. Instead of presenting financialization as a process of structural transformation in which corporations derive more and more of their profits from financial activities, these scholars present financialization as an ideological change whereby corporate executives and investors think of the corporation itself in financial terms.[23] According to these scholars, the conglomerates convinced subsequent generations of managers and entrepreneurial financiers to think of the corporation as a bundle of financial assets to be bought and sold in the pursuit of large personal fortunes.[24] While these arguments do provide valuable insight into the role corporations themselves played in financialization, they require further contextualization.[25] Conglomerate managers and their peers in more established companies did embrace finance in the 1960s, but they did so as a means to traditionally managerialist ends.[26] Beyond an instinctual understanding of the virtues of diversification, conglomerate managers had a limited theoretical understanding of financial markets. Conglomerate-era managers viewed financial markets as tools, sources of funding they could manipulate in order to build the kinds of large, diversified corporations their rivals had built over the preceding decades.[27] Though they used different methods than their more traditional counterparts, conglomerate managers shared the same objectives. Ultimately, conglomerate managers wanted to create companies that could predictably deliver steady growth and employment while bearing as little risk as possible. When the conglomerates began to falter at the end of the 1960s, financial economists, who were some of the conglomerates' earliest and sharpest critics, used their failure to craft an entirely new concept of the business firm that was rooted in financial theory.[28] To finance scholars, the rise and fall of the conglomerates was just the clearest example of managers' inability to harness the power of financial markets to serve their own ends. The very existence of the conglomerates only exposed a much deeper flaw with the prevailing understanding of what a corporation was and what its purpose should be. Financial economists pointed to the conglomerates as evidence that the postwar ideal of a risk-minimizing corporate institution that sought to tame markets in service of balancing the interests of workers, investors, and communities was economically inefficient.[29] Instead, they claimed that corporations were nothing more than legal fictions that existed to generate wealth for shareholders, and that the sole purpose of corporate management was to maximize shareholder value. This financial theory of the firm is what truly brought about the ideological transformation that marked the financialization of the American corporation.[30] The conglomerates brought this about not because the people who built them made such liberal use of finance, but because they failed so spectacularly in doing so. In the wake of their failure, people who did have a deep understanding of financial theory were able to use that knowledge to redefine what a corporation was.

To explore the history of the conglomerates and the legacy of their failure, this chapter examines the story of the one of the conglomerates that rose the highest and fell the furthest: Litton Industries. Litton, a massive defense and technology conglomerate, was founded by some of the nation's brightest young managers, and along with other large conglomerates such as Gulf and Western or International Telephone & Telegraph, it seemed to be at the cutting edge of modern management. During its meteoric rise from 1954 to 1968, Litton embodied a combination of both the respectability of postwar managerialism and the entrepreneurial energy of a high-tech startup as it entered into willing partnerships with dozens of different businesses. At the company's peak, Litton's managers claimed that their mixture of numbers-driven management and loose organizational style could be applied not only to any commercial industry, but also to social problems beyond the business sector such as unemployment or poverty. Litton seemed to represent the newfound ability of American managers to tame the power of markets as the firm harnessed the power of the stock market to purchase new businesses and deliver impressive financial results to investors quarter after quarter.

Unfortunately for Litton and its investors, the company's streak of good fortune did not last beyond the 1960s. By the end of the decade Litton was revealed to be just as disorganized and inefficient as any other big company might have been. As Litton and the other conglomerates began to unravel, investors and media observers turned sharply against them. The excesses of the conglomerate movement and the grandiose promises of the people who assembled the conglomerates, as embodied in the stories of Litton and other organizations like it, discredited not only the conglomerate as a form of corporate organization, but American management itself. Importantly, however, the conglomerates' failure did not discredit some of the methods conglomerate managers used to build their fleeting corporate empires. Though the 1960s ended with a strong public backlash against creatively financed mergers, plenty of entrepreneurial financiers, managers, and lawyers had learned how powerful they could be. With the fall of the conglomerates calling the entire structure of the corporation into question and new financial theories of the firm gestating in the minds of economists, American businesses were poised for another merger wave in the years that followed, one that would elevate shareholders to the center of the nation's political economy.

The Rise and Fall of Litton Industries

Few firms embodied the outsized hopes and bitter disappointments associated with the conglomerate movement better than Litton Industries.

Between 1954 and 1968, Litton grew from a small microwave-tube manufacturer to the fortieth largest company in the United States, with more than 100 different businesses united under the Litton umbrella. Litton's remarkable growth was due in large part to the technology-focused strategy for the company developed by Charles "Tex" Thornton, the company's founder and chairman.[31] Thornton was born in a small Texas farming town in 1913 and his rise to the heights of success he achieved at Litton exemplified the kind of technocratic optimism the conglomerate movement celebrated. Thornton's father, Word Augustus Thornton, abandoned Tex and his mother at an early age and made and lost a fortune in the Texas oil fields before being murdered by a pair of hitchhikers. Tex's mother was determined to raise her son to follow a different path, and when Tex was twelve years old, she encouraged him to work odd jobs so that he could save up money to buy land. By the age of fourteen, Thornton had purchased forty acres of land, and at nineteen he and a friend started a gas station and auto dealership. Thornton used the money he earned from these businesses to attend Texas Technological College, where he majored in business administration. By his junior year Thornton had grown impatient with college, and he chose to drop out and move to Washington, DC, where in 1934 he was hired as a clerk at the Department of the Interior. While working as a clerk and finishing his degree at night, Thornton demonstrated an impressive mastery of statistics and an ability to condense a great deal of numerical information into easy-to-understand summaries. Thornton's statistical skills were on full display in a report he wrote in the late 1930s on low-cost federal housing that was circulated in the federal government and eventually reached the desk of Robert Lovett, a fellow Texan who was serving as the assistant secretary of war for air. Lovett, who was trying to improve the efficiency of the nation's emerging air force, reached out to Thornton and convinced him to join the Army Air Corps as a second lieutenant. Thornton accepted a commission as a second lieutenant in 1941 at the age of twenty-eight, and through a series of rapid promotions he rose to the rank of colonel before the end of the year, becoming one of the youngest people in the military to reach that rank.

With his new command, Thornton established the first program of "statistical control" used by the military.[32] Though Thornton himself described statistical control as "a fancy name for finding out what the hell we had by way of resources and when and where it was going to be required," the technique would become a cornerstone of postwar corporate and government management.[33] Statistical control programs allowed planners like Thornton to map out an entire process, such as a bombing run or the production of an automobile, identify the individual inputs and outputs relevant to that process, and then track the quantity of those elements and their movements across the process. This meant that Thornton and his statisticians were able to tell Lovett exactly how many supplies would be needed to complete the massive buildup that the American Air Force—which was quite small at the onset of the Second World War—required to wage war on several different continents. Moreover, once those new planes were in the air, Thornton's unit calculated the amount of fuel, ammunition, and equipment commanders would need to enable their pilots to fly the maximum number of missions, even factoring in inevitable losses due to mechanical breakdowns and enemy fire. To accomplish this enormous task, Thornton partnered with the Harvard Business School, where he established his headquarters, to train Army officers in statistical control methods. Thornton also recruited Harvard faculty members, including eventual Secretary of Defense Robert McNamara, to join the Army Air Corps as statistical control officers.[34] Once the war ended in 1945, Thornton convinced nine of his best officers, including McNamara, to join together and offer their services as a unit to any company that was interested in hiring them for their statistical expertise. Henry Ford II, who had recently taken over control of the disorganized Ford Motor Company, jumped at Thornton's offer and hired his entire team in 1946. As Thornton, McNamara, and the other eight members of the group swarmed through Ford, collecting data on seemingly everything and peppering their fellow executives with questions, they acquired the nickname that would follow them for the rest of their professional lives: "the Whiz Kids."[35]

Used to being in command, Thornton quickly grew frustrated at Ford, and in 1948 he left the company to work for Howard Hughes as a vice president of Hughes Aircraft. At Hughes, Thornton led a campaign to reorganize the company around high-tech research, including the development of emerging missile technology. While Thornton's efforts did boost Hughes's sales by an impressive amount, he frequently clashed with his fellow executives, who took issue with the amount of money he was spending on research programs and new business lines. In 1953, Thornton chose to leave Hughes to start a company of his own. On his way out the door, Thornton convinced two other Hughes executives—Roy Ash, a statistician with an MBA from Harvard whom Thornton had lured to Hughes from Bank of America, and Hugh Jameson, an engineer—to join him in his new endeavor, which he named Electro Dynamics Corporation. To finance his ambitions Thornton approached Lehman Brothers, one of Wall Street's most prestigious investment banks, for funding. As Thornton later recalled, he told the representatives of Lehman Brothers "that I wanted to start a company that would become a strong blue chip in the scientific and technological environment of the future. It would be a balanced company—not just engineering, not must manufacturing, not just financial. You can't win a ball game with only a pitcher and a catcher, and you can't have a strong company unless it's balanced."[36] Thornton promised that, if Lehman Brothers provided him funding, he would be able to generate $100 million in sales within five years—a wildly optimistic projection that sparked doubts among the partners at Lehman. Even with their doubts about how fast Thornton would really be able to grow his company, Lehman's partners provided Electro Dynamics Corporation with $1.5 million in financing Thornton could use to establish his new company.

When Thornton, Ash, and Jameson surveyed the business landscape of 1953, they believed that the rush of technological advance and economic growth let loose by the end of the Second World War made it necessary to rethink how to build up a company. As Thornton and Ash (Jameson left the company in 1958) explained in a statement to Congress in 1969, "when we were planning the company, it was our belief that this nation was entering a new era of scientific and technological advancement which would far exceed anything in the past. We believed there was an opportunity and a need for new concepts and plans which, in whole or in part, would differ from those of most other industrial companies."[37] To this end, the original three partners decided to use the money they received from Lehman Brothers to grow their company through acquisitions instead of investing in Electro Dynamics itself. The trio decided to purchase a microwave-tube manufacturing company with approximately $3 million in sales located south of San Francisco which was named after its founder, Charles Litton. With the purchase, which was completed in 1954, Thornton decided to change his company's name to Litton Industries, and he moved Litton's headquarters to a stately mansion in Beverly Hills, California. From this base in Beverly Hills, the company embarked on a rapid program of acquisitions, financed with a mixture of cash purchases and stock swaps, that grew Litton from a minor technology firm into a major industrial corporation. By utilizing both the cash they had on hand and Litton's highly valued stock, Thornton and his management team were able to go on a shopping spree for small electronics and technology companies, and Litton successfully purchased six additional companies within fifteen months of Thornton's original acquisition. Fueled by consistent acquisitions, Litton's revenues shot past Thornton's promised $100 million in just three years. Litton's growth leapt forward again in 1958 with the purchase of Monroe Calculating Machine, a calculator company, which had about $40 million a year in sales. The purchase of Monroe won Litton entry to the increasingly lucrative business machines market, and the company sought to capitalize by purchasing several other firms in this market including Svenska Dataregistrar, a Swedish cash register manufacturer with a small market presence in the US. By 1960, Litton's total revenues had reached $188 million—a 6,166 percent increase from the $3 million a year Litton was generating at the time of its acquisition.[38]

Litton was able to achieve these impressive growth figures by following the strategy of acquisitions its founders had crafted in the company's earliest days. The strategy behind Litton's success was one that several other conglomerate firms would emulate over the course of the 1960s, though, as Litton's managers took pride in pointing out, they developed their philosophy "many years before the word 'conglomerate' came to be used to categorize some, but by no means all, multi-industry companies."[39] While Litton's leadership, like almost all corporate managers, bristled at the term "conglomerate" being used to describe their business, Thornton and Ash's statement of their philosophy was a nearly perfect summary of the optimistic promise of managerial superiority that drove so many of the conglomerate acquisitions of the 1950s and 1960s.[40] As Thornton and Ash recalled, "we planned to acquire other companies whose products and future might also benefit from technological innovations and management concepts which we then envisioned or believed would be forthcoming. We believed that it would be necessary for Litton, over a period of years, to become a multi-product, multi-industry company with sufficient resources to support its operations; otherwise its technological development and competitive capability would be materially limited."[41] Acquisitions were central to this strategy since, as they explained, the electronics industry "consisted of a few giants with capability in electronics and a great many small companies. Many of the giants were mostly preoccupied with meeting the pent-up demand for civilian goods following the war and were slow to develop the emerging technologies into useful products. The small companies generally lacked the management and capital resources to do so."[42] In keeping with this observation, Litton focused its acquisitions activity on smaller firms, and as late as 1970 it had never acquired any company with assets greater than $50 million. Litton's role was to give these small companies the management know-how and financial resources necessary to compete against the ponderous large companies that dominated the electronics market.[43] Like other conglomerates who extolled the virtues of synergy, the idea that mergers between companies could create efficiencies that were unavailable to either company individually, Litton's managers claimed that their expertise in marketing and finance, as well as their supposed ability to find cross-applications for new technologies, would allow them to raise the value of each individual company they acquired beyond what that acquisition could ever be worth as an independent entity.[44]

Since none of the contemporary players in the market seemed capable of meeting the rapidly changing demands of consumers, Thornton and Ash believed that the American market needed a new style of corporate organization, one that blended two things that seemed very much at odds: Thornton and Ash's belief in rigorous statistical control and a decentralized management structure. Unlike those corporate "giants" that were too bogged down in bureaucracy to respond to technological developments, Litton was organized to encourage a sense of entrepreneurial dynamism among its various managers. As Ash explained in 1963, "this day of change and opportunity is a time for entrepreneurs, men who can convert opportunities into success. This can't be done by one person or two, or from a central source."[45] The building blocks of Litton's corporate structure were its divisions, each an autonomous business headed by divisional manager responsible for the profits and losses of their unit. In most cases these divisional managers were the same people who had been running that division when it was still an independent company prior to its acquisition by Litton. Divisions operating in similar industries were collected into groups, each headed by a corporate vice president, who reported directly to Litton's executive management at the company's headquarters. Each of these group vice presidents were responsible for supervising their divisional managers, allocating additional capital and professional services to divisions in need of them, and lending their supposed managerial expertise to divisional managers in need of their skill. The company's top executives provided an additional level of management support for both its group vice presidents and its divisional managers in order to "inspire division managers to exhibit personal entrepreneurship, to assume responsibility for results, and to exercise leadership and initiative." As part of this effort, Litton's top executives offered each divisional manager the "broader perspective and strategical planning skills" needed for each divisional manager to set long-term goals for their division.[46] Most important meetings at Litton were done face-to-face, which placed tremendous travel demands on its various managers, and the company's executive management prided itself on being easily available for meetings with group and divisional leaders. Litton took its anti-bureaucratic ethos a step further by actively discouraging its managers from writing things down. As Thornton and Ash explained, "there is hardly anything less productive among executives than writing notes to each other," which they believed served to do little more than offer executives a chance to protect their image. As the company's leaders explained, "in Litton Industries we have little patience with such defensive and nonproductive activity. The man who spends his time writing justification papers in Litton is not likely to be with us very long."[47]

The entrepreneurial, free-wheeling side of Litton existed alongside the company's very demanding system of financial controls, which the company's top managers called a "management information system."[48] This system, which borrowed heavily from the statistical control program run by Thornton and his fellow whiz kids during the Second World War, was overseen by Ash, who was even more numbers-oriented than Thornton and lacked his good-natured personality.[49] Paradoxically, given the company's stated aversion to paperwork, divisional managers were required to submit reports detailing their financial results and progress toward their long-term goals every month. At the beginning of every fiscal year, each divisional manager had to draft a detailed plan of operations and forecast of results for the upcoming year. This yearly plan had to be approved by both the manager's group vice president and Litton's so-called "murder squad" of top executives led by Ash. Even after the murder squad approved a manager's plan, the document had to be updated and revised every three months.[50] Litton's top managers believed their management information system offered the company a powerful advantage over its less sophisticated rivals. As they put it, "although management information systems don't of themselves produce sales or profit, or solve problems, our very extensively developed information system does provide detailed, accurate, and current information by which management actions can be taken, if necessary."[51] Litton's top managers believed that their system allowed them to identify which individual parts of the firm's overall business were struggling so that a team of management experts from higher up in the organization could be dispatched to resolve the issue before it weighed down the company's profits. In this way, Litton could always be

THE CONGLOMERATES   29

one step ahead of the market and effectively outpace both its competition and macroeconomic pressures. Instead of waiting for problems to develop and then trying to respond to them, Litton's future-oriented managers would be able to know when trouble was developing in one of their businesses and to take whatever actions were necessary to avoid it.

For most of the 1960s, Litton seemed to live up to its managers' lofty promises. Between 1960 and 1967 the company's revenues grew from approximately $187 million to $1.56 billion, a 732 percent increase, while its net income grew from $7.46 million to $70 million over the same period.[52] Even more impressively, Litton accomplished all of this without posting a loss in any single quarter before 1968, a winning streak rarely seen in American business. Though Litton's managers self-consciously sought to differentiate their company from the supposedly lethargic firms that made up the nation's corporate establishment, they ran their business largely in keeping with the managerialist spirit of the 1960s. Litton never engaged in a hostile takeover, financed its merger activity through either direct cash purchases or traditional stock swaps, and maintained a conservative level of corporate debt, which made the company's successes between 1960 and 1968 seem all the more impressive.[53] During these years Litton established itself as a major player in the defense industry thanks in part to its internal development of advanced navigation systems for military aircraft. With the military as a reliable customer, Litton was able to fund a rush of acquisitions. Between 1960 and 1968, Litton purchased 104 companies with some combination of cash and stock on its path to becoming the fortieth largest company in the United States.[54] In addition to projecting an image of managerial expertise and dynamism, Litton also actively courted investors through a sophisticated public relations campaign built around the company's glossy annual report, which was distributed to more than 200,000 investors and business leaders in the United States and abroad. The report, which contained little in the way of specifics, was full of optimistic projections about the company's future arranged around an annual theme, some of which included: "man's eternal struggle for freedom," "the era of opportunity," "leadership," and "managing ideas," all of which were intended to give investors an impression of Litton as a powerhouse of innovation and respectability.[55] Between Litton's outreach efforts and the company's seemingly endless growth, investors rewarded Litton with a generous stock valuation. Between the first quarter of 1964 and the last quarter of 1967, Litton's stock price rose from $39 to $120 a share. Litton's valuation of $120 a share at the end of 1967 was nearly fifty times the company's earnings, which represented a tremendous vote of confidence in the ability of Litton's managers to run their increasingly scattered corporate empire even as it continued to expand.[56] For their part, the press also cheered Litton, with the *Los Angeles Times* calling the company "Legendary Litton" in 1963 as part of an admiring profile of the company and its top managers.[57] Litton's management style was held in such esteem that the company's executives were in high demand as other companies sought to emulate Litton's managerial style. The practice of hiring Litton alumni was so widespread by the end of the 1960s that these former Litton executives became known as "Lidos"—short for "Litton Industries Drop Out"—and the sight of a company hiring a Lido was likely to send its stock price higher.[58]

According to Litton's executives, all of the acquisitions the company made over the course of the 1960s somehow adhered to the technology-first strategy Thornton had established at the company's founding, but a close look at the record of Litton's acquisitions revealed several instances where it was nearly impossible to argue that Litton was at the forefront of new technology. During its acquisitions binge, Litton acquired a low-cost office furniture manufacturer, a dental tools business, a typewriter manufacturer whose products were conspicuously outdated when compared to IBM's electronic typewriters, and a photocopier company that manufactured obsolete machines that were a generation behind Xerox's latest offerings.[59] Many of Litton's acquisitions seemed to be motivated as much by often-futile attempts to find synergies with previous acquisitions as by any inherent potential that may have existed in each individual business. An example of this "snowball effect" could be seen in Litton's decision to acquire Stouffer Foods in 1967. Prior to the Stouffer's acquisition, Litton had developed its original microwave-tube technology to support the construction of microwave ovens, a product category Thornton believed was primed for rapid growth. Litton's microwave division competed well in both industrial and commercial markets, but the company's top management wanted to find a way to break into the presumably lucrative home consumer market.[60] To accomplish this, Litton chose to approach Stouffer's, which made frozen food in addition to running a chain of restaurants and hotels, with an acquisition offer in 1966 that was eventually accepted in 1967.[61] The companies justified the merger with a vague appeal to the potentials for synergy that supposedly came from uniting a food company and a microwave company. In a statement to *The New York Times* at the time the merger between Stouffer's and Litton was announced, the two companies claimed that "by coordinating food preparation and electronic cooking, breakthroughs could be achieved in home, commercial, and institutional meal preparation."[62] While this acquisition did not lead to any breakthroughs in the world of microwave cooking, it did lead Litton to get involved in running cafeterias, managing restaurant chains, and constructing new hotels and motels, none of which fit with Litton's image as a high-tech company on the cutting edge of scientific development.[63]

While moves into hotels or office furniture certainly seemed far afield from Litton's original technology focus, those were nothing compared to the company's grandest attempts to apply its managerial techniques to the problems of poverty and international development. In keeping with managerialist commitments to corporate social responsibility, Litton was a major supporter of President Lyndon Johnson's War on Poverty. A Litton vice president named John Rubel, a former assistant secretary of defense, was involved in creating plans for Johnson's Job Corps, which was intended to provide job training for supposedly "unemployable" people. In an internal Litton memo issued in 1964, Rubel proposed applying the same "weapons system" approach the company had used to develop the Polaris submarine missile to the problem of unemployment. Under Rubel's direction, Litton set up both a conservation camp program that would offer opportunities for manual labor, "basic remedial education," and "spiritual revitalization" for young men deemed "unfit for useful work or military service," and job training centers designed to provide vocational training and job counseling for draft rejects who did not require "remedial education."[64] Litton's grandest example of a commitment to corporate social responsibility was the company's choice to diversify into international development, which it termed "nation building."[65] In 1967 Litton reached an agreement with the newly installed military government of Greece under which the company would take the lead on an $830 million development program in the western Peloponnesus and the island of Crete designed to spur both agricultural and industrial development and to create a tourist industry for the island.[66] Though Litton expected to make a profit on the deal, its leadership described its participation in the project in far grander terms than just profitability. In a speech to the Los Angeles Chamber of Commerce in November 1967, Ash claimed that corporate leadership in international development was necessary for the United States to stave off impending crises of overpopulation and hunger that would jeopardize global stability and provide avenues for communist powers to spread their influence.[67] As with Litton's sponsorship of the Job Corps, Ash claimed that the company could apply its "systems management techniques" to the problems of international development in a more effective way than governments ever could. Instead of just saddling the Greeks with impractical development plans or inefficient government aid, Litton would provide Greece with the "capital and know-how" not only to raise economic productivity, but also to infuse the people of Greece with the motivation required to take control of their own destiny and ensure their country's future stability and prosperity.[68]

The mismatch between Litton's various business activities and its high-tech strategy would have mattered little to investors or media observers as long as Litton continued its streak of unbroken earnings growth. Unfortunately for Litton, the company did post its first drop in quarterly earnings at the beginning of 1968, which began a dramatic reversal of fortune for both the company and the broader conglomerate movement.[69] On January 22, Litton sent a letter to its shareholders informing them that the company's earnings would be "substantially lower than planned" largely due to "the result of certain deficiencies of management personnel." When Litton released its actual results at the end of the month things only got worse. Litton's second fiscal quarter earnings for 1968 were $7.2 million, which was a 56 percent drop from 1967 second-quarter earnings of $16.43 million.[70] Though Litton tried to reassure its investors that the company's managerial problems had been addressed and that the company planned to continue its aggressive acquisitions program, these reassurances fell on deaf ears.[71] Litton's stock price went into a free fall, dropping twenty points after the letter was released and eventually falling from an all-time high of $120 per share at the end of 1967 to a low of $67.13 per share by March 1968.[72] The damage was not confined to just Litton's stock either; other major diversified companies also saw their stock prices tumble as investors began to sour on the very concept of conglomerates.[73]

Part of why investors punished Litton so much for its earnings drop was that conglomerate companies were assumed to be immune from large drops in earnings. As *Forbes* asked its readers, "wasn't Litton's diversification supposed to protect it against having any one business seriously hurt over-all profits?"[74] In theory, conglomerates, by virtue of their diversification, were supposed to be able to withstand shortcomings in any handful of their businesses or even the downward pressures of a bear market by balancing any underperforming companies they might have owned with others that could make up for the slack. Litton was supposed to benefit not only from diversification, but also from possessing management sophisticated enough to identify and solve potential problems before they affected earnings. The fact that Litton's executive management purposely cited "deficiencies of management personnel" when explaining why its earnings growth had fallen seemed to directly challenge most observers' belief in the superiority of Litton's management.[75] For whatever it was worth, the inclusion of that acknowledgment of management problems in the letter was likely a veiled jab at William McKenna, a former Litton vice president who, before leaving the company to become president of Hunt Foods, had headed the company's business equipment group, which had accounted for a good deal of the drop in earnings.[76] While Litton's top managers may have intended their language about managerial deficiencies to be a way of settling scores with McKenna, investors interpreted it as a more general confession that Litton's managers were not up to the task of running the company. Almost nothing could have been more disastrous for Litton than this. On paper, Litton was little more than a collection of increasingly dissimilar companies. The reason investors once valued this collection of companies at fifty times their combined earnings was that they believed Litton's management possessed a unique ability to weave these companies together in a way that would make the whole far more valuable than the sum of its parts.[77] If this was not the case, as Litton's management seemed to be acknowledging, then there was little reason for the conglomerate to exist in the first place.[78] If conglomerates offered nothing more than a diversified "portfolio" of companies for investors to purchase, they were unnecessary, since it was far more efficient and less expensive for an investor to simply invest in a diversified portfolio of companies on their own than for someone to construct a conglomerate in order to offer investors the benefits of diversification. Conglomerates could only be justified if managers could truly create synergies and dramatically improve companies' operations through advanced management systems. If not, they had little reason for existence.

    A look at the factors that depressed Litton's earnings at the beginning of 1968 revealed that, in many cases, Litton's management could not create the kind of synergies or efficiencies that were central to their stated reason for existence. It is important to note, as Litton's managers often did, that several labor strikes at Litton plants contributed to Litton's earnings shortfall in 1968—but strikes, even when combined with a general decline in stock prices at the beginning of 1968, did not explain the extent of the drop.[79] Instead, the dramatic reversal in earnings growth was related to problems with several of Litton's more questionable acquisitions. Many of Litton's most problematic businesses were in the firm's business equipment group, which included the company's office furniture division as well as its calculator, typewriter, and fax machine units. As noted above, these businesses were not at the cutting edge of technology, and they mostly sold outdated and inferior products in very competitive markets, often with small market shares. Litton justified its acquisition of these companies by claiming that the company could create synergies among these different businesses and that its systems management approach would enable these businesses to better compete against industry rivals. By 1968, reality had caught up to Litton's optimistic projections. Instead of transforming its office furniture or copy machine businesses into high-tech dynamos, Litton was simply stuck with poorly performing companies that had changed very little since they were first acquired.[80]

Litton's dismal performance running a shipyard demonstrated better than anything else the gulf between the company's optimism and the more conventional—sometimes disreputable—ways the company actually operated. In 1961 Litton acquired the Ingalls Shipyard in Pascagoula, Mississippi, which represented a move into an industry that was, according to Litton's executive leadership, "as moribund as any" in the United States.[81] To offset the cost of the acquisition, Litton's management convinced the state of Mississippi, which was desperate for economic development, to give the company free rent for five years and to finance, by floating a $130 million bond, the construction of a cutting-edge modular shipbuilding facility at Ingalls that would allow for the mass production of ships, while Litton invested only $3 million.[82] Before Litton had even constructed a single ship at its new facility, the Navy awarded the company two contracts, and thanks to the generous terms of Navy contracts—one Litton vice president explained that when working with the military, "your chances of losing money are not too great"—Litton was able to overlook serious problems with the shipyard, including high labor turnover and an ineffective cadre of shipyard managers sent from other divisions within Litton who often had no experience in the industry.[83] When Litton did try to increase its production volume in 1964 and 1965 with large civilian contracts, the problems that had dogged the company in previous years became harder to ignore, and the shipyard was beset by cost and production overruns. Even as Litton's management privately acknowledged in 1967 that the Ingalls shipyard was not competitive with other defense contractors such as General Dynamics, the company continued to solicit large contracts from the Navy and civilian buyers.[84] Litton's inability to keep up with these contracts proved costly. A substantial portion (nearly $8 million) of the company's earnings shortfall in early 1968 was due to a write-off the company took in response to cost overruns related to a contract it won for fourteen cargo freighters.[85] Even after Litton's management confessed to some of the problems at the Ingalls shipyard, the company continued to fall behind schedule in its major contracts with the Navy; eventually, in 1970, the Navy cancelled a large order for helicopter landing ships even though it was forced to pay Litton a $109.7 million "cancellation fee." As late as 1972, Litton was still months behind schedule for its major shipbuilding contracts. Even after several government investigations into its operations, including a Defense Department audit that discovered that Litton had fraudulently billed the Pentagon for $7 million in work it had done on unrelated projects, the company continued to muddle along in the shipbuilding business and to win Navy contracts.[86] While Litton's many shortcomings were apparently not enough to scare off military procurement officers, they did highlight many of the endemic problems that Litton and other conglomerates faced, including over-hyped claims about technological innovation and efficiency; sometimes inept management that had little understanding of the businesses they were running; and cozy relationships with the government—especially the military—that allowed the conglomerates to grow despite their obvious inefficiencies.

Once Litton had lost its sheen of invincibility at the beginning of 1968, investor and media opinion swiftly turned against the company. In the months that followed the release of its letter, Litton was battered by a series of media profiles that voiced deep skepticism about the company's prospects while quoting several former executives who were frustrated with the company's top management, and particularly with Ash.[87] Litton's struggles continued into 1969. At the beginning of the year, Richard McLaren, who had been appointed assistant attorney general in charge of antitrust enforcement by the newly inaugurated President Richard Nixon, announced that he would seek to expand antitrust enforcement to block conglomerate mergers, which further dampened investors' enthusiasm for conglomerate companies.[88] Litton itself ran afoul of the Federal Trade Commission, which sued to block its acquisition of two German typewriter manufacturers in April 1969.[89] In May, the company was strongly criticized by Senator William Proxmire (D-WI) for its practice of hiring Defense Department officials as soon as they left their jobs in the Pentagon and then putting them in charge of military contracts.[90] In October, Litton and the Greek government mutually agreed to scrap its international development contract after Litton was unable to raise the funds it had promised for the first round of projects; as *The New York Times* reported, both parties "privately agreed that the idea of entrusting regional economic development to private enterprise had failed."[91] In December, *Forbes* published a scathing profile of Litton, titled "Litton's Shattered Image," which argued that, apart from Litton's genuine, internally developed successes in the defense market, the company was mostly a collection of obsolete technologies acquired from other people and showed little ability to continue to innovate. As the article stated, "none of this is to say that Litton is a bad company. Its top people are able, dedicated and shrewd. Litton's trouble is that it has oversold itself. It simply never was worth 46 times earnings. But it has compounded its problem by continuing to talk as if it were."[92] Investors seemed to agree with this assessment, and by the end of 1969, Litton's stock was selling for below $40 per share, which represented a loss of about $2 billion in market value from the company's high in 1967. Litton had enough assets and managerial skill to remain profitably in business, but as the *Los Angeles Times* put it in December 1969, "the market magic of Litton itself is gone, at least for now. The veil has been lifted."[93] Instead of viewing Litton and its managers as the way of the future, investors had decided that Litton was just another company run by people who were perhaps talented, but not special—a judgment they had increasingly extended to other conglomerates as well.

"America the Inefficient"

The Third Merger Wave itself came to an end not long after Litton's fall from grace. Investors' growing skepticism about conglomerates in the wake of Litton's downfall combined with reinvigorated antitrust litigation, a paperwork crisis on Wall Street that crippled the nation's leading brokerages, and the onset of a recession had by the end of 1969 placed a dramatic curb on further merger activity.[94] The economic slowdown, in turn, exposed even more of the problems associated with the conglomerate movement and American management as a whole.[95] In June 1970, the Penn Central Railroad, the nation's sixth largest company, fell apart in what was to that point the largest bankruptcy in American history. Penn Central was itself a product of the Third Merger Wave, formed in a merger of the New York and Pennsylvania Railroads in 1968—the largest merger in American history at the time.[96] Prior to its bankruptcy and bailout by the US government, Penn Central had attempted to emulate the conglomerates by diversifying into several non-railroad businesses including hotels and real estate.[97] As the company fell apart, government regulators and investigative reporters discovered that it was plagued with catastrophic mismanagement, including allegations of fraud and insider trading.[98] After two years of bad publicity for American managers on the heels of Litton's fall from grace at the beginning of 1968, the Penn Central bankruptcy served to reinforce a growing distrust of managers across broad swathes of the American public.[99] As *The New York Times* put it, "the wreck of the Penn Central is much more than a railroad story. It is the story of much that is wrong with the American corporate structure, with regulatory agencies, and with the existing 'partnership' between business and government. It reveals the inadequate representation of stockholder and broad public interests within great corporations and within self-regulatory bodies, such as New York Stock Exchange."[100]

Penn Central's demise was a spectacular coda to the Third Merger Wave; though Penn Central did not survive the onset of the 1970s, most conglomerate firms did. Beyond the select group of high-profile conglomerates like Litton, most large companies had diversified over the course of the 1960s, and the American economy was dominated by large collections of disparate businesses. Unfortunately for these companies, by 1970 the image of any widely diversified company, whether it had been considered a conglomerate or not, was read as shorthand for everything wrong with American business, and the years that followed would be no kinder, as the public discovered that many of the problems that bedeviled Litton were endemic to American business.[101] In March 1970, *Time* magazine ran a cover story titled "America the Inefficient" that captured the nation's growing frustration with postwar management by cataloguing the public's numerous grievances with the nation's faltering institutions, including big business.[102] In 1971, the House Antitrust Subcommittee released a damning report on the nation's leading conglomerates that catalogued the numerous management failures associated with the conglomerates.[103] This was followed up the next year by a report from the Federal Trade Commission which found that the conglomerates made almost no improvements to the businesses they acquired and often hid their inefficiencies behind shoddy financial reporting.[104] With the merger markets dormant and the nation's economy in the grips of inflation and recession, investors had little choice but to sell their stocks and either sit out of the market or search for better returns with so-called institutional investors—the large firms such as banks, insurance companies, pension funds, and mutual funds that made up a growing portion of the investment community.[105] With growth by merger effectively closed off by the economic downturn, the managers of the nation's conglomerates had to turn their attention to attempting to run the collections of businesses they had assembled during the go-go years of the 1960s.[106] The American political economy may still have been dominated by managerialism, but the public support for managerial control had been badly shaken. Managers had attempted to usurp the power of financial markets and had clearly fallen far short.

With the nature of the corporation in doubt after the failure of the conglomerates, business managers were left to muddle through the ensuing decade with little in the way of public support. While managers were busy contending with economic crises, increased government intervention, and an aggressive consumer movement during the 1970s, a small group of financial theorists was creating a new theory of the firm that would shape the future of the American corporation for the remainder of the twentieth century and into the twenty-first. This new theory of the firm was the product of financial economics, an academic discipline that was younger than some of the conglomerates. From its origins in the 1950s, amid the same postwar optimism about scientific management that helped to fuel the rise of the conglomerates, financial economics would, by the 1990s, become not only the dominant academic discipline within business schools but also the guiding paradigm for understanding corporate strategy, corporate law, and the very nature of the corporation itself.

CHAPTER TWO

Can the Corporation Survive?

By almost any measure, the 1970s were a difficult decade for American businesses. Non-financial profits for American firms peaked in 1965, and as foreign competition from Japan and West Germany continued to make inroads in American markets, businesses saw their profit rates continue to decline.[1] The end of the postwar growth boom only made things worse.[2] The United States posted its first trade deficit since World War II in 1970 and entered a mild recession in the same year. Increasing foreign growth rates also contributed to the Nixon administration's decision to abandon the Bretton Woods gold standard system in 1971, and by 1973 the entire Bretton Woods system of monetary controls had collapsed, ushering in a new era of monetary instability.[3] Additionally, the OPEC oil embargo of 1973 threw the US back into a deeper recession, and the quadrupling of energy prices ate into corporate profits.[4] To make all of this worse, the US also experienced high rates of inflation for most of the 1970s, which depressed the value of financial assets, kept interest rates higher (making investment more expensive), and contributed to a heightened sense of economic uncertainty that made corporate planning difficult.[5] Politically, the experience of inflation and low growth fatally wounded the mixed-economy Keynesianism that had denoted American economic policy since the end of World War II, as both the Democratic and the Republican Party prioritized fighting inflation over boosting employment.[6] As part of this bipartisan reconfiguration of American economic policy, the free-market ideas of Chicago School thinkers like Milton Friedman began to fill in the gaps left by the demise of Keynesianism, and leaders of both parties adopted deregulation and capital liberalization as a solution to the nation's woes.[7] While these political transformations were worked out, Americans and American businesses had to suffer through most of the 1970s in a period of economic pain and uncertainty as the government seemed to flounder from one failed solution to the next.

No amount of macroeconomic trouble was likely to win business leaders much sympathy from the public either. Through the 1970s, the damage the business community's reputation suffered from the downfall of the conglomerates was compounded by revelations of corporate misbehavior, including several bribery cases and campaign finance violations and the mounting public awareness of some of the environmental and human costs of corporate misbehavior, all of which fueled growing public anger at the corporate sector.[8] Inspired in part by this anger, a new generation of labor activists broke with both management and their own union leadership to launch a wave of strikes that culminated in 1974 in the highest incidence of strikes since World War II.[9] These strikes were motivated by the dehumanizing nature of the work demanded of employees, and this younger generation of labor activists made attempts to work across racial and gender lines to create a more egalitarian workplace.[10] The sociologist Daniel Bell summed up the public's changing opinions on business in his book *The Coming of Post-Industrial Society* when he wrote that "a feeling has begun to spread in the country that corporate performance has made the society uglier, dirtier, trashier, more polluted and noxious."[11] As Bell saw it, corporate power was "clearly . . . the predominant power in the society," and "the concern for public policy, summed up in the phrase 'social responsibility,' derives from the growing conception of a communal society and the controls which a polity may have to impose on economic ventures that generate unforeseen consequences far beyond the intentions, or powers of control, of the initiating parties."[12] Bell predicted that, to combat this perception, corporations would soon need to adopt a more "sociological" mode of existence in which they "made the effort to judge a society's needs in more conscious fashion, and to do so on the basis of some explicit conception of the 'public interest.'"[13]

While Bell's prediction about a "sociological" future for business did not come to pass, he did accurately identify the question of business's social responsibility as a key point of contention in debates about American political economy during the 1970s. Whatever consensus about the role of large corporations in American society might have existed in previous decades evaporated during the 1970s.[14] In the words of Douglas Eicher, a scholar of the history of corporate social responsibility (CSR), in the 1970s the corporation once again became a "contested institution" as activists, managers, academics, and politicians argued about what corporations owed to society.[15] It is useful to split this debate over CSR into three camps: supporters of politically enforced, progressive-minded CSR on the left, the defenders of Cold War–era managerialist CSR in the center, and the opponents of any kind of CSR on the right. The key fault line in this debate was the issue of managerial autonomy. Consumer rights advocates like Ralph Nader, as well as environmentalists and antidiscrimination activists, argued that managers could not be counted on to voluntarily implement socially responsible policies, and that those policies they did implement were woefully insufficient given the range of harms business was responsible for. This camp argued that since businesses were created by the state in the incorporation process, the state should take a more active role in policing their behavior, and the state should be explicit about what business's responsibilities were. Meanwhile, opponents of the idea of CSR were incensed that managers had the autonomy to spend money that was not rightfully theirs on things not directly related to their business. Opponents of CSR believed that business's contribution to society came from the fact that it produced goods and services people wanted and it generated wealth for shareholders, who in turn invested that wealth in other productive activities.

Though for most of the 1970s it seemed like the champions of a more expansive vision of CSR were likely to see their hopes for a more socially conscious corporation come to fruition, it was the conservative opponents of CSR who ultimately won out. This conservative critique of CSR is most often associated with Milton Friedman and the University of Chicago, but the most consequential work on the social responsibilities of the corporation was done across the Great Lakes from Chicago, in Rochester, New York. During the 1970s, it was Rochester's faculty, not Chicago's, that led the way in applying financial theories to matters of corporate finance and business strategy. The financial theories developed at Rochester during this time, including Michael Jensen and William Meckling's landmark "Theory of the Firm," published in 1976, were only the most visible aspects of a grander effort on the part of Rochester's faculty to address what they saw as a crisis in democratic capitalism. This perceived crisis was fueled by the dire economic situation of the 1970s combined with growing public mistrust of business and increased government regulation of business. The decision of many business executives to seemingly discount the profit motive in the name of an expanded conception of CSR that went beyond the conservative version of Cold War–era responsible management as a means of coping with the public's mistrust was especially worrisome to the faculty at Rochester. In their minds these trends all seemed to point to the elimination of market freedoms at the hands of a democratic process that had been corrupted by popular politics. In their own efforts to save free markets, the professors at Rochester sought to make the case that efficient markets, not popular will or politics, should regulate economic activity.

It is important to note that in no way did Jensen and Meckling's work cause the corporate takeover wave of the 1980s. Indeed, judging from the pessimism they expressed in the 1970s about the future of free markets Jensen and Meckling had little faith in their ideas' ability to change the nature of American political economy. But these ideas did have the power to make sense of the chaos of the 1980s—something Jensen and Meckling had not seen coming. Jensen and Meckling's "Theory of the Firm," along with the work they and their colleagues did to support it, provided a powerful conceptual weapon that later generations of activist investors, legal theorists, entrepreneurial academics such as Jensen himself, and media commentators could use (and sometimes manipulate) to justify insulating corporations from democratic pressure and redirecting toward investors the profits those firms generated.

Debating Social Responsibility

The theoretical work done at Rochester needs to be understood in the context of a heated debate over the idea of CSR. With the public turning against business and the costs of several decades of sometimes reckless growthsmanship becoming harder and harder to overlook, critics of managerial autonomy and corporate excess had an opportunity to push their demands for greater regulation of corporate activity. These corporate reformers won an early victory in 1970 with the creation of the Environmental Protection Agency (EPA) and the Occupational Safety and Health Administration (OSHA), both of which had the power to investigate workplace conditions and set rules for how a business could be run.[16] These new regulations in turn inspired a fierce backlash on the part of some business owners who were incensed at the idea of government regulators interfering in what they considered their prerogative to run their businesses in whatever way they saw fit.[17] Leaders of large and small businesses united in their opposition to federal regulations they saw as "arbitrary" and "costly." These agencies were the targets of a sustained campaign of criticism from business leaders, as well as conservative intellectuals and politicians. Though this conservative counterattack did blunt the momentum of the environmental and safety movements, federal regulations stayed in place throughout the 1970s, 1980s, and beyond.[18]

This burst of new regulatory activity and the subsequent backlash against it raised the stakes in the debate on CSR and fueled advocates on both sides of the issue to press their case. For the champions of an expanded version of CSR, the creation of the EPA and OSHA confirmed their belief that the negative externalities generated by corporate growth necessitated a political solution that would force managers to act in prosocial ways. The autonomy that managers cherished was exactly what Ralph Nader identified as one of the central problems with postwar political economy. With the help of his fellow consumer activist Mark Green and Joel Seligman, an attorney, Nader spent most of the 1970s attempting to build public support for a federal incorporation act that would break the power of what Nader called the "management autocracy," which he argued had run American companies inefficiently and was unaccountable to either shareholders or the public.[19] The federal chartering act would eliminate the system of state-level incorporation and replace it with a single federal incorporation process in which companies would have to include social responsibilities in their charters and include representatives from both their communities and labor on their boards of directors.[20] The theory behind these proposals was that by including explicit curbs on managers' autonomy in federally issued corporate charters and forcing managers to answer to community and labor leaders on their boards of directors, the government would be able to ensure that managers operated their businesses in the best interests of society as a whole, not just those of shareholders or a narrow group of corporate insiders. After making the case for their idea in the book *Taming the Giant Corporation*, which was published in 1976, Nader, Green, and Seligman spent the rest of the decade trying to build support for the idea of federal chartering.[21] Though Nader's campaign ultimately fizzled and a federal chartering law died without a vote in the House of Representatives in 1980, the threat Nader's activism posed to managerial autonomy was a powerful call to action for both business executives and free-market academics.[22] The fact that Nader's ideas were being taken seriously at all meant that there was a real possibility that the government could become even more involved in the regulation of business.[23] For those business elites committed to managerial power and unwilling to fully embrace—at least publicly—the reactionary politics of their more conservative anti-government counterparts, the lesson learned from the political activism of the 1970s was that business had to take action to address the public's concerns about it, or government was going to do it for them.[24]

Judging from their expressed attitudes on CSR, many executives did try to get ahead of any government action by voluntarily adopting new, more expansive socially responsible practices. In a survey of 644 presidents of American corporations conducted by the American Management Association in 1975, 68 percent of executives agreed on a definition of CSR as "seriously considering the impact of the company's actions on society," and 63 percent of executives claimed that "many social responsibility programs introduced during the past few years have become integral, rather than peripheral to corporate functions."[25] When asked to identify their firm's socially responsible policies and predict which of them would see increased activity in the future, large percentages of executives predicted that they would be dedicating more resources to: "responding to the changing aspirations of minority groups and female employees (59 percent); improving physical working environments (55 percent); job enrichment programs (53 percent); better consumer relations (52 percent); and increasing employee participation in decision making (43 percent)."[26] The president of a small agricultural firm explained the imperative behind this expansion of CSR by reminding fellow executives that "corporations are entities created by the state; they may be taken away by the state. Therefore, corporations must evolve along the general lies wished by, perhaps, the US House of Representatives, assuming that the American public, though more or less imprecisely, elects people to that body who reflect their current wishes."[27] The president of a small consulting firm drove this point home by warning that "there must be a general dedication by business, completely within the framework of our capitalistic democracy (including the profit motive), to the total attainment of social justice. Only then can the corporation survive."[28] While most of the respondents made similar calls for change, some were more pessimistic than others. The president of one industrial firm agreed with the need for more CSR but felt that "it's a pipe dream.... In the year 2000 the corporation will be identical except that we will have figured out how to make a profit out of being socially conscious."[29] Finally, the president of a financial services company hit on one of the key unanswered questions about the future of the corporation and CSR when they remarked that "the 1976–2000 time period relates to the need for our society and the Western world to learn to live with changing obligation in which performance will be emphasized rather than growth.... Perhaps new measures of corporate performance would be appropriate—*the question is how does that make stockholders happy?*" (emphasis added).[30]

"A Moderate-Sized University of the First Rank": The University of Rochester's Graduate School of Management

Ironically, the University of Rochester became the site of the conservative counterattack against CSR thanks in large part to the generosity of one of mid-century CSR's greatest champions. Joseph C. Wilson, the founder of Xerox Corporation, was a major champion of the university during the 1960s until his untimely death from a heart attack in 1971, and it was his support that allowed Rochester to grow from an obscure regional private university into, for a time, one of the leading centers of social science research in the United States. Wilson personified the managerial ideal of a corporate statesman better than almost anyone. As president and CEO of Xerox from 1946 to 1967, Wilson oversaw the development of modern photocopying technology and, with the release of the Xerox 914 in 1959, grew the company into a worldwide information technology giant by the 1960s.[31] While corporate success alone would have secured Wilson's legacy, he was also deeply committed to the ideals of CSR and he worked to encourage businesses to attempt to solve the nation's most pressing social issues. In 1964, Wilson spent Xerox's entire advertising budget on a series of television ads in support of the United Nations even after the ultraconservative John Birch Society and conservative business leaders threatened Xerox with boycotts.[32] In an interview with the *New Yorker*'s John Brooks, Wilson argued for an expansive vision of CSR when he told Brooks that "issues like university education, civil rights, and Negro employment clearly *are* our business. I'd hope that we would have the courage to stand up for a point of view that was unpopular if we thought it was appropriate to do so."[33] Wilson also began the slow process of integrating the company and sponsored a series of television programs on the contributions of African Americans to national life—though he also publicly defended Eastman Kodak, Rochester's other industrial giant, when they were criticized for moving even slower than Xerox had on integration.³⁴ In both his actions and his statements Wilson embodied the *noblesse oblige* of the managerial elite, and he was quoted by his biographer as saying that "business leaders—because they will direct the new technologies—will be held accountable in larger part for the total quality of society, for the kind of life people live throughout much of the world. We therefore cannot give lip service to social progress. We must be committed to it, work for it and achieve it ... else we shall lose our power to be free."³⁵

As the founder of a technology company, Wilson had a deep belief in the power of science and research to transform society for the better, and he brought this commitment to scientific progress to his work as a trustee and benefactor of the University of Rochester.³⁶ Beyond his belief in the power of scientific research to transform society, there were also more practical reasons for Wilson to be supportive of the university. Wilson himself was a graduate of the University of Rochester, and the university was a valuable source of employees for Xerox.³⁷ Wilson joined the university's board of trustees in 1949 and was made chairman of the board in 1959. During his time on the board, Wilson and his family made several large donations to the university and successfully raised millions of dollars with the intent to transform the university into a "moderate-sized university of the first rank."³⁸ To meet these ambitious goals, Wilson shifted the university's endowment into high-growth stocks, including a large amount of stock in local stalwarts Xerox and Kodak.³⁹ This aggressive investment strategy did exceptionally well during the boom years of the 1960s, and by January 1967 the university's endowment was valued at $268,680,000, making it the sixth largest in the United States.⁴⁰ This bedrock of financial success enabled Wilson to raise the funds necessary to expand the university into a major research center. Ironically, Wilson's desire to fund a university that would produce useful social science research ended up creating the institutional launching pad for a theory of the corporation that explicitly rejected the values of corporate social responsibility that Wilson held dear.

One of the most consequential moves Wilson made as part of this effort was to hire Allen Wallis, then the dean of the University of Chicago's business school, as president of the University of Rochester in 1963. Wallis, who was well-connected to the national security state via his time as the head of Columbia University's Statistical Research Group during World War II, aligned very well with Wilson's desires to both grow the university and make sure that the work done at Rochester would be designed with an eye toward practical application.[41] Upon his arrival, Wallis set about trying to replicate the institutional environment of Chicago. One of his first acts was to establish a business school, and in 1964 the Graduate School of Management (GSM) welcomed its first class of MBA students.[42] Wallis turned to his friend William Meckling to be the GSM's first permanent dean. Meckling had done his graduate work at the University of Chicago, and he staffed the GSM with several Chicago PhDs (fourteen between 1970 and 1995), including Michael Jensen, the Swiss monetary economist Karl Brunner, the accounting professor Ross Watts, and the public finance economist Ronald Hansen as part of an effort to replicate in Rochester the scientific qualities of Chicago's business school.[43] Both Meckling and Wallis had very high standards for what they considered to be good, scientific research, and they were disappointed by what most management PhDs at the time were producing. As a consequence of these high standards, the original faculty of the GSM was staffed mostly by economists in the Chicago mold who specialized in public policy as opposed to management. The academic background of the faculty meant that the GSM produced far more research on politics and public policy than most other business schools.[44] In fact, the GSM first made national news for the work Wallis, Meckling, and Hansen did as part of the President's Commission on the All-Volunteer Force set up by President Nixon in 1969 to study ending military conscription, in which they provided the economic justification for ending the draft.[45]

The GSM's commitment to a vision of economics as a science led the sociologists Marion Fourcade and Rakesh Khurana to claim that "Rochester was a satellite of Chicago, and perhaps the most zealous and loyal satellite."[46] Like their counterparts in Chicago, the professors in Rochester's business school made a claim to scientific legitimacy as part of their own project of institution-building. To raise the academic profile of the school's faculty and their research, Rochester faculty members also founded several academic journals, including the *Journal of Accounting and Economics*, the *Journal of Financial Economics*, and the *Journal of Monetary Economics*; the pages of these journals were dominated by authors from Chicago and Rochester.[47] Flush with cash and armed with new ideas about how to transform the social sciences, the University of Rochester had entered into heady times. The school's faculty mobilized a mathematically complex and theoretically rich version of economics to claim scientific legitimacy and predictive power and to denigrate prior work as normative and unscientific.[48] Even more than their Chicago counterparts, the faculty at Rochester trumpeted the scientific nature of the work in a bid to both establish the legitimacy of their school and present their work as practically useful. Like their friends in Chicago, Rochester's economists saw themselves as outsiders who, by virtue of their superior intellect and scientific sophistication, were challenging and discrediting conventional practice in both economics and investment.

As the following chapters will demonstrate, no one embodied this spirit more than Michael Jensen.[49] A natural iconoclast (Jensen abandoned religion relatively early in life because he distrusted tradition and organized hierarchies, which he believed were "bullshit") and an abrasive personality—by his own admission Jensen spent most of his professional and personal life being "a jerk"—Jensen fit in perfectly at the University of Chicago and later at Rochester, where he arrived in 1967.[50] Jensen was born in Rochester, Minnesota, in 1939 to a deeply Catholic and conservative blue-collar family.[51] After attending vocational high school, Jensen was recruited to go to college close to home at Macalester College, where he studied economics and graduated in 1962. After finishing his undergraduate studies, Jensen enrolled in the University of Chicago's MBA program in the fall of 1962. During his undergraduate years and his time as an MBA student, Jensen also worked nights as a linotype operator to make enough money to pay his tuition. Jensen's experience in the MBA program exposed him to research and the Chicago method of economics, and he chose to remain in Chicago after finishing his MBA in 1964 to do doctoral work. Jensen earned his PhD after completing a dissertation that was the first empirical test of the Efficient Markets Hypothesis (EMH), a theory developed at Chicago by his doctoral advisor, Eugene Fama, that claimed that stock prices accurately and nearly instantaneously report information on the intrinsic value of a corporation. This meant that stock prices were an accurate and complete "scoreboard" for corporate performance: anything a company's managers did to raise the stock price created value, and anything they did to lower it destroyed value.[52] The EMH was central to Jensen's academic work and his worldview. As Jensen and other proponents of Chicago School finance theory saw it, efficient markets, powered by the rational, self-interested actors that operated within them, would be able to provide almost immediate accurate information about decision-making and to generate wealth for society. When markets failed in this task, it was not a flaw of the market, but the fault of something impeding the efficient operation of the financial markets. From this premise, Jensen's mission—one he shared with his colleagues at Rochester and Chicago—was to identify what was impeding market efficiency and make the case for its removal.[53] This mission led Jensen to turn his eye first toward government and then to the corporation itself as he sought to identify the things standing in the way of efficient markets.

Freedom, Capitalism, and Human Behavior

Though Rochester's business school was on the periphery of the nation's academic life in the 1960s and 1970s, this distance from more established schools afforded its faculty a high degree of freedom in setting their research agendas. Even more than their colleagues at Chicago, Rochester's faculty were free to make bold, sometimes shocking arguments against ideas like democracy in the service of protecting markets. Through the early years of the school's existence, members of the business school collaborated with their fellow social scientists both on and off campus to defend capitalism from what they perceived as existential threats to both economic prosperity and human liberty.[54] Karl Brunner, Meckling, and Jensen developed a wide-ranging critique of "sociological" understandings of mankind that they identified as the root cause of the growth of the state and the erasure of personal responsibility. Meckling and Brunner argued that scientific economics had developed the best understanding of human beings in the social sciences, and they christened this model of the individual REMM (Resourceful, Evaluating, Maximizing Man).[55] When critics like Brunner, Meckling, and Michael Jensen applied this form of social scientific analysis to the political questions of the 1960s and 1970s, they determined that democracy—as embodied in the extension of the franchise and the proliferation of rights claims by social "interest" groups—stood in tension with market capitalism. One of the distinguishing features of the form of social science to which these thinkers were committed was the refusal to accept that REMMs, either in government or in business, would consistently act in accordance with some kind of "general good" instead of acting to advance their own interests above all else.[56] Given the supposed nonexistence of any meaningful kind of public-spiritedness in human affairs, these thinkers sought to examine the inner workings of public institutions, including businesses, to determine how the REMMs that comprised them could be incentivized to act in the most efficient way.

Within Rochester's business school, Brunner and Meckling played key roles in focusing part of the faculty's research on issues related to public policy and the economics of politics and public institutions and in setting a combative tone for the kind of research done at the school. Though he had earned distinction as a monetary economist, Brunner's interests were wide-ranging. Brunner maintained that "intellectual life remains embedded in a social and political context," and this embeddedness led him to seek to understand the institutions that shaped intellectual and public life through economics.[57] Within the business school Brunner headed a research workshop titled the Center in Government Policy and Business that was the co-sponsor of a semiannual conference held jointly with Allan Meltzer and Carnegie-Mellon University known as the Carnegie-Rochester Public Policy Conference.[58] Though most management students might not have expected to have to concern themselves too deeply with issues of public policy, Brunner believed that they should, and the official description of the Center reminded MBA students that "they have a role to play as participants in the game [of business], and a role to play as participants in the rule-making process. From both points of view, it is important that we (1) forge a solid scientific basis for delineating what the effects of particular policy measures are or will be, and (2) impart that knowledge to students, particularly those whole aspire to business leadership in the future."[59] In addition to this group, Brunner also organized an annual conference of economists, theologians, philosophers, and public intellectuals called the Interlaken Seminar on Analysis and Ideology, which began in 1974 and was named after the resort town in Switzerland that hosted the event. As Brunner himself explained, the seminar "was deliberately planned as a forum for the 'imperial' application of 'economic analysis' over the whole range of the social sciences," and his decision to found two academic journals (the *Journal of Money, Credit, and Banking* and the *Journal of Monetary Economics*) was "similarly motivated."[60]

Brunner's "imperial" ambitions spoke to the fact that he saw his work, and the work of economists like him, as having very high stakes. In 1970, while he was still a member of Ohio State's Economics Department, Brunner published an essay in the journal *Kyklos* titled "Knowledge, Values, and the Choice of Economic Organization" which presented the stakes of his work in stark terms.[61] In the essay Brunner claimed that human beings had always sought to understand their place in the universe through a mixture of valuation judgments about things like morals and norms, often associated with religion, and cognitive evaluations of the world around them performed by scientists. To Brunner, the development of modern science since the Enlightenment represented the ultimate victory of the cognitive side of human nature, which left many of the world's intellectuals feeling "lost, naked, and cold" as "meanings vanished" and "objects, events, and human situations appeared pointless."[62] To cope with the seeming pointlessness of life once things like religious dogma were stripped away, intellectuals searched for ways to revive an understanding of the universe based around "cherished values" instead of observable facts, and often landed on utopian schemes to improve the world around them.[63] This effort mattered to people like Brunner because "the search for new orientations and new values exhibits dangerous undercurrents obstructing and beclouding the only source of systematic and reliable knowledge we can reasonably acquire in human affairs. This is perhaps nowhere so clearly expressed as in our conflicts bearing on the choice of economic organization."[64] After aligning himself and other scientific economists on the side of cognition, Brunner used the rest of the essay to tear into the cognitive shortcomings of a range of contemporary critics of market society, including the counterculture movement, Catholicism, Marxism, the New Left, technocrats and futurists, artists, and "the preachers (in churches and universities) of 'social involvement.'"[65] When these critics charged the market with being unfair or exploitative, Brunner believed they were engaged in an anachronistic attempt to substitute moral judgment for science by declaring how they wanted the world to be and then developing often counterproductive policies that sought to mold reality to their own moral judgment. This was dangerous because "the intelligent choice between economic organization requires a detailed assessment of empirical theories bearing on the working of organizational patterns. Values and valuations alone yield no rational decision and cannot guide intelligent action by themselves."[66]

Meckling, with Jensen's assistance, elaborated on Brunner's critique by detailing how the scientific economists viewed human nature. According to Meckling's REMM model, every human being was a rational agent who would assign values to all aspects of life relative to all potential alternatives and then seek to maximize the things they valued highly. Importantly, an REMM was also capable of the ingenuity and creative thinking necessary to adapt to ever-changing environments so as not to simply be a utility-maximizing automaton.[67] In Meckling's argument, human beings operated as REMMs in all aspects of life, meaning that there was no separation between the economic, political, and personal spheres, and that economics could best explain the range of observed human behavior. This idea of human beings always being self-interested meant that Meckling could not accept what he called the political understanding of human beings in which those placed in leadership positions (private or public) would act toward any sort of "general good."[68] For Meckling, politicians and political activists were just another set of entrepreneurial REMMs who would be willing to do anything, up to and including "inciting violence," to create a demand for their services as a means to grow the power they found so desirable. This belief that human beings could never be counted on to act for a "greater good" was the bedrock of the political and economic theory developed at Rochester during the 1970s and 1980s. In a world of REMMs, politicians and civil servants could not be trusted to do anything other than serve their own interests, just as managers could not be trusted to do anything other than self-aggrandize. For theorists at Rochester and similar institutions, human beings would only respond to incentives, and a scientific approach to organizations would need to discover the incentive structures within an organization and then devise ways to mold it toward whatever end was most desirable.

This articulation of the REMM model was paired with a wide-ranging attack on what Meckling termed the "sociological" view of human nature. Those who adopted a sociological view of human nature supposedly believed that "man is conformist and conventional. His behavior is a product of his cultural environment; the taboos, customs, mores, traditions, etc. of the society in which he is born and raised."[69] In this way, people could not be held individually responsible for their actions or circumstances, since so much of their lives were determined by societal factors. Meckling did not believe that people could rationally justify a sociological understanding of human behavior; instead he believed that this viewpoint was adopted by those who either wanted to expand the power of the state or were unwilling to face the consequences of their actions. Since the sociological view obliterated the individual as a meaningful actor, Meckling believed that those who subscribed to this view were guilty of elevating the state to a position of supreme importance over human life, since only state action could have any meaningful effect on people's lives.[70] In this way, talk of values and equality was really just a smokescreen — a seemingly virtuous cover for those who would rather subsume themselves to the state or any other coercive institution than face consequences for their actions as individuals.[71]

The ideas of individual responsibility and individual ownership were at the core of Meckling's and Jensen's political philosophy, and the two spent over a decade attempting to distill this philosophy into a book, which they titled *Freedom, Capitalism, and Human Behavior*.[72] Though the book was never published, the materials they developed for it did form the basis of a seminar Jensen conducted in the summer for Rochester alumni in which participants remember him being "studiously and deliberately provocative, inveighing against the abuses of big government which had brought us to a 'Crisis of Democracy.'"[73] The Jensen and Meckling definition of freedom could be reduced to two parts: freedom of use, and freedom of expression and exchange, most often through contracts. Any infringement on how an individual used their property was an attack on their freedom.[74] In Jensen and Meckling's own examples, rulings by courts that people had the right to solicit commuters in a train station were not protecting some imaginary right to free speech, but rather redistributing some part the station owner's rights to their property to someone else. In a more extreme example, the authors claimed that allowing homeless people to sleep or beg in public was a redistribution of land rights held by government or private owners, thus diminishing human freedom by removing the landowners' rights to use their property in whatever way they saw fit.[75] Jensen and Meckling also combined this example of homeless people with their earlier critiques of "sociological man" when they noted that "in addition to reassigning scarce legal rights to homeless people, the shift from labeling them 'vagrants' to 'homeless' significantly reduces the approbation such people received from others in society. This shift in the language used to refer to such people changes their social acceptance by subtly suggesting that they have no choice or responsibility in the matter. Such a shift reduces the social cost of such behavior and will therefore increase the number of homeless."[76]

The train station and homelessness examples help shine some light on how Jensen and Meckling's definition of freedom related to the broader critiques of society and politics coming out of Rochester in the 1970s. In Jensen and Meckling's example, the sociological understanding of mankind led a group of well-intentioned reformers to socialize responsibility for some people's poverty and then implement laws and policies that reduced individual freedom in a misguided attempt to alleviate others' misfortune. This dynamic made freedom especially vulnerable in political democracies since, as Brunner argued, the sociological model of man had become broadly popular, especially among intellectuals, the media, and the policy elite.[77] Jensen publicly addressed this issue on interpretation in a debate with John Kenneth Galbraith in 1977 in which he claimed that freedom was not equivalent to democracy, and that in fact "that there exists a fundamental conflict between a political democracy as we know it and freedom. They appear to be incompatible and it seems only a matter of time until the political sector succeeds in eliminating many of the freedoms that we still have."[78] In a two-part article titled "Between Freedom and Democracy" that Jensen and Meckling published in the financial magazine *The Banker*, Jensen revealed that his fundamental issue with democracy came from his observation that people could advance their situation in one of two ways: "by expending time and other resources operating in the private sector to produce goods and services which other people wish to buy" or "by expending resources in the political sector to get government and the courts to change the rules of the game to reallocate wealth from others in society to themselves."[79] Since redistribution necessarily involved infringing on individuals' freedom, these temptations to get ahead by political lobbying put freedom at risk and elevated normative concerns about things like equity or justice above the rights of individuals.

The emphasis Jensen and Meckling put on personal responsibility and the need for people to be punished for their actions spoke to the important link between this individualist conception of human existence and a sweeping denunciation of contemporary society's supposed permissiveness—a denunciation that put this vision of society and politics firmly within the camp of the conservative backlash to the rights movements of the 1960s and 1970s.[80] The most troubling aspects of this opposition were on display in a conversation between the economist James Buchanan and a group of his colleagues including Meckling, Wallis, and Brunner at a conference celebrating the ten-year anniversary of the publication of Milton Friedman's *Capitalism and Freedom* held at the University of Virginia in 1972. At the conference Buchanan presented a paper titled "The Political Economy of Franchise in the Welfare State" in which he argued that political interest groups would lobby for the expansion of the franchise in order to use newfound voting rights to win redistributive legislation.[81] A conversation between Buchanan and Lecis Kochin, an official with the Federal Reserve Bank of New York, made the coded criticism of the Voting Rights Act of 1965 even more clear. Kochin warned the assembled economists: "If the franchise is used for redistribution, then people will bend much of their efforts towards obtaining more votes. Perhaps this helps explain some of the social disturbances we have had in the past decade. If you can buy franchises by being more disruptive or speaking louder or better, and therefore transfer income to yourself, then people will bend their efforts in this direction rather than in some direction which is beneficial to the community at large." Buchannan agreed with this sentiment and followed by claiming that "in the last decade we have allowed people to get whatever they want through redistribution. They could not do that thirty years ago."[82]

In all their criticisms of government action, Jensen and Meckling made special mention of policies like affirmative action or equal employment legislation as emblematic of the fundamentally misguided nature of contemporary political action. Wallis argued that the enfranchisement of African Americans provided a market for political entrepreneurs to offer ever-expanding welfare benefits in an effort to win votes.[83] Though no one at Rochester claimed to have an objection to the intent behind antidiscrimination laws or other prosocial policies, they did object vigorously to the actual policies put in place to support these ends. Government actions to combat discrimination in the workplace drew the ire of Jensen and Meckling, who both saw things like affirmative action and the Equal Employment Opportunity Commission as curbs on managers' freedom to run their workplaces in whatever way they saw fit.[84] Products of the environmental movement such as the EPA were similarly presented as inefficient restrictions on peoples' freedom and a revocation of businesses' rights to their own property. Brunner believed the political battle over racial discrimination in mortgage lending epitomized by the practice of redlining had "evolved with little concern or interest about the nature and the validity of the issue," and that instead "the motor force behind the rhetoric [is] systemic attempts to exploit the political process for redistribution at a new front."[85] A theory of human freedom based on property rights and the supposed violence of redistribution simply could not accommodate movements to address systemic inequalities. In a world where economic, political, and social power were disproportionately concentrated among White men, any attempt to address these inequalities would be read by those who defined the term as Jensen and Meckling did as an attack on freedom. In this way economists like Jensen and Meckling and their political allies in the modern conservative movement could recast the rights movements of the 1970s as attacks on the freedom of dominant social groups.

Principals and Agents: A New Theory of the Firm

Ironically, the professors in Rochester's business school who trained future business managers took a rather jaundiced view of management as a profession, and they held managers partly responsible for the erosion of freedom and the expansion of government. Jensen and Meckling's "Theory of the Firm" was the most significant result of this view, but it was by no means an isolated phenomenon. In much the same way that Brunner had created a supposedly scientific conception of politics as just another venue for rational self-advancement, Jensen and Meckling developed a market-based definition of the business firm that was very much in keeping with the individualistic understanding of human nature and of politics embodied in the REMM model and the examinations of politics detailed above. The argument that managers were just as self-interested as anyone else meant that all of the managerialist rhetoric around corporate social responsibility and business and managers' commitment to the public good was nothing more than a self-righteous delusion at best. Since managers, workers, and owners would naturally have a different set of interests, Jensen and Meckling argued, the purpose of corporate organization and management was to design incentive structures to minimize these conflicts of interest.

Jensen and Meckling began to draft their theory of the firm in response to an invitation from Brunner to write an academic paper, to be presented at his Interlaken seminar, that would address the same issues that Milton Friedman had in his *New York Times Magazine* article titled "The Social Responsibility of Business Is to Increase Its Profits," which had brought anti-CSR arguments into the mainstream when it was published on September 13, 1970.[86] Though this article was written in the same spirit as Friedman's arguments against government, the target of Friedman's ire was businesspeople themselves.[87] Friedman opened his article by claiming that businesspeople who spoke of being concerned with more than profit were "preaching pure and unadulterated socialism" and were acting as "unwitting puppets of the intellectual forces that have been undermining the basis of a free society these past decades."[88] In the next paragraph, Friedman attacked the very foundations of the managerialist ideal of corporations as socially responsible by remining his readers that "only people have responsibilities. A corporation is an artificial person and in this sense may have artificial responsibility, but 'business' as a whole cannot be said to have responsibilities."[89] From this beginning, Friedman went on to define the so-called principle-agent problem that would be at the heart of Jensen and Meckling's theory of the firm. In Friedman's conception of a business firm, managers were hired by shareholders (acting through a board of directors) to serve as their agents, specifically to run the firm and make as much money as possible for their principals (the shareholders) on whose behalf they act.[90] Unfortunately for shareholders, managers often valued some sort of social cause such as environmentalism or poverty reduction, and as self-interested individuals they would seek to direct some of the resources at their command toward those causes. As Friedman saw it, this amounted to little more than managers imposing a kind of tax on shareholders whereby socially oriented managers would confiscate some amount of money that was invested in a profit-seeking corporation and redistribute it. This amounted to socialism because wealth was being distributed not according to the market, but according to the political decisions of a set of unaccountable managers. Business leaders might have gained praise in the short term by talking about their social responsibilities, but in the long run this behavior helped "to strengthen the already too prevalent view that the pursuit of profits is wicked and immoral and must be curbed and controlled by external forces." According to Friedman, "once this view is adopted, the external forces that curb the market will not be the social consciences, however highly developed, of the pontificating executives; it will be the iron fist of Government bureaucrats."[91] Whether because of their vanity or their naïve good intentions, business managers were in Friedman's mind partly to blame for the ills capitalism was beginning to experience in the 1970s.[92]

Friedman's article was the jumping-off point for Jensen and Meckling's work, but they quickly went beyond Friedman's critique to craft their own theory of what a corporation really was. The pair presented an early draft of the paper to Brunner's seminar in 1974, and the final version, after being rejected for publication in the *Bell Journal of Economics*, was published at Fama's insistence in the *Journal of Financial Economics* (which Jensen had founded in 1974) in 1976.[93] Jensen and Meckling stated that the purpose of their paper was to develop "a theory of ownership structure for the firm" that could explain a firm's capital structure (amount of debt, equity, etc.) and how the ownership of a firm was divided between "insiders" (managers and employees) and "outsiders" (shareholders).[94] Though this was the main purpose of the paper, the authors also acknowledged that they had much more on their minds than just the issue of ownership structure, and they claimed their work would have implications for such topics as "the definition of the firm, the 'separation of ownership and control,'" and "the 'social responsibility of business.'"[95] In keeping with these broad ambitions, the two seminal contributions of the paper to the debate on the structure and obligations of firms were: the definition of a firm as a "nexus of contracts," and the argument that "agency costs" generated from the separation of ownership and control were a significant determinant of overall corporate value.

Jensen and Meckling began their "Theory of the Firm" paper by arguing that the economics profession had not developed a useful theory of how firms operated, and too often treated the firm as a "black box" that simply produced profits.[96] As a first step toward solving this problem, Jensen and Meckling used the first section of their paper to make some general points about the nature of a firm that echoed the arguments Meckling and Brunner had made earlier. The most important and oft-cited of these observations was the claim that "the private corporation or firm is simply one form of a *legal fiction which serves as a nexus for contracting relationships and which is also characterized by the existence of divisible residual claims on the assets and cash flows of the organization which can generally be sold without permission of the other contracting individuals.*"[97] Though this definition might have seemed abstract, its implications were profound. If a firm was nothing more than a nexus of contracts, then "it makes little or no sense to try to distinguish those things that are 'inside' the firm (or any other organization) from those things that are 'outside' of it."[98] Understood this way, it would be impossible for a firm to be the kind of lasting social institution the defenders of CSR claimed it to be; indeed, it would be hard to say that the firm truly existed as much of anything at all. Jensen and Meckling continued with this line of reasoning to argue that "*the firm is not an individual*"—it was a market, and therefore it made no sense to ask what the social responsibly of the firm should be, since markets had no existence beyond that of the numerous individuals who populated them.[99] This "nexus of contracts" definition of the firm complemented the numerous attacks Rochester theorists had made on the "sociological" understanding of firms by giving a definition of the firm that fit perfectly within the REMM model of human behavior Jensen and Meckling had developed. After years of claiming what a corporation was not, the market critique of managerialism and CSR had a definition of what the corporation was.

Jensen and Meckling's efforts to explain the ownership structure of the firm hinged on the same conflict of interest between agents and principles that Friedman had discussed in his *New York Times Magazine* article. Discussions of the so-called "agency problem" in corporate organization dated back to at least Bearle and Means's discussion of the issues raised by the separation of ownership and control and had recently been investigated by the economists Armen Alchian and Harold Demsetz.[100] Jensen and Meckling saw the issue of agency costs as a key determinant of the overall value of a firm. In a hypothetical example, Jensen and Meckling asked their readers to imagine a company owned controlled by a single manager-owner.[101] If this imaginary entrepreneur wanted to grow their company, they would need to raise money from the stock market by selling off some amount of their claims to profits in the form of shares in the company. If the manager sold 5 percent of their company, that meant that they would only get 95 percent of the company's profits and would therefore be incentivized to either slack off or spend some of the corporation's resources on their own wants (perhaps by buying a bigger office or a private jet) to make up for what they had lost in claims to the corporation's profits. Naturally, as the entrepreneur sold off more of their company in the form of stock, these problems would become more and more acute. Of course, shareholders were not fools, and "prospective minority shareholders will realize that the owner-manager's interests will diverge somewhat from theirs, hence the price which they will pay for shares will reflect the monitoring costs and effect the divergence between the manager's interest and theirs."[102] Therefore the stock price of any public firm was determined in part by what Jensen and Meckling termed "agency costs." Jensen and Meckling defined these agency costs as "(1) the monitoring expenditures by the principal, (2) the bonding expenditures by the agent, and (3) the residual loss."[103] In simple terms, this meant that agency costs would be the sum of whatever the shareholders had to spend in time and money to keep their managers in line; the cost of any managerial confidence-building measures or self-imposed constraints managers placed on themselves to ease shareholders' concerns; and the dollar amount of efficiency lost due to divergences of interest between principles and agents that could not be accounted for. The more likely managers of a firm were to act against the interest of shareholders, the greater the agency costs would be, and the less people would be willing to pay for shares of that firm since their wealth was likely to be "taxed" away from them by managers acting in bad faith or spent trying to keep managers in line. Therefore, if shareholders were able to closely monitor their managers' behavior and have mechanisms in place to discipline those managers who did seek to expropriate wealth, then the value of the firm would be higher as a result.

Jensen and Meckling explicitly linked their theory of the firm to their criticism of democracy in an article they wrote for the *Financial Analysts Journal*, titled "Can the Corporation Survive?"[104] Jensen and Meckling presented the public's desire for CSR as little more than the scheming of various interest groups to extort wealth and privilege from corporations and shareholders through a skillful manipulation of politics. In this conception of politics and CSR, everything from environmental standards to rent control, OSHA regulations, and affirmative action programs were all attacks on the rights of business by the government at the behest of self-interested political minorities who had the support of the press and social activists. To Jensen and Meckling, socially responsible behavior on the part of either corporations or the government was simply redistribution of wealth from those who were willing to produce things in the private sector to those who chose to use the public sector to have wealth reallocated to them.[105] Since shareholders only invested money in corporations to have a residual claim on corporate profits, the danger in corporate profits being siphoned off toward socially responsible ends was that "when potential investors become convinced that the rights of managers to use the assets of corporations in the interest of stockholders and creditors [are] very tenuous, or when they become convinced that the contractual rights represented by their shares, bonds, or other financial instruments are likely to be abrogated, they will simply stop investing in corporations."[106] The authors attributed the declining stock market of the past decade to exactly this phenomenon, and they declared that "the most spectacular period of economic growth in our history is over" precisely because investors had lost faith in the corporation.[107] The erosion of faith in the free enterprise system meant that "large corporations will become more like Conrail, Amtrak, and the Post Office. One likely scenario begins with the creation of a crisis by the politicians and the press. In some cases, the crisis will be blamed on the 'bad' things corporations do or might do. The remedy will be more and more controls on corporations."[108] Though Jensen and Meckling predicted a future in which private corporations would be destroyed and people would be "much poorer" and "much less free," they did leave room for some small amount of hope when they claimed at the end of their article that "although we believe that our forecasts have a high probability of being realized, their realization is not a certainty. Indeed, we hope that bringing the problem to the attention of the public will generate a solution."[109]

By Jensen and Meckling's own admission, their work on the theory of the firm contained little in the way of specific or actionable ways to solve the problems they identified in their theoretical and political writings. Even among economists, the "Theory of the Firm" was fairly marginal in the years immediately after its publication.[110] Instead, it was the article

"Can the Corporation Survive?" that initially won Jensen and Meckling a degree of public prominence. Its relatively simple language, in conjunction with its pointed criticism of government regulation, resonated among corporate leaders and political conservatives who were increasingly active in decrying supposed government overreach during the 1970s.[111] Though Jensen and Meckling's "Theory of the Firm" eclipsed this work in later decades, it has to be understood as part of their broader political project of protecting capitalism from democracy. A commitment to shareholder value maximization insulated businesses from the kinds of democratic pressures Jensen and Meckling warned about in their political work, which in turn had a profound effect on the nation's political economy.

By the time Jensen left Rochester for Harvard Business School in 1985 thanks to the fame he had gained as the most visible intellectual champion of the hostile takeover wave discussed in the following chapters, the theoretical framework necessary to justify the shareholder value imperative was in place. As the takeover wave called the normative foundations of American business into question, consultants, academics, and management gurus all began to latch on to the ideas first developed at Rochester in the 1970s as a justification for corporate takeovers and restructurings. Jensen and Meckling's mixture of finance and political theory, which dismissed CSR and insisted that the corporation was nothing more than a nexus of contracts, became the intellectual foundations of the shareholder value revolution. The takeover artists who began the shareholder value revolution may never have heard of Jensen or Meckling or Manne when they began the process of making the market for corporate control into reality, but by the end of the 1980s when these changes were being consolidated their work was routinely cited by the consultants and lawyers who brought market discipline into corporate boardrooms.

CHAPTER THREE

The Fourth Merger Wave

Jensen, Meckling, and their fellow finance theorists could not have known it when they were creating their financial model of the corporation, but the hostile takeover movement that would place shareholder value maximization at the heart of the American political economy was already underway. The explosion of hostile takeover activity in the 1980s—which marked a revival of a controversial practice that had captured Americans' attention during the third merger wave in the 1960s— that marked the ascent of shareholder value was part of a larger wave of mergers that began in 1974.[1] This fourth merger wave was itself sparked by a transformation of the nation's financial sector as Wall Street struggled to cope with the effects of the conglomerate crash and stagflation during the 1970s. As the relatively sedate version of Wall Street created in the aftermath of the Great Depression and the New Deal gave way to one marked by intense competition between firms and hyperactive trading, a cohort of aggressive young takeover specialists won fame and riches as the stars of a new generation of financial professionals. Though the investment community embraced hostile takeovers during this period, the early years of the fourth merger wave were still a far cry from the shareholder-focused takeover binge of the 1980s. It is helpful to think of the fourth merger wave as being divided into two parts: a less controversial period running from 1974 to 1981, and a much more disruptive phase marked by mega-deals and contentious hostile takeovers from 1982 to 1989.

Compared to the voluminous literature on the hostile takeover wave of the 1980s, the early years of the fourth merger wave have received relatively little scholarly treatment.[2] The most complete accounts of these years — and their connection to the broader shareholder value revolution — have been provided by journalists.[3] These journalistic accounts do an admirable job of locating the origins of the takeover wave in the 1970s, and they do call attention to an important shift in power within investment banking as traders and merger specialists supplanted their colleagues who focused on more traditional activities such as underwriting at the top of banks' internal hierarchies; but, in presenting this narrative as a prologue to the takeover mania of the 1980s, they elide some key differences between the types of mergers being conducted in the 1970s and those in the 1980s. During the 1970s, hostile takeover activity was being driven by large companies looking to purchase the presumed benefits of corporate diversification by taking over other, often smaller companies. Instead of focusing on things like shareholder value, takeover artists in the 1970s were attempting to hedge against the economic headwinds of the decade by purchasing their rivals and gaining market share.[4] These corporate-led takeovers generated enough opposition from state legislatures, congressional antitrust advocates, and federal regulators to throw their future in doubt had Reagan not been victorious in 1980. Instead, as chapter 4 will reveal, Reagan's election paved the way for the second phase of the fourth merger wave, in which individual corporate raiders were the driving force behind the largest takeover battles.[5] It was during this second phase that corporate raiders and shareholder value theorists formed their alliance to defend takeovers from legal challenges as well as congressional and media critics.[6] This alliance between free-market economists and takeover financiers also reflected a shift in power within the nation's business community as the financial sector gained influence in Washington at the expense of the industrial companies that for decades had formed the core of the business lobby. The evolution of the fourth merger wave from its corporate origins in the 1970s to the ideological crusade for shareholder value maximization it became serves as a valuable reminder of how the progress of the shareholder value revolution was shaped by the intersection of ideas and politics. This chapter does not dispute the common argument that it was the second period of the fourth merger wave, and especially the rise of hostile takeovers, that drove the ascent of shareholder value maximization in American political economy; rather, it complements this argument by examining the early years of the fourth merger wave to identify the necessary political and economic antecedents to the rise of shareholder value ideas in the 1980s.[7] In doing so, it highlights the important ways in which the hostile takeover wave of the 1980s was different from what came before and explains why business leaders embraced shareholder value maximization in the wake of the failure of the diversification mergers of the 1970s. Shareholder value theory did not spark the fourth merger wave or the hostile takeovers of the 1980s, but the theory did provide an economic explanation of takeovers, one that could link takeovers to a broader project intended to reshape the American political economy.

A New Financial Landscape

Like their cousins in corporate America, Wall Street banks and investment firms also struggled to cope with the difficult macroeconomic environment of the 1970s. As the decade began, the nation's financial community was still digging itself out of the so-called back-office crisis of the late 1960s.[8] The crisis had been caused by brokerages' inability to keep up with the paperwork created by the unprecedented surge in trading volume associated with the conglomerate mania of the late 1960s.[9] As paperwork continued to pile up, New York Stock Exchange (NYSE) member brokerages generated billions of dollars in liabilities due to lost or bungled orders. By 1970, these losses threatened to overwhelm the NYSE as many of its members teetered on the brink of failure. In response, the NYSE's board created an executive committee to address the crisis. The committee created an emergency fund it could draw upon to bail out failing members, forced NYSE members to increase the amount of capital they had on hand to cover potential losses, and arranged for over eighty mergers between failing smaller firms and larger concerns that had enough capital to absorb them.[10] The committee also pledged to use its emergency fund to pay the costs associated with liquidating ten member firms that were insolvent and could not be sold off. The committee's triage work, and Congress's decision at the end of 1970 to create a federal insurance program for brokerage orders, brought the worst of the crisis under control, but at a cost.[11] Between 1969 and 1970, over 100 member firms of the NYSE disappeared through mergers or liquidations, and a substantial number of non-member brokerages failed as well. These failures cost thousands of securities industry workers their jobs, including many working-class clerks who had to work under incredibly demanding conditions during the worst of the crisis.[12]

Beyond the effect it had on individual brokerages and their employees and customers, the back-office crisis also marked the end of an era on Wall Street. Prior to the crisis, brokerages had relied on armies of poorly managed clerks who worked under intense pressure to manually process orders.[13] While this system was remarkably inefficient and error-prone, the bull markets of the postwar years allowed brokerages to prosper despite their many operational shortcomings. The avalanche of paperwork that buried the brokerages' back offices at the end of the 1960s forced those firms to reckon with their own inefficiencies, and in response they scrambled to invest in both the computers necessary to automate their order processing and improved management systems. The high costs of the automation process trapped brokerages in a cycle of expansion as firms broadened into new lines of business to generate the capital needed to pay for new computers, only to discover that each expansion also required them to purchase more computers to keep up with the increased volume of work. The need for capital also accelerated the consolidation of the brokerage industry, as giant firms like Merrill Lynch bought up their smaller competitors.[14] In response to the increased demands for capital they faced, the leaders of NYSE brokerages lobbied the Exchange's board to allow them to sell stock in their companies to the public for the first time.[15] Under pressure from its members, the NYSE's board agreed to amend the Exchange's rules in late 1969, and on April 10, 1970, a small brokerage named Donaldson, Lufkin & Jenrette became the first NYSE member firm to conduct an initial public offering (IPO).[16] A little over one year later, in July 1971, Merrill Lynch, the nation's largest brokerage, followed suit with an IPO that Donald Regan, the chairman of the company, described as "an historic moment in the history of Merrill Lynch and indeed in the history of Wall Street."[17] Merrill Lynch's IPO marked the beginning of the end for the privately held financial services firm, as other leading brokerages, including Bache & Co., the nation's second largest brokerage, quickly followed suit and held their own IPOs. This initial burst of public offerings among brokerages created a momentum toward public ownership that swept through the rest of Wall Street in the decades that followed as other brokerages—and, by the 1980s, investment banks as well—sought to expand their businesses (as well as the fortunes of their partners) by becoming publicly traded companies.[18]

Public ownership was a mixed blessing for brokerage firms. Being able to sell stock allowed brokerage firms to raise previously unobtainable amounts of money to expand their businesses, and the limited liability that came with being a publicly traded corporation meant that brokerage partners no longer needed to risk their own capital when making investments on behalf of their firms. However, these benefits came at the cost of increased pressure from shareholders to deliver consistent earnings growth. Pressure from shareholders combined with the consolidation of the brokerage industry put firms in an increasingly competitive fight for investors' business that stood in marked contrast with the clubby atmosphere on Wall Street in the 1950s and 1960s.[19] The SEC heightened this competition on May 1, 1975, when they prohibited brokers from setting fixed commissions on trading activity because of the Commission and Congress's belief that fixed commissions favored institutional investors who could leverage economies of scale at the expense of individual shareholders.[20] With brokerages no longer able to set an industry-wide fixed price for trading activity, these firms were forced to compete against each other on price to attract investors' business. As brokerages slashed their commission prices to attract customers, they saw their profit margins shrink and they had to rely even more heavily on increasing volume to keep themselves afloat.[21]

Despite the effects they had on the nation's financial industry, neither the back-office crisis nor the SEC's decision to end fixed commission rates did anything to reverse the most powerful trend reshaping Wall Street: the continued growth of institutional investors. Since the end of the Second World War, individual investors had been steadily selling their shares to institutions as they sought to gain the advantages of diversification without having to pay the costs in time and effort to manage their own portfolios. In 1970, the NYSE reported that institutions owned 27.2 percent of all stocks on the Exchange, and by the end of the decade they were estimated to own around 36 percent of US equities.[22] High rates of inflation at the end of the 1960s and throughout the 1970s accelerated the movement toward institutional investors, since the interest commercial banks could offer on deposits was capped by the Federal Reserve's Regulation Q at a level that often fell below inflation. In response to the inflationary environment, mutual funds companies began offering new products such as money market mutual funds to lure people away from bank accounts. These new products were received well by customers who were hungry for any investment opportunity that could potentially outpace inflation, and Americans gladly entrusted their money to institutional investors in ever-increasing numbers.[23]

Institutional investors were no less demanding of their fund managers than other clients, and they demanded proof that their investments were generating steady returns. To demonstrate their supposed effectiveness, fund managers increasingly used a concept known as "alpha," which Jensen had invented in his dissertation, to measure their performance.[24] In simple terms, alpha represented the degree to which a specified investment portfolio outperformed the market portfolio, meaning that it provided fund managers with a way to quantify the degree to which they may have been able to beat the market in a given quarter. As ambitious fund managers sought to generate alpha each quarter by constantly reshuffling their portfolios in order to beat that market—an especially ironic turn, given that Jensen invented alpha to demonstrate that it was not possible for fund managers to consistently beat the market—institutional investors began to gain a reputation for being focused on short-term results and quarterly performance above all else.[25] During the 1970s, however, fund managers' demands for quarterly performance did not translate into institutional investors directly challenging corporate managers as they would sometimes do in later decades. Instead, when a company's management or share price disappointed them, institutional investors generally followed a tradition known as the "Wall Street Rule," in which they simply sold the stock of the disappointing firm and moved on.[26] The combination of the Wall Street Rule and fund managers' constant search for alpha helped to push trading volumes even higher as investors found themselves pitted against each other in a fierce battle for high returns.

The Birth of M&A

All the changes described above helped to transform Wall Street into a more consolidated and competitive place amid the worst decade for the nation's financial community since the Second World War. Though the United States was only officially in a recession from 1969 to 1970 and from 1973 to 1975, stock prices remained often far below the peak they hit at the end of the 1960s for the entirety of the 1970s. This difficult macroeconomic environment offered no small number of challenges and dangers for people working in the financial industry, but it also created a chance to change the way finance was done in the United States. For a rising cohort of aggressive young traders, brokers, and investment bankers the 1970s was a golden moment of opportunity. The disruptions caused by years of economic crises cleared the way for these finance professionals to engage in the kinds of risky behavior that would have been impermissible in previous decades when Wall Street was a more "gentlemanly" place.

Perhaps the clearest sign that times had changed on Wall Street came on July 23, 1974, when readers of *The Wall Street Journal* discovered that Morgan Stanley, Wall Street's most prestigious investment bank, was managing a hostile takeover bid for ESB Inc., a Philadelphia-based battery manufacturer, on behalf of the International Nickel Company of Canada (INCO).[27] The idea that a member of the "House of Morgan" would sponsor a takeover would have been unthinkable even five years prior. Since Morgan Stanley's creation in 1935 when the Glass-Steagall Act forced J. P. Morgan & Co. to split its investment banking business off into an independent company, the investment bank had occupied the top spot in Wall Street's unofficial social hierarchy. Like their brethren at J. P. Morgan, the partners of Morgan Stanley were almost uniformly sober-minded Ivy League patricians in the mold of J. P. Morgan Jr. and his son Henry Morgan, who was one of the founders of the firm.[28] Though the federal government had forced it to legally separate from J. P. Morgan & Co. with the passage of the Glass-Steagall Act, Morgan Stanley remained closely tied to its former parent company. J. P. Morgan's bankers advised their clients, a laundry list of the nation's industrial giants that included General Motors, General Electric, AT&T, and US Steel, to use Morgan Stanley as their investment banker.[29] Connections to J. P. Morgan also helped Morgan Stanley become the preferred investment banker for state and local as well as foreign governments and even international institutions like the World Bank. For their part, Morgan Stanley's partners believed in the idea that large multidivisional corporations were durable social institutions, and these companies were the only type of non-government client Morgan Stanley needed. From its founding, the core of Morgan Stanley's business was underwriting new securities issues on behalf of its clients.[30] When Morgan Stanley participated in an underwriting syndicate—an ad hoc group of investment banks and brokers working together to sell a securities issue—its partners almost always ensured that it was the lead syndicate member, with its name at the top of the so-called tombstone ad that announced the offering and provided a ranked list of syndicate members. Morgan Stanley's name at the top of these syndicate lists was a tangible sign of its importance to the closely connected world of American finance prior to the 1970s. It was no exaggeration to say that the center of the investment banking world in the United States was the syndicate department at Morgan Stanley. Even though other investment banks may have been larger, no other bank could draw upon the same levels of prestige and social connections that were available to the partners of Morgan Stanley.[31]

Given Morgan Stanley's pedigree and genteel reputation, it was quite surprising that it was also one of the first major investment banks to adapt to the cutthroat, sometimes crass realities of Wall Street in the 1970s. The driving force behind the transformation of the firm was Robert H. B. Baldwin, a partner who had served as undersecretary of the Navy from 1965 to 1967 and became the bank's president in 1973.[32] Though Baldwin had attended Princeton University and had started his career as a protégé of one of Morgan Stanley's founding partners, he always viewed himself as different from his upper-class colleagues. Baldwin liked to remind his fellow partners that he had worked his way through Princeton and that his grandfather was a railroad conductor.[33] Baldwin was also acutely aware that the economic environment for investment banks was changing rapidly during the 1970s. During his presidency Baldwin reportedly kept a copy of an old tombstone ad in his desk drawer that had the names of over 100 investment banks listed on it, and he would cross out the name of each firm that had gone out of business since the ad was printed. Whenever one of his colleagues challenged him about the changes he was trying to make to the bank, Baldwin would show them this ad—which by the end of the decade had more crossed out names on it than not—to drive home the need to change or die.[34] In a symbolic move designed to distance the firm from its patrician heritage as much as anything else, one of Baldwin's first acts as president was to move the bank's headquarters away from its home on Wall Street to midtown Manhattan. Baldwin believed that the bank's traditional focus on only serving its corporate clients was no longer viable and that, to survive, Morgan Stanley had to do more to cater to the interests of investors, particularly institutional investors such as pension funds and mutual funds. Given their power and the pressures they faced to deliver alpha, institutional fund managers were demanding clients for an investment bank. Fund managers wanted Morgan Stanley to provide them with detailed research reports on any potential investments, and wanted the bank to be able to buy and sell large blocks of stock at a moment's notice.[35] To satisfy these demands, Baldwin created sales and trading desks within Morgan Stanley and staffed them all with hyper-aggressive young bankers, mostly in their twenties, who were overseen by partners who were themselves only in their thirties. The sight of these young bankers working at all hours of the day and screaming orders into the telephone led *The New York Times* to begin a profile of the bank published in May 1975 by stating that "the investment banking game as it is being played these days by Morgan Stanley & Co. resembles a sweaty arm-wrestling match in a barroom far more than a gentlemanly croquet contest on a manicured law in the Hamptons."[36]

One of the men who was a leading contributor to the new barroom atmosphere at Morgan Stanley was Robert Greenhill, a partner who, while still in his thirties, received permission to set up a semi-autonomous mergers and acquisitions (M&A) department of the firm in 1972. Greenhill, who had received his undergraduate degree at Yale and an MBA from Harvard Business School, was far more flamboyant than Morgan Stanley's older partners. A fitness devotee, he started his days with a two-mile jog, and his favorite vacation activities were 500-mile canoe trips in the waters north of the Artic Circle. When working, Greenhill liked to be photographed wearing suspenders with dollar signs stitched into them that his daughter had made for him, and he became something of a minor fashion icon for wearing them.[37] People who worked with Greenhill, and those who found themselves on the other side of the table from him in merger deals, described him as "brilliant," "abrasive," "ruthless," and "the ultimate samurai."[38] When Greenhill won permission to set up his business at Morgan Stanley the idea of a top-tier investment bank doing M&A work for a profit was alien to Wall Street. Traditionally, when the client of a bank like Morgan Stanley wanted to merge with another company on friendly terms, the bank would advise them on the deal free of charge as a way of maintaining a good relationship.[39] Instead of seeing merger work as simply a favor to be offered to loyal blue-chip clients, Greenhill believed that M&A was a potentially lucrative business. Many of Morgan Stanley's clients were interested in growing via mergers, and Greenhill realized that these clients would be willing to pay quite heavy fees for Morgan Stanley's services if the bank started charging them for its help. When INCO, one of Morgan Stanley's long-standing clients, approached the bank in 1974 to see if it would advise them on a hostile takeover attempt for ESB, it was Greenhill who convinced the bank's senior partners to look past the stigma associated with hostile takeovers and approve the first takeover bid sponsored by a top-tier investment bank.[40]

INCO's takeover of ESB was a good preview of just how contentious, and how profitable, hostile takeovers could be. When INCO announced that it was planning to issue a tender offer—a public solicitation to a company's shareholders offering to purchase their shares for a set amount of money—to purchase ESB stock at $28 per share on July 18, 1974, ESB's board issued a statement the next day denouncing the bid as "hostile" and pledging to "take every possible step to see that this foreign company will not succeed in taking advantage of the current depressed state of the stock market." ESB's leadership also hinted in the statement at the possibility of legal action by noting that a takeover could violate American antitrust laws because of INCO's dominant position in the international nickel market.[41] From this point, the battle between the two firms quickly escalated. On July 22, INCO filed a lawsuit against ESB claiming that the company had made false statements about its tender offer and announced that it had hired Morgan Stanley to manage its tender offer.[42] ESB responded on July 23 by revealing that it had solicited a so-called "white knight" bid for $34 per share from United Aircraft, an aerospace conglomerate, and ESB's management planned to accept this offer.[43] ESB also filed a lawsuit of its own against INCO on July 25 that sought to prevent any future bids from INCO so that the board could sell ESB to United.[44] As lawyers on both sides geared up for battle, INCO and United sought to outbid each other as the takeover contest transformed into an auction for ESB. This bidding war made ESB's stock the hottest item on Wall Street, and shares of the battery maker rose from a pre-takeover value of $19.50 per share to $41.25 when the contest ended on July 30 after United refused to match INCO's offer to buy the company for $41 a share and ESB's board immediately recommended that its shareholders accept INCO's offer.[45] The spike in ESB's stock price was driven in part by a community of Wall Street traders known as risk arbitrageurs, or "arbs," who bought ESB stocks in large numbers once takeover rumors started in the hopes that a bid (ideally an inflated one) would go through and they would receive a premium for their shares from the winner of the takeover contest.[46] Along with the arbs and ESB's regular investors, investment bankers were among the biggest winners from the takeover contest. Since the advisory fees Morgan Stanley and other banks charged were a percentage of the overall value of a merger, whether it was successful or not, the ballooning price of the ESB takeover meant that Greenhill and his M&A team made a greater profit for themselves every time the takeover got more expensive. By the time the ESB contest was over, Greenhill and his team were estimated to have made between $1 and 2 million on the deal, while a competing group at Goldman Sachs who had represented ESB likely made an equivalent amount even though their side had lost.[47]

Propelled forward by the success of the ESB takeover, Greenhill's M&A department quickly became the most profitable business in all of Morgan Stanley.[48] Greenhill's success did not escape the attention of other investment banks, and success quickly bred imitation as other major banks rushed to set up M&A practices of their own. Thanks to Greenhill's success, M&A was no longer a relatively unimportant part of investment banking work; buying and selling companies became a business in and of itself.[49] Across Wall Street, young people in their twenties and thirties such as Steven Friedman at Goldman Sachs, Joseph Perella and Bruce Wasserstein at First Boston, and Martin Siegel at Kidder Peabody began to specialize in hostile takeovers. The oldest member, and unofficial figurehead, of this group of takeover specialists was Felix Rohatyn, a mergers specialist at the highly prestigious investment bank Lazard Freres who was forty-six years old in 1974.[50] In addition to the stature he had already won through his work with Lazard, Rohatyn was also able to leverage the prestige and political connections that came with being named the head of the Municipal Assistance Corporation that was formed in 1975 during the New York City bankruptcy crisis to help lend some amount of establishment credibility to the emerging hostile takeover business.[51] These bankers were also supported by an emerging class of takeover specialists within the legal profession. At the forefront to this group was Joseph Flom, a brilliant lawyer who had built his law firm, Skadden, Arps, Slate, Meagher, & Flom, from modest origins when he first joined it in 1948 into one of the most powerful corporate law firms in the United States by being one of the first lawyers to specialize in hostile takeovers during the 1950s and 1960s. Flom, who was willing to work for either the offensive or defensive side of a takeover battle, may have been the most in-demand takeover lawyer of the 1970s, but he was challenged every step of the way by his arch rival, Martin Lipton of Wachtell, Lipton, Rosen, & Katz, who specialized in defending against hostile takeovers and frequently argued against Flom in court.[52]

M&A professionals like Flom and Greenhill were able to become stars so quickly because demand from American companies for mergers began to rebound by the mid-1970s after several fallow years following the conglomerate crash. High rates of inflation during the 1970s depressed stock prices while also making capital expenditures like new production facilities often prohibitively expensive for companies. In this environment, many companies—even large, "respectable" ones—looking to expand found that it was "cheaper to buy than to build," meaning that it was less expensive and often easier to simply purchase an existing business than it was to grow their own.[53] The low prices at which many companies' stocks were trading may also have contributed to the rise of hostile takeovers in particular, since incumbent managers believed their companies were

THE FOURTH MERGER WAVE

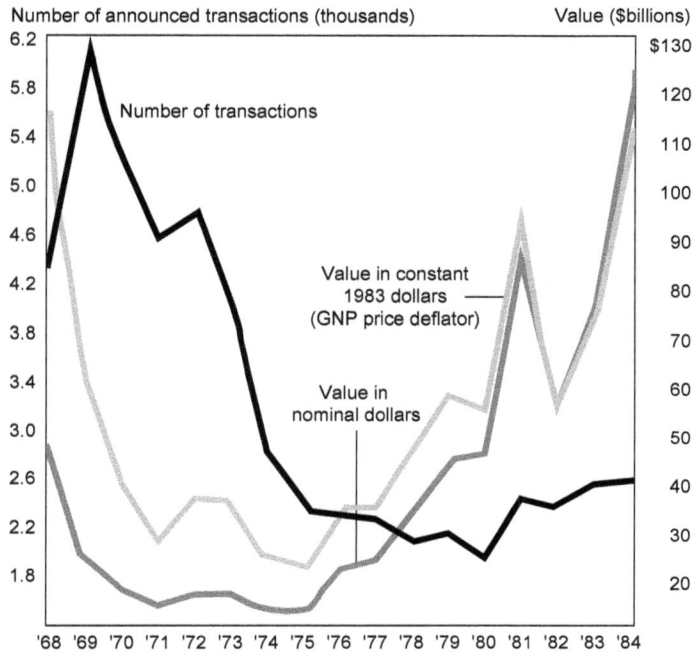

FIGURE 3.1. M&A activity 1968–1984. Data recreated from Allan Sloan, "Why Is No One Safe?," *Forbes*, March 11, 1985, 137. Source: US Council of Economic Advisers. W. T. Grimm & Co.

being undervalued by the market and were thus more likely to resist attempts to purchase their businesses at prices they felt were too low.[54] Despite incumbent managers' objections, it seemed that plenty of investors wanted to get in on the early years of the M&A boom. As seen in figure 3.1, even as the number of overall transactions declined from the highs of the late 1960s, the value of transactions being completed in the second half of the 1970s rose steeply. Though there may have been fewer mergers than in past decades, the deals being made during the fourth merger wave were far more lucrative than those that came before.[55]

Ironically, given the experience of the conglomerate wave, some of the most active participants in the M&A market were large firms seeking to purchase companies outside their main lines of businesses in the hope that these acquisitions would help to offset the losses they were experiencing in their core business.[56] As Greenhill explained, "very often the acquiring company is looking to make an investment in a business that

	Market share	
	HIGH	LOW
Growth HIGH	★ STAR	? QUESTION MARK
Growth LOW	$ CASH COW	X PET

FIGURE 3.2. BCG's growth share matrix. Recreated from Bruce Henderson, "The Product Portfolio," Boston Consulting Group Perspectives, January 1, 1970, https://www.bcg.com/publications/1970/strategy-the-product-portfolio.

is countercyclical to its other business so that if one portion of its business turns down, it still has other legs to stand on."[57] The dominant model of corporate strategy during the 1970s that guided these acquisitions was the Boston Consulting Group's (BCG) growth-share matrix (figure 3.2), which was introduced by the consulting company's founder, Bruce Henderson, in 1970.[58] As developed by Henderson, the growth share matrix divided a firm's various businesses into a 2 × 2 matrix with high and low market share on the horizontal axis and high and low growth potential on the vertical axis. Within the matrix, a business could fall into one of four categories: stars (high market share and high growth), cash cows (high market share and low growth), question marks (low market share and high growth), and what Henderson originally termed as a "pet," but which is much more often referred to as a "dog" (low market share and low growth).[59] In Henderson's telling, a company would only be able to "truly capitalize on its growth opportunities" if it could assemble a balanced portfolio of stars, question marks, and cash cows while ridding itself of any dogs.[60] Once a company had a balanced portfolio assembled, it could use the money generated by its cash cows (which it had stopped investing in) to feed the growth of its stars and question marks. Businesses could also move from one square of the matrix to another over the course of their lifetimes. This meant that building a balanced portfolio was a continuous process in which managers always had to be ready to acquire a needed cash cow, star, or even question mark, while also being ready to shed any business that became a dog.

Henderson's introduction of the growth matrix in 1970 proved to be especially well-timed, since it seemed to offer exactly the kind of insights companies needed after the economic crises of the 1970s caused them to reevaluate their long-term strategies.[61] The simplicity of the growth-share matrix also undoubtedly helped it, and other consulting firms' variants, to catch on. A *Harvard Business Review* survey found that by 1979 around 45 percent of Fortune 500 companies were using some form of portfolio planning to determine their corporate strategies.[62] In practice, firms' decision to adopt portfolio planning often meant diverting investment away from mature "cash cow" business lines in the industrial sector toward businesses with higher growth potentials while also seeking to sell off underperforming "dogs."[63] The widespread adoption of portfolio planning also fed into the growth of the M&A sector as firms sought to create their balanced portfolios by buying and selling various businesses.[64] However, for all its importance, corporate portfolio planning did not represent a significant change in corporate objectives from previous decades. Much as it had been in the 1950s and 1960s, the dominant corporate goal during the 1970s was still growth, specifically market share growth.[65] BCG's matrix and similar models allowed managers to claim they were moving in a different strategic direction from the days of the conglomerate craze, but in reality portfolio planning was mostly a new way for companies to achieve the same goals they had sought for decades.[66] The fourth merger wave would eventually transform corporate objectives once corporate raiders and financial economists raised the issue of shareholder value, but in these early years of the M&A boom this transformation had not happened yet. Instead, at its outset, the fourth merger wave seemed to be picking up where the third wave left off.

Hostile Takeovers Return

The return of hostile takeovers that came along with the birth of the M&A industry was an alarming event for the managers of the smaller and medium-sized firms being targeted by their larger rivals. Though most mergers were nominally friendly, by the end of the 1970s a growing percentage of deals were overtly hostile.[67] Any effort to produce an accurate count of hostile takeovers was fraught with difficulty as well, since the distinction between friendly and unfriendly mergers was much blurrier in practice than it may have seemed at first glance. In an interview with

Fortune, Lipton estimated that "at least half of the ostensibly friendly acquisitions are unfriendly at heart."[68] Many of these "friendly" mergers were actually thinly disguised hostile takeovers in which the acquired company's management felt that they had no choice other than to accept a purchaser's bid. These takeover bids were also quite attractive to shareholders. Bidders generally offered shareholders a hefty premium for their stocks, and unlike the third merger wave in which bidders financed their tender offers with stocks, fourth wave tender offers were almost always paid for with cash obtained from loans that commercial banks were increasingly willing to offer to would-be takeover artists.[69] Tender offers were also very lightly regulated by the federal government and the SEC. The only meaningful regulations on tender offers came from the Williams Act, which Congress passed in 1969 amid the spike in hostile takeovers during the third merger wave. The Williams Act mandated that anyone who purchased more than 5 percent of a company's shares was required to file disclosure forms detailing their identity, source of funding, and reason for acquiring the shares they purchased to both the target company's management and the SEC within ten days of acquiring those shares.[70] Bidders planning to issue a tender offer were also required to file a different, confidential disclosure form with the SEC at least five days prior to issuing their offer that outlined much of the same information.[71] In light of the financial advantage takeover bidders usually enjoyed, the Williams Act offered incumbent managers little protection beyond giving them ten days to either scrape together a defense or find a "white knight" to which they could sell their company on friendlier terms.[72]

Being generally unable to defeat takeover attempts on the financial front, managers at target companies chose to mount their defenses in the political arena instead. Because corporate law was created at the state level, companies focused their attention on lobbying state legislatures to pass laws that would make hostile takeovers more difficult, sometimes to the point of effectively banning them. Prior to the passage of the Williams Act in 1968, only Virginia had passed an anti-takeover statute. Between 1968 and 1974, as hostile takeovers remained mostly dormant, only a handful of other states (Nevada, Ohio, Wisconsin, Minnesota, Hawaii, and Kansas) followed suit and passed laws of their own. However, as the number of hostile takeovers began to swell in the second half of the 1970s, states rushed to pass anti-takeover laws at the urging of local business leaders and labor groups. By the end of 1978, thirty-six states, including Delaware and New York, had anti-takeover laws on their books.[73] The passage of these laws created a somewhat bewildering patchwork of regulation that provided creative management teams with ample opportunities to frustrate their would-be acquirers. Even if these defenses did not prevent a merger from taking place, they did allow target firms to gain some negotiating leverage over their would-be acquirers that enabled incumbent managers to force a higher price for a merger or potentially line up competing bids from other companies. Thanks to their ability to raise costs, these laws served as a deterrent force, one that could dissuade takeovers at the margins and help to put a check on the continued growth of the practice.[74]

While the individual states did the most to protect incumbent managers from corporate takeovers, there were signs that policymakers in Washington might also step in to curtail takeovers. At the broadest level, the rising number of mergers signaled a worrying trend toward market concentration and monopoly for champions of antitrust enforcement.[75] Throughout the second half of the 1970s, opponents of corporate concentration in both houses of Congress held hearings to accuse large businesses of attempting to destroy competition and consumer choice by purchasing their smaller rivals.[76] Senator Edward Kennedy (D-MA) attempted to capitalize on the renewed interest in antitrust reform as he sought to bolster his progressive credentials ahead of his run against President Jimmy Carter for the Democratic Party's presidential nomination in 1980.[77] As part of his effort to attack Carter from the left, Kennedy introduced an ultimately unsuccessful bill that would have regulated mergers based on corporate size instead of their effect on competition, which would essentially have banned any mergers, friendly or hostile, beyond a certain size.[78] While some congressional leaders focused their legislative activity on antitrust issues, individual members of Congress also used the power of their offices to intervene in hostile takeover attempts. Senator William Proxmire (D-WI) held a hearing in 1976 to urge Congress to consider expanding the SEC's ability to regulate tender offers in the wake of the General Cable Corporation's attempt to take over Microdot Incorporated, a tool parts manufacturer, using money borrowed from a four-bank syndicate led by Microdot's own bank, the Irving Trust Company of New York.[79] In 1979, in response to lobbying from McGraw-Hill, a publishing company facing a takeover attempt from American Express, Representative Henry Reuss (D-WI), the chairman of the House Banking Committee, tasked one of his subcommittees with investigating the proposed merger in the hope of dissuading banks from lending to American Express. Between Reuss's threats and the timely intervention of both the Federal Trade Commission (FTC) and the Federal Communications Commission, American Express's takeover attempt quickly fell apart as the company's leaders realized that pursuing an acquisition might lead to disastrous retaliation from the federal government.[80]

As takeover artists fretted about the increasing danger Congress might pose to their business, they also had reason to fear that the SEC might also lend its support to tender offer reform. On January 17, 1980, SEC Chairman Harold Williams broadcast his numerous displeasures with the conduct of both incumbent managers and takeover artists in a speech to a securities industry conference that immediately raised alarm bells within the M&A industry.[81] Williams began his address by unfavorably comparing the takeovers of the 1970s to the merger boom of the 1950s and 1960s. As he saw it, "in the '50s and '60s, when the securities markets were far more buoyant than they are today, many of the acquisitions which were effected resulted in net gains to the economy measured in terms of the combined companies." Williams acknowledged that hostile takeovers did occur during this period, but "the idea of seizing control of a corporation over the objections of incumbent management probably struck most executives as an ungentlemanly tactic best left to a small group of notorious raiders." In contrast to this supposedly more genteel time, Williams believed that "it has become acceptable to treat corporations as the sum of their properties and to assume that corporate control may change hands with no greater concern about the consequences than accompanies an exchange of property deeds in a game of Monopoly." Williams dismissed this financial view of the corporation out of hand and reminded his audience that "a corporation is more than the aggregate of its tangible assets—and more than the equity of its current shareholders—it is an institution with a complex of interpersonal and contractual relationships that create legitimate interests in the corporation among employees, suppliers, customers, communities, the economy and society at large."[82] While Williams did note that "this new crop of corporate takeovers has been fueled—if not caused by low stock market prices," he also believed that the increase in takeover activity was being driven, at least in part, by self-interested corporate executives who sought the "ego satisfaction, prestige and remuneration" they could win through successfully acquiring their rivals.[83] According to Williams, it was this self-serving attitude among corporate managers and the "financial inbreeding" it engendered that was causing American firms to lose their economic competitiveness with the rest of the world as they wasted their capital on financial transactions instead of using it for productive investment.[84]

Despite his many criticisms of takeovers, at the time of his speech Williams was not quite ready to endorse legislation designed to slow down or halt the practice. Instead, he appealed to corporate directors, especially independent directors, to act responsibly when faced with a takeover attempt by taking the time to rationally evaluate the offer and its potential effects on corporate stakeholders without resorting to disreputable tactics like defensive amendments to corporate charters.[85] While Williams believed that his vision of a lightly regulated marketplace populated by responsible actors was preferable, he did warn his audience that if corporate managers and takeover artists did not behave in socially responsible ways, "a society which places as much reliance as does ours on government as an instrument to check the perceived excesses of business is unlikely to tolerate indefinitely business behavior which the public regards as contrary to its interests."[86] Between Williams's threats of potential regulation and congressional Democrats' attempts to expand the nation's antitrust laws, there seemed to be a real possibility that the nascent boom in hostile takeovers could unravel at the hands of the federal government.

The macroeconomic environment also seemed to be turning against hostile takeovers at the start of the 1980s thanks to the actions of Paul Volcker, the newly appointed chairman of the Federal Reserve. On October 6, 1979, Volcker announced his intention to wring inflation out of the American economy by raising interest rates. As Volcker made good on his promise and pushed the Federal Funds Rate toward its all-time high of 20 percent at the end of 1980, the nation slid into a brief recession between January and July 1980 that was soon followed by a much deeper recession that ran from July 1981 to November 1982.[87] Additionally, Volcker himself publicly discouraged banks from issuing loans intended to fund takeovers, since he did not believe that they were a productive use of capital.[88] The economic and political situations for takeovers at the beginning of the 1980s looked dire enough that *The New York Times* declared on July 29, 1980, that "the era of simple cash corporate takeovers ended when soaring interest rates made such takeovers costly and the Federal Reserve Board moved to discourage them."[89] For their part, investment bankers predicted that the takeover business would adapt to the challenging circumstances it was facing by moving away from large deals and focusing on mergers for small and medium-sized companies. Bruce Wasserstein of First Bank of Boston claimed that takeover bids for medium-sized companies would resume once the macroeconomic situation stabilized, but he admitted that "aggressive billion-dollar transactions might be too politically charged to be workable at present."[90] Steven Friedman of Goldman Sachs predicted that "there's still going to be plenty of deals in the $35 million to $100 million range." Felix Rohatyn tried to put a positive spin on the seemingly narrowed horizons for M&A work by claiming that "I enjoy smaller deals. They're more fun. They bring me back to my youth," though he did admit that any deal, regardless of size, was more difficult now since "the economics keep shifting."[91] Almost no one predicted that hostile takeovers would disappear altogether, but the prevailing wisdom held that hostile takeovers would be mostly confined to smaller companies, and that the 1980s would not be a decade of mega-deals.

CHAPTER FOUR

The Reagan Revolution

Ronald Reagan's election to the presidency in November 1980 rendered all the speculation about the relatively modest future of the hostile takeover business obsolete. Reagan's victory kicked off the "deal decade" of the 1980s and was followed by a string of favorable economic and political shifts that rejuvenated the market for corporate control and made hostile takeovers front-page news.[1] As Reagan appointees, with the help of the US Supreme Court, removed political and regulatory obstacles to hostile takeovers, the passage of Reagan's signature tax cuts in 1981 and the end of the recessions engineered by the Federal Reserve to tamp down inflation in 1982 left the financial sector primed for a bull market that ran for the rest of the decade and fed capital into the hands of takeover practitioners. Takeover artists had no shortage of potential targets either. Conglomerates, including those constructed with the aid of BCG's growth matrix, had been especially hard hit by the recessions at the beginning of the 1980s. By the time the economy recovered, there was ample evidence available to investors that conglomerates tended to underperform their more focused rivals.[2] By 1982, the stocks of conglomerate firms were trading at a significant discount relative to their more focused peers as investors increasingly soured on the idea of corporate diversification amid widespread criticism of the conglomerate companies by management theorists and economists.[3] This "conglomerate discount" meant that many conglomerates were literally valued at less than the sum of their parts. As investors increasingly came to believe that corporate diversification was now destroying rather than creating value, entrepreneurial financiers discovered that they could generate tremendous profits for themselves by attempting to take over and break apart the conglomerates.[4]

With seemingly unlimited funding at their disposal and plenty of corporate targets available to them, takeover specialists like T. Boone Pickens, Carl Icahn, and Ronald Perelman became a new generation of "corporate raiders," larger-than-life celebrities who were viewed with some combination of admiration, fear, and disgust by judges, politicians, and the news media.[5] Newspapers were filled with the strange, sometimes playful, sometimes violent language M&A professionals used to describe takeover tactics such as "Pac-Man defense," "white knights," "scorched earth," "sharks," "Romeos," "gunslingers, " and "war" between "heroes" and "villains."[6] When media coverage focused on the employees of companies targeted for corporate takeovers, it often referred to the experience of workers as a traumatic one, with one middle-level manager describing his experience going through a takeover to *The New York Times* as "like a death in the family."[7] Beyond the easy-to-construct media narratives of takeover battles, the sheer scale of the market for corporate control during the 1980s demanded attention from government officials and academics as well as the general public. Nearly $1.3 trillion of assets changed hands during the hostile takeover wave of the 1980s, and 143 of the 500 largest firms in the United States were acquired in either a hostile or a friendly merger by the end of the decade, which made the second phase of the fourth merger wave an almost inescapable fact of life for those involved with corporate America during the 1980s.[8]

The sight of so much money changing hands for such seemingly dubious reasons during takeover battles, and the widespread association of takeovers with layoffs, meant that corporate raiders and their allies had to struggle to define what the takeover wave represented and what economic or social purpose it served. During the 1980s, the popular press was filled with denunciations of both raiders and managers as being emblematic of a new age of "Me-First" management in American business marked by greed and a lack of morality.[9] The opponents of hostile takeovers, who were an odd alliance of corporate executives (represented by advocacy groups like the Business Roundtable and the National Association of Manufacturers [NAM]) and labor unions, leveraged this critique of corporate raiders' supposed greed to lobby Congress, state legislatures, and courts for protection from takeovers.[10] As these critics of takeovers explained it, takeovers were nothing more than opportunistic attempts on the part of well-financed raiders to make a quick fortune by dismantling well-run companies. A spokesman for the NAM testified before Congress that hostile takeovers were "dangerous, unbridled speculative activity" that risked "thwarting the entrepreneurial spirit that creates new products and services in favor of financial gamesmanship and speculation."[11] The chairman of the Business Roundtable's Corporate Responsibility Task Force argued that hostile takeovers were "causing serious damage to the economic system," all because "a small group is systematically extracting the equity from corporations and replacing it with debt."[12] In a rare instance of labor unions taking the side of corporate managers, the AFL-CIO joined in this criticism of hostile takeovers, arguing that "there are rarely, if ever, any new jobs created by takeovers. The incentive for raiders and others who seek to gain control of a company is generally to profit by gaining control over existing assets of the company being taken over. It is not to the advantage of the community or the national economy to have such takeovers consummated."[13] In all of these denunciations of takeovers, critics made a point to emphasize that they were financially outmatched by raiders, and that they needed the federal government to step in and protect them.

To prevent this from happening, corporate raiders needed an alternative explanation of what they were doing if they hoped to beat back the charges being leveled against them in the press and in Congress. Unlike the M&A practitioners of the first part of the fourth merger wave in the 1970s, raiders could not claim to be following some sort of corporate portfolio planning. In fact, some raiders did not even seem interested in actually managing the companies they ostensibly set out to purchase. Raiders could make a fortune without even taking over a company thanks to the widely despised defense tactic known as "greenmail," in which a target company bought back its shares from a raider at a greatly inflated price for a promise that the raider would leave the target alone. Indeed, most corporate raiders did not succeed in taking over companies, and even those who did often showed little aptitude, or even interest, in running large businesses.[14] With older justifications for mergers unavailable to them, corporate raiders attempted to cast themselves as the champions of dissatisfied shareholders who, in challenging incumbent managers, were seeking to redistribute corporate profits to investors.[15] These efforts often took the form of bombastic statements to the press, such as when the famed corporate raider T. Boone Pickens told *The Washington Post* that his life legacy would be summarized by the slogan: "shareholders own companies. Management are employees of shareholders."[16] In a different attempt at populism, Carl Icahn summed up his view of American businesses by telling *The Wall Street Journal* that managers "take money from the peasants [the stockholders], and then hire mercenaries [lawyers] to protect their castle, mainly by browbeating the peasants. So we attack the castle." After a moment of thought, Icahn quickly added to the reporter interviewing him, "I don't want to call shareholders 'peasants,' don't put that in the article. Call them an 'oppressed majority.'"[17]

Fortunately for corporate raiders, financial economists—with Jensen in the lead—were ready to offer their own "scientific" explanation and defense of hostile takeovers, one that was much more persuasive than the raiders' own often clumsy attempts at populism. Instead of framing hostile takeovers as corporate greed gone amok or as a kind of populist crusade against big business, economists argued that the seemingly baffling developments of the 1980s could be explained by the work Jensen and Meckling had done in the 1970s. In this telling, hostile takeovers were simply the signs of a market for corporate control at work: after decades of driving up investors' agency costs through wasteful spending on acquisitions and the redundancies associated with mid-century CSR, entrenched corporate managers were finally being subjected to market pressures and forced to either raise stock prices or cede control to someone who would. Thanks to the intense political debates around hostile takeovers, and the massive public interest in them, these economists were able to find a much broader audience for their arguments than they ever could have hoped for even only a few years prior. Indeed, it was the hostile takeover wave of the 1980s that made agency theory, and by extension shareholder value maximization, useful not only to academics, but to corporate raiders, politicians, media commentators, consultants, and eventually corporate executives as well. More than just offering an explanation of why the hostile takeover wave had happened, these theories offered nervous executives a way to avoid the chaos of corporate raiders and activist shareholders: raise share prices by whatever means necessary.

Explaining Hostile Takeovers

The most immediate effect of Reagan's victory was to kill off the political momentum for takeover reform at the federal level that had been building for the past several years. The Republican Party's control of both the White House and the Senate following the election in November marked the end of congressional Democrats' antitrust efforts and seemingly lessened the danger of congressional action on takeover reform.[18] Reagan's victory also meant that takeover artists had less to worry about from existing antitrust laws. Once in office, Reagan filled the ranks of the executive branch with people committed to transforming antitrust enforcement, including William Baxter (whom Reagan named as assistant attorney general for antitrust) and James C. Miller III (whom Reagan installed as the head of the FTC).[19] Both Baxter and Miller were devotees of Robert Bork's "Chicago School" of antitrust law, which held that mergers should be regulated based solely on how they affected consumer welfare.[20] While the Reagan administration's embrace of these arguments did not lead to an abandonment of antitrust enforcement altogether, as some critics claimed, it did signal an effective end of federal opposition to horizontal mergers as regulators shifted their attention away from merger enforcement toward aggressively prosecuting price fixing instead.[21]

Reagan did his best to install pro-business figures at the SEC as well, most notably by pressuring Williams to resign and replacing him with John S. R. Shad, who became a key figure in the political and regulatory battles over hostile takeovers that dominated the commission for the next several years. Before his appointment, Shad had been an executive at E. F. Hutton & Co., a stock brokerage, where he had set up a successful M&A business. Shad had come to Reagan's attention after a chance meeting at the Bohemian Grove, a men's social club dominated by prominent conservatives, where the two bonded over their shared belief in small government and the power of free markets. Shad was one of the first members of New York City's financial establishment to endorse Reagan when he ran for president in 1980, and Reagan named him the chair of his New York campaign.[22] Shad's appointment to the SEC after Reagan's victory was not without controversy, however. During the transition period, documents from a report on the SEC that Reagan's transition advisers prepared for the president-elect leaked to the press. The report recommended that the new president force Williams, who still had almost two years left in his term as chairman, to resign so that Reagan could appoint a chair closer to his own political preferences.[23] The report went on to recommend that the president-elect instruct this new chairman to "make sweeping changes in senior staff promptly" in order to remove staff members hired in "previous Democratic administrations" because of "philiosophic [sic] incompatibilities."[24] The report's most extreme recommendations included a blanket

30 percent reduction of the SEC's budget and the effective dismantling of the commission's enforcement division, which investigated potential violations of securities law. When Williams bowed to the political pressure coming from the president-elect and announced his resignation in a letter to Reagan on December 31, 1980, Democratic senators were furious over Reagan's supposed meddling in an independent agency and vowed to defeat any nominee who endorsed the transition report's recommendations.[25] Though he anticipated a difficult confirmation process, Shad managed deftly to diffuse the controversy surrounding his nomination by disavowing the transition team's recommendations during his confirmation hearings.[26] After averting a political fight, Shad sailed through the rest of the process and was confirmed by a voice vote on May 6, 1981.

In office, Shad proved to be not quite the ideologue that some of his opponents had feared. Shad was undoubtedly a pro-business conservative, but he was also very much a believer in a gentlemanly and relational form of doing business—one that had been disappearing on Wall Street for much of the last decade in large part because of hostile takeovers.[27] Though Shad himself was an M&A professional, he had always favored friendly mergers, and his own standards of conduct were so high that he had never been party to a lawsuit as part of his M&A work. In Shad's mind, a properly conducted merger would leave everyone better off, and the cutthroat nature of hostile takeovers was alien to his own experience on Wall Street.[28] As the head of the SEC, Shad believed his primary duty was to protect the value of stockholders' investments. Given that trust and fair play were central to Shad's worldview, insider trading and abusive business practices were anathema to him, and his tenure at the SEC is best remembered for his successful criminal investigations into the financiers Ivan Boesky and Michael Milken.[29]

Beyond his law enforcement duties, Shad wanted to understand the effect that SEC actions had on stock prices and urged his staff to focus on crafting light-touch regulations that would boost investors' confidence in the markets, encourage liquidity, and lead to higher stock prices.[30] This desire to understand costs and benefits led Shad to develop a particularly close relationship with economists, especially those trained at the University of Chicago. One of the biggest changes Shad made at the SEC was to push the commission, which had been dominated by lawyers since its founding, to hire more economists who could study the economic impact of any potential regulations.[31] Even though he had a law degree himself, Shad made no secret of the fact that he preferred the quantitative and relatively straightforward advice of economists to the often convoluted legal analyses of regulations offered to him by the commission's lawyers. Though Shad himself was far too moralistic and trusting in the better parts of human nature to classify as a true devotee of the Chicago School, he deeply respected the work of Chicago economists. In the fall of 1982 Shad established the Office of the Chief Economist within the SEC and named Charles Cox, a law and economics scholar who studied under George Stigler at Chicago and had organized a law and economics program at Texas A&M, as the commission's first chief economist.[32] Shad set up the Office of the Chief Economist to report directly to the chairman, and to make room for Cox to have an office near his, Shad moved the commission's equal opportunity director to the basement—a symbolic act that would come back to haunt Shad later in his tenure when the commission was rocked by several cases of racial and gender discrimination.[33]

As he set about trying to transform the commission, hostile takeovers quickly rose to the top of Shad's agenda thanks to the aftermath of the US Supreme Court's decision in the case of *Edgar v. MITE*, which was announced in June 1982.[34] The *MITE* case stemmed from a hostile tender offer issued in 1979 by the MITE Corporation, a machine parts conglomerate based in Connecticut and chartered in Delaware, for control of the Chicago Rivet & Machine Company, which was located in Illinois. Under Illinois law, MITE was required to issue a public notice of its intention to make a tender offer for Chicago Rivet at least twenty days in advance of the offer. During that twenty-day advance warning period, Chicago Rivet's managers were permitted to issue announcements to the company's shareholders as part of a defensive campaign, while MITE was prohibited from communicating with shareholders. MITE's management chose not to comply with Illinois's anti-takeover law and instead only filed disclosure forms with the SEC ten days before their tender offer, as required by the Williams Act. When the state of Illinois moved to block MITE's offer, the company sued and claimed that the state's anti-takeover law was unconstitutional since it was superseded by the Williams Act and violated the Commerce Clause in the US Constitution. After MITE won favorable rulings in lower courts, the case reached the Supreme Court, which ruled by a 6–3 decision that all state-level anti-takeover laws, not just Illinois's law, were unconstitutional. The court's decision instantly removed some of the strongest deterrents to hostile takeovers and left the Williams Act as the sole law governing tender offers.[35]

It did not take long after the MITE decision for the inadequacies of the Williams Act to make themselves apparent. In the fall of 1982, the national media was transfixed—one columnist called it better than football—by the bizarre merger battle between the Bendix Corporation and Martin Marietta that seemed to reveal the very worst aspects of the hostile takeover movement.[36] The Bendix saga began when William Agee, a forty-four-year old "whiz kid" graduate of Harvard Business School who was sometimes described as "America's first yuppie" due to his informal way of dressing and interacting with staff combined and his brash style of conducting business, made an offer to purchase Martin Marietta, a defense contractor based in Maryland, for $1.5 billion.[37] What started as a single takeover attempt blossomed into a four-way affair as two other conglomerates, United Technologies and Allied Technologies, leapt into the fray in an attempt to purchase the weakened companies.[38] After weeks of back-and-forth that included such humorous details as a meeting being held on the side of a suburban Maryland highway and an angry shareholders' meeting cut short by someone shutting off the power, the contest ended with Allied purchasing control of Bendix, Bendix's chairman receiving a $4.1 million "golden parachute" severance payment, and Martin Marietta having taken on $990 million in debt to remain independent. In addition to the monetary cost, Allied's acquisition of Bendix was soon followed by a series of layoffs that cost hundreds of jobs.[39]

With the media already primed to make a big story out of the Bendix fight, the cartoonish behavior of the people involved sent the press into overdrive, and the experience of a high-profile fracas in an industry with deep ties to the federal government raised alarm bells in the popular press and in Washington.[40] That the Williams Act seemed to do nothing to affect the behavior of the participants and the courts refused to do anything to curb the excesses of the merger battle only added to the sense that something had to be done to rein in takeovers.[41] *Time* magazine labeled the entire affair "merger theater of the absurd," while newspapers were full of union heads, business leaders, investment bankers, and academics claiming that hostile takeovers had been allowed to go too far.[42] One law professor went so far as to label the entire affair "a cannibalistic orgy."[43] Importantly, even the bankers who worked on the deal realized that their behavior put the entire M&A community in jeopardy. Rohatyn, who had advised United Technologies, warned his colleagues that "there's a general perception that investment banks' fees are too high, and that they don't earn them. . . . That opinion is so widespread that the investment banking community had better pay attention to it or someone else will."[44]

Though some corporate raiders such as T. Boone Pickens, who called the Bendix fight an example of "the free enterprise system" in action, tried to argue that no additional regulation was needed, the spectacle of the takeover battle made a political debate over hostile takeovers all but inevitable.[45] At the SEC, Shad knew that there would be public calls for new regulations on tender offers in the wake of Bendix. In an attempt to get ahead of the debate, Shad announced in February 1983 that the SEC would form an expert committee to study the hostile takeover issue.[46] The committee would be made up almost entirely of lawyers, business executives, and investment bankers who had been deeply involved in takeovers.[47] Academia was represented by two Chicago alumni: Frank Easterbrook, a law professor at Chicago who had received his JD at Chicago's law school; and Gregg Jarrell, a finance professor at Rochester's business school who had received an economics PhD from Chicago's business school.[48] Given the committee's makeup, it was no surprise that they decided hostile takeovers were "a valid method of capital allocation." Having established the validity of hostile takeovers, the commission declared that they sought "neither to promote nor to deter takeovers," but rather to smooth out imperfections in the market.[49] Despite these modest aims, the committee did propose, on July 8, 1983, fifty regulatory changes that ranged from minor tweaks to existing regulations to a handful of major changes that would require congressional action.[50] Aside from one major recommendation that would strengthen disclosure requirements for bidders, most of the committee's substantial recommendations sought to limit defensive tactics.[51] None of these recommendations were more controversial than the set that sought to create a national market for corporate control by effectively banning state anti-takeover laws, which put the Reagan administration in the awkward position of advocating for increased federal regulation at the expense of the individual states.[52]

Despite the committee's claims of neutrality, two dissents from the members of the commission not directly involved in takeovers revealed the difficulty any reform package—much less one designed by the M&A sector—would encounter. On one side, the former Supreme Court Justice Arthur Goldberg took the committee to task for failing to include any "significant reference to the protection of the public interest" thanks to their "misconception that only shareholders" were involved in takeovers.[53] Easterbrook and Jarrell issued a lengthy competing dissent, written in startlingly mocking language designed to catch Shad's eye, in which they provided a summary of Chicago financial theory and sharply criticized the commission for its supposed choice to ignore the "science" that proved the economic value of takeovers. In light of the pro-takeover "science," Easterbrook and Jarrell claimed, the only thing the committee should have recommended was deregulation.[54] Though the extreme nature of Easterbrook and Jarrell's position may have made them a minority within the advisory committee, it did raise their profile. In 1984 Easterbrook was nominated by President Reagan to be a federal judge, while Jarrell was hired by Shad as the SEC's next chief economist after Shad had successfully asked President Reagan to promote Cox to a seat on the SEC.[55]

After the commission issued its recommendations in July 1983, the next significant moment for reform came in March 1984 as congressional inquiries into hostile takeover reform began. Even before Shad had the opportunity to testify before Congress about the committee's recommendations, House Judiciary Committee Chairman Peter Rodino (D-NJ) and Senator Arlen Specter (R-PA) both introduced reform bills of their own that went beyond the SEC's recommendations.[56] Congressional action was driven in no small part by a seemingly widespread desire on the public's part for some version of hostile takeover reform. In a series of hearings that began in March, House Finance Subcommittee Chairman Timothy Wirth, a market-friendly "Atari Democrat" from Colorado who would emerge as the leading congressional voice for takeover reform, released the many letters his committee had received from labor unions, investment banks, and business executives all expressing some degree of support for reform to strengthen disclosure and ban some of most controversial defense tactics.[57] While all of these groups were pressing for reform, the staff of the White House Council of Economic Advisers (CEA) began crafting their own response to the takeover issue. A letter sent on March 23 from the CEA's legal counsel, Stephen Halpert, to CEA Chair William Niskanen, a famously blunt free-market economist who would later go on to head the libertarian Cato Institute, warned that attempts to curb takeovers would "leave us with (almost) the worst of all possible worlds" and that the CEA needed to come up with a counterargument quickly.[58]

On May 22, the day before he reconvened his hearings on takeovers, Wirth introduced three bills in the House that sought to implement a jumbled range of reform proposals.[59] These bills combined the recommendations of the SEC with a measure to ban a coercive tactic known as a two-tiered tender offer that had been proposed to Wirth's subcommittee by Martin Lipton.[60] As a complete package, the bills seemed to amount to a scattershot approach to reform in which Congress was attempting to stamp out a long list of practices that angered people without doing anything to address the effects takeovers were having on the broader economy. Wirth admitted as much in his opening statement for the second day of his hearings when he claimed that "we are not addressing today the question of whether takeovers are good or bad for the economy as a whole, but whether we should be strengthening the law to make the takeover process more fair."[61]

After Wirth's statement, a parade of witnesses representing the highest echelons of the business and financial worlds testified as to the need for takeover reform, with several going further than Wirth had in denouncing takeovers. NAM blasted the SEC advisory commission as nothing more than the representatives of Wall Street and demanded that Congress take a closer look at the takeover issue in light of the harms that takeovers could cause.[62] Charles Munger, Warren Buffet's longtime business partner and a self-professed "right-wing Republican," told Congress that most hostile takeovers were "not in the public interest" and demanded that the subcommittee make up their minds quickly about the value of hostile takeovers and not "wait for a lot of social science research."[63] Rohatyn reiterated the warnings he had issued after the Bendix merger fight and called for Congress to impose even stricter limits on takeover bids and defenses than the SEC commission had recommended.[64] Even Irwin Jacobs, a feared corporate raider, agreed that disclosure deadlines for bidders should be shortened.[65] On the political front, Anthony Celebrezze Jr., the attorney general of Ohio, testified on behalf of the National Association of Attorneys General that the association was opposed to hostile takeovers in general due to their damaging effects on communities and would prefer that Congress enact no new federal regulations, but rather pass legislation that would allow the individual states to regulate and likely prohibit takeovers.[66] Though organized labor was excluded from these hearings, a representative of the Consumer Federation of America announced the Federation's strong opposition to takeovers and called on Congress to do all it could to pass Lipton's anti-takeover measure.[67] Given the amount of public support for reform, it was not surprising that on June 22 *The Wall Street Journal* claimed that a reform bill would stand "a good chance of passage" in the current Congress.[68]

Takeover reform's prospects seemed especially bright because in June Shad had surprised everyone in the Reagan administration by seemingly throwing his weight behind reform in a speech titled "The Leveraging of America" he delivered to a group of New York City financial writers.[69] Though Shad had gravitated toward the advice of Chicago School adherents like Cox and Jarrell within the SEC, he also remained in close contact with his former colleagues in the financial world, including the former SEC commissioner A. A. Sommer and Lipton, who urged him to support takeover reform by appealing to his sense of propriety and to worries he held about skyrocketing levels of corporate debt.[70] Judging by the content of Shad's speech, these appeals may have had the desired effect. Though Shad claimed that he only wanted to "ventilate some of the major issues" associated with hostile takeovers, his remarks made it clear that he had serious problems with them. He began the speech by noting that within the past year institutional investors had begun to take an active role in voting against managers' anti-takeover proposals and supporting corporate raiders. This change in behavior led Shad to project that "a rising number of institutions will not only oppose future anti-takeover proposals by managements, but also begin to support corporate break-ups and mergers, with a view to enhancing the value of their investments."[71] This worried Shad because most takeovers were financed by very large loans. As Shad saw it, "the more leveraged takeovers and buyouts today, the more bankruptcies tomorrow," which meant that "the leveraging-up of American enterprise will magnify the adverse consequences of the next recession or significant rise in interest rates."[72] Shad also made it clear to his audience that he was quite skeptical of the supposed benefits of hostile takeovers when he told them that "the theory that contested takeovers discipline incompetent managements is of limited veracity."[73] In Shad's opinion, many of the companies being threatened with hostile takeovers were well-run and on economically sound footing; they were only being threatened because the financial and regulatory environments favored corporate raiders. To Shad, this meant that "in today's corporate world, Darwin's 'survival of the fittest,' has become — acquire or be acquired."[74] As a sign of his pride in these remarks, on his return to Washington Shad asked his aide to mail a copy of the speech to other government officials and business leaders across the country, including the CEOs of the Fortune 500.[75]

Shad's speech set off a firestorm among free-market advocates in the White House and in the SEC. Between Shad's speech and the continued progress of takeover reform in Congress, Reagan's economic advisers sensed that they were losing control over the takeover issue in a critical period before the 1984 election. With the pressure mounting on them, Reagan's advisers felt that they needed to quickly put together a solid position on takeover reform.[76] At the end of June, Wirth's subcommittee consolidated their three takeover bills into a single bill and added a provision that would force takeover bidders to disclose any plans they might have to lay off workers or reduce their pay.[77] On June 28—the same day Wirth's subcommittee approved their reform bill—the President's Cabinet Council on Economic Affairs (CCEA), which included Treasury Secretary Donald Regan and Niskanen, met to discuss Wirth's proposed legislation and how best to oppose it.[78] The discussion of the takeover issue was led by Christopher DeMuth, a Chicago-trained lawyer who worked as Reagan's "deregulation czar" in the Office of Management and Budget (OMB) and would go on to lead the American Enterprise Institute in 1986 after leaving government.[79] In this meeting, DeMuth led the CCEA through an explanation of the economic benefits of hostile takeovers by presenting them with evidence that takeovers boosted stock prices. On July 19, DeMuth presented the CCEA with a draft of the Reagan administration's response that would announce the administration's opposition to takeover reform. In that July meeting, DeMuth also informed the CCEA on meetings that Reagan administration officials held with Shad in which they pressured him to back down from his earlier statements, and worked with the chairman to hammer out a response to Wirth's bill.[80]

Within the SEC, Jarrell took on a leading role in the Reagan administration's campaign to blunt the progress of takeover reform.[81] Though Jarrell was prone to overstate his importance to the policymaking process in interviews with journalists, his activities within the SEC did demonstrate how he was well positioned to help nudge Shad's thinking away from the sentiments he voiced in his "Leveraging of America" speech and back toward the free-market views the chairman instinctively held. As a member of what he (with tongue in cheek) called the "cabal" of Chicago School thinkers scattered throughout the Reagan administration, Jarrell knew that he could use his position within the SEC, as well as Shad's seemingly unlimited willingness to indulge him, to push Shad away from takeover reform.[82] As part of this effort, Jarrell convinced Shad to consult with other pro-takeover members of the administration including Assistant Attorney General Douglass Ginsburg, a Chicago-trained antitrust scholar who, with Jarrell's help, formed a close working relationship with Shad. Jarrell also sought to leverage his own work as the commission's chief economist in an effort to derail reform. During the height of the political debate over takeovers, Jarrell's office produced a steady stream of academic studies that demonstrated the positive effects takeovers had on stock prices and R&D spending as well as the negative effects that defensive tactics had on shareholder value.⁸³ Jarrell did not hesitate to leak the details of these confidential studies to the press before the commission had issued them, either. In September 1984, only a few months after Shad's speech, Jarrell provided a reporter from the financial magazine *Barron's* with the details of a confidential study his office had just conducted that claimed to demonstrate that even greenmail had economic value because it too raised stock prices.⁸⁴

While leaks like this were a well-established part of the policymaking process in other parts of the government, they were quite rare in an agency as tightly-knit and publicity-averse as the SEC. Jarrell's willingness to transgress institutional norms and publicly advocate for hostile takeovers may have alienated him from some of his colleagues, but it also won him the attention of T. Boone Pickens, who reached out to tell him how much he admired his work. Jarrell and Pickens formed a friendship, with Pickens nicknaming the youthful Jarrell "the boy economist." When Pickens was in Washington, he often came to the SEC's headquarters in a limousine to pick up Jarrell for racquetball matches while Jarrell was on his lunch break.⁸⁵ Within the commission itself, Jarrell sought to obtain advance copies of reform proposals that would be presented to meetings of the agency's five commissioners from the head of the Commission's Office of Tender Offers and then hurriedly prepared rebuttals he could submit to the commissioners at those same meetings, sometimes with the help of Cox. In every instance when Jarrell stepped over a line, Shad would chastise him and sometimes even threaten to take action against him, but he never did; and the other members of the commission marveled at their boss's willingness to indulge his mischievous chief economist. Shad's affection for Jarrell combined with Jarrell's consistent advocacy of takeovers led the commission's takeover staff to view him as the single most important figure within the commission when it came to takeover issues, and they believed he had a great deal of influence over Shad's thinking on the issue.⁸⁶

From outside the policymaking process, Michael Jensen also attempted to do what he could to slow the pace of reform by publishing an article in the November 1984 issue of the *Harvard Business Review* titled "Takeovers: Folklore and Science."⁸⁷ Jensen used the article to combine his previous work on agency theory and the nature of the corporation with evidence that supposedly proved the benefits of hostile takeovers. Since it was published in the *Harvard Business Review* Jensen knew his work would reach a large audience, and he used this opportunity to fully leverage the argumentative power he could gain from claiming the mantle of "scientific" research. Much of the article consisted of a point-by-point takedown of the "folklore" and "myths" about takeovers which Jensen said worked to "distort the public's perception and render a meaningful dialogue impossible," such as the idea that takeovers were a waste of corporate funds or that they caused socially damaging job losses.[88] In language very similar to his earlier work with Meckling, Jensen blamed the continued existence of these "myths" about takeovers on a combination of the public's ignorance and "the actions of individuals and groups that wish to use the corporation's assets for their own purposes, without purchasing them."[89] Instead of believing in "folklore," Jensen urged his audience to pay attention to "science"—namely, the EMH and a large body of empirical studies which demonstrated that hostile takeovers raised stock prices and therefore improved social welfare. The punchy nature of Jensen's article also caught the eye of Pickens, who reportedly handed out copies of it to his friends and began to incorporate references to Jensen's work into his own defenses of hostile takeovers before Congress.[90]

Jensen followed his attack against the "folklore" offered by critics of hostile takeovers with his own theory of why takeovers happen, which he published in 1986. After reviewing recent takeover battles, Jensen decided that instead of being motivated by more nebulous problems like a supposedly undervalued stock price or perceived managerial incompetence, hostile takeovers were, at their core, a fight between incumbent managers and activist investors over control of a company's cash. From this insight, Jensen created a theory of takeovers that hinged on the concept of Free Cash Flow (FCF). In mathematical terms, FCF was simply the amount of cash left in a business's account after it had paid for all of its capital expenditures—which for these purposes encompassed all money spent on productive activities, including buying new facilities, research and development, and even workforce training.[91] As Jensen saw it, FCF was one of the major causes of conflict between investors and managers, and as a result, it was a significant driver of the agency costs he had written about in "Theory of the Firm." The reason investors cared about free cash flow so much was that, according to shareholder value theorists like Jensen, it belonged to them. In Jensen's telling, one of the greatest agency costs shareholders were forced to bear was created by managers seeking to hold cash in a company's account or wasting it on unproductive activities.[92] As Jensen explained in a piece for *The New York Times* in March 1986, "free cash flow must be paid out to shareholders if the company is to be efficient and to maximize shareholder values.

Companies with high agency costs due to high free cash flows and poor future investment prospects are highly likely to be takeover candidates."[93] A business was already required to pay out FCF to cover legal obligations against the firm, which included wages, taxes, and debt payments. Shareholder value theorists argued that all FCF that remained in a company's coffers after making these required payments belonged to shareholders, and that managers should disburse it to them in the form of either share buybacks or dividend payments. If managers chose not to give shareholders sufficient FCF, then it was only natural to expect those shareholders to try to replace those managers in a hostile takeover.[94]

Not with a Bang, but with a Whimper: The End of Tender Offer Reform

The counterattack against reform from raiders, academia, and the White House, and within the SEC, began to make progress during the late summer and fall of 1984. On August 2, the full House Committee on Energy and Commerce approved Wirth's bill with a voice vote and sent it to the House floor in the hope of securing its passage before the end of the legislative session on October 12.[95] On September 7, Shad began to take a harder stance against reform and made his opposition to Wirth's bill final by sending a letter to Representative John Dingell (D-MI), the chairman of the Energy and Commerce Committee, announcing that the SEC had withdrawn its support for the proposed reforms and urging the House to support only the SEC's original legislative proposals instead.[96] On the same day, Shad also notified Senator Alfonse D'Amato (R-NY), the chairman of the Senate Subcommittee on Securities and an ally of Wirth in takeover reform efforts, that he had opposed Wirth's bill and hoped to discourage the Senate from considering it.[97] When D'Amato held his own hearings on October 2, the Treasury Department sent an announcement that it opposed any attempt to regulate takeovers since they were too "complex and their implications are too important to be dealt with hastily" and Congress needed to "give these issues the thorough analysis and careful debate they deserve."[98] These warnings seemed to have worked, and D'Amato voiced his displeasure with the House bill and announced that he would be leading his own effort to design a competing reform bill.[99] Though the Senate was no less supportive than the House of the general need for takeover reform, and three senators—one Democrat and two Republicans—did announce their own reform proposals in the October hearing, the fact that D'Amato had announced his opposition to Wirth's bill killed off any hopes of takeover reform in the last few days of the congressional session before the general election of 1984.[100]

Though takeover reform suffered a setback at the end of 1984, its prospects only seemed to brighten in the new year thanks to another messy high-profile takeover battle. In December 1984, Pickens launched a takeover bid for Oklahoma-based Phillips Petroleum that ended with him accepting a greenmail payment for a quick $87 million profit in return for his promise that he would not buy any Phillips stock for fifteen years. As soon as Phillips had bought their freedom from Pickens, however, they were hit with another takeover bid from Carl Icahn, who had secured $8.1 billion in funding, much of it from risky debt often referred to as "junk bonds" sold by Michael Milken, who almost singlehandedly created the hyperactive market for junk bonds during the 1980s from his position at the investment bank Drexel Burnham Lambert.[101] In the end, Icahn also accepted a greenmail payment for a profit of $52.5 million in March 1985 after he led a shareholders' revolt that defeated an anti-takeover charter amendment the board of Phillips had attempted to implement.[102] Icahn's junk-bond-fueled raid revealed just how dramatically the hostile takeover wave had escalated. Milken's ability to raise billions almost overnight through selling junk bonds sent a signal to corporate America that almost no company was too big to face a takeover attempt.[103] Moreover, Icahn's successful bid to defeat Phillips's anti-takeover provision was backed a wide array of institutional investors, who by 1985 controlled around half of all shares listed on the NYSE.[104] The defeat of Phillips's anti-takeover amendments by these institutional investors at Icahn's behest was the most prominent example of these financial powerhouses being willing to use their stock holdings to force managers to behave in shareholder-friendly ways, and a sobering reminder to corporate managers of the potential dangers they faced from increasingly restive shareholders.[105]

Once again, the titans of the business and financial worlds issued calls for Congress to rein in hostile takeovers in response to the Phillips battles.[106] In 1985 the Business Roundtable threw its considerable political influence behind congressional action and was joined by NAM as well as the AFL-CIO, Warren Buffet, and Rohatyn.[107] The NYSE went so far as to propose abandoning its long-standing commitment to "one-share-one-vote" and allowing its listing companies to issue non-voting shares of stock as a way to protect management.[108] Within Congress itself, there was a flood of bills (at least thirteen in 1985) introduced in both Houses from Republicans and Democrats that ran the gamut from minor restrictions on abusive practices to an outright ban on effectively all hostile takeovers.[109]

Unlike in 1984, the Reagan administration and its allies in academia were more than prepared for the pro-reform onslaught they faced in the press and Congress. In February 1985, the CEA dedicated an entire chapter of the Economic Report of the President, the official statement of the administration's economic policy to "the market for corporate control."[110] The report, which was signed by Reagan and primarily written by Niskanen and William Poole, an economist who had received his PhD in finance from the University of Chicago, read like "a carbon copy of the free-market academic arguments," in the words of financial journalist John Brooks.[111] The report drew heavily on the landmarks of financial theory, like the EMH and agency theory, as well as several event studies conducted by Jensen, among others, to supposedly prove the economic value of takeovers. In language reminiscent of Easterbrook and Jarrell's SEC dissent in 1983, the report suggested that if Congress wanted to address hostile takeovers it should seek deregulation, not regulatory attempts to slow down the market for corporate control.[112] Jensen himself had the opportunity to testify before Wirth's committee in March, and he used his testimony to present the committee with a forceful defense of the full range of takeover behavior and an argument for so-called "raiders" to be celebrated for their value to society.[113] Jensen also reminded his audience that "we know from modern capital theory that we want to look at stock price changes in measuring the welfare implications of takeovers.... Congress should take actions which maximize the value of the assets in the country. That is exactly why stock prices are the best measure we have of what those values are."[114] Though Jensen did not completely win over the room with his argument, it is clear that he made a good deal of headway, and at the end of the day's testimony, Wirth admitted to him "that members of the subcommittee would like to agree with you, Professor Jensen, when you say that there is one measure that we can depend upon."[115]

With the unified opposition of the executive branch and the ability of academics like Jensen and Jarrell to sow doubt in the minds of pro-reform legislators and regulators, the scattered efforts of takeover reformers went down to an anticlimactic defeat. The death knells for takeover reform came in the spring and summer of 1985. On May 20, after a hearing dominated by pro-takeover testimony from institutional investors and the OMB, the five commissioners of the SEC voted unanimously to oppose any further attempts to regulate the market for corporate control and Shad declared all legislative proposals "obsolete."[116] The final sign that momentum had shifted decisively away from the pro-reform camp came on July 1, when FTC Chairman James Miller penned a *New York Times* op-ed in which he announced that the Reagan administration officially supported the deregulation of hostile takeovers.[117] Though Congress continued to hold hearings—and indeed held them for the remainder of the decade—not a single anti-takeover bill ever came to a vote on the floor of either chamber.

To expert observers of congressional politics, the failure of Congress to pass takeover legislation would likely not have come as a surprise. Given the opposition of the executive branch, the diffuse nature of support for takeover reform, and the unwillingness of Atari Democrats like Wirth to advocate for strong government interventions in the market, takeover reform was always going to face an uphill battle in congressional committees.[118] Despite the inherent difficulties involved in passing takeover reform, however, Congress's failure to do so in the 1980s does offer several lessons for students of American political economy. The entire episode is a reminder of the importance of what the political scientists Jacob Hacker and Paul Pierson call "drift," which they define as deliberate government inaction in the face of dynamic economic change.[119] Congress's failure to act allowed corporate raiders and institutional investors to continue to force managers to reckon with the power of shareholders and the economic arguments in favor of shareholder value maximization. For their part, Hacker and Pierson identified business lobbyists and wealthy political donors as the people most responsible for encouraging drift, since inaction was likely to benefit these wealthy interest groups. Historians interested in the politics of deregulation and economic liberalization in the late 1970s and 1980s have similarly focused their attention on business lobbyists and their connections to movement conservatives in the Reagan administration, and have identified these relationships as a key factor in driving economic liberalization.[120] The case of hostile takeovers adds an important wrinkle to these narratives about America's shift to the right in the 1980s, since both the Business Roundtable and NAM, along with even some of the investment banking community, actively lobbied Congress for takeover reform. Yet this effort was unsuccessful, thanks in part to the activism of a small group of pro-takeover intellectuals and a shift in power away from traditional bastions of the business and financial lobbies toward more aggressive financial traders and M&A specialists. Though mainline business leaders had often found free-market intellectuals to be useful allies in their fights against what managers considered to be bothersome government regulation, the battle for tender offer reform reminds us that free-market ideologues could also be quite dangerous to managers. Business managers often found value in government regulation, especially when it insulated them from destructive pressures from financial markets or competitors. Scholars like Jensen or Jarrell cared little for the plight of managers threatened by corporate takeovers; their concern was ensuring that neither government regulations nor entrenched corporate managers could stand in the way of efficient markets as they restructured American business.

Coordination, Control, and the Management of Organizations

Though they generated no response from the federal government, the political debates over hostile takeovers did leave a lasting legacy for American political economy by sparking a transformation in business education, one that was spearheaded by Jensen and his fellow financial economists. Jensen's colleagues in the world of business academia did not fail to notice that he seemed to have one of the most in-demand intellectual explanations of, and justifications for, the phenomenon that was likely at the front of most MBA students' minds during the 1980s. Jensen had a knack for publicity, and he was frequently cited in both the business press and mainstream newspapers during the first half of the 1980s as an expert on hostile takeovers.[121] Jensen's growing public profile brought him to the attention of Harvard's Dean John McArthur, who invited Jensen to come to the school and take a visiting professorship in 1984—a position which was made permanent the following year.[122] McArthur's decision to approach Jensen was part of his broader effort to bolster the school's reputation after it had begun to slip over the preceding decade. In 1976, *MBA Magazine* published a poll of US business school deans asking them to rank the nation's graduate business schools. Harvard's faculty was shocked to see that their school came in a distant second place to Stanford in these rankings, and that both Chicago and MIT were close behind Harvard at third and fourth place, respectively. The reason for Harvard's slip in these rankings was the school's stubborn adherence to a focus on teaching—particularly its cherished case method of classroom instruction—and its relative lack of attention to research.[123] Moreover, Harvard's adherence to managerialism made it seem out of step with the world of American business in the 1980s, as agency theory began to be cited in government reports, congressional testimony, and the mainstream press. By associating themselves with Jensen, the school's administrators hoped they could shake off the perception of Harvard as being out of touch and capitalize on Jensen's research success as well as his popularity with both students and the press.[124]

Aside from lending the school his star power, Jensen's major contribution to Harvard was importing an elective course titled "Coordination, Control, and the Management of Organizations" (CCMO) that he and Meckling had developed at Rochester. When Jensen and Meckling first began to develop CCMO in 1973, they envisioned it as a way to teach price theory to Rochester's young MBA students from a managerial perspective instead of the perspective of a policy maker.[125] After the first two years of teaching the class, Jensen and Meckling found that their students were far more interested in the organizational problems their professors were using as examples than they were in price theory.[126] Jensen and Meckling redesigned the course and integrated their research on political economy, human nature, and the theory of the firm into the syllabus as a way to provide students with a general framework for understanding business problems. As part of this redesign, Jensen and Meckling established what Jensen would later identify as the two key traditions of the course: "first . . . the idea that *real learning leads to (and is evidenced by) changes in behavior*," and second, a commitment to bring new faculty in to learn the course material and teach it to students.[127] To this end, Jensen and Meckling compiled a long list of "course notes" that were shared with new faculty when they were assigned to teach the course and were, in 1998, made public by Jensen to spread the course to other interested professors.[128] By the time Jensen left Rochester in 1985, CCMO was the school's most popular elective, a feat Jensen would duplicate at Harvard as shown in the enrollment numbers displayed in figure 4.1.

CCMO was designed by Jensen and Meckling to have three modules that built on each other: a "foundations" module that introduced students to the assumptions on which the course was built; a second module that sought to define how corporations were structured; and a final module that related what the students had learned to "organizational governance and corporate control."[129] These three modules amounted to "nothing more nor less than a set of propositions about how the world behaves," in the words of the Organizations and Markets Unit of Harvard, which

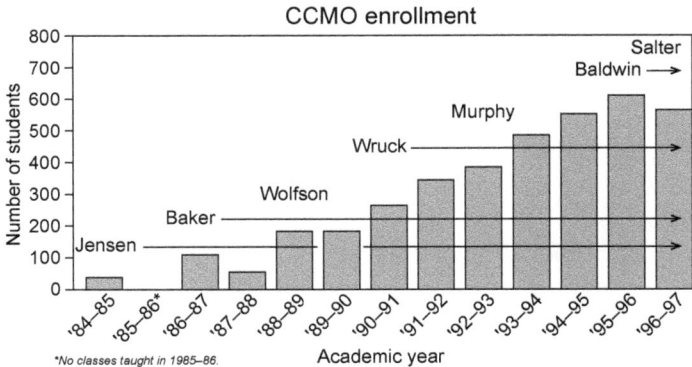

FIGURE 4.1. Historical enrollments in CCMO and teaching faculty for the period 1985–1996. The names of the HBS faculty that taught sections of CCMO are Michael Jensen, George Baker, Mark Wolfson, Karen Wruck, Kevin Murphy, Carliss Baldwin, and Malcolm Salter. Recreated from Jensen et al., "Organizations and Markets: History and Development," 7.

was responsible for administering the course once Jensen moved there.[130] The course began with Jensen and Meckling introducing students to the REMM model of human behavior and the idea of agency costs, with the instructor taking a deliberately confrontational stance with students to get them to abandon other understandings of human behavior. The course notes published by Jensen revealed that this first module contained many of the same arguments against sociological and political conceptions of mankind that Meckling and Brunner had made in their earlier published work.[131] From these foundations, Jensen and Meckling moved into the second module, which was a discussion of the theory of the firm and how decisions were made in economic organizations. This second module presented students with a contractual definition of the firm that could be adapted to the various economic organizations that made up the modern economy, from private family businesses to large public companies and even nonprofits.[132] The final module then took students through the various ways in which they as managers could structure their companies to incentivize efficiency and minimize agency costs in the interest of maximizing shareholder value.[133] These lessons included sessions on designing compensation plans, delegating decision-making rights, and selecting the proper performance evaluation measurements for different parts of a multidivisional firm. By the end of the course students were supposed to have "a clear understanding of how organizational rules of the game affect a manager's ability to resolve problems, increase productivity, and achieve his or her objectives" as well as "an understanding of how organizational structure affects performance and how current economic and social forces are reshaping the role of managers."[134] All in all, the course aimed to provide students with "an integrated worldview that starts at a very basic level by describing the characteristic of the individuals who are actors, agents, managers, employees, and customers in a system and the nature of information (its inherent scarcity and the differential cost of moving it between people); and builds a structure—describing organizations, markets, and social systems—that we think is a logical consequence."[135]

In Jensen's own telling, this first module was an intense experience and students "were far from uniformly happy with the CCMO experience. In fact, many were (and are today) often shocked, depressed, and even angry, especially in the early weeks of the course."[136] Jensen attributed these negative responses to the fact that he used the logic of the course to challenge some of his students' deeply held beliefs. As an example, Jensen explained that many of his students came into his course supporting the idea of rent controls to secure affordable housing. Jensen confronted his students with the observed effects of rent controls—in his telling, that it destroyed housing stocks and raised prices—as a means of demonstrating to his students that their normative evaluations of issues were insufficiently rigorous when compared to the scientific evaluations used by economists. Jensen went on to describe how "this gap between hoped-for outcomes and reality is disconcerting, especially when it is applied to concepts—such as the 'stakeholder model'—that are dear to the hearts of many of our students."[137] These traumatic first few weeks included the introduction of the REMM model and the demolition of the sociological model of behavior that Meckling and Brunner were so concerned about, as well as the introduction of principle-agent problems and the argument that politicians and other people in positions of authority only acted in their own self-interest. In a paraphrasing of William James, the people responsible for teaching the course claimed that it served to separate the "tough-minded" students who were willing to tackle hard facts and face the world as it was from the "tender-minded" who did not have the intellectual or moral courage to do so.[138]

Judging from the fact that CCMO was the most popular course at both Rochester and Harvard, and that by 1997 the course was also being taught at the University of Southern California and the University of Chicago, there must have been an ample supply of "tough-minded" future executives who were ready to have their ideals challenged.[139] The course material did evolve from its beginnings in the 1970s. For instance, Jensen's acceptance in the 1990s of behavioral economics and the idea that not all human behavior was rational was a major departure from the early work he had done with Meckling and was a source, along with Jensen's move to Harvard, of a falling out between the two that lasted for the rest of Meckling's life.[140] Despite these changes, the course did not depart from the vision of political economy that developed out of Rochester in the 1970s. A generation of future executives and managers learned to think of business problems in terms of REMMs, agency costs, and the irrationality of trusting in politics or society. Even at universities where the CCMO course was not taught, the theory of the firm that was developed at Rochester became a fundamental part of any academic program in finance or management.[141] It is impossible to fully gauge just how effective Jensen and the other professors who taught CCMO were at convincing their students to adopt a new worldview, but the massive demand for the course among students is certainly an indication that there was an audience for these arguments. Those who taught the class certainly felt that it was effective, and a statement from the Harvard faculty claimed that "it is clear that CCMO changes students' behavior."[142]

Survey data and insights from scholars of management education lent credence to the boasts of those who taught CCMO that their work, and the work of business professors who taught similar content, changed students' behaviors. Surveys of MBA students conducted in 2001 by the Aspen Institute, a think tank, found that 75 percent of MBA students identified maximizing shareholder value as the primary responsibility of a company. Richard Preim and Joseph Rosenstein, a pair of management professors, found in an experiment they conducted in which they asked participants to select business strategies for different hypothetical situations that participants who had received business school educations were significantly more likely to base their decisions on academic theory than either businesspeople without an MBA or the general public.[143] Even if MBA graduates did not fully remember what they learned in business school, the theories they learned may still have influenced their behavior through a process known as "imprinting," which was defined by the sociologists Christopher Marquis and András Tilcsik as "a process whereby, during a brief period of susceptibility, a focal entity developed characteristics that reflect prominent features of the environment, and these characteristics continue to persist despite significant environmental changes in subsequent periods."[144] The sociologists Jiwook Jung and Taekjin Shin applied this concept to business education by pointing out that MBA students, who were often early in their careers and sequestered in an intellectually intense environment, were quite susceptible to imprinting, especially since MBA curricula placed such a strong emphasis on shareholder value maximization and finance.[145] Moreover, the pair specifically investigated the behavior of CEOs who enrolled in Jensen's CCMO course at Harvard and found that their business decisions matched closely with the business strategies suggested by a deep understanding of agency theory, including an avoidance of diversification and a focus on "core competencies," which they took as evidence of psychological imprinting.[146] This process of imprinting, along with those students who self-consciously chose to follow the insights of the theories they learned in business school, helped explain some of the ways in which financial theory became a "self-fulfilling prophecy" in which rising executives who learned agency theory and shareholder primacy in their MBA coursework managed their companies according to these theories even when the pressures of corporate raiders were removed.[147]

The successes shareholder value theorists enjoyed during the 1980s capped off a remarkable rise both for them and for financial economics as a whole. While the strength of their research agendas combined with generous financial backing undoubtedly best explains their rise over the long run, the hostile takeover wave of the 1980s does deserve credit for accelerating the ascendancy of financial economics, and of shareholder value theorists like Jensen in particular. During the 1980s, scholars such as Jensen and Jarrell saw their careers advance rapidly thanks to the relevance of their work to hostile takeovers. While some like Jarrell chose to take part directly in policymaking debates about hostile takeovers, many more chose to exercise their growing influence by reshaping professional education around shareholder primacy. Shareholder-centric curricula in business schools amplified the work corporate raiders were doing to champion the cause of shareholder value maximization. Perhaps even more importantly, the rise of financial economics provided shareholder value maximization with an institutional home at the very heart of the American corporate establishment. While the immediate work of restructuring American business around shareholder value maximization detailed in the following chapters was carried out largely by corporate leaders educated before shareholder value ideas achieved intellectual hegemony in professional education, subsequent generations of business leaders—thanks in part to what they had learned in the formative years of their careers—would carry on the work of the shareholder value revolution into the 1990s and the twenty-first century.

CHAPTER FIVE

The Eclipse of the Public Corporation

As important as financial economists' theories were in shifting the intellectual environment of American business, they were of little immediate use to business managers in the 1980s and 1990s who sought to protect their companies from corporate raiders and restless investors. The pronouncements of academics like Jensen and raiders like Pickens made it clear to managers that they needed to focus on delivering value to shareholders, but these exhortations offered little in the way of concrete steps managers could take to achieve this goal. Fortunately for managers who were searching for ways to protect themselves by maximizing shareholder value, the hostile takeover wave of the 1980s also gave rise to a series of organizational and managerial techniques that offered to teach corporate leaders "value-based management."[1] The most prominent and potentially transformative of these techniques was the leveraged buyout (LBO), which offered corporate managers, or enterprising takeover artists, the ability to take a company private at the cost of tremendous amounts of debt. Though the rise of leveraged buyouts was inextricably linked to the hostile takeover boom, LBOs' effects on American business were even more profound than those of hostile takeovers. LBOs were the preferred tool of investors and managers looking to break up conglomerates, and by the end of the 1980s buyout artists had largely succeeded in "deconglomerating" American business.[2] LBOs also seemed to be the perfect tool to resolve the problem of agency costs, and shareholder value theorists became some of the most ardent supporters of the emerging buyout industry. Jensen was so enamored of buyouts and their ability to create value that he went so far as to predict that leveraged buyouts would largely eliminate the public corporation from the American economy. Though the end of the fourth merger wave in 1989 may have dashed Jensen's hopes for an economy dominated by LBOs, the buyout boom of the 1980s did reshape American political economy through its two greatest legacies: the emergence of the modern private equity industry, which has used buyouts to reshape large swaths of the American economy; and the rise of a cohort of so-called value consultants who offered the managers of public companies restructuring programs designed to help them adopt some of the managerial strategies associated with LBOs. These consultants believed that the public corporation itself could be remade into a vehicle for shareholder value maximization if managers focused on some of the same key issues—namely, cash flow and the cost of capital—that were prioritized by companies going through leveraged buyouts. Between these restructuring programs and LBOs, corporate leaders learned how to manage for value throughout the second half of the 1980s and the 1990s, and in the process brought the shareholder value revolution into the very heart of American business.

Though leveraged buyouts were instrumental in both advancing the cause of the shareholder value revolution and reshaping entire sectors of the American economy, the historical literature on them is remarkably diffuse. Most of the scholarly writing on buyouts has been done by social scientists or management scholars, and much of this work—though certainly not all—is quite laudatory of buyouts given their demonstrated ability, if used correctly, to create both financial profits and economic value.[3] Management scholars have written a great deal about how buyouts work and which firms may be good candidates for one, and LBOs are now a standard part of most business school curricula.[4] For their part, economists, especially financial economists, have long been interested in measuring how buyouts may create or destroy economic value, and there is a sizeable empirical literature examining these questions.[5] Beyond scholarly work, the largest segment of literature on buyouts comes from journalists who have written several, usually quite negative, profiles of buyout firms or case studies of companies that went through buyouts.[6] Historians writing on the history of late twentieth-century American political economy have either omitted buyouts from their work or given them only passing mention as just one aspect of the larger takeover movement of the

1980s.[7] Undoubtedly, one of the major factors explaining the lack of historical work on leveraged buyouts is the fact that these transactions are shrouded in a degree of secrecy that goes beyond what even traditional businesses—many of which do not part with archival information easily, if at all—employ. Leveraged buyout firms and the people who run them are notorious for their secrecy, and thanks to the fact that they take companies private when they purchase them, LBO specialists are required to disclose very little about the businesses they purchase. Moreover, until the passage of the Dodd-Frank Act in 2010, buyout firms themselves were completely unregulated by the SEC, and were therefore exempt from most financial disclosure requirements.[8] The tight control buyout specialists exercise over their work has meant that only a very few authors have been able to gain access to the internal records of buyout firms or the people who run those businesses, and this access has come only with the approval of buyout specialists themselves.

Two of these insider accounts of leveraged buyouts that this chapter, and indeed many other historical treatments of leveraged buyouts, draw from—*The New Financial Capitalists: Kohlberg Kravis Roberts and the Creation of Corporate Value* and *Merchants of Debt: KKR and the Mortgaging of American Business*—focused on one firm in particular, Kohlberg, Kravis, Roberts (KKR); and the differences between these two books highlighted the broader divide in the literature on buyouts.[9] *The New Financial Capitalists* was written by George P. Baker, a professor at Harvard Business School, and George David Smith, a professor at New York University's Stern School of Business, and was born out of a consulting engagement in which George Roberts, one of KKR's founders, hired the authors to create a history of the firm.[10] Though Smith and Baker's work was a serious piece of scholarship that sought to tell the story of KKR and explain why the firm had been successful and the book did contain many useful and otherwise inaccessible details about the firm, the authors' admiration for their subject was clear and the book was written in part to defend KKR from its critics in the press and government.[11] *Merchants of Debt*, on the other hand, was written by George Anders, a *Wall Street Journal* reporter who covered leveraged buyouts, and Anders took a much more critical look at KKR's history in order to understand why American businesses had come to embrace what he saw as dangerously high levels of debt. Like many good journalists, Anders's greatest strength was his ability to present the men who ran KKR as complex human beings, and his book was full of details concerning how KKR's leaders interacted with each other as well as their clients and competitors, though this detail came at the expense of Anders's ability to fully place KKR within the context of transformations in American political economy going on in the final decades of the twentieth century.[12] Though different in both their approaches and their perspectives, the two books did make a convincing case that KKR was centrally important to the rise of the overall leveraged buyout market and that buyouts were a major force in reshaping American capitalism.

This chapter also focuses on the history of KKR, but it does so in order to place both that firm and the broader leveraged buyout movement in the context of the shareholder value revolution. Leveraged buyouts were the most transformative practice associated with the Fourth Merger Wave. Theorists like Jensen and hostile raiders like Pickens may have convinced corporate managers that they needed to focus on shareholder value, but it was leveraged buyouts that provided them with an idea of how they could do so. Unlike hostile takeovers, which did not necessarily involve changes in managerial or organizational strategy, buyouts, and the restructuring programs they inspired, required managers to drastically change the way they organized and ran their businesses. Like the shareholder value revolution itself, the modern leveraged buyout industry began in the wake of the conglomerate crash of the 1960s. As conglomerate managers began to sort out their businesses according to tools like BCG's Growth Share Matrix during the 1970s, they created a class of "cast-off" companies that did not fit comfortably into their new portfolios. Some cast-offs had been acquired during the rush of the conglomerate craze and made little sense in their parents' overall business strategy, while others may simply have been too small to meet the performance demands of a large corporate head office.[13] While they may not have been the right fit for their parent company, the fact that some of these corporate cast-offs were well managed and could be profitable on their own presented an opportunity for enterprising investors who realized they could make a profit by breaking these businesses away from their corporate parents.[14]

"The New J. P. Morgans"[15]

KKR was formed by a trio of investment bankers who broke away from Bear Sterns, a New York investment bank, in 1975. The senior member of the group was Jerome Kohlberg, a former lawyer who switched to a career in banking and joined Bear Sterns in 1955 after becoming disillusioned with the "cutthroat" nature of the legal profession and finding the doors to most of New York's most prestigious law firms—and later investment banks—closed to him because he was Jewish.[16] Kohlberg radiated the kind of genteel integrity associated with his more patrician counterparts at blue-chip banks, and for the entirety of his career Kohlberg's reputation for integrity would be among his greatest assets as he assumed the role of elder statesman overseeing deals and reassuring nervous clients.[17] While working at Bear Sterns, Kohlberg met a young lawyer named George Roberts, who proved to be especially skilled at strategizing potential deals and arranging financing, and the pair formed a productive partnership working on what were known as "bootstrap" deals, an early form of the LBOs they would work on later in their careers.[18] After working side by side with Kohlberg for about a year in 1969 and 1970, Roberts, who had been born in Texas and attended school in California, found that he could no longer contain his extreme distaste for living in Manhattan, and in 1970 he asked Kohlberg if he could move to San Francisco and work on buyouts from the West Coast. Kohlberg agreed, but only on the condition that Roberts find someone to replace him in New York. Roberts chose his cousin, Henry Kravis, who had received an MBA from Columbia University and had been working odd jobs on Wall Street for the last several years, to be his replacement.[19] Kohlberg initially disliked Kravis, who was a gregarious charmer who sometimes neglected the details of his work in favor of trying to charm potential friends and clients; but once the two realized that their contrasting personalities could anchor an effective partnership, they developed a strong working relationship. With Roberts working from his office in San Francisco, the three buyout specialists formed a potent team with Roberts as the strategist who lined up potential deals, Kravis as the salesman who closed them, and Kohlberg as the statesman who oversaw the whole affair and reassured everyone involved that things would work out to everyone's advantage.[20]

After breaking away from Bear Sterns, Kohlberg and his partners got to work on refining their approach to buyouts as they strung together a series of small deals in the second half of the 1970s. In these early years, the company's partners created a business model so powerful that it could deliver profits almost regardless of how any individual buyout worked out. Perhaps the greatest testament to the power of this model was that it formed the basis of the entire LBO industry during the 1980s and is still in use today as the template for private equity firms.[21] Since an LBO was, at its core, an exercise in purchasing a company using almost entirely borrowed money, KKR's partners knew that a company's cash flow was one of the key features in determining whether a buyout could be successful. If the target of a buyout was going to have any hope of paying off the massive amount of debt placed upon it by an LBO, it needed to have a predictable stream of earnings in place to generate the cash needed to pay its loans on time. To compensate for the risk that the buyout target might not be able to pay off its loans on time, banks were also likely to require that the company put up its own assets as collateral. Given these requirements, the ideal candidates for leveraged buyouts were what Kohlberg described as "fairly mundane industrial companies with a good record of stable earnings and good management."[22] According to corporate portfolio models, these "mundane" companies were the cash cow businesses many conglomerates and diversified firms had incorporated into their corporate portfolios.[23] When it came to a leveraged buyout, cash cows' lack of growth or R&D potential were actually assets, since these businesses supposedly had very few profitable places to invest the cash they were generating, and the opportunity cost of using every available dollar of corporate earnings to pay off debt would therefore be low. The fact that many of these cash cow businesses operated in "mundane" industries with few prospects for technological innovation, such as traditional manufacturing or retail, also meant that they were likely to own large amounts of physical assets such as real estate or equipment and vehicles that could be put up as collateral to creditors. Finally, it is important to note that Kohlberg and his partners' involvement with the companies they purchased extended beyond just the financial engineering required to purchase the company. KKR made sure that the new managers of their acquisitions invested a significant portion of their own money to take an equity stake in the company so that they would be incentivized to think like owners and prioritize servicing the firm's debt.[24] To this end, Kohlberg was always very clear that, in his view, an LBO was only suited to a particular kind of company: one with steady cash flows, a secure market position, and reliable managers with whom he could partner.[25]

One of KKR's earliest and most important breakthroughs came in 1978 when the partners created their first equity fund for future deals. Unlike traditional funds, which were raised for specific transactions, KKR modeled theirs after the "blind pools" common in the world of venture capital. In pools like these, the heads of a buyout firm such as KKR served as "general partners," who would contribute some amount of their own money—usually around 1 percent of the fund's total—in return for having control over the fund and assuming all of its risks.[26] To obtain the remainder of the fund's capital, the general partners offered investors the chance to become "limited partners" in the fund. These limited partners, generally institutions and wealthy individuals, turned their money over to the general partners, who were free to use it in whatever way they saw fit. After the fund was fully subscribed to, it was locked for the duration of its lifespan (usually ten years), meaning that the limited partners could not withdraw their money and new investors could not buy in. Once the limited partners' money was locked in, the general partners used it to pay for the equity portions of leveraged buyouts, thereby making both the limited and the general partners into the stockholders of the companies that were bought out. At the end of the equity fund's lifespan, the general partners distributed whatever profits it might have made among the investors and returned any money they were unable to spend.[27] Buyout firms typically operated several funds at once as well, ensuring that their investments were spread out across several different groups of investors, and these firms typically raised a new fund every three to five years.[28]

What made this business model so powerful, beyond the autonomy it gave to a fund's general partners and the potential for profits if a buyout was successful, was the tripartite fee structure that underpinned it.[29] Though variations existed between LBO firms, the industry's basic fee structure was remarkably similar across the entire sector. A fund's general partners charged their investors an annual management fee that typically ranged from 1.5 to 2 percent of assets under management (KKR's usual fee was 1.5 percent).[30] A fund's general partners also awarded themselves fees based on the cost of any successful buyout they conducted. For KKR, these acquisition fees were usually 1 percent of the total cost for a company, a not insignificant amount given that the firm would soon be conducting buyouts worth hundreds of millions and even billions of dollars.[31] Finally, even after a buyout was completed, a fund's general partners collected advisory fees from the company they purchased. These fees, which were negotiated independently as part of each individual buyout, forced the purchased company to pay a fund's general partners for the advice they offered to management as they sought to pay off their company's debts, and could also include additional payments for general partners who took a seat on the purchased company's board of directors.[32] All of these fees provided a steady stream of cash to the fund's general partners that would hopefully culminate in a windfall of profits when a buyout reached its successful conclusion, most often in the form of either the purchased company being acquired by a third party at a higher price or an IPO. The profits from a successful buyout—which were classified as "carried interest" and thus taxed as capital gains at a lower rate than ordinary income—were split as well, typically with 80 percent going to the limited partners and 20 percent going to the general partners.[33] Finally, it should be noted that buyouts did not just generate revenue for the members of an equity fund. A successful buyout, especially a large one, typically required a small army of investment bankers and lawyers to assist with the financial and legal nuances of any large transaction, and every one of these supporting players charged their own fees. The partners at KKR and their counterparts at other LBO firms used these fees as one of their most powerful relationship-building tools, and they made sure to spread their business around to several investment banks and law firms on each transaction.[34]

As critics of the leveraged buyout industry have pointed out, the fee structure associated with buyouts seemed to create a no-lose scenario for the partners who ran a private equity fund. Even if their investments did not pan out, the general partners were guaranteed fees from both their investors and the companies they purchased. In a study of buyout funds' performance from 1993 to 2006, the economists Andrew Metrick and Ayako Yasuda found that almost two-thirds of buyout funds' revenues came from "fixed revenue" sources—namely, management fees.[35] Since investment profits were generated from any appreciation to the purchased company's value either in the form of a sale price or stock value, the upside of a buyout was theoretically limitless and a fund's general partners were assured a portion of that profit far out of proportion to the initial capital they contributed. Conversely, the general partners were well protected from downside risks. Buyout funds were legally distinct from the firms like KKR that sponsored them, and it was the individual funds that purchased and advised companies, not the buyout firm. If a business that KKR's partners purchased through one of their buyout funds went bankrupt or ran into legal trouble, the partners could only lose the money that they contributed to that individual fund. This meant that the downside risk of any leveraged buyout was capped for the buyout specialists who ran them and they could not lose any money beyond what they put in at the beginning.[36] In essence, the leaders of a buyout firm needed to do two things to ensure that they received a healthy stream of revenue from fees: convince investors to contribute to a buyout fund, and ensure that they were able to spend their investors' money far enough in advance of the end of the fund's lifespan for any companies the fund purchased to be sold off. Given these requirements, salespersonship and confidence-building were two skills that could be just as important to the buyout business as the more mechanical competencies involved in sizing up potential acquisitions and arranging financing.

The power of KKR's business model was on full display in the firm's first major deal, a leveraged buyout of a troubled Fortune 500 conglomerate named Houdaille Industries. Houdaille began its life as an auto parts manufacturer, but by the 1970s it had followed the path of other American industrial firms to become a diversified conglomerate incorporating automobile parts, construction materials, industrial pumps, and machine tools.[37] As was the case for the many other conglomerates forced to muddle through the stagflation of the late 1970s amid rising competition from abroad, Houdaille's earnings and profit growth were stagnant through these difficult years, and by the end of the decade its stock was valued below the book value of the company's assets.[38] Like other companies saddled with a so-called "conglomerate discount," Houdaille was a tempting target for a hostile takeover, and on July 7, 1978, *The New York Times* ran an article in its "Market Place" section identifying the company as an ideal takeover candidate.[39] Indeed, corporate raiders—including the Jacobs family of Buffalo, New York, who had been secretly buying shares of Houdaille—were indeed circling the company, and Houdaille's managers tasked their bankers with finding them a friendly buyer to which they could sell the firm rather than allowing it to be taken over.

As it turned out, Houdaille's managers did not need to find a buyer—a buyer found them. Kohlberg, who regularly scanned the business press for potential buyout opportunities, had read the *New York Times* article on Houdaille, and he approached Houdaille's team about negotiating a sale. After some difficult negotiations, KKR convinced Houdaille's management to sell the company in an LBO with KKR paying $40 per share, which was well above the $25 per share the company was currently trading at. Given the fact that KKR had never attempted a buyout of this scale before, the partners had to overcome a great deal of skepticism from potential lenders, and they worked on financing for almost an entire year from August 1978, when Houdaille agreed to be bought out, to May 1979, when KKR was finally able to announce that they had secured $335 million in financing.[40] The equity portion of the deal was split between an investment group made up mostly of KKR's partners, the firm's equity fund, and the top managers of Houdaille which purchased $25 million in stock (approximately 7 percent of the total purchase) and a sale of preferred stock to a handful of banks that netted an additional $10 million (around 3 percent of the total purchase). Of the $35 million in equity, KKR itself only paid $1 million, meaning that the firm was purchasing Houdaille while paying only slightly less than 0.3 percent of the purchase price out of its own account. The remaining $300 million, 90 percent of the purchase, came from debt.[41] Once they had all of the pieces in place, KKR, with all of their trademark secrecy, simply issued a joint statement with Houdaille on March 7, 1979, stating that they had secured financing for the buyout and that, on the advice of counsel, they would provide no details about where the money came from.[42] Once all was said and done, everyone involved was also able to collect their portion of the approximately $6 million in fees that the buyout generated. Goldman Sachs, which had been the primary investment banker for the buyout, took $3.4 million; a handful corporate law firms that advised the deal divided up $1.6 million; and KKR themselves took home $1 million.[43]

While successfully completing a buyout on the size of the Houdaille deal was a feat in and of itself, it was only the first step in a much longer process for KKR's partners and the company's new managers. Houdaille now had hundreds of millions of dollars in debt to pay off, and the company needed to generate as much cash as possible in order to service this debt. Fortunately for Houdaille and KKR, they had an unlikely ally in this effort: the US tax code. Under federal tax law, interest payments on corporate debt were tax deductible, which meant that making payments on Houdaille's new mountain of debt had the beneficial side effect of slashing the company's tax bill nearly in half.[44] Kravis compounded these initial savings by turning to an associate of his named Tom Hudson who worked at the accounting firm Deloitte, Haskins & Sells in Greensboro, North Carolina. Hudson helped KKR's partners pull off a very complicated maneuver in which they re-depreciated Houdaille's assets at their current market value, and then made use of the series of shell companies that carried out different stages of the buyout to push the company's tax bill down to almost zero, where it remained for the lifetime of the buyout. Hudson's tax wizardry effectively turned the $22.3 million that the company had paid in taxes before the buyout into profits.[45] This meant that without changing a thing about how Houdaille operated, and just changing how it was financed, KKR's partners could claim to have generated millions of dollars in profit growth simply by borrowing money. In the words of buyout specialists like the partners at KKR, being able to reduce or eliminate a company's tax obligations through debt was a manifestation of buyout artists' ability to "unlock value" through leverage.[46] To critics of buyouts, the whole process seemed to amount to little more than creative accounting and tax evasion, which delivered a boost to corporate profits at the expense of government revenues.[47]

Houdaille's new management team was not content to simply reconfigure Houdaille's capital structure either. KKR's buyout of Houdaille kicked off a complete restructuring of the company's corporate portfolio. The new management team quickly divested themselves of Houdaille's construction materials and chrome-plated auto bumpers businesses, and in 1981 Houdaille purchased John Crane, a mechanical seals manufacturer, for $204 million, paid for in new debt issues. With these moves, the KKR-backed management team transformed Houdaille from a diversified conglomerate into a more specialized company exclusively focused on making high-value industrial parts.[48]

Between this new focus and the company's progress toward paying off its debt, Houdaille briefly seemed to be on the path to success. Unfortunately for Houdaille, its run of good fortune did not extend into the 1980s. The surprisingly deep recession that lasted from 1981 to 1982 cut into Houdaille's profits, while at the same time Japanese firms were making startlingly fast inroads into the American machine tools market, a market Houdaille's managers thought was well insulated from foreign competition. By 1985, Houdaille's position was so bad that it decided to simply give up on machine tools altogether, and it spun off its entire machine tool business through another leveraged buyout that sold off those businesses to their current managers at the cost of approximately 2,200 well-paying jobs.[49] Even after this latest restructuring, Houdaille's equity investors demanded that the company "recapitalize"—in essence, perform a second buyout that would allow equity investors to cash out—and Houdaille piled on even more debt to purchase these investors' shares. For the company's former equity investors, who had paid $2.52 per share in 1979, this recapitalization was quite lucrative since it allowed them to sell their shares back to the company for $11 per share.[50] For Houdaille, however, the recapitalization was the beginning of the end. In August 1987 the company was acquired by the TI Group, a British industrial conglomerate, for $500 million.[51] In their announcement, the TI Group made it clear that they were only interested in keeping Houdaille's mechanical seals business and that they intended to dispose of the rest of the company, which meant that Houdaille would cease to exist.[52]

The end of Houdaille underscored the often ambiguous or even contradictory legacies of many buyouts. For KKR, its investors, and the Houdaille management team that partnered with them, the buyout was undoubtedly a success; investors were able to sell their shares for far more than they had been worth originally, and KKR was able to successfully offload the company. The legacy of the Houdaille buyout was much less positive for the people who used to work for the company, however. The high debt loads associated with the buyout and the multiple rounds of recapitalizations and divestitures caused Houdaille to fall apart, and it ended its buyout experience by ceasing to exist altogether. For the thousands of workers employed by Houdaille, many of whom had held highly skilled and high-paying jobs, as well as the communities where Houdaille's operations were based, it was hard to see the buyout as anything other than a failure.[53]

For all the complicated legacy of KKR's first large-scale buyout, the immediate effects of the deal were nothing but positive for Kohlberg and his partners. The fact that KKR had been able to purchase a Fortune 500 company almost entirely with debt sent a signal to the rest of Wall Street that buyouts did not have to be limited to small companies at the margins of the nation's economy.[54] KKR's creative financing and accounting—which had been the butt of jokes on Wall Street in 1979—became a model to be imitated by accountants and investors who began exploring how to arrange LBOs themselves.[55] The Houdaille buyout also let managers know that an LBO could be a profitable and friendly alternative to a hostile takeover, which was especially welcome news during the early days of the takeover boom of the 1980s. All of these positives were tempered somewhat by the fact that the Houdaille deal had obviously been very difficult to arrange and that KKR held on to its stake in the company for several years before cashing out, but for ambitious financiers and managers the appeal was there regardless.

With KKR leading the way, LBO activity began to accelerate rapidly and continued to rise over the course of the 1980s. The majority of buyout activity during this decade was made up of divestiture buyouts, in which a large, diversified firm sought to sell off one or more of its business units.[56] These buyouts tended to escape public attention—unless they either went terribly wrong or delivered eye-popping profits—since they usually involved smaller businesses being spun off from large conglomerates, and the managers of the businesses being bought out often stayed in place. These divestiture buyouts offered beleaguered conglomerate managers an easy way to disassemble their collections of disparate businesses while receiving a quick windfall of cash, and according to the Congressional Research Service there were 931 divestiture buyouts between 1979 and 1987, with an average value of $79.68 million.[57] Though most individual divestiture buyouts were relatively small affairs, the cumulative effect of hundreds of these transactions over the course of the 1980s amounted to the "de-conglomeration" of American business.[58] In 1980, 52 percent of large American firms operated in three or more industries; but by the end of the decade only 30 percent of firms did so.[59] Conglomerates may have been out of favor since the end of the 1960s merger mania, but it was LBOs that provided managers and investors the financial tools needed to break them apart.

While divestiture buyouts were relatively uncontroversial, the same could not be said for the other main class of LBOs carried out during the 1980s in which buyout specialists purchased an entire business firm. These "going private" buyouts, though numerically fewer than divestiture deals, often involved much larger companies and higher purchase prices, as in KKR's buyout of Houdaille. Between 1979 and 1987 there were 365 of these "going private" buyouts, with an average value of $286.62 million.[60] Since investors purchased an entire firm in a going-private buyout, these transactions often resulted in the new ownership group making more drastic changes to the firm's operations which could include shutting down plants, selling off businesses, or layoffs.[61] Most controversial of all, going-private buyouts were intimately tied up with the broader hostile takeover movement. A management-led buyout (sometimes referred to as an MBO) was a powerful, if risky, defensive move for managers to take if they were worried about a potential hostile takeover, since corporate raiders would not be able to displace incumbent managers if those managers succeeded in taking their firm private. However, raiders themselves could also use a leveraged buyout to take control of a firm, and some of the highest-profile takeover battles of the 1980s, including the infamous fight over RJR Nabisco in 1989 chronicled in the book and made-for-TV-movie *Barbarians at the Gate*, were hostile LBOs.[62] Hostile buyouts were, if anything, even more controversial than more traditionally financed takeovers due to their outsized reliance on risky debt and the fact that they were even more likely than traditional takeovers to result in the dismantling of the acquired company.[63]

Just as most of the mergers that took place during the fourth merger wave were friendly deals and most takeovers did not involve corporate raiders such as Pickens or Icahn, most of the leveraged buyouts of the same period were also friendly, and buyout firms like KKR participated in only a small fraction of the overall number of transactions.[64] However, in much the same way that raiders had an outsized effect on the hostile takeover market, buyout firms like KKR, despite being only one piece of a much bigger market, were instrumental in structuring the leveraged buyout industry and setting the standard for other players in the market.[65] KKR, and the buyout market more broadly, won an important victory in 1981 when the firm acquired Fred Meyer, Inc., a Portland, Oregon-based chain of department stores, with money acquired in part from Oregon's public pension fund. The fact that KKR had been able to win the support of a state pension fund was a sign of the newfound respectability of leveraged buyouts, and other states' funds soon followed Oregon's lead in investing part of their money in buyouts.[66] With the nation's major institutional investors, including the politically powerful and deep-pocketed public pension funds, increasingly willing to fund buyouts, KKR soon found itself locked in a much fiercer competition for acquisitions. During the first half of the 1980s, KKR largely followed the partners' original requirements that the firm only acquire companies with strong, reliable cash flows with the cooperation of incumbent management. Even though KKR may have avoided initiating a takeover contest, they were increasingly being drawn into them as a white knight incumbent managers under threat of a hostile takeover could turn to in order to arrange a friendly buyout that would fend off raiders.[67] By the end of 1983, buyouts had become one of the hottest markets on Wall Street, with new deals "popping up like dandelions," in the words of an executive at Prudential Insurance, one of the largest institutional supporters of LBOs. According to one vice president at the brokerage firm Smith Barney, competition for buyout deals had become so fierce that "hardly a day goes by that Fortune 500 companies don't get a flood of phone calls from (leveraged buyout) entrepreneurs begging them to put subsidiaries on the market so a buyer can be arranged."[68]

As buyouts began to get more mainstream attention, and the controversy that came with it, KKR's partners were forging a partnership with Michael Milken and his junk bond team at Drexel Burnham Lambert that allowed them to send the buyout movement into overdrive.[69] The KKR and Drexel teams began to explore a collaboration after they both unsuccessfully tried to acquire Gulf Oil, a Philadelphia-based petroleum company. In February 1984, Gulf was bogged down in a takeover attempt being led by T. Boone Pickens, who was offering $1.5 billion for the company — funds he had raised with Milken's help.[70] With little to defend themselves from this junk-bond-fueled attack, Gulf's directors put the firm up for auction and paid KKR a $7.5 million fee to design a leveraged buyout of the company that would allow them to fend off Pickens. Though KKR had been invited to bid for Gulf, its involvement in the takeover contest turned into a frustrating embarrassment when Gulf's board of directors and their investment bankers, in a meeting with KKR, vigorously questioned KKR's ability to raise the funding required for their $15.4 billion bid, and Kravis lost his temper and stormed out.[71] After KKR's presentation wrapped up, Gulf's investment bankers advised the company to turn down the buyout firm's offer, which they claimed—with no small amount of condescension toward KKR—was too risky, in favor of a $13.4 billion, all-cash purchase offer made by Standard Oil.[72]

This unexpected defeat in what would have been their largest deal to date convinced KKR's partners that they needed to find a way to secure large amounts of financing if they wanted to have a chance at closing larger buyouts in the future. Fortunately for KKR, Drexel was ready to help them, and Milken's team began offering their services to the buyout firm immediately after the Gulf battle. For Milken and his team at Drexel, KKR seemed like an ideal client: a well-run, aggressive player in the M&A market that was hungry for bigger deals and in desperate need of financing that would allow them to realize these ambitions.[73] After seeing how much money Milken could raise, KKR's partners realized that he could be the solution to their financing problems. In the Gulf battle Milken had been able to raise enough money for Pickens to credibly threaten one of America's largest companies; if Milken could do the same for KKR, they too might be able to compete at the very highest levels of the M&A market.[74] In August 1984, only a few months after crossing paths in the Gulf deal, Kravis accepted an invitation to go to Milken's Beverly Hills office to consider Drexel's offer to help KKR raise $100 million for a buyout of Cole National, a Cleveland, Ohio-based retail chain, and was stunned to see Milken almost effortlessly sell the bonds necessary to fund the buyout in a single afternoon. Having seen Milken's legendary fundraising firsthand, Kravis returned from this meeting to sell the rest of his colleagues on working with Drexel, and after months of internal discussion, KKR embarked on a partnership with Milken.[75]

KKR chose to capitalize on its alliance with Drexel by spending $6.2 billion to acquire Beatrice Companies, a sprawling food and consumer goods conglomerate that was the twenty-sixth largest company in the United States. KKR's buyout of Beatrice was, to date, the largest buyout in history, and arguably the firm's first hostile takeover.[76] KKR's shift to blockbuster-sized hostile acquisitions marked a turning point for both the firm and the LBO market in general. Within KKR, Kohlberg became more and more estranged from his other partners due to his disapproval of the firm's relaxation of its strict guidelines for acquisitions and his personal distaste for the excesses of the merger market best embodied in the decadent "Predators' Balls" Milken hosted each year.[77] In 1986 Kohlberg went with the rest of the KKR team to the first Predators' Ball to which they had been invited; while there he was visibly uncomfortable with the raucous parties that accompanied what was ostensibly a business conference, and spent most of the festivities huddled in a corner.[78] Kohlberg was also increasingly feuding with Kravis, who, unlike the other partners, reveled in the riches he had won in the buyout business and was frequently featured in the society pages as he socialized with figures like Donald Trump and went through a messy public divorce before marrying an up-and-coming fashion designer named Carolyne Roehm.[79] Kravis's jet-setting lifestyle was far too much for Kohlberg, who, like Shad, Rohatyn, and other financiers who made up the older ranks of the M&A business, straddled the line between mid-century notions of managerial respectability and the more vulgar ruthlessness of the 1980s.[80] The working relationship between Kohlberg and his younger partners deteriorated to the point that by the beginning of 1987, the firm's partners decided Kohlberg had to go, and Kravis broke the news to his former mentor and friend in February. Deeply hurt and angry at what he perceived to be a betrayal, Kohlberg spent his last month at the firm negotiating what one KKR associate called "the biggest golden parachute ever" in advance of his official retirement in March.[81] Though Kohlberg officially left in March, he announced his retirement in May in a speech to KKR's investors that left no doubt that he was leaving due his deep displeasure with what buyouts had become. In that speech he lamented the "overpowering greed that pervades our business life," and insisted that KKR and the rest of the buyout market needed to recommit themselves to high ethical standards "or we will kill the golden goose."[82] Despite plenty of hurt feelings on both sides, Kohlberg and his former partners kept most of the details about Kohlberg's departure from the press. When asked by *The New York Times* why he was leaving, Kohlberg would only admit to "some philosophical differences" with his former colleagues, while Roberts simply remarked that "Jerry may have felt that the deals were getting too big."[83]

In retrospect, Kohlberg's worries about buyouts getting out of hand were well founded. Thanks to the injection of Milken's junk bond financing, the buyout market continued to expand throughout the second half of the 1980s as financiers and incumbent managers tried to cash in on the LBO craze. With more and more money chasing after fewer and fewer high-quality deals, the LBOs of the second half of the 1980s were far more likely to involve riskier targets with uncertain cash flows and, as a consequence, to make even greater use of high-interest debt than those from earlier in the decade. Indeed, a study published in 1993 by the financial economist Steven Kaplan and the macroeconomist Jeremy Stein found that 1985 was a turning point for the buyout market after which an "overheated" demand for buyouts pushed financiers to rely increasingly on junk bond financing, which resulted in overpriced deals that were more prone to financial distress.[84] With Kohlberg out of the way, KKR's remaining partners were free to fully indulge these outsized expectations, and they embarked on a buyout spree that culminated in their purchase of RJR Nabisco, the nation's nineteenth-largest company, in 1988 for $25 billion, of which KKR provided only $15 million.[85] All of this frenzied buyout activity did raise concerns for some participants in the market; one consultant warned that the market had become "a feeding frenzy," and the investment director of Wisconsin's investment board wondered "if there are as many deals out there as there are people chasing deals."[86] Despite plenty of reasons to be skeptical, many investors felt they had no time to waste thinking about risks, especially as the Reagan presidency was nearing its conclusion and investors did not know who would follow his remarkably market-friendly administration. As one investor put it, "there's an element of let's get this done today, because we may not get to tomorrow"; another characterized the buyout market as the "financial version of an all-you-can-eat night."[87]

The End of Equity

As the end of the 1980s drew near, investors were not the only ones who entertained grandiose ideas about the potential for leveraged buyouts. Jensen saw buyouts as a potentially era-defining force that would reshape American capitalism by bringing the age of managerial capitalism and the public corporation itself to a close. Buyouts were a critical source of inspiration for Jensen's theories about what motivated hostile takeovers and his predictions about what takeovers meant for the future of American business. Jensen's vision of what he called "the eclipse of the public corporation" pushed the ideas behind the shareholder value revolution to their extreme.[88] In fact, Jensen's hope for an economy dominated by LBO firms—which he termed "LBO associations"—moved entirely beyond the existence of widespread public stock ownership in large companies.[89] In Jensen's mind, buyout specialists like the partners at KKR had solved the problems associated with the public corporation he had been writing about for the past decade. As he saw it, buyout artists' focus on cash flow, their heavy use of debt, and their willingness to take large ownership stakes in the companies they acquired largely solved the agency problems that had bedeviled corporate theorists since Berle and Means. By unifying ownership and control and pressing managers to pay attention to cash flow in order to pay off their companies' high debt loads, LBOs forced managers to focus on creating economic value above all else.[90] Though Jensen's hopes for the eclipse of the public corporation did not come to pass after the buyout market crashed at the end of the 1980s, his ideas about an economy dominated by LBO associations were not entirely wrong. Though the public corporation's dominance endured beyond the 1980s, many of those companies voluntarily chose to adopt the managerial techniques associated with buyouts. Moreover, once leveraged buyouts returned to prominence in the early years of the twenty-first century under the more genteel name of private equity, several sectors of the American economy did get reorganized under the direction of the LBO associations Jensen admired.[91]

One of the features of buyouts that attracted Jensen was the way LBOs called attention to free cash flow, the issue he believed to be at the center of all takeover battles. In Jensen's mind, the debt LBOs forced onto acquired companies reduced "the agency costs of free cash flow by reducing the cash flow available for spending at the discretion of managers."[92] What made debt especially powerful at reducing agency costs was that, unlike divided payments or share repurchases, which were both voluntary actions taken at corporate managers' discretion, debt payments were legal obligations that managers had to meet if they wanted to avoid bankruptcy. These obligations were particularly beneficial for companies with high agency costs, which were exactly the type of firm most likely to be targeted for a hostile takeover or buyout. According to Jensen, the ultra-high levels of debt firms took on during takeovers and buyouts was, despite critics' protestations, "desirable," since "leveraging the firm so highly that it cannot continue to exist in its old form yields benefits by providing motivation for cuts in expansion programs and the sale of divisions that are more valuable outside the firm. The proceeds are used to reduce debt to a more normal or permanent level."[93] This process of "overleveraging" and then deleveraging through selloffs had the power to completely remake the organization. As Jensen put it, "this process results in a complete rethinking of the organization's strategy and structure. When it is successful, a much leaner, more efficient, and competitive organization results."[94]

Despite the widespread gains that could come from highly leveraging a company, Jensen did make sure to point out that high debt loads, while beneficial for many types of businesses, would not be appropriate for all firms. Specifically, Jensen claimed that high debt loads would not be helpful for "rapidly growing organizations with large and highly profitable investment projects but no free cash flow." Debt could choke off the ability of these types of firms to fund the ideally plentiful number of profitable investment opportunities they possessed, and these companies were better off relying on the financial markets to obtain capital. If debt was relatively unimportant for growth firms, it was extremely important for companies at the other end of their economic life cycle. According to Jensen, "the control function of debt is more important in organizations that generate large cash flows but have low growth prospects, and it is even more important in organizations that must shrink. In these organizations the pressure to waste cash flows by investing them in uneconomic projects is most serious."[95] No one seemed to understand the value of the "control function of debt" better than buyout artists, either. Jensen found that "many of the benefits in going-private and leveraged buyout transactions seem to be due to the control function of debt. These transactions are creating a new organizational form that competes successfully with the open corporate form because of advantages in controlling the agency costs of free cash flow."[96]

Jensen pulled his thoughts on LBOs together in an article he published in the September/October 1989 issue of the *Harvard Business Review* titled "The Eclipse of the Public Corporation."[97] In this article Jensen made the case that "the publicly held corporation, the main engine of economic process in the United States for a century, has outlived its usefulness in many sectors of the economy and is being eclipsed."[98] Specifically, Jensen claimed that "the public corporation is not suitable in industries where long-term growth is slow, where internally generated funds outstrip the opportunities to invest them profitably, or where downsizing is the most productive long-term strategy," which included a laundry list of businesses that likely made up the majority of the American economy, including "aerospace, banking, and food processing," as well as "steel, chemicals, brewing, tobacco, television and radio broadcasting, wood and paper products," and even the petroleum industry and automobile manufacturing.[99] The reasons the public corporation was no longer suited to these industries boiled down to the twin issues of agency costs and free cash flow. With too much cash on hand and not enough profitable opportunities to invest it, the managers of public corporations, insulated from any real accountability due to share ownership being concentrated in the hands of "powerless" institutional investors, were free to waste this money on whatever uneconomic or self-aggrandizing projects they desired to the detriment of their own organizations' long-term health and their investors' wealth.[100]

With public companies having outlived their usefulness for large swaths of the American economy, Jensen predicted that they would be replaced by active investors at the head of LBO associations. In an inversion of the argument once made by the proponents of conglomerates, Jensen claimed that "with its vast increases in data, talent, and technology, Wall Street can allocate capital among competing businesses and monitor and discipline management more effectively than the CEO and headquarters staff of the typical diversified company."[101] The economy dominated by LBO associations that Jensen envisioned combined what he felt were the best aspects of pre–New Deal corporate governance with the insights of modern financial economics. As he saw it, "LBO partnerships and the merchant banks are rediscovering the role played by active investors prior to 1940, when Wall Street banks such as J. P. Morgan & Company were directly involved in the strategy and governance of the public companies they helped to create." Though this emerging model of corporate ownership dominated by LBO associations harkened back to the start of the twentieth century, Jensen was pleased to note that "consistent with modern finance theory, these organizations are not managed to maximize earnings per share but rather to maximize *value*, with a strong emphasis on cash flow."[102] In practice, this meant that buyout managers could take actions that Jensen felt were long overdue—namely, breaking apart the massive corporations constructed in previous decades, ending unproductive investment programs, and shrinking corporate workforces in the name of efficiency. What made these changes truly extraordinary in Jensen's mind was that they seemed to come at almost no cost. As he put it, "to date, the performance of LBO associations has been remarkable. Indeed, it is difficult to find any systematic losers in these transactions, and almost all gains appear to come from real increases in productivity."[103] According to Jensen, buyouts created large gains for shareholders at almost no expense to bondholders or the US Treasury and improved operating efficiency without "massive layoffs or big cuts in research and development."[104]

Importantly, Jensen thought that all of the gains coming from LBO associations could be maintained without LBO partners having to take their acquisitions public again—something LBO firms had been doing with increasing speed over the course of the second half of the 1980s.[105] Jensen acknowledged that most buyouts were done with "a goal of returning the reconfigured company to the public market within three to five years," but he urged the investors behind these transactions to recognize that "LBO sponsors do not have to take their companies public for them to succeed." Instead, Jensen argued that "huge efficiency gains and high-return asset sales produce enough cash to pay down debt and allow LBOs to generate handsome returns as going concerns."[106] Jensen made this argument because he worried that the managerial discipline and focus on cash flow buyouts were able to impose on corporate managers would be undone if companies that were acquired in an LBO were let go after only a few years.[107] Jensen admitted that it was possible for public companies to "learn from LBO Associations and emulate many of their characteristics," but he warned that this would require "major changes in corporate structure, philosophy, and focus." Though some companies might be able to perform this feat, Jensen maintained that "only a coordinated attack on the status quo will halt the eclipse of the public company" and concluded that "it is unlikely such an attack will proceed fast enough or go far enough."[108] Jensen may have made this argument in a slightly more diplomatic tone than he had used in his work with Meckling or his CCMO class, but the message was the same: corporate managers, just like any other economic actor, could not be trusted to act in anyone's interest but their own. In Jensen's mind, investors and American society had been forced for decades to bear the agency costs that came with the public corporation because of a lack of creditable alternatives. Thankfully, advances in technology, deregulation, and innovations in financial and organizational theory—all of which were powering what Jensen would later term "The Third Industrial Revolution"—had provided dissatisfied investors with a clearly superior alternative in the form of the LBO association.[109] If LBO associations did indeed replace the public corporation as the dominant institution in American political economy, it would represent the triumph of efficient markets over unreliable and self-interested human beings. With corporate managers brought to heel by active investors who understood the insights of modern financial theory, corporate decision-making would be regulated by perfectly efficient financial markets.[110] For someone like Jensen who had spent his entire professional life championing the virtues of the efficient markets hypothesis, this was exactly what was needed to revitalize the American economy, as long as nothing happened to slow the pace of buyout activity and buyout specialists did not give in to the temptation to abandon value-creating practices in favor of easy profits, as corporate managers had done decades ago.

Unfortunately for Jensen, his argument about the eclipse of the public corporation rested on two fatal misconceptions: he underestimated the ability of public corporations to change, and he overestimated how willing buyout specialists would be to pass up short-term profit maximization in favor of embarking on a long-term campaign to remake American political economy. Jensen also had the misfortune of publishing his article at almost the same time that the political and economic forces that brought the fourth merger wave to a close were gaining ground.[111] In 1987 the US Supreme Court overturned its ban on state anti-takeover measures with its decision in the case of *CTS v. Dynamics*, and in 1989 the Delaware Supreme Court issued a verdict in the case of *Paramount v. Time* that provided incumbent managers with additional legal protections against takeovers. As the political and legal environments began to sour, federal law enforcement agencies were also closing in on Milken, who Jensen believed was indispensable to the health of the buyout market.[112] After years of investigations by the SEC, the Justice Department indicted Milken on ninety-eight counts of racketeering and fraud in March 1989, and he pled guilty to six charges in April 1990.[113] Milken's downfall prompted a crash in the junk bond market that cut LBO specialists off from the vast pools of cheap debt they needed to wage expensive buyout campaigns.[114] To make matters even worse for buyout artists, the American economy entered a recession in July 1990 that marked the formal end of the Fourth Merger Wave. The recession made buyout financing, already difficult to find in the wake of the junk bond crash, even harder to come by and forced the LBO market into retreat.[115] The economic downturn also forced several notable LBOs, many of which had targeted firms in the retail industry, into bankruptcy, including buyouts of Federated Department Stores, R. H. Macy & Co., and the drug store chain Revco.[116] These high-profile failures, combined with the disappointing performance of the RJR Nabisco buyout, which was compounded by a growing public backlash against investing in tobacco companies, tarnished the image of leveraged buyouts and LBO firms such as KKR.[117]

Even as buyout activity cooled down from the fever pitch of the 1980s and buyout firms lost some of the esteem they had commanded from investors, buyouts did not disappear in the 1990s. Though hostile buyouts and mega-deals were largely impossible in the first several years of the 1990s, buyout firms like KKR were able to survive the downturn by refocusing their work on smaller, friendly deals and taking a slightly less standoffish stance toward press and public inquiries about their work.[118] In 1990, KKR published the first issue of *KKR Review*, a magazine intended to give the public a better picture of how the firm operated in order to deflect criticism of buyouts. In the preface of the first issue, Kravis and Roberts wrote that "while we know our investors will judge us first on our financial success—and rightly so—we believe the people, products and services found within our portfolio of business are important to recognize because they are key to the success of our investments. We are publishing *KKR Review* for our investing partners so you, too, have an opportunity to know more than the bottom line."[119] In addition to abandoning some elements of the firm's secrecy, KKR's partners also shifted their strategy away from the hostile takeovers and corporate divestitures that had brought them a great deal of criticism at the height of the takeover wave.[120] Instead of pursuing contentious or high-profile deals that often ended in large companies being broken apart, KKR announced that they would focus on creating large companies "by finding an experienced management team, backing them financially, and helping them build a business from scratch by acquiring several small companies in a related industry."[121] KKR started rolling out this new strategy in 1991 with the acquisition of the Bank of New England and several publications from Rupert Murdoch's News Corporation.[122] Even when KKR returned to multi-billion-dollar deals, as it did in 1994 with the $2 billion purchase of Borden Inc., a food and beverage maker, these acquisitions made far fewer headlines than during the 1980s, thanks to KKR negotiating the deal on friendly terms and paying for the buyout with RJR Nabisco stock.[123] By 1995, KKR had fully unloaded its RJR Nabisco stock—thanks in no small part to the Borden purchase—and, no longer weighed down by the disappointing remnants of its largest buyout, was free to expand its acquisition activity for the remainder of the decade.[124] However, even as the firm stepped up its acquisition activity, it focused its efforts on the unglamorous kind of businesses Kohlberg had insisted on in the early days of the buyout industry. Instead of attacking large firms at the heart of the nation's economy, as it had in the 1980s, KKR acquired a portfolio of lower-profile firms in sometimes marginal industries such as daycare, sporting equipment, and movie theaters.[125]

Acquiring these less glamorous businesses still allowed KKR to earn handsome profits from both equity sales and its steep fees, but these successes did not inspire the same degree of interest that the firm's marquee deals from the 1980s had. Instead, KKR's record—along with those of its competitors who largely followed suit—at the end of the 1990s and into the 2000s marked the creation of the modern-day private equity industry.[126] Indeed, it was sometime in the late 1990s that the term "private equity" was adopted by buyout specialists as a new, more genteel way to refer to the work they did.[127] Instead of trying to remake or eclipse the public corporation, newly rechristened private equity firms like KKR or Bain Capital, which had been founded in 1984, sought to generate profits from the same cash cows Kohlberg had originally focused on as far back as the 1970s, albeit on a much broader scale. In the decades since the 1990s, private equity partners have been among the nation's highest earners as they have assembled sprawling portfolios of cash cow businesses, many of which generated their revenue from some of the nation's poorest citizens, including mobile home parks, ambulance services, snack food companies such as Hostess, dollar stores, mortgage providers, and even fire departments.[128] Along the way, all of the major private equity firms, including KKR, went public themselves, allowing them to tap public equity markets for financing even at the expense of separating ownership and control and subjecting investors in these firms to the same agency costs that buyout partnerships were supposed to solve.[129]

The evolution of the swaggering buyout partnerships of the 1980s into the more respectable publicly traded private equity firms of the present day showcased why Jensen's hopes for the end of the public corporation ended in frustration, and why the broader shareholder value revolution would fall short of its ideological champions' hopes. In adjusting to unfavorable changes in the macroeconomic and political environments at the start of the 1990s, buyout specialists proved much more adaptable and opportunistic, and less ideologically committed to the idea of the shareholder value revolution, than Jensen or other heralds of the eclipse of the public corporation would have hoped. Buyout artists were never interested in remaking American political economy or displacing the public corporation. Instead, buyout specialists like Kravis, Roberts, and even Kohlberg were much more interested in finding the opportunity to make profits. When buyout specialists could make profits by launching hostile buyouts for giant firms like RJR Nabisco, they did so; when the operating environment changed and profits were more easily achieved by acquiring smaller companies, buyout specialists did so to great effect. Similarly, despite Jensen's hopes that buyout firms might pass up the short-term profits to be gained by taking businesses public only a few years after a buyout, buyout specialists were generally not interested in holding on to their acquisitions beyond three to five years if possible.[130] Nothing underscored the difference between Jensen's image of LBO associations and the reality of the buyout market more than buyout firms' decision to go public. The fact that buyout firms were willing to accept public investors and to introduce agency problems into their own businesses was proof that they were not really interested in disciplining unaccountable managers. Indeed, between the decision to go public and the high fees firms like KKR charged, Jensen increasingly felt like there was little difference between the heads of major buyout firms and traditional corporate managers; they both seemed to be more interested in pursuing their own enrichment than in creating value or fostering efficient markets.[131] Though Jensen was quite surprised and angry to see what became of his dream of an economy dominated by LBO associations, he should not have been surprised by this outcome given the fact that buyout specialists themselves were quite honest about what motivated their work. The mismatch between Jensen's hopes and the reality of the buyout market was on full display in a back-and-forth between brokerage founder Charles Schwab and George Roberts at an event during the height of the 1980s buyout boom. According to *Fortune*, Schwab had personally complimented Roberts on all that KKR was doing to restructure American business and to take companies out of the hands of self-interested managers and put them in the care of owner-managers. After hearing Schwab's effusive praise, Roberts simply looked at him sideways and told him, "that's not why we do it, Chuck."[132]

A Quest for (Economic) Value

Though leveraged buyout specialists had little interest in restructuring the public corporation beyond whatever deals they could win for themselves, there were plenty of other people who were ready to take up the banner of shareholder value maximization and carry it into the boardrooms of some of America's largest public corporations. Management experts and consultants pointed out that many of the changes associated with LBOs, such as selling off business units to focus on a firm's "core competencies," laying off supposedly unproductive headquarters staff in the name of efficiency, and focusing on cash flow, were things managers could do without necessarily undertaking a risky buyout.[133] To help managers make these changes, a host of consulting firms began to offer advice on what was sometimes termed "managing for value" beginning in the 1980s.[134] At the forefront of this group was Stern Stewart, a specialized consulting firm started in 1982 by two former Chase Manhattan executives, Joel Stern and Bennett Stewart, who both had attended the University of Chicago's business school and sought to apply the economic theories they had learned there to consulting work.[135] As part of their efforts to generate business for their firm, Stern and Stewart hosted conferences and seminars designed to bring academics and managers together. They even published their own journal intended for corporate managers called the *Journal of Applied Corporate Finance*, which was designed to provide executives with easy-to-understand summaries of the latest scholarship in academic finance. One of Stern Stewart's closest academic partners was Jensen, who often participated in conferences with Stewart as one half of what Stewart described as a "tag-team" of financial experts. According to Stewart, the ideas behind Jensen's "Free Cash Flow Theory of Takeovers" article originated at one of Stern Stewart's roundtable discussions on corporate takeovers.[136]

Though translating academic scholarship was a central part of their work, value consultants did not simply transmit other peoples' ideas to managers. Instead, they used the insights of economic theory to craft management programs they could sell to executives looking to restructure their businesses. Stern Stewart's consultants urged managers to focus on creating economic profits with a program they named Economic Value Added (EVA), a term Stern Stewart copyrighted in 1987 that then quickly became the most popular way to describe the concept of economic profit. EVA forced managers to calculate firm profits by accounting for both the regular costs of doing business and the costs of raising capital from investors.[137] For a manager to calculate their firm's EVA they first had to calculate the standard accounting profit (revenue minus costs of operations, interest, and taxes), and then they needed to subtract the opportunity cost of their investors' capital from that accounting profit.[138] The cost of capital for debt was simply the interest rate on a loan. For stocks, the cost of capital was the average rate of return an investor could expect to make investing in a similar asset in the marketplace.[139] If a company used both debt and equity to fund its operations, its cost of capital would be an average of the cost of debt capital and the cost of equity capital, weighted to reflect the balance of the two. Given its emphasis on economic value instead of accounting value, EVA could produce startling results for corporate: a firm that generated reliable accounting profits could still be guilty of destroying economic value if those accounting profits were less than the cost of the firm's capital. By introducing the cost of capital into profit calculations, EVA forced managers to think of their businesses as being locked into a fierce competition for investors' money, one they could only win by generating cash in excess of what their shareholders demanded.

EVA was mathematically equivalent to a firm's projected FCF once it had been "discounted" for a firm's cost of capital. Both value consultants and academics like Jensen were adamant that shareholders would search for companies that could generate the highest amounts of FCF, since the more cash a business had left in its account, the more shareholders would expect to receive.[140] If managers wanted to maximize shareholder value, then they would be forced to invest only in projects and activities that had positive projected cash flows over a set period of months or years, depending on the type of project. The reasoning behind this all boiled down to the opportunity cost of capital. To have positive projected cash flows, a project had to generate returns in excess of both what the project cost and investors' cost of capital year after year. As with EVA, a project could make more than it cost on paper—but if it failed to generate more than investors' next best alternative, it was economically "unproductive." If a company invested in a project with a projected negative cash flow, it was taking its investors' money and spending it on something investors would not have chosen themselves. Therefore, shareholder value advocates argued that once the company had exhausted its economically profitable investment opportunities, it should return that money to shareholders, who could then invest it in other projects that would provide their required rate of return.[141]

By the 1990s the pressures managers faced to maximize shareholder value existed independent of either corporate raiders or buyout specialists. Even after the hostile takeover wave ended, institutional investors, especially public pension funds, continued to demand shareholder-friendly changes in American companies.[142] Since they could claim to directly represent the interests of millions of everyday American investors, institutional investors proved to be much more adept than the corporate raiders at making populist demands for managers to redistribute corporate wealth to shareholders. Institutional investors' demands for corporate managers to maximize shareholder value were not merely idle threats, either. Institutional investors engineered a series of high-profile CEO firings in 1992 and 1993 that cost the leaders of corporate giants such as GM and IBM their jobs because of their perceived inability to deliver value to shareholders. As unsettling as these firings were for corporate managers, they were still quite rare, and even during the 1990s most institutional investors had little direct influence over corporate decisions. Instead, they found that the mere threat of action was enough to keep the pressure on managers to maximize shareholder value.[143]

The consistent pressure corporate managers faced to maximize shareholder value in the wake of the takeover wave drove the demand for the services of value consultants like Stern Stewart. By the 1990s, thanks in large part to the work of people like Jensen, Pickens, and Kohlberg, value consultants' clients had already been convinced that they needed to maximize shareholder value, and they hired management consultants to design restructuring programs that would make their goal a reality.[144] Often a decline in profits or some other indicator of poor performance prompted managers to seek out the services of management consultants. For example, in 1989 Briggs and Stratton, a manufacturing firm based outside of Milwaukee, Wisconsin, that specialized in making small engines for devices such as lawn mowers, posted a $20 million loss, its first in sixty years.[145] For the preceding decade, the company had been struggling to respond to the emergence of fierce competition from Japanese rivals who were able to produce similar engines at lower costs. In 1988, Fred Stratton Jr., the company's chairman and the grandson of its founder, began to worry that the company could be the target of a hostile takeover, and he contemplated taking the company private through a management buyout. Stratton's bankers at the Continental Illinois National Bank, who had a close relationship with Stern Stewart, recommended that he meet with Bennett Stewart, so that Stewart and his fellow consultants could help Briggs and Stratton explore their options for restructuring. Stewart presented Stratton with a proposal for a management buyout and also offered him an EVA analysis that demonstrated that the company had been destroying economic value over the course of the last decade, even when it had been profitable in accounting terms. After considering their options, Stratton and his management team rejected the idea of going through a buyout, in part because they saw Stewart's EVA analysis as a credible and less risky alternative to an LBO. Having decided to keep their company public, Briggs and Stratton's executives hired Stern Stewart to design a restructuring program for the company based around promoting EVA.[146]

Briggs and Stratton began to roll out its EVA program in 1991. In the company's annual report for that year its leadership opened its letter to shareholders by claiming that cash flow was the most important metric of the company's success, and that "our main goal is to add economic value by earning more than our cost of capital."[147] To incentivize the managers of its seven operating units to focus on EVA, the company's top leadership introduced a new bonus plan for 100 of its managing executives that based those executives' bonus pay on their ability to generate improvement in their operating units' EVA. These bonus programs could be very lucrative to executives who managed to boost EVA since they were uncapped: as long as EVA kept rising, an executive's pay would rise along with it. In pursuit of bonus payments executives tried to follow the mantra of John Shiely, one of the company's vice presidents, who urged them to "build, operate, and harvest." In Shiely's telling, managers needed to "build" EVA-positive investments, "operate" their respective businesses more efficiently so that they could generate more cash without increasing their use of capital, and "harvest" those business lines that were not generating economic value by selling them or shutting them down.[148]

It was this commitment to "harvesting" economically unprofitable operations that created a labor crisis for Briggs and Stratton between 1993 and 1994. As part its cost-cutting efforts, the company laid off around 2,000 workers between 1988 and 1992. In the summer of 1993, it announced plans to reorganize its Milwaukee factories into new "focus factories" that would specialize in one product category.[149] Fearing that these "focus factories" would threaten union workers' seniority and potentially lead to layoffs, the company's workforce—which had signed a no-strike contract—engaged in a work slowdown beginning in September.[150] As the labor tensions deepened, Shiely warned union leaders that the company was committed to using EVA to decide where its workforce should be located, and that might mean moving jobs out of the area unless labor costs declined.[151] After months of bitter fighting between the two sides, Briggs and Stratton made good on Shiely's threat and announced in May 1994 that it would move 2,000 jobs from the Milwaukee area to lower-cost, non-union factories in Missouri, Kentucky, and Juarez, Mexico.[152]

While it engaged in this campaign to defeat workers who refused to accept EVA, Briggs and Stratton also sought to teach its remaining workforce to adopt EVA themselves. Beginning in 1994, the company started requiring salaried and shop-floor-level workers to attend classes on EVA conducted by the company's head of corporate training. In these classes, workers received simple lectures on what EVA was, brainstormed ways to increase the company's EVA, and even took part in simulations in which they pretended to be the managers of a convenience store and tried to maximize their store's EVA. Between 1994 and 1997, 3,000 workers passed through these classes. As this program of education spread throughout the company, corporate managers gleefully reported stories of line workers debating ways to improve EVA during their breaks or designing ways to improve the efficiency of their respective tasks. To reinforce the lessons taught in these classes, the company also began to tie workers' pay to EVA by offering bonuses to workers if their plants met EVA targets or performed well on operating metrics thought to be associated with EVA growth.[153]

Briggs and Stratton's restructuring was an undeniable accomplishment in economic terms and a valuable success story that Stern Stewart could point to when advertising its services. After suffering a loss in 1989, the company posted consistent profit growth for the next five years, with profits rising from approximately $35.4 million in 1990 to $104.8 million in 1995.[154] The company's leaders became evangelists for EVA in the Milwaukee area, and Shiely even coauthored with Joel Stern a book based on his experience with EVA. Titled *The EVA Challenge*, the book was published in 2001.[155] Those workers who remained employed by Briggs and Stratton generally benefited from their company's improved economic position in the form of EVA bonuses and profit-sharing agreements, as well as the opportunity to have more say in how to organize their workplace to boost efficiency.[156] However, these gains came at a tremendous cost for those workers who lost their jobs and for the Milwaukee area as a whole. Briggs and Stratton's Milwaukee-based workforce shrank from approximately 8,000 people in 1989 to around 3,000 by the end of 1996.[157] The fact that Briggs and Stratton was the Milwaukee area's largest private sector employer meant that its decision to lay off thousands of local workers had an outsized effect on the community. The 2,000 jobs lost because of the labor standoff in 1993 and 1994 alone were estimated to have cost the city somewhere between $71.8 million and $73.2 million, while those individual workers who lost their jobs were often forced to find lower-paying work in the city's service sector or rely on overburdened charity networks.[158]

Though the particulars of downsizing and shareholder value promotion differed from industry to industry and firm to firm, stories similar to

Briggs and Stratton's played out across the entire American economy in the 1980s and 1990s. Stern Stewart was hardly unique in offering restructuring programs based around economic profit and shareholder value maximization. Indeed, one the greatest testaments to Stern Stewart's influence was the degree to which their ideas were imitated by other management consulting firms and accounting firms. In 1987, McKinsey & Co., perhaps the world's most influential management consulting firm, hired a Stern Stewart consultant named Tim Koller to create a value consulting business for their firm.[159] As part of his effort to advertise McKinsey's new line of business, Koller and two other McKinsey partners published a textbook for managers and business students titled *Valuation: Measuring and Managing the Value of Companies*, which by 2016 was in its sixth edition, having become a mainstay of business education with more than 700,000 copies sold.[160] Other major consulting firms, including the Boston Consulting Group and a host of boutique firms, joined the crowded market for value consulting and offered their own programs for corporate restructuring and valuation.[161] The major accounting firms also sought to offer value consulting to their clients, including accounting giant KPMG, which was sued by Stern Stewart in 1996 for allegedly stealing Stern Stewart's intellectual property by setting up an EVA practice of their own in 1995.[162] In a sign of just how ubiquitous the ideas behind EVA were by the mid-1990s, the judge in the lawsuit ruled against Stern Stewart in 1996 because she believed the firm had done such a good job of spreading awareness of EVA that it was hard to argue that it was a truly proprietary product. She concluded that "no evidence was advanced to show that Stern Stewart embarks upon a client analysis in any defined way different from the methods used by its current competitors."[163] Stern Stewart was a victim of its own success. By 1996, the ideas behind EVA had thoroughly permeated American business and no one firm or individual could reasonably claim to have ownership of them. Having already become dominant in professional schools, shareholder value ideas had taken root in boardrooms and executive suites as well. The shareholder value revolution had nearly won the battle for American political economy. Shareholder value ideas were hegemonic, and corporate managers were turning to value consultants and buyout specialists to help them restructure their companies around the promotion of shareholder value, but these victories could still be undone. To ensure that corporate managers did not revert to their old ways, investors and shareholder theorists knew there was one issue they still needed to address: executive pay.

CHAPTER SIX

Give Stock a Chance

As far as state visits go, President George H. W. Bush's trip to Japan in January 1992 was one of the more disastrous in American politics. Though nothing captured the attention of Americans more than when Bush, who was ill with the flu, vomited and fell unconscious onto the lap of Japanese Prime Minister Kiichi Miyazawa during a state dinner, it was the issue of CEO pay that ended up causing Bush the bigger political problems as the 1992 presidential campaign got underway.[1] Bush's purpose for the visit was to lobby the Japanese government for greater trade restrictions on cars made in Japan, since Japanese automakers were outcompeting the ailing American automotive industry. To help make his case, Bush invited twelve CEOs, including the heads of GM, Ford, and Chrysler, to accompany him on the trip. The sight of these twelve executives—whose combined annual pay was around $25 million even as the country was in a recession and their companies were laying off workers—protesting unfair competition from Japanese CEOs who made on average around $300,000 to $400,000 was a political disaster for Bush. Japanese officials were quick to point out that "in Japan, you'd cut executive pay before eliminating jobs," and they blamed America's supposed lack of competitiveness on executives who were more interested in short-term results and high pay than in productivity.[2]

The domestic reception of the trip was not much better than the reception in Japan. In response to the trip, Paul Gigot, a columnist for *The Wall*

Street Journal, called high executive pay "an embarrassment for free marketers."³ Democrats, who sensed that executive pay could be a favorable issue for them in the 1992 elections, lined up to denounce Bush's decision to align himself with highly paid CEOs. Mario Cuomo, the Democratic governor of New York, called the trip "a truly dumb idea."⁴ Bill Clinton, then the governor of Arkansas and a leading contender for the Democratic presidential nomination, put this question to voters: "How can we run a country with a president who's coddling people he ought to be kicking in the fanny?" For his part, Clinton pledged that, if elected, he would eliminate corporate tax deductions for undeserved executive compensation. This condemnation of high CEO pay was a bipartisan affair as well. Pat Buchanan, the right-wing commentator who was challenging Bush in the Republican primary, told an interviewer that "you can't have executives running around making $4 million while their workers are being laid off." Even Bush's vice president, Dan Quayle, criticized "some of these exorbitant salaries paid to corporate executives unrelated to productivity" at an event before the president left for Japan.⁵ What united these critics was the feeling that the executives accompanying Bush on the trip to Japan had not earned their pay. Quayle, Clinton, and many other executive pay critics were not railing against high executive pay per se; rather, their objection was that it seemed to have no connection to corporate performance. By and large, executive pay critics did not mind if executives made good money when their companies had a good year; the problem was that all too often executives were making good money when their companies had bad years.⁶

Executive compensation reform had been a part of the shareholder value revolution since its very earliest days, and changes to managerial pay packages were a part of many LBO and restructuring programs. By the early 1990s, it seemed like the conditions were right for academics, consultants, investors, and politicians to press for widespread compensation reform and to force companies to tie executive pay to performance. The power of institutional investors and populist resentment at high CEO pay amid the ongoing recession provided reformers with favorable conditions, and it seemed like pay for performance could become a reality in the 1990s. However, executive compensation reform efforts between 1992 and 1994 did not play out the way academics or reformers thought they would. The proliferation of simplistic stock option compensation in the 1990s—something financial economists and consultants had warned against—did not impose market discipline on CEO pay; instead, it allowed CEOs to make unprecedented sums of money regardless of performance.

Likewise, political attempts to limit executive compensation through new taxes and disclosure requirements backfired and ended up sending executive compensation rates higher as firms competed to pay their CEOs more than their rivals.[7]

While the disclosure and tax reform attempts were controversial, nothing compared to the controversy started when the Financial Accounting Standards Board (FASB) attempted to require companies to record the value of the stock options they granted as an expense on their annual financial statements. FASB's attempt to force firms to account for stock options brought the nation's high-tech, "new economy" firms located in places like Silicon Valley and along Massachusetts's Route 128 corridor fully into the politics of shareholder value.[8] Until this point, tech firms had barely been involved in the shareholder value revolution, aside from the fact that new-economy companies were held up as a model for older companies being pressured into restructuring.[9] The fight over stock options changed this. In response to the FASB's efforts, tech companies leapt into the vanguard of the shareholder value revolution to champion stock options. Tech companies' participation in the fight over the FASB's actions also allowed executives at other, older companies and politicians to paint stock options as a uniquely American way to spur innovation and entrepreneurship, and in turn to justify ever-increasing options grants across the corporate landscape.[10] The tech sector's involvement also helped foster a political realignment in favor of shareholder value maximization within the Democratic Party. Tech companies had been important allies for Clinton in his election campaign, and as the Democratic Party fully embraced its new constituency of what Lilly Geismer called "suburban liberals," many of the party's most influential members lined up to denounce FASB while extolling the virtues of stock options.[11] Though there was a firm consensus in favor of FASB's proposals among shareholder value theorists, no amount of academic support could overcome the tidal wave of criticism FASB faced between 1992 and 1994 from Congress, investor groups, and businesses. In the face of such opposition, FASB had little choice but to back down and abandon its proposal, which it did in December 1994. FASB's defeat marked a new era in the nation's political economy. The shareholder value revolution had triumphed; managers and investors had arrived at a tremendously profitable—if still uneasy—alliance held together by stock options. By the time the Business Roundtable got around to formally endorsing shareholder value maximization in 1997, it was simply ratifying what had already been done.

Paying for Performance

Even with the victories they had won during the hostile takeover wave and their success in prodding businesses to commit to restructuring, shareholders groups still had plenty to be upset about in the 1990s, especially in terms of executive compensation. Evidence from academia and renegade compensation consultants that executive pay had little connection to corporate performance had continued to pile up, and institutional investors were increasingly frustrated with CEOs' record-breaking pay. Investors' criticism of executive pay was much more than just frustration with managerial excess. Investors feared that if managers could find a way to insulate their paychecks from corporate performance, all the gains made by shareholder value advocates over the past decade could be undone. If managers were all but guaranteed to receive ever higher levels of pay regardless of how their companies were performing, then they would have little incentive to do the unpleasant things like layoffs that managing for value entailed. This would essentially combine the worst aspects of the managerial era and the "era of greed" in the 1980s: managers would have little accountability to shareholders, and they would not be held back by the managerial era's normative commitment to some degree of self-restraint.[12]

Institutional investors had no shortage of experts they could point to when discussing the problems of executive pay. A former compensation consultant named Graef Crystal made a second career for himself as the most high-profile—and in the minds of executives, the most infuriating—critic of executive pay.[13] Crystal had spent most of the 1980s working at Towers, Perrin, Forster & Crosby, an executive compensation consulting firm. During his career as a consultant, Crystal earned a reputation as one of the nation's leading experts in designing lucrative compensation packages laden with stock options. Crystal was the one who designed Michael Eisner's original contract with Disney in 1984, which Crystal predicted would make Eisner the highest-paid CEO in history—a prediction that came true when Eisner made $203.1 million in 1994 (Eisner had already been the highest-paid CEO in America in 1989).[14] After becoming disenchanted with this work, Crystal took an early retirement from Towers, Perrin in 1988 and began amassing evidence that executives, by and large, did not deserve the pay they were receiving.[15] To these ends, he started collecting the financial statements of over 500 leading companies and tried to calculate how much of a CEO's pay was connected to corporate performance. With this information in hand, Crystal then reported how much pay he thought CEOs deserved to demonstrate just how much some CEOs were over- or underpaid. To publicize his findings Crystal started publishing a newsletter called "The Crystal Report" and wrote a book titled *In Search of Excess* that he published in 1992, and he quickly became a near-omnipresent figure in media discussions on executive pay.[16]

In addition to his inside knowledge of executive compensation, what made Crystal such a powerful critic of CEO pay was his knack for self-promotion and the often irreverent ways in which he described the executive compensation process. Crystal even compared his former profession to prostitution, claiming that compensation consultants like him were partly to blame for runaway CEO pay since they were often more interested in pleasing their clients than in recommending sensible pay arrangements.[17] Boards of directors also came in for a good amount of criticism from Crystal. According to Crystal, boards were unwilling to challenge CEOs, and since many boards included the CEOs of other companies, they often needed little convincing to decide to issue pay raises.[18] Notwithstanding all of these other criticisms, though, Crystal took the most delight in criticizing CEOs themselves. For example, when asked about the $75.1 million that Anthony J. F. O'Reilly of Heinz was paid in 1990, Crystal replied, "if they [Heinz] gave him one more dime, the 60th floor of the building would collapse."[19] In another instance, Crystal claimed that German and Japanese CEOs were paid less than American CEOs because "their greed glands are smaller."[20] Though these jibes poisoned Crystal's relationships with executives and former clients, he was a hit with the media, investors, and even politicians. *Fortune* hired Crystal to publish an annual list of which CEOs were overpaid and which were underpaid according to his calculations, and Crystal was frequently cited in newspaper articles about compensation.[21] Even more impressively, Crystal spoke personally with Bill Clinton during his presidential campaign, met with Vice President Dan Quayle's advisers, and testified several times before Congress as well.[22]

Shareholder activists looking for academic support of their criticisms of executive pay could also turn to Michael Jensen. Jensen had been making the case for paying managers in some form of stock since publication of his "Theory of the Firm" paper in 1976.[23] Jensen's interest in CEO pay grew over the course of the 1980s as executive pay levels began to rise rapidly amid protests from media commentators and shareholders groups.[24] In a break from form, Jensen's first comments on managerial pay in the 1980s were actually in defense of managers and their large paychecks. Jensen and another colleague named Kevin Murphy, a finance professor at Rochester's business school who would later join Jensen at Harvard Business School, aggressively defended rising CEO pay levels in both *The New York Times* and the *Harvard Business Review* (*HBR*) as well-deserved since, theoretically, CEO pay was being determined by a "market for managerial talent."[25]

Though they were both convinced that managers deserved high pay, Jensen and Murphy realized they had little in the way of empirical data to support their claims. To address this problem, the two decided to investigate CEO pay to see if it truly was set by an efficient managerial labor market. In 1990, Jensen and Murphy published an article in the *HBR* titled "CEO Incentives—It's Not How Much You Pay, but How."[26] Jensen and Murphy's article was arguably as influential as Jensen and Meckling's "Theory of the Firm," and far timelier.[27] Unlike "Theory of the Firm," which was a theoretical exploration of an issue that would not become hotly contested until years later, Jensen and Murphy's article was an easy-to-follow guide to how to structure executives' compensation written for an audience of business executives and consultants.[28] As the authors reported in the article, what they found when they looked closer into CEO pay was quite disappointing. It turned out that "in most publicly held companies, the compensation of top executives is virtually independent of performance. On average, corporate America pays its most important leaders like bureaucrats."[29] According to their calculations, the median change in a CEO's pay for a $1,000 change in shareholder value at the 250 largest companies in America was only $2.59. This meant that if a CEO made all the right moves in a given year and boosted their company's market value by $100 million, they would receive a two-year increase in salary that amounted to $6,700. Conversely, if a CEO made terrible investment decisions and wiped out $10 million in market value, they stood to lose $25,900, which given the fact that the average CEO was making $20,000 a week did not amount to much at all. The reasoning for this was that the majority of CEO pay came in the form of a yearly salary and easy-to-achieve bonus payments that the executive received regardless of how well or how poorly their company did.[30] According to Jensen and Murphy, CEO incentive targets were usually pegged to simplistic accounting figures like earnings growth—exactly the kind of thing shareholder value consultants had been urging executives to abandon.[31] Jensen and Murphy were very clear that they had no problem with high executive pay, only executive pay that was not tied to performance. As Jensen told *The Wall Street Journal*, "better performers should be paid more, and poorer performers should be paid less."[32] To make this happen, Jensen and Murphy advised boards that instead of paying their executives like "bureaucrats" on a salary, they needed to pay executives like "value-maximizing entrepreneurs"—namely, by paying them in stock, thus giving them a stake in the organization.[33] If managers were paid in stock, they would personally benefit from any increase in their firm's stock price, agency costs would be reduced, and managers would be paid for demonstrating performance, rather than collecting a fixed salary.

Investor groups seized on this evidence of managerial unaccountability to press for reform.[34] Neil Minnow, the president of Institutional Shareholder Services, a consulting firm that advised investors in corporate governance disputes, declared that even "Marie Antoinette would have been embarrassed" by CEO pay in the United States. According to Minnow, this scandalous state of affairs was due to the fact that "only CEOs pick the people who set their salary," and that CEOs' hand-picked boards were willing to give CEOs whatever they wanted. The end result of this "cozy system" was that "when a CEO does badly, his pay almost never goes down, indeed, it often goes up. When the company does well, the board raises the CEO's pay. The justification is 'because he deserves it.' When the company does badly, the board still raises his pay—and the justification is usually 'to make sure he stays' or 'because he has to make difficult decisions.'"[35] Instead of allowing this "cozy system" to continue, investors wanted to make sure that CEOs would only get paid if shareholders were getting paid. As Ralph Whitworth, the president of the United Shareholders Association, put it, "the only way the shareholders can get rich is by appreciation in the stock price or by dividends. And so that's the only way the top officers of the company should be able to get rich. Then you've got the interests aligned." Lest anyone mistake Whitworth or any other shareholder advocate for a populist railing against the very principle of high pay, Whitworth also reassured CEOs that he and his fellow shareholders "hope they [executives] do get rich, by the way. We want them to be multimillionaires. But they've got to make that money right alongside the shareholders in the form of either stock options or some plan that's linked to the stock price."[36]

"Excessive" Pay

After Bush's disastrous trip to Japan in January 1992 highlighted the fact that many American executives had made their money quite independently of their shareholders, Democrats sensed that executive compensation would be a hot-button issue in the upcoming elections, and they moved to capitalize on it.[37] The political fight over executive compensation, which would determine the overall direction of the shareholder value revolution, centered on attempts to reform three aspects of executive compensation: stronger disclosure mandates for CEO pay, tax penalties for "excessive" levels of pay, and accounting reforms that would force companies to expense the value of stock options in their financial statements. These three issues fractured the politics of shareholder value maximization and exposed the limited influence of shareholder value theory. Predictably, corporate managers opposed all three of these reforms, and the Business Roundtable lobbied strongly against each one. Shareholder groups were the greatest champions of stronger disclosure requirements, yet they opposed both tax hikes and accounting reform for fear of what these might do to their own profits. For their part, economists largely opposed tax penalties for high CEO pay, but they were supportive of both stronger disclosure requirements and accounting reform—a stance that proved to be very lonely by 1994. Both political parties tried to position themselves as the champions of shareholders, and it was the Democratic Party that was most directly responsible for putting all three of these reforms on the political agenda. However, Democrats were also quite divided over these reforms, and it was the actions of Democratic politicians responding to their constituents in the nation's booming tech sector that cleared the way for stock options to power CEO pay levels to an all-time high by 2001.[38]

Forcing companies to disclose what they were paying their executives in a transparent way was by far the easiest of the three fights executive compensation reformers engaged in at the beginning of the 1990s. The lack of meaningful disclosure requirements had been a perennial complaint of investors and had often been included in their reform proposals.[39] Shareholders hoped that if companies were required to faithfully report the amount of money they were giving their executives, and if shareholders could express their displeasure with these plans, companies would rein in executive pay lest they open themselves up to criticism from shareholders and the public. The principle of open disclosure was at the heart of the nation's securities laws, and the Securities Act of 1934 already forced firms to disclose top executives' compensation.[40] However, thanks to decades of rule changes and corporations' attempts to camouflage what they were paying their executives, these requirements had been rendered almost meaningless.[41] By 1991, even though firms were technically required to report all types of executive compensation in the proxy statement forms they submitted to the SEC and investors each year, this information was next to worthless since the SEC had no clear guidelines as to how this information needed to be presented. Firms exploited this loophole to the fullest and provided the required information on executive compensation in such a convoluted way as to be essentially unreadable. For his part, Crystal made sport of this process by awarding an annual "proxy obfuscation award" to the company that did the best job of concealing its CEO's pay.[42]

Senator Carl Levin (D-MI) chose to make the issue of proxy statement disclosure the first step in his broader campaign against high executive compensation. From his position as the chairman of the Senate oversight subcommittee, Levin was able to establish himself as the leading congressional voice for reining in CEO pay.[43] Levin was especially adept at using his ability to call hearings and the introduction of legislation that would usurp the authority of independent regulatory agencies to prod regulators into taking action. In May 1991 Levin held a hearing on "The SEC and the Issue of Runaway Executive Pay" that was designed to pressure the SEC into taking action on disclosure requirements.[44] Crystal was Levin's star witness, and he provided the subcommittee with the reasons he believed executive pay "has gone out of control" by citing both unreasonably high levels of CEO pay and the fact that CEO pay had little connection to corporate performance.[45] Following Crystal, Neil Minnow, Ralph Whitworth, and Robert A. G. Monks, a former Labor Department official who now headed a consulting firm named Institutional Shareholder Partners, all testified as to institutional shareholders' displeasure with the lack of accountability in executive pay and impenetrable proxy statements. This testimony was a laundry list of shareholders' grievances with executive pay: CEOs set their own pay, boards rubber-stamped whatever a CEO asked for, pay disclosure was meaningless, and managers so completely dominated the shareholder voting process that it was impossible for investors to challenge them.[46] After this litany of complaints, the subcommittee called on Linda Quinn, the SEC's director of corporation finance. In her written testimony, Quinn discussed how the SEC was considering both reforming disclosure requirements and granting shareholders an advisory vote on executive compensation.[47] Subcommittee members used their time questioning Quinn to repeatedly ask her when the SEC might adopt these changes—noting that the last regulatory change in this area had taken seven years—and Quinn refused to provide any specific timetable amid this obvious congressional pressure for action. To drive home the point of the hearing, Levin closed the day's proceedings by telling Quinn that he hoped the SEC would act soon and warning her that if it did not, he would.[48] To underscore this threat of preemption, Levin introduced what he called the Corporate Pay Responsibility Act just days after the hearing, on June 4, 1991, which would have mandated the SEC to both tighten its disclosure rules and allow shareholders to hold non-binding votes on companies' executive compensation plans.[49]

Levin's hearing was followed by a hearing on "Shareholder Rights" held by the Senate Securities Subcommittee, which was chaired by Senator Christopher Dodd (D-CT), in October 1991.[50] During this hearing SEC Chairman Richard Breeden was questioned about Levin's bill. Unsurprisingly, Breeden testified that he opposed the bill since it would cut into his agency's prerogatives; but he did signal his sympathy with Levin's concerns, likely in an effort to mollify Levin and win his agency more time to conduct their own reform process.[51] After Breeden testified, representatives from both the United Shareholders Association and the Council of Institutional Investors had another opportunity to reiterate their complaints about executive pay and managerial unaccountability and to voice their support for Levin's bill.[52] What made Dodd's hearing different from Levin's was that representatives from both the Business Roundtable and the National Association of Manufacturers (NAM) testified. Though both organizations were opposed to proxy reform, the ways in which they voiced this opposition were a clear sign that shareholders had achieved a dominant position in the politics of corporate governance. John Hartley, the CEO of the Harris Corporation and the chairman of NAM, testified that "we strongly support the overriding principle that companies should be run primarily for the benefit of their shareholders."[53] Bruce Atwater, the chairman of General Mills and the head of the Roundtable's task force on corporate governance, told the senators that "clearly, the purpose of corporate governance and the purpose of shareholders banding together to form corporations, is to build shareholder wealth. This was perhaps a controversial issue a few years ago, but I think there's general agreement on this today."[54] Despite their commitment to shareholder value maximization, both Atwater and Hartley still maintained that managers themselves were more than capable of accomplishing this goal without any increased oversight from institutional investors, especially when it came to the issue of compensation. As these hearings revealed, the debate over shareholder value maximization was no longer about whether companies should do so, but about how they should do so.

With a good deal of legislative support for reform already in place, once executive pay became a major campaign issue in 1992 the SEC was all but forced to act. In February, in an effort to "bring a market solution to a market problem" in the words of Chairman Breeden, the commission allowed shareholders to propose holding non-binding advisory votes on companies' executive pay plans so that shareholders would have a mechanism to formally protest pay packages they found objectionable.[55] In October, the agency's commissioners went further, voting unanimously to require companies to disclose the full value of their executives' compensation arrangements, including stock options, in an easy-to-read table. In their October decision the commission also allowed shareholders to vote for individual candidates instead of a slate of candidates when electing directors and loosened some of the regulations on proxy contests, which made it easier for institutional investors to pressure managers at companies' annual meetings.[56] Though hailed by both investors and academics at the time as a meaningful step toward corporate governance reform, it is possible that enhanced disclosure actually pushed CEO pay upward instead of reining it in. Though some investors and reformers hoped companies might have been embarrassed to have to disclose just how much they were paying their executives, these hopes were not borne out. Boards determined CEO pay in large part by looking at what other firms were paying their executives and trying to match it, and the SEC's new disclosure requirements made this process much easier.[57] Moreover, since the SEC now required firms to report the value of executives' stock options in their proxy statements, many of them had to report much higher levels of executive compensation, which only made it easier for executives and compensation consultants to justify higher salaries and larger options grants.[58]

President Clinton's attempt to limit executive compensation through the tax code backfired even worse than the SEC's attempt did. Clinton seized on the executive pay issue during the 1992 campaign in an attempt to paint Bush as elitist, and as part of this effort Clinton pledged that he would eliminate the corporate income tax deduction for all executive compensation over $1 million.[59] House Democrats had passed a similar measure in March 1991, but President Bush vetoed it.[60] During a campaign address to NAM Clinton tried to win business support for his plans by claiming that his tax on CEO pay was part of a larger effort to encourage companies to spend more on job creation amid ongoing recession.[61] These efforts were largely unsuccessful, and corporate executives were predictably upset with Clinton's plan to attack their pay levels. Perhaps no part of the business world was more opposed to Clinton's tax plan than Wall Street.[62] Major Wall Street investment banks, all of which (except for Goldman Sachs and Lazard Freres) had at this point gone public, worried that Clinton's plan would be the end of the generous bonus payments banks traditionally offered their top executives, as well as the stock option grants firms had recently been able to take advantage of by going public. Notably, Robert Rubin, then the head of Goldman Sachs and soon to be the head of Clinton's National Economic Council, kept silent about the plan even as the rest of his colleagues on Wall Street threatened to take their firms private if Clinton followed through on his tax pledge. Meanwhile compensation consultants were far more relaxed, and on the eve of the election they told their clients that no matter what happened, consultants would be able to find some form of loophole.[63]

It turned out that consultants did not have to look very hard to find a loophole in Clinton's tax plan once the first details of it were announced in February 1993. Before Clinton was even sworn in, executives voiced their displeasure with any potential tax by rushing to cash in as many of their options as possible. Michael Eisner was at the front of this pack; he made over $200 million from options in December 1992 to—in his telling—protect Disney from potential tax liabilities in the new year.[64] By the time Clinton was inaugurated in January, Secretary of Labor Robert Reich was the only member of the president's economic team who still supported Clinton's campaign pledge to end deductions for all pay over $1 million.[65] Instead, Clinton's economic advisers, led by Rubin and Treasury Secretary Lloyd Bentsen, convinced the president that his tax plan should include an exemption for any form of executive pay that could be tied to corporate performance. Clinton agreed to this caveat, and in February he promised executives that his tax plan would only target executive pay above $1 million if it was not tied to corporate performance. Though Clinton did not specify during his remarks in February what pay for performance might mean in relation to his tax proposal, compensation consultants predicted that stock options would certainly be exempt from his tax plan and that executives' pay would not fall, even though the composition of their pay packages might shift toward more options.[66]

These predictions were validated when the Treasury published the formal language of the tax plan in April. In the final text of the proposal, any compensation over $1 million provided to the five highest-ranking executives in a company was defined as "excessive" and not tax deductible unless it was tied to a defined performance goal, which could include either stock price or accounting metrics like earnings. Additionally, performance plans had to be set in advance of any payment by a compensation committee comprising only independent directors, and any plan had to be ratified by shareholders.[67] Even with these modifications, the tax plan was not popular in the business community, and NAM announced their opposition to it in congressional hearings on the tax bill in June.[68] Shareholders were not pleased with the tax plan either. Wentworth called it a "wrongheaded solution" to the problem of high executive pay that would likely shift companies' tax burden to shareholders, since he believed firms were likely to still pay salaries above $1 million and accept higher taxes, which would leave less corporate cash flow available to shareholders in the form of dividend payments or share buybacks.[69] Economists were also upset with Clinton's plan. Jensen and Murphy both opposed the tax, and Murphy claimed that any tax increase would "further undo the relationship between pay and performance."[70] Dennis Aigner, the dean of University of California Irvine's business school, called the plan "ill-timed, illogical, probably superfluous, and hopefully ill-fated" and warned that it would impede job creation and disincentivize executive effort.[71] Still, the Clinton administration pressed ahead with the tax plan and included it as part of the president's omnibus deficit reduction plan. Once the omnibus bill passed by extremely narrow margins in both the House and the Senate, the executive pay deduction limit was officially added to the nation's tax laws as Section 162(m).[72]

The supporters of Clinton's compensation tax were quite clear that the new tax was designed not to raise revenue, but to discourage high CEO pay. In Clinton's own words, his plan would have a "relatively small dollar impact," but he promised that it would be of "great significance to the American working people," who were upset with high CEO pay.[73] The House Ways and Means Committee was even more explicit about the tax's intended purpose. In the final report on the bill, the committee wrote that "the amount of compensation received by corporate executives has been the subject of scrutiny and criticism. The committee believes that excessive compensation will be reduced if the deduction for compensation (other than performance-based compensation) paid to the top executives of publicly held corporations is limited to $1 million per year."[74] Judged by these standards, the tax law was an abject failure. At the most basic level, the tax did not stop executive pay levels from rising, and executive pay increases continued to accelerate for the remainder of the decade.[75] This tax plan very likely fueled those pay increases as well. One side effect of setting the standard for "excessive" pay at $1 million was that firms could argue that any pay under $1 million was, by default, not excessive.[76] In an analysis of executive compensation rates after the tax law was passed, the accounting professors David Harris and Jane Livingstone found that companies that had been paying their executives under $1 million pushed their executives' pay right up to the $1 million limit.[77] Many firms which were paying their executives over $1 million in salary did lower their executives' pay below the $1 million threshold, but they more than offset these reductions with even more generous options grants.[78] This acceleration in the use of stock options was the most significant consequence of the law. This governmental endorsement of stock options came just as the nation's economy was accelerating toward a period of robust growth that would last for the rest of the decade. As the stock markets continued to set record highs, corporate boards seemingly had few reasons not to offer their managers generous grants of stock options.[79]

The Trouble with Options

The controversies over disclosure requirements and taxation paled in comparison to the war between the nation's business community and FASB over the accounting treatment of stock options between 1992 and 1994. Options were, by far, the most popular way to tie pay to performance, and with the encouragement of both institutional investors and the federal government boards came to rely on them as the best way to attract the star CEOs they were searching for.[80] At the beginning of the decade, CEO incentive pay in S&P 500 firms was split about evenly between stock options and cash bonus payments tied to accounting benchmarks. By 1996, options had become the largest single component of CEO pay, and by 2001 options were accounting for more than half of all money paid to CEOs.[81]

Given how popular stock options had become, FASB's attempt to regulate options prompted attacks from almost every corner of the nation's business and political establishments. FASB itself was a small private-sector organization headed by a seven-member board nominated by the trustees of the Financial Accounting Foundation, who were drawn from business, government, and academia.[82] Though FASB was not a government agency, it had de facto legal authority since the SEC had outsourced its statutory authority to set the nation's accounting rules to the group upon FASB's founding in 1973.[83] Though it could technically override FASB's decisions, the commission made it very clear that it would support whatever decisions FASB made, and the ability to make independent regulatory decisions was at the heart of FASB's existence.[84] FASB's attempt to mandate options expensing provoked one of the most furious business lobbying campaigns of the 1990s. The Business Roundtable, all six major accounting firms, institutional investors, the tech sector, Wall Street, venture capitalists, the Treasury Department, the government of California, and eighty-eight US senators all opposed forcing companies to expense the value of the options they granted in their annual financial statements. Aligned against this juggernaut were FASB, economists, a handful of US senators led by Carl Levin, and executive compensation critics like Crystal. For over two years, opponents of FASB's proposal did everything in their power to convince the American people that stock options were responsible for the nation's growing economy, and that forcing firms to account for their cost would jeopardize not only the nation's economic growth, but also the very existence of free markets themselves. In making these claims, FASB's opponents transformed stock options from a (deeply flawed) way to tie executive compensation to corporate performance into one of the very foundations of American capitalism.

Stock options—like all financial derivatives—can be dizzyingly complex, but (fortunately for scholars interested in studying executive compensation) unrestricted stock options, which are the type most commonly granted to executives by boards, are remarkable for their simplicity.[85] In their simplest form, stock options grant whoever holds them the right to purchase newly issued shares in a company at a predetermined price by some date in the future. Options generally have some minimum holding period (called the "vesting period") that must pass before people can exercise them and an expiration date by which the holders need to exercise them or they will become invalid. Typically, boards chose to use a four-year vesting period and set the expiration date of options at ten years from the day they were granted. For purposes of illustration, imagine a company whose stock is selling for $10 on January 1. The board of the imaginary company decides on January 1 to issue stock options to its CEO that allow them to purchase 100 shares of its stock at $10 per share in the future. Five years later, the company's stock price is $20, and the CEO's stock options are said to be "in the money" since the market price exceeds the exercise price. With their options in the money, the CEO chooses to exercise their options and purchase 100 shares with money they obtained from an ultra-low-interest-rate loan so that they do not have to spend any of their own capital. At the moment the CEO exercises their options, the company issues 100 shares of stock and sells them to the CEO at $10 per share. At this point, the CEO could immediately sell their shares at the $20 market price, thus making a profit of $1,000, or they could hold on to those shares and incorporate them into their portfolio as regular stocks.

Despite options' popularity with boards and corporate managers, executive compensation experts were often quite skeptical of them.[86] In January 1990, *Fortune* ran a story titled "The Trouble with Stock Options" that featured several compensation consultants and investment managers listing out the various ways in which stock options did not link managers' pay to performance.[87] In theory, stock options could do a good job of mitigating the principal agent problem Jensen and other economists had been warning about since the 1970s, but they needed to be used carefully.[88] For starters, if stock options were truly going to force executives to think like shareholders, then executives should have to hold on to their options until very near their expiration date, and ideally would then hold onto the shares they received instead of selling them immediately. If executives held their options for the full duration and then retained their stock, they would be meaningfully exposed to the risk that the firm's share price might fall and so would have a real stake in the long-term performance of the company. However, if executives cashed in their options early when the price looked appealing or if they sold their stock immediately upon receiving it, then stock options would amount to little more than a deferred paycheck—with tax and accounting benefits—that an executive could cash in at a time of their choosing. Unfortunately for boards and shareholders that might have hoped managers would treat their options like ownership stakes in the company, the accounting professors Steven Huddart and Mark Lang found in a study of over 50,000 employees with stock options published in 1996 that most options holders exercised their options years before the expiration date and that this decision was based on short-term stock price movements.[89] Additionally, a study of 8,516 top executives in 1,646 companies between 1993 and 1995 conducted by the economists Eli Ofek and David Yermack revealed that "executives retain approximately none of the shares acquired on the exercise of options."[90] Even if executives did choose to hold on to the shares they received from options, they could use complex financial hedges known as "collars" to protect their new shares from price drops and to lock in the gains they would have received if they had sold upon exercise.[91]

Even if boards did a good job of designing options packages, there was still the problem that most boards simply gave out far too many options. As Murphy himself would later admit with regret, companies took his and Jensen's pay-for-performance "mantra a little too literally: adding increasingly generous grants of stock options on top of already competitive pay packages, without any reduction in other forms of pay and showing little concern about the resulting inflation in pay levels."[92] If executives were truly going to have their pay exposed to market risk, then options would need to replace their salaries, not augment them. Even with their flaws, stock options were at least somewhat risky and might end up being worthless; however, if an executive was making $1 million or more a year in guaranteed salary, plus whatever they could earn from easy-to-achieve bonus payments, they had little to fear if their options wound up underwater. Amanda Bennet, a *Wall Street Journal* reporter, summed this up colorfully in 1988 when she wrote that options programs "are almost always additions to rather than substitutes for other compensation, and they almost always lift total pay simply because they're ladled like gravy on top of base salaries, bonuses, and other fixed benefits."[93]

Beyond these problems brought about by the behavior of managers and boards, there was the deeper problem that simple stock options did not do a very good job of linking managers' pay to their performance.[94] Aside from the perennial debate over what effect, if any, CEOs can have on corporate performance, the fact that the vast majority of stock options issued to top executives were not indexed to some external benchmark meant that options rarely reflected a company's real performance.[95] If an option was indexed, that meant its exercise price would move along with whatever it was benchmarked to. For example, if an option were indexed to the S&P 500 and the value of the S&P 500 rose by 2 percent, the exercise price of the indexed option would also rise by 2 percent, meaning that the issuer's stock would need to rise by a greater percentage than the index in order for the option to gain value. Without an index, anything that caused a company's stock price to rise would automatically increase the value of managers' stock options. The sustained bull markets of the 1980s and 1990s were already putting upward pressure on firms' stock prices, and managers reaped the rewards regardless of how their firms were performing. This meant that a company could dramatically underperform its competitors or the overall stock market, while its management team still made a handsome profit from their options. For example, if a company's stock price rose by 1 percent in a given year and the S&P 500 Index rose by 5 percent, then, all other things being equal, investors would likely consider the imaginary company to be an underperformer and a bad investment. However, as long as the stock options of that underperforming company's management were in the money, its managers would still be rewarded by having their stock options appreciate in value. Given the large size of many options grants, even a small gain in a firm's stock price could deliver hundreds of thousands or millions of dollars for executives.[96]

Large grants of stock options could also provide managers with perverse incentives to obsess over quarterly earnings targets, even to the point of committing fraud.[97] In the 1990s, Thomson Financial / First Call, a financial consulting firm, began to compile analysts' predictions about companies' quarterly earnings performance to generate what it called a "consensus estimate." These projections were largely based on analysts' readings of firms' accounting statements and focused on EPS growth instead of cash flow—something that, as already discussed, infuriated economists and shareholder value consultants.[98] Regardless of what shareholder value theorists might have said, the money managers who controlled the funds of institutional investors eagerly bought up these consensus estimates in their efforts to keep generating above-market performance each quarter.[99] On Wall Street and among corporate managers, a firm's projected earnings became known as "the number." Hitting "the number" became one of the most important goals for corporate managers in the 1990s. If a firm hit or exceeded its number quarter after quarter, it would be rewarded with higher stock prices; if a firm fell below its number in a given quarter, the stock price would drop. Stock options did not create the earnings game that developed in the 1990s, but they helped grow the corporate obsession with earnings into what the financial journalist Harris Collingwood called "The Earnings Cult" by the end of the decade.[100] Given that executives had so much of their potential wealth tied up in stock options, they had extraordinarily strong incentives to spend their time working to make sure that they hit their number, though they often resented having to spend so much of their working day dealing with analysts.[101] Regardless of how time-consuming the earnings process was, if a CEO could reliably hit her numbers, their stock options would dramatically appreciate in value and they might even be granted more by an appreciative board. If they missed their firm's number, they could lose millions. With stakes as high as these it is easy to see why executives might be tempted to manipulate their firms' accounting statements—something that would become very apparent in the wave of accounting scandals that swept through corporate America at the beginning of the 2000s.[102]

This host of potential problems with large grants of simple stock options seemingly did nothing to dull boards' enthusiasm about granting them in the 1990s. One important reason why boards may have issued simplistic unrestricted stock options plans was because these plans, and these plans alone, had no cost—at least as far as accounting standards were concerned. This peculiar state of affairs was due to the complicated interaction between the nation's changing tax laws and the accounting standards-setting process.[103] Between 1950 and 1969 firms almost exclusively issued restricted stock options, a special class of options created by Congress in 1950 that were treated as a capital gains transaction instead of a compensation expense, and therefore were not treated as an expense for either tax or accounting purposes. The Accounting Review Board (ARB, FASB's predecessor) paid little attention to unrestricted stock options during this time, since they were functionally nonexistent. Once Congress killed off the restricted stock option at the end of the 1960s and firms started issuing unrestricted options again, the ARB was forced to reckon with unrestricted options, which it attempted to do in 1972. According to a Supreme Court ruling in 1945, unrestricted stock options provided to executives were a compensation expense, which meant that the money individuals made from selling their stock options was taxed as personal income, and that companies would be allowed to deduct that amount from their corporate taxes as a business expense.[104] Since unrestricted stock options were a compensation expense, this meant they would need to be expensed on a company's income statement as well. One of the underlying principles of accounting was that expenses should be reported over the same time period in which the services rendered for those expenses were performed. For executive compensation, the expense would be the value of the stock option at its grant date and the time period would be the vesting period of the option. In 1972, it was seemingly impossible to determine what the value of a stock option was at its grant date (sometimes called its "fair value"), since the ultimate value of the option would vary depending on the movement of the company's stock price.[105]

Since determining the fair value was impossible, the ARB chose to have firms expense the option's "intrinsic value," which was simply the market value of the stock on the day it was issued minus the exercise price of the stock option.[106] Therefore, as long as a firm issued a stock option whose exercise price matched the market price on the day it was issued, it would mark an expense of $0 for the option in its financial statements. What made this even more peculiar was that this $0 cost only applied to unindexed options—exactly the kind that economists and compensation experts were least supportive of—since accountants could measure the value of an indexed option by simply calculating how much an option would pay off each year as its price changed, and firms were required to deduct this amount as an expense on their income statement. The nation's tax laws also worked to disincentivize using indexed options, since indexed options did not meet the Treasury Department's standards for performance-based compensation in Section 162(m) because the exercise price of an indexed option could potentially drop below the market price on the day the option was granted.[107] This meant that only unindexed options could be deducted from corporate taxes if they pushed executive pay over $1 million, and only indexed options did not have to be charged against earnings. The result of all of this was that if an executive made $2 million by selling simple unrestricted options granted to them by their firm, the firm would record an expense of $0 and would take a $2 million deduction from its taxes. This tax deduction meant that, on paper (not in reality), options were even better than free—they actually saved a company money.[108]

Of course, as academics and knowledgeable observers pointed out, this was all a game of smoke and mirrors. Options did indeed have value, and they did impose a cost on companies in the form of stock dilution as well as the opportunity cost of not being able to sell stock at market prices.[109] What made the situation especially infuriating was that the University of Chicago's finance department had invented what should have been the obvious solution in the minds of many of these experts. In 1973, Fischer Black, a Harvard Economics PhD who taught finance at the University of Chicago and MIT before joining Goldman Sachs in 1984, and Myron Scholes, who had received his PhD from Chicago in 1969, published their landmark options pricing formula (known as "Black-Scholes") in the *Journal of Political Economy*.[110] The Black-Scholes model, which was a complex partial derivative used to estimate the value of stock options, was, along with the EMH, one of the crowning achievements of Chicago's finance program. By the 1990s, Black-Scholes was already widely taught in business schools and used every day on Wall Street and at the Chicago Mercantile Exchange, and had revolutionized financial markets by enabling the creation of a hyperactive derivatives market.[111] After the SEC set new disclosure requirements in 1992, most firms were using the formula in their proxy statements as well, since Black-Scholes was one of the models the SEC allowed firms to use when reporting the value of stock options granted to executives.[112] Compensation reformers argued that Black-Scholes would allow firms to calculate the fair value of stock options, and that this fair value, not an intrinsic value of $0, should be expensed on firms' financial statements.[113]

Showdown in Silicon Valley

FASB had been considering requiring firms to use Black-Scholes to expense the value of stock options since 1984, but due to disagreements amongst the seven members of the board over technical matters and fear of the controversy any reform attempt would bring, the board had abandoned the idea in 1988.[114] Here again, Levin used the power of his chairmanship to spur FASB into taking action. Levin's Corporate Pay Responsibility Act, which he had introduced after his disclosure hearings in 1991, had already included a provision that would have forced companies to expense the value of stock options. After six months without any sign that the SEC or FASB had taken action on this issue, Levin called another hearing in January 1992 to call renewed attention to what he termed the problem of "Stealth Compensation of Corporate Executives."[115] Since FASB was subject to the SEC's oversight, Levin was able to use his subcommittee to directly pressure the group's board into taking action. At the end of a hearing dominated by critics of the SEC's and FASB's inaction on stock options, Levin concluded by pressing both the SEC's head accountant, Walter Schuetze, and FASB's vice chairman, James Leisenring, on why their organizations had not acted. In a contentious back-and-forth between Levin and Leisenring, the senator demanded that Leisenring provide an estimate of how long it would take to reform accounting standards. Leisenring said that the soonest it could be done was "two years," which "would be a very quick decision of this type in the world of accounting standards today."[116] This clearly did not please Levin, and he ended the hearing by warning Leisenring and Schuetze that "when you [FASB] fail to act after a certain length of time, the SEC has an obligation to act. It has not. If the SEC fails to act after a certain length of time, Congress, I believe, should act."[117]

Given that FASB's authority depended in large part on the perception of it as an independent and objective body, this threat of legislative interference posed an existential threat to the organization. In response to Levin's threat, FASB Chairman Dennis Beresford restarted the group's stock option project in January, and in April 1992 the seven members of FASB's executive board voted unanimously that they would craft new regulations that could take effect in 1994.[118] At this early date, it seemed to Beresford and the rest of FASB's board that the group had a good chance of passing these reforms. As Beresford himself recalled in an oral history interview conducted in 2011, "we just felt that we were technically or theoretically correct, sort of on the side of the angels. I think we felt we had some support in Washington through Senator Levin or otherwise. Ultimately, if we did the right thing, that somehow would be enough." Given what happened, Beresford admitted that, in retrospect, this stance was "a little politically naïve."[119] Beresford and his colleagues could be forgiven for their naiveté, however, given that it seemed investors would have been on their side. Since stock options grants involved creating new shares, they had always been subject to shareholder approval, and in the early 1990s shareholders had been voting against options plans with increasing frequency, with the percentage of "no" votes rising from 3.5 percent in 1988 to 12 percent in 1991.[120] As chronicled in *Fortune*, many investors knew that companies were being too generous with stock options. Warren Buffet had long mocked the idea that stock options were not expensed, and liked to joke that he was considering paying all of Berkshire Hathaway's expenses with options so that he could report zero expenses year after year.[121] Sarah A. B. Teslik, the executive director of the Council of Institutional Investors, also acknowledged that the misuse of options was creating problems for executive accountability, and she told *The Washington Post* that "the options are where the problem is. You can put a lot more money into an options package than into a plain pay package."[122] In an even more encouraging development, in written testimony submitted to Levin's hearing on "Stealth Compensation" Elizabeth Holtzman, the comptroller of New York City and a member of the Council of Institutional Investors, declared that she and the City's pension funds encouraged "efforts through Financial Accounting Standards Board and the Securities and Exchange Commission to require companies to deduct from their income the cost of granting stock options to their top executives."[123]

Convinced that they were "on the side of the angels," FASB walked into a storm of opposition. As soon as FASB's board started giving indications that they were considering a change to options rules, they received a swift response from the business community and from pro-business members of government. In June 1992, John Robson, the deputy secretary of the Treasury, used an address to a biotechnology trade group to rally opposition to what he called FASB's "bean-counter mentality." Robson likely found a great deal of agreement with him among the audience.[124] The biotech sector—much like the electronics and software firms of Silicon Valley—relied heavily on stock options to compensate both executives and lower-level engineers and scientists, since the startup firms that dominated the sector often did not make enough cash to adequately pay talented employees.[125] Robson warned that if FASB did require firms to expense stock options, then biotech startups, along with the rest of the tech sector, would likely have to abandon the use of stock options lest they drag down startups' earnings and jeopardize their ability to attract funding and potential acquirers. Though high-tech firms may have been the most vigorous opponents of FASB, the Business Roundtable was not far behind. By August 1992, over a dozen Roundtable CEOs had written Beresford personally to express their displeasure with FASB, and the relationship between FASB and the Roundtable had soured to the point that Beresford wrote to Roundtable member John Reed, the head of Citicorp, to protest the "unfortunate" ways Roundtable members had described FASB in the press.[126]

The pressure on FASB only intensified in 1993 as the board prepared to release the specifics of its reform plan. In January, Levin once again threatened FASB's independence by introducing a bill that would force companies to expense the value of stock options.[127] Unfortunately for FASB, in the same month the Council of Institutional Investors announced its opposition to the board's options plan, thereby costing the board its most important potential ally.[128] In February the Council, along with the heads of the nation's six major accounting firms, the United Shareholders Association, the National Venture Capital Association, and companies such as GM, GE, Apple, and AT&T, among others, signed a letter to Beresford indicating their opposition to FASB's reform plan.[129] Instead of a charge to earnings, the signatories recommended that FASB require firms to disclose the value of options in one of the numerous footnotes that accompanied firms' financial statements, where curious investors could find the information but it would have no effect on earnings. Given investors' traditional opposition to high CEO pay and their previous criticisms of the abuses of stock options—not to mention their earlier support for FASB—their opposition to FASB's proposal came as a surprise to many observers.[130] Investors' objection to the proposal boiled down to a fear that it might cost them money. If expensing options did depress earnings, stock prices could drop in response, and then there would be less money available for shareholders to receive in the form of dividends or share buybacks. In a similar vein, the accounting firms' decision to oppose reform likely reflected a desire to please their corporate clients, since accounting firms depended on managers' good graces for continued business and companies were not shy about retaliating against consultants who threatened their pay practices.[131]

While FASB was losing potential allies, its opponents were mobilizing. As firms began compiling their annual proxy statements in the winter of 1993, the Roundtable urged them to use the statements to try to sabotage FASB. As per the disclosure rules the SEC implemented in 1992, firms were required to disclose the value of their options plans in their proxy statements. To calculate the value of the options, the SEC allowed firms to report either the single Black-Scholes value of the options or estimates of how much executives could earn if the firm's stock price rose by either 5 or 10 percent. Even though the Black-Scholes value was generally significantly lower than the estimates, the Roundtable urged its members to use the more costly estimates in spite of the risk that higher reported values could expose firms to backlash from shareholders and the public. The Roundtable's leadership figured that these risks were justified since if firms overstated the value of their options it would, first, inflate the potential effect FASB's decision could have on earnings, and second, discredit FASB by making it seem that Black-Scholes was too complicated to use.[132] This charge that Black-Scholes was too complicated for anyone to use was common among executives. Even though, as proponents of reform liked to point out, compensation committees and consultants often used the formula to tell executives what their options might be worth, CEOs often claimed that the formula was unworkable and that complex formulas had no place in the world of executive pay.[133]

FASB's opponents also built up a powerful political lobbying campaign. Thirty-two large corporations, including many leading tech firms, formed an advocacy group called the Coalition for American Equity Expansion (CAEE) to lobby Congress to block FASB's attempts to change accounting standards.[134] CAEE developed a plan not only to attempt to block FASB, but to launch a counterattack in which they would convince Congress to pass legislation making options even easier to use. Ken Hagerty, a Washington lobbyist and a founder of CAEE, wrote the groups' members on February 1, 1993, shortly after Levin introduced his bill, that "since the best defense is a good offense, CAEE is developing a legislative initiative to *improve* the current tax and regulatory treatment of employee stock options.... Companies will be able to help by persuading their constituent House and Senate members to cosponsor the bill."[135] In the same memo, Hagerty included a draft of legislation which he titled the "Equity Expansion Act of 1993" that would have banned the SEC from forcing firms to expense traditional unrestricted options and created a new class of options called "Performance Share Agreements"(PSAs) that would not be deducted from corporate taxes, but would instead be taxed upon the sale of the options at a reduced rate instead of upon the exercise of options at regular personal income tax rates. To help sell the bill, Hagerty also included a three-page statement titled "Why We Need Stock Option Reform." In the statement Hagerty argued that options tied "pay to performance" while also enhancing "productivity, innovation, and shareholder value," and he pointed out that the new economy stalwart Microsoft had created "over 2,200 employee millionaires" through stock options. Hagerty warned that success stories like these were threatened by both the government's insistence on taxing options when their holders exercised them and FASB's attempts to make "options plans prohibitively expensive."

Urged on by Hagerty, executives and representatives of the tech and venture capital sectors descended on Washington in droves. Given that their paychecks were at stake, executives held nothing back in these lobbying efforts. The head of Raychem, a high-tech radiation chemistry firm based in California, said that his first response to the plan was "total rage."[136] Arthur Levitt, the chairman of the SEC, recalled that one CEO who opposed FASB's plan warned him, "Arthur, if you let this happen, it means the end of capitalism."[137] FASB's opponents scored an early victory in April when Treasury Secretary Bentsen wrote FASB that he had reservations about forcing companies to take "a highly debatable charge" to earnings on the day before FASB was to vote on new standards.[138] Despite this warning, FASB's members voted 6–1 on April 7 that they would force companies to expense stock options. In an attempt to appease business leaders, FASB's board decided that the rule would not take effect until 1997, though firms would need to disclose the value of stock options in a footnote to their financial statements starting in 1994. Though the delay until 1997 was intended to give firms time to adapt to FASB's changes, corporate executives made it clear that they intended to use the extra time solely to continuing their lobbying efforts against the board's proposal.[139]

These lobbying efforts escalated dramatically in the summer of 1993 as CAEE made significant inroads with several members of Congress, including Senators Barbara Boxer and Diane Feinstein, California's two Democratic senators. CAEE's closest ally in the Senate was Joseph Lieberman (D-CT), and he was the one who took the lead on opposing FASB. On June 29, Lieberman took to the floor of the Senate with Feinstein to introduce the Equity Expansion Act of 1993, which was sponsored by himself, Feinstein, Boxer, and Connie Mack (R-FL).[140] Lieberman's bill, which was derived from Hagerty's original draft, forbade the SEC from allowing options to be expensed and created "Performance Share Options" (PSOs) which offered the same tax advantages as Hagerty's PSAs. In an effort to cast the bill as a populist measure, Lieberman included a provision which mandated that half of any PSO grant had to be given to workers who were classified by the IRS as "non-highly compensated." In his floor speech, Lieberman claimed that the Equity Expansion Act was a "jobs bill" since stock options encouraged people to start new companies and hire workers they might not be able to otherwise afford.[141] Lieberman said that FASB's proposals may have been defensible "as a matter of abstract accounting theory," but "from a public policy, job creation, and competitiveness perspective, it is simply unnecessary and unusually disruptive" since it would likely force companies to either discontinue stock options altogether or only issue them to their highest-ranking executives.[142]

The claim that stock options were widely issued to employees at all levels was at the center of the anti-FASB campaign. According to FASB's opponents, companies routinely made stock options available to all their employees, and the decision to expense options would hurt lower-level workers the most since their options would be the first ones revoked.[143] In one instance, FASB's opponents ran an advertisement in *Roll Call*, a newspaper focused on Capitol Hill, with pictures of four ordinary workers and an invitation to readers to "meet the 'fat cats' who benefit from stock options."[144] Though there was some truth to the claim that ordinary workers were starting to receive options in the early 1990s, the situation was much more complicated than the members of the anti-FASB coalition made it seem. While startups did offer many of their workers options, this was not the case in most American firms. According to a study of 5,891 public companies conducted by Institutional Shareholder Services and commissioned by Levin, all the companies surveyed offered options to executives, but only 1 percent offered options to lower-level employees.[145] Some major companies, such as the Walgreens drug store chain, did start offering stock option plans to all full-time employees in the 1990s, and while these plans did seem to boost morale, they could come with substantial risk.¹⁴⁶ As *Fortune* pointed out in June 1993, options plans — which were much riskier for lower-level workers than for executives — often came in lieu of wage increases, which meant that workers were being asked to risk a portion of their compensation on the stock market instead of receiving risk-free cash in the form of a raise.¹⁴⁷ These issues did not stop people like Lieberman from supporting "stock options for all employees," however, and the opponents of FASB continuously pounded home the idea that companies should be expanding their use of stock options, not curtailing it.¹⁴⁸

A hearing called by Dodd in October 1993 drove home just how lopsided the debate was becoming.¹⁴⁹ The hearing began with a parade of senators from both parties that included Dodd, Lieberman, Boxer, Mack, Bill Bradley (D-NJ), and Phil Gramm (R-TX), all denouncing FASB, while Levin, who was called as a witness, was the lone senator who supported the organization. After the senators expressed their displeasure with FASB, representatives from the Council of Institutional Investors, CAEE, the American Electronics Association (AEA), the Biotechnology Industry Organization, the National Venture Capital Association, Microsoft, General Electric, and NAM all expressed their firm opposition to FASB and defended the centrality of stock options to American business and economic growth. Beresford and Leisenring, who were both called to testify at the hearing, did their best to answer these criticisms. Whenever pressed on the board's proposal, Beresford claimed that the board had a duty to the truth and needed to force firms to expense options in accordance with economic reality.¹⁵⁰ Moreover, Beresford reminded critics that FASB had rolled out its proposal according to proper procedures and that it was under no obligation to appease the business community.¹⁵¹ Though Beresford and Leisenring were badly outnumbered at the hearing, they were not entirely alone. Mary Barth, an accounting professor at Harvard Business School who represented the American Accounting Association, was one of the only witnesses to support FASB. Barth's defense of FASB was similar to what other academics offered. She claimed that options had an economic value that needed to be disclosed; Black-Scholes was more than capable of estimating the value of options; and since markets were efficient, investors would not unreasonably punish firms for depressed earnings as long as they thought executives were being compensated fairly.¹⁵²

Academics like Barth made up one of the few constituencies FASB could reliably count on for support.¹⁵³ Joseph Stiglitz and the rest of the economists on the president's Council of Economic Advisers supported FASB's reforms, but they were ignored by the president and both the Treasury and Commerce Departments.[154] Nobel Prize winner Merton Miller, one of the founders of financial economics as a discipline, also voiced his support for FASB in an article for *The Washington Post* that he coauthored with Crystal. Miller and Crystal claimed that the lack of accounting standards for options was creating market distortions and "bizarre results" in the managerial labor market by incentivizing boards to issue more options than they should have issued, which helped to divorce pay from performance. Miller and Crystal defended Black-Scholes as well and reminded critics that income statements already contained several estimates, including allowances for depreciation, that were much more imprecise than what Black-Scholes produced for options. They also attempted to use the EMH to sooth people's worries by telling worried executives that sophisticated investors already knew how many options firms had granted, and any adjustments to firms' share prices after FASB's rule took effect would just be investors resolving any lingering distortions as they moved the stock price closer to its correct value.[155]

These academic arguments were increasingly drowned out as FASB began holding public hearings on its plan in 1994.[156] At a public meeting in March at FASB's headquarters in Connecticut, the seven board members were met with a largely hostile audience of executives, financiers, and even their fellow accountants. At the start of the meeting Beresford acknowledged the hundreds of angry letters FASB had received on their stock options plan and complained that his secretary suffered several papercuts from opening 600 letters sent from a single company. During the meeting, Bernie Marcus, the chairman of Home Depot, told the board members that FASB had driven "a stake into the heart of current and future entrepreneurial endeavors," and that being forced to expense options would hurt his firm's stock price. When a board member tried to calm Marcus's fears by citing academic work on efficient markets that said changes in accounting standards did not affect stock prices, Marcus shot back, "you're trying to confuse me with logic here . . . it's not going to work. I deal with the emotional side of the street. I deal with Wall Street."[157]

The shouting matches that broke out in Connecticut were nothing compared to what happened when FASB's board decided to hold a public meeting in Silicon Valley at the end of March. In response, the American Electronics Association (AEA) called on its members to turn out for a massive public rally in front of the San Jose Convention Center across the street from the hotel where the meeting would be held. In a flyer announcing the rally, the AEA warned its members that "your stock options/ stock purchase plans are threatened because of 7 bureaucrats." According to the AEA, stock options were at the very heart of Silicon Valley's entrepreneurial culture; or, as the organization put it on the flyer, "What sets Silicon Valley Apart? **Stock Options**. Why do we get the best people? **Stock Options**. What's the one incentive left? **Stock Options**."[158] On March 25, the day of the FASB meeting, the organization's members were met with a carnival-like atmosphere outside the hotel where the meeting was taking place. Around 3,000 people, a high school marching band, and the Toys'R'Us mascot Geoffrey the Giraffe (Charles Lazarus, the CEO of Toys'R'Us, had made millions with stock options) all turned out to protest. California's Treasurer, Kathleen Brown, a Democrat who was the co-chair of the Council of Institutional Investors and a candidate for governor, was one of the featured speakers at the event. Brown called on FASB to "give stock a chance" and urged the Board not to "stop the engine of growth that has absolutely fueled this California economy!"[159] The meeting itself was equally hostile. Joseph Graziano, the CFO of Apple, called FASB's plan "the most ridiculous thing I've ever heard." James Morgan, an officer of the National Venture Capital Association, railed against the plan and warned FASB that "the National Venture Capital Association will stop it. It will deeply hurt venture capital, and we cannot allow this to happen." Gordon Moore, the co-founder and chairman of Intel, chastised FASB's board and told them that "stock options should not be sacrificed for the sake of accounting purity, even if that were possible."[160]

The death knell for FASB's efforts came from the Senate. On May 5, 1994, Lieberman introduced a non-binding Sense of the Senate resolution to formally express the chamber's displeasure with FASB and urge it to abandon its reform effort. Lieberman's resolution passed 88–9, with every Republican voting in favor and only nine Democrats, including Levin, voting against.[161] After this latest setback, FASB announced in June that it would delay its requirement for firms to report the value of their options in their financial statements' footnotes until 1995.[162] By this point, FASB was almost entirely without friends in government. Aside from Levin and the handful of Senate Democrats who had voted against Lieberman's bill, almost every other government official was either explicitly opposed to FASB or trying to avoid the issue. Treasury Secretary Bentsen and Secretary of Commerce Ronald Brown both officially opposed FASB, as did SEC Commissioner J. Carter Besse Jr.[163] President Clinton tried to avoid the issue altogether, and in a letter to Levin that the senator was forced to release after Hagerty told the press that Clinton opposed FASB, he wrote that he supported FASB in principle, but did not favor any reform that might hurt the competitiveness of the tech sector.[164] FASB finally began to admit defeat when SEC Chairman Levitt told Beresford—in what he would later characterize to Beresford's successor as the biggest mistake of his career—that while he personally supported FASB's rule change, the Board should drop the issue lest the Senate abolish it.[165] It did seem that FASB's future truly was in jeopardy. After his Senate resolution passed, Lieberman began discussing new legislation that would force the SEC to take formal votes on every recommendation FASB made, which would essentially put FASB out of business. FASB's prospects worsened after the 1994 midterm elections when Republicans took control of the Senate. Senator Phil Gramm, who would head the Senate Securities Subcommittee in the new Congress, vowed that if FASB did not abandon its proposal, he would pass a bill to override FASB's decision-making authority.[166]

On December 14, 1994, Beresford finally announced that FASB had given up. Though Beresford maintained that "the board remains convinced that employee options have value and are compensation," he acknowledged that "in the final analysis, there simply isn't enough support for the basic notion of requiring expense recognition." To try to salvage something from the whole process, FASB did vote 5–2 to still require firms to put the value of their options in the footnotes of their financial statements. FASB's supporters were predictably disheartened. Levin once again denounced the accounting rules for options as a "sham" and lamented that "honest accounting lost out to the pressure of the rich and the powerful."[167] Business groups and their allies were quick to celebrate, and Hagerty declared that FASB's defeat "may usher in the golden age of employee equity and employee ownership."[168]

"The End of History"

Even if FASB had been able to push through these reforms, it is hard to imagine that they truly would have killed off stock options, especially given the fact that most major US companies voluntarily began expensing options after 2002 in the wake of the Enron scandal and there was still little change in their use of options or in CEO pay. Even after FASB did pass official rules forcing all companies to expense options in 2006, this had no

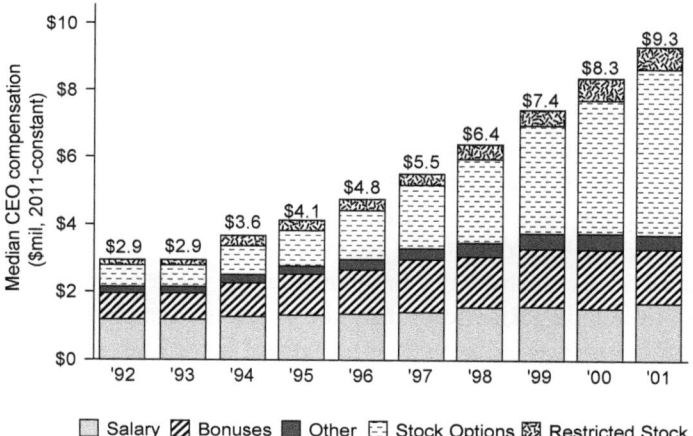

FIGURE 6.1. Median grant-date compensation for CEOs in S&P 500 firms, 1992–2001. Recreated from Murphy, "Executive Compensation," 73.

demonstrable effect on CEO pay levels either.[169] Regardless of what effects, if any, being forced to expense options would have had on managerial behavior in 1994, the more than two years that companies, investors, and politicians spent championing options did have a significant effect on the nation's political economy. The anti-FASB campaign changed the nature of the national debate over executive pay and compensation in general. Thanks to the efforts of tech companies in particular, Congress went from debating how to rein in high CEO pay to looking for ways to encourage firms to use more stock options in part to supposedly reward executives for their performance.[170] As seen in figure 6.1, the use of options exploded after 1994 due in part to the massive amount of favorable publicity they had received in the preceding years. Though investors never completely stopped complaining about high CEO pay, as the decade continued and the value of their shares continued to rise they became much less vocal in their complaints, and the contentious annual shareholders meetings of the early 1990s were replaced with sedate and friendly affairs by 1998.[171] Shareholders and managers still may not have entirely trusted each other, but as the fight against FASB revealed, they both had plenty to gain from the expansion of stock options, and they realized that partnership and not opposition would be more profitable for both.[172]

The alliance forged between shareholders and corporate managers—as uneasy as it may have been—during the fight against FASB marked the end of the shareholder value revolution. In a retrospective of the 1980s and 1990s published in 2001, the economists Bengt Holmstrom and Robert Kaplan nicely encapsulated the role stock options played in bringing the shareholder value revolution to a close. As the two saw it, beginning in the 1990s "thanks to lucrative stock option plans, managers could share in the market returns from restructured companies. Shareholder value became an ally rather than an enemy. This explains why restructurings continued at a high rate in the 1990s, but for the most part on amicable terms."[173] Compensation consultants put the matter in more pointed terms by reminding Americans that they were in part to blame since institutional investors were using their retirement funds to demand that corporate executives restructure their companies. As *The Washington Post* put it, "if you are among the majority of working Americans who earn a middle-class or upper-middle-class income and invest some money for retirement ... you have to accept much of the blame for the growing paycheck gap. As you fret about your own flat salary, you forget how much you contributed—just by investing in stocks—to the changes that have made your company's chief executive officer so rich."[174] Stock options helped to pave the way for even the diversified conglomerates of the industrial era to shrink and attempt to become the lean, shareholder-focused companies that investors and elected officials celebrated. As the recession of the early 1990s became a seemingly distant memory by the middle part of the decade amid robust growth, especially in the stock market, worries about declining national competitiveness were replaced with triumphal celebrations of the new economy and the seemingly unlimited potential of globalization and technological innovation to deliver economic growth.[175] Thanks to the campaign against FASB's accounting reforms, stock options were now celebrated for their ability to encourage entrepreneurship and innovation, and were now included as one of the hallmarks of new economy firms alongside lean organization, flexible employment practices, and a focus on knowledge work. Mortimer Zuckerman, the editor-in-chief of *U.S. News and World Report*, writing in *Foreign Affairs*, even cited American companies' use of stock options as one of the reasons why the twenty-first century would be "a second American century."[176]

Though the signs of growing economic and racial inequality in the United States were certainly visible by the turn of the century, and some commentators did sound alarm bells, most policymakers were more interested in celebrating the ascendancy of shareholder value than in reflecting on its costs.[177] By the end of the 1990s, elite observers across the corporate, legal, and academic sectors all were ready to acknowledge the obvious: shareholder value maximization had triumphed. Given that the Business Roundtable had already testified as to their commitment to shareholder value maximization in 1992, their formal adoption of shareholder value ideology in 1997 was less a turning point in corporate governance and more a belated acknowledgment that the world had already changed.[178] In a telling example, when David Coulter became CEO of Bank of America in 1996 the first decision he made as CEO was to announce "that the governing objective of B of A would be to maximize shareholder value." When some of his fellow executives questioned whether it was wise to say this, Coulter responded by asking, "well, if we don't say that, what do we say? I don't see any alternative."[179] The greatest testament to the degree to which these arguments became conventional wisdom by the start of the twenty-first century was an article published in 2001 in the *Georgetown Law Journal* by Henry Hansmann, a professor at Yale Law School, and Reinier Kraakman, a professor at Harvard Law School, proclaiming "The End of History for Corporate Law."[180] Hansmann and Kraakman claimed that they had noticed a "growing consensus" among "academic, business, and governmental elites" that

> ultimate control over the corporation should be in the hands of the shareholder class; that the managers of the corporation should be charged with the obligation to manage the corporation in the interests of its shareholders; that other corporate constituencies, such as creditors, employees, suppliers, and customers should have their interests protected by contractual and regulatory means rather than through participation in corporate governance; that noncontrolling shareholders should receive strong protection from exploitation at the hands of controlling shareholders; and that the principal measure of the interests of the publicly traded corporation's shareholders is the market value of their shares in the firm.[181]

Based on their observations of this growing consensus, the authors proclaimed that "the triumph of the shareholder-oriented model of the corporation over its principal competitors is now assured, even if it was problematic as recently as twenty-five years ago."[182] Though this may have been an overstatement, a look at American business and legal schools could have provided Hansmann and Kraakman with plenty of evidence for their claim. By 2001, 75 percent of MBA students surveyed by the Aspen Institute emphasized that a corporation's primary responsibility was to maximize shareholder value.[183] In the world of legal academia, students were routinely taught that corporate managers had a fiduciary duty to maximize shareholder value.[184] By the beginning of the twenty-first century, shareholder value ideology was so widespread that Lynn Stout, a legal scholar and prominent critic of shareholder value maximization, claimed it "became dogma: an omnipresent belief system that was seldom questioned, rarely justified, and so widely accepted."[185]

CONCLUSION

The End of Enron and the Last Man

In *The End of History and the Last Man*, Francis Fukuyama announced the historical triumph of democratic capitalism over its alternatives. Writing during the last decade of the twentieth century, Fukuyama's claim became a cautionary tale for political hubris by the time of the events of 9/11, which ushered in decades of warfare and geopolitical challenges for the United States and its model of liberal governance.

At almost the exact same time, the rapid demise of Enron, once one of the nation's most admired companies, in October 2001 provided a stark rebuke to Hansmann and Kraakman's celebration of the end of history for corporate law.[1] Before its downfall, Enron had been a stock market darling, as analysts and investors marveled at the ability of the company's leadership team (especially CEO Kenneth Lay, Chief Operating Officer Jeffery Skilling, and Chief Financial Officer Andrew Fastow) to combine high-tech financial trading with the energy business to generate impressive profits and high growth potential. After enjoying runaway success during the 1990s, the company was hit by a series of crises as the new millennium started. Enron's manipulation of California's energy markets after the state's disastrous experiment with deregulation in the summer of 2000 created rolling blackouts and skyrocketing energy prices for consumers that eroded some of the goodwill the company had generated over the past decade and prompted media investigators to take a closer look at its financial practices. At the same time, the end of the dot-com bubble in the summer of 2000 revealed that many high-tech companies investors had flocked to in the heady days of the 1990s relied on overly optimistic growth projections to attract investment and were financially unsound and often mismanaged. The reckoning caused by the end of the dot-com bubble prompted Wall Street analysts to press Enron about its opaque accounting practices as suspicions about the company's record began to mount.[2] The beginning of the end for Enron came in March 2001, when *Fortune* writer Bethany McLain published an article titled "Is Enron Overpriced?," in which she struggled in vain to answer the question "how exactly does Enron make its money?"[3] As other journalists, and eventually regulators and law enforcement officials, began to dig through the network of thousands of shell companies known Special Purpose Entities (SPEs) that Enron created to hide losses and manipulate accounting figures, it became clear that the company was built on an elaborate fraud.[4]

On October 16, 2001, Lay announced that the company needed to take a charge to earnings in excess of $1 billion to account for the losses it had been attempting to hide. On November 8, Enron was forced to restate its earnings for the years between 1997 and 2000, revealing that it had earned $591 million less that it had originally claimed during those years.[5] These revelations immediately cast serious doubts on the work of Enron's auditor, Arthur Andersen, one of the world's largest accounting firms. As subsequent investigations demonstrated, Arthur Andersen's accountants had signed off on Enron's manipulations for years and had tried to destroy evidence related to their work on Enron's fraudulent accounting statements. The damage caused by the revelation of Enron's fraud and Arthur Andersen's role in it proved fatal to both companies. With Enron's reputation in tatters and law enforcement closing in, investors fled from the company in droves. As its stock price cratered, Enron declared bankruptcy on December 2 and ceased to exist shortly thereafter, putting more than 4,000 people out of work almost overnight.[6] Arthur Andersen limped on for a little while longer, shrinking from a high of 85,000 employees in 2002 to about 200 employees, mostly working on the company's various legal challenges, in 2005 before it was dismantled and ceased to exist in any meaningful form.[7]

Beyond being arguably the largest corporate scandal in American history to date, the Enron story also perfectly captured the unintended consequences of the shareholder value revolution and galvanized even some of shareholder value's greatest champions to rethink their support for it. It was especially problematic for some shareholder value theorists because, before its downfall, Enron was held up as an exemplar of the kind of good corporate governance the shareholder value revolution was supposed to have produced. In 2000, *Fortune* rated Enron as the 25th most admired company in the world and put the company first in its "innovativeness" rankings.[8] By the time scandal enveloped the company, Enron had already implemented most of the governance reforms shareholder value activists and institutional investors had been calling for in the 1980s and 1990s. The company's top executives were generously compensated with stock options that were supposed to link their pay to corporate performance.[9] Aside from Lay and Skilling, Enron's board of directors was composed entirely of extremely skilled external directors. The board's audit committee, which was in charge of internally policing the company's financial statements, was staffed with highly respected figures from academia, government, and management.[10] At an ideological level, Enron embodied the spirit of the shareholder value revolution, and the company was fully committed to maximizing shareholder value at any cost.[11] Enron's executives aggressively pushed for economic deregulation and championed the spread of American-style economic liberalization to other nations.

This combination of Enron's aggressive pursuit of growth, its focus on technology and financial trading, and its shareholder-friendly organizational structure made the company appear to be a model of what the shareholder-focused company of the future might look like. A fraud on the order of Enron should have been impossible given managers' professed commitment to shareholder value maximization and the presence of several supposedly independent "watchdogs" such as the board's audit committee and an independent financial auditor who were supposed to protect the interests of the company's shareholders. Yet despite the fact that, as the legal scholar William Bratton put it, "Enron stumbled into its end period while following the book of good governance practice, at least nominally," this was not enough to prevent Lay and other top executives from breaking the law and wasting billions of dollars of shareholders' money.[12]

Once the Enron scandal broke, the press and government investigators searched for a way to understand how a company that once seemed to have done everything right in corporate governance could have been responsible for perhaps the greatest failure of governance in American business history. The press was immediately drawn to the colorful stories of outlandish behavior within Enron, including stories of executives awash in sexual excess and indulging in over-the-top adventure sports and conspicuous consumption. As the press reported on the culture of the company and federal prosecutors pressed successful criminal cases against the company's leaders, the Enron saga became a morality tale, one in which greedy and short-sighted executives chose to break the law to satisfy their own egos and desires for self-aggrandizement.[13] Though the personal failings of Enron's executives were the dominant theme in the popular narratives of the Enron scandal, corporate governance reformers saw a broader problem with the ways the company was run. Investigators and reformers catalogued the ways in which Enron's governance procedures failed to measure up to how they looked on paper. According to these investigations, Enron's nominally independent directors actually had financial ties to the company and the board's audit committee scheduled meetings that were too short to accomplish anything of substance.[14]

These reformers' efforts to shore up the nation's corporate governance standard were supercharged by a rush of even more similar corporate scandals in the following year.[15] As media investigators and regulatory watchdogs began to pay closer attention to companies' financial statements in the wake of Enron, they discovered that many of the nation's largest businesses, including giants like IBM, GE, and Coca-Cola, had published misleading financial reports in an effort to meet analysts' earnings projections.[16] Even more alarming, an internal audit at the telecommunications company WorldCom in the summer of 2002 revealed that the company's leaders had committed large-scale accounting fraud by improperly accounting for more than $3.8 billion in expenses to protect the company's stock price. In the wake of these revelations, WorldCom, which had assets of more than $107 billion, was forced to declare bankruptcy, thus displacing Enron as the largest bankruptcy in American history.[17] In the immediate wake of WorldCom's bankruptcy, Congress passed the Sarbanes-Oxley Act in July 2002 which sought to restore investors' confidence in the nation's large corporations by requiring stricter board procedures and more transparent corporate accounting and auditing in what President George W. Bush described, upon signing the act into law, as "the most far-reaching reforms of American business practices since the time of Franklin D. Roosevelt."[18]

While Sarbanes-Oxley did address some flaws in the nation's corporate governance structure by strengthening the role of boards of directors and independent auditors (and thus became a perennial target of criticism from business executives), neither it nor the criminal prosecution of a handful of executives addressed the deeper issues raised by the corporate scandals of 2001 and 2002.[19] Explanations for corporate scandals centered on either individual misbehavior or shortcomings in the existing regulatory framework were built on the assumption that the investor-focused corporation created in the wake of the shareholder value revolution could be counted on to behave properly and create wealth for society as long as the right people were in charge and the rules were clear. A deeper look at the scandals that began the twenty-first century revealed that this was not the case. Enron's leaders did not engage in fraud in spite of their commitment to shareholder value maximization; instead, their commitment to shareholder value maximization motivated them to engage in criminal activity.[20]

In the language of agency theory, the interests of principals and agents were aligned: managers were working for their shareholders, and those same shareholders were quite pleased with their managers' performance, until everything fell apart. The analysts and fund managers who followed Enron were entranced by the image Enron's leaders created of their company as a high-tech innovator. Having been convinced that Enron could do almost anything and make a profit, these analysts issued a series of increasingly ambitious earnings forecasts while advising their clients to invest in Enron stock.[21] Enron's managers, meanwhile, were left to figure out how to meet the unreasonable earnings expectations they had a part in creating. The fact that those same managers were also given high levels of compensation in the form of stock options meant that they had personal reasons for being willing to do anything to meet earnings targets and keep stock prices high.[22] The company's board members had little incentive to look closely at the accounting work being done by Enron's managers, lest they depress the company's share price and cause their own stock options to lose value. Similarly, Enron's auditors, who were locked in a vicious competition with other large auditing firms, did not want to risk losing Enron's business by pushing back against the company's financial manipulations.[23] Finally, investors themselves had little interest in pushing Enron to be more transparent about its financial information as long as the company was seemingly hitting its earnings projections and creating value for them. Even though Enron's managers had been publishing opaque financial statements for years and outside observers were never entirely certain how the company was making the money it claimed it was earning, very few people had the desire to seriously challenge these practices until the company was already mired in crisis.[24]

Enron and the other corporate scandals of 2001 and 2002 were tremendous disappointments for Michael Jensen in particular. Jensen had spent three decades as the intellectual face of the shareholder value revolution. Throughout his academic work, consulting, and public advocacy, even as his approaches and ideas changed, Jensen believed his work was contributing to the creation of an efficient corporate system that could create wealth for society.[25] In the 1970s, efficiency meant fighting against big government and the idea that corporate managers had responsibilities to society beyond making money. In the 1980s, Jensen's quest led him to support hostile takeovers and LBOs as a way to get rid of self-aggrandizing managers and undo the damage caused by the separation of ownership and control.[26] During the 1990s, Jensen cheered on companies like Enron that appointed independent directors and paid their top managers in stock to supposedly make sure managers' interests were aligned with those of shareholders. The shareholder value revolution was supposed to discipline managers and prevent them from wasting shareholders' money, yet by the end of 2001 Enron, a poster child of the revolution, had produced a greater degree of fraud and waste than Penn Central or Litton Industries ever could have. Jensen told the financial journalist Nicholas Lemann that, at some point during the seemingly endless parade of accounting scandals at the beginning of the twenty-first century, he reflected on his advocacy work in favor of shareholder value maximization and told himself, "holy shit, now it's doing more damage than good; anything can be corrupted."[27] Jensen could not simply blame unaccountable managers or government bureaucrats for Enron's downfall. It was clear that something deeper—something fundamental—had gone wrong.

Jensen's sense that the shareholder value revolution had been corrupted led him to make a public break with the cause. In early 2002, Jensen and Joseph Fuller, the CEO of the Monitor Group, the management consulting firm Jensen had co-founded, published an article in the *Journal of Applied Corporate Finance* titled "Just Say No to Wall Street: Putting a Stop to the Earnings Game."[28] In the article, Jensen and Fuller blamed Enron and similar accounting scandals on the pressure corporate managers faced from investors and analysts to meet often unrealistic earnings targets every quarter. In Jensen and Fuller's minds, the analysts setting earnings projections simply did not understand the true value of the businesses they were writing about, and they had personal incentives to issue aggressive earnings projections to gain attention and higher bonus payments when companies managed to live up to their inflated expectations. Jensen and Fuller urged corporate managers to stand up to analysts who were pushing them to do anything—including breaking the law—to meet earnings projections. The authors asked managers to "witness the part that Wall Street's rising expectations played in the demise of once high flyers like Enron, Cisco, and Nortel. With analysts pushing these companies to reach for higher and higher growth targets, the managements of these companies responded with actions that have generated long-term damage. To resolve these problems, managers must abandon the notion that a higher stock price is always better and recognize that an overvalued stock can be as dangerous to a company as an undervalued stock."[29] On the face of it, this argument was hardly radical. The "earnings cult" had been a frequent target of criticism from journalists and academics since the 1990s.[30]

What made the criticism in "Just Say No to Wall Street" truly remarkable was that it was coming from Jensen. It would have been unthinkable in the 1980s or even the 1990s to imagine that Jensen, once one of the fiercest champions of the EMH, would ever write the words "managers must abandon the notion that a higher stock price is always better." In this short article, Jensen was admitting that the EMH was wrong; he was saying that a company's stock price was not always the best indicator of a company's true value.[31] Incredibly, Jensen was now saying that corporate managers, the same people he had denigrated for decades, actually knew more about the true value of their companies than the stock market. This was a complete inversion of the arguments Jensen had made in favor of hostile takeovers during the 1980s. Moreover, Jensen's change of heart fatally undercut the intellectual justification for the shareholder value revolution. If the stock market could be wrong, if a company's share price did not always reflect that company's true value, then what reason did managers have for making it the focal point of their work?

Jensen found the solution to the problems created by the shareholder value revolution in the work of the eccentric and controversial self-help guru Werner Erhard, the founder of the Erhard Seminars Training (est) program that operated during the 1970s and 1980s. Jensen attended one of Erhard's Landmark seminars (the successor program to est) in 1998 at the suggestion of one of his daughters, with whom he had a fraught relationship, and was transfixed by Erhard. Jensen credited an impromptu public therapy session with Erhard at one of his seminars with helping him to realize that he had spent most of his life being a "jerk," which had estranged him from many of his friends, family, and colleagues.[32] After his conversion experience, Jensen formed a close relationship with Erhard and the two began a collaboration to design a new philosophy of management and leadership centered around what they called "integrity."[33] According to Jensen and Erhard, "integrity," which they defined as an individual "condition of being whole and complete," was the fundamental prerequisite for success in any kind of human endeavor.[34] In a combination of Jensen's scientific mode of argumentation and Erhard's eclectic mixture of self-help and pop psychology, the pair claimed to have developed a "positive model of integrity" that incorporated "the normative phenomena of morality, ethics, and legality" to demonstrate the importance of "honoring one's word" and not subjecting one's decision-making to the rational kind of cost-benefit analysis that Jensen and Meckling had once celebrated in their writings on REMMs.[35] This newfound focus on integrity allowed Jensen to redeem his previous work on efficient markets and agency theory even as he discarded much of the intellectual content of that work. With his new model of integrity, Jensen could blame the problems created by the shareholder value revolution on dishonest individuals who corrupted what might otherwise have been efficient financial markets and well-designed organizational structures. After a lifetime of trying to remove the barriers to human beings' pursuit of their own rational self-interest to create a more efficient and productive world, Jensen realized that human beings themselves were flawed. If markets or corporations were ever going to work as Jensen and the champions of shareholder value maximization hoped, then human beings themselves would have to be reformed; they would have to learn how to live with "integrity."[36]

Unsurprisingly, given Erhard's dubious reputation and Jensen's radical departure from his previous scholarship, the pair's often impenetrable writings about integrity and leadership were almost completely ignored by mainstream academics and most business leaders. Though Jensen and Erhard managed to create a successful business in leadership seminars out of their collaboration, the pair made no discernible impact on debates about business management or corporate purpose, and this later act of Jensen's career was mostly viewed as an odd sort of coda to his academic work.[37] Though Jensen and Erhard's "positive model of integrity" was largely irrelevant, Jensen's change of heart was illustrative of the complicated, and often problematic, legacy of the shareholder value revolution. On the one hand, the shareholder value revolution undeniably succeeded in generating tremendous profits for American corporations and for their shareholders, and its supporters credit it with reviving the American economy during the 1980s.[38] At the same time, however, this movement to rein in the power of corporate managers and to combat wastefulness and fraud instead incentivized managers to commit some of the largest cases of corporate fraud in history. Similarly, despite all of the energy institutional investors, corporate raiders, and financial economists put into critiquing corporate managers' lavish lifestyles and unearned pay, the rise of stock option compensation that was cheered on by economists and investors resulted in CEOs and other top managers making previously unthinkable amounts of money, often with little connection to either individual or corporate performance.

The broader effects of the shareholder value revolution on American society have been similarly problematic. Between 1978 and 1999, Fortune 100 companies laid off more than five million employees, and the average Fortune 100 company went through about one round of layoffs per year.[39] The gains from these restructurings were unevenly shared. Though CEOs' pay outpaced everyone except for entertainment superstars and Wall Street's largest traders, plenty of other Americans also shared in the riches of the shareholder value revolution.[40] Knowledge workers, skilled professionals, and those workers fortunate enough to survive corporate restructurings saw their paychecks increase and their working conditions improve, and often were granted the ability to work with greater autonomy on personally fulfilling creative tasks.[41] In contrast, lower-level workers and those who were laid off had a much different experience of the 1990s and beyond. According to the Department of Labor's Bureau of Labor Statistics (BLS), though the nation's employment rate grew by 15 percent between 1989 and 1999, wages grew by only 6.9 percent, all of which came between 1997 and 1999, whereas between 1989 and 1996 wage growth was either zero or negative.[42] When broken down into high-paid workers (mostly executives and skilled professionals), mid-level workers (technicians, machine operators), and lower-paid workers (frontline retail and service sector workers and support staff), these results pointed to worrying trends in the American economy. According to the BLS, though employment grew substantially from 1989 to 1999, "nearly all of the growth was concentrated among relatively high- and low-paid workers, with the strongest job growth occurring in the highest earnings group. There was scant employment growth among workers with midlevel wages."[43] Likewise, wages grew 6.3 percent for high earners, 11.6 percent for low earners, and only 2.4 percent for middle-income workers.

Taken together, these trends all pointed to the hollowing of the American economy brought about by restructuring and the promotion of shareholder value. As mid-level jobs were gradually eliminated, outsourced, or automated, many of these workers found themselves forced to find lower-paid work in the expanding service sector.[44] Unfortunately for the growing ranks of lower-paid service workers, the sharp wage increases they received at the end of the 1990s were an aberration, and wage growth remained stagnant for these workers in the twenty-first century.[45] The growing separation between the "winners" and "losers" of the shareholder value revolution was also represented in wage differentials across education levels and racial categories as well. According to the Congressional Research Service, only workers with bachelor's degrees or higher experienced a rise in their real median wage between 1980 and 2018. Those workers with some college or less, who constitute around 65 percent of the overall workforce, saw their real median wage decline between 1980 and 2018.[46] Women did make some progress in closing the wage gap with men during this time period; the median wage of a female worker grew from 62.8 percent of a man's wage in 1979 to 83.2 percent of a man's in 2018. However, these gains were driven primarily by gains in White women's wages; both Black and Hispanic women made far more modest progress. Overall, the burdens of the shareholder value revolution and restructurings fell disproportionately on Black and Hispanic workers. The median wage for Black workers fell from 80 percent of the median wage of White workers in 1979 to 71.5 percent in 2018, while the median wage for Hispanic workers fell from 80.6 percent of the median White wage in 1979 to 69.8 percent in 2018.[47]

The wealth generated by rising stock prices has been similarly concentrated among already wealthy Americans. Though many Americans depend on the stock market as a major part of their retirement savings, only a small percentage of Americans own large blocks of stock. According to the Federal Reserve, in the second quarter of 2024 the wealthiest 10 percent of Americans owned 87.1 percent of all stocks, and the top 1 percent alone owned 49.8 percent. Despite the outsized importance policymakers and commentators have given to the stock market in recent discussions of economic policy, the bottom 80 percent of Americans own only 12.93 percent of all stocks, and the bottom 50 percent of Americans own 1 percent.[48] While the massive imbalance in stock ownership by itself was bound to widen economic inequality once businesses chose to focus on shareholder value as their primary objective, recent trends in monetary policy have supercharged these effects. The Federal Reserve's embrace of asset purchases, known as quantitative easing (QE), and ultra-low interest rates to combat the economic downturns brought about by the financial crisis of 2007–2008 and the COVID-19 pandemic sent stock prices soaring to all-time highs while disadvantaging Americans trying to save money through more conventional means such as savings accounts.[49] Though these actions were intended to help restore economic prosperity after two devastating crises, according to the Bank of International Settlements, QE's benefits were ten times greater for stock prices than for economic growth as a whole.[50] Though the federal government did deliver several rounds of fiscal relief to Americans in 2020 and 2021, the effects of stimulus payments and spending increases still paled in comparison to the money the government's monetary policy delivered to the relatively small number of Americans who owned large amounts of stock.[51] The rise in inflation beginning in 2021 stemming from a combination of this fiscal relief, the effects of the COVID-19 pandemic, and the Russian invasion of Ukraine, along with the Federal Reserve's decision to raise interest rates to tamp down price increases promises to add further challenges to Americans' economic standing, especially for those most disadvantaged by the shareholder value revolution, as they see the cost of living and financing the debt needed to purchase things like cars or homes rise.[52]

Shareholder value maximization has been a guiding principle behind these transformations in American society over the past half-century. Decisions by publicly traded companies to dismantle businesses, lay off employees, and force those who remain employed by them to do more with less have all been made in its name. When combined with the efficient markets hypothesis, shareholder value ideas produced an almost inescapable logic in favor of shareholder value maximization. If a business executive, management consultant, or government official accepted that stock prices accurately reflected a company's intrinsic value, it would be hard to argue against the idea that companies should try to maximize the value of their stock price without resorting to the kind of arguments economists like Jensen or Meckling could ridicule as sentimental and unscientific. Theories about shareholder value maximization did not cause American firms to lose money in the face of renewed foreign competition or the outbreak of the hostile takeover wave, but these ideas did provide an easy-to-understand explanation for American firms' struggles. Shareholder value ideas gave narrative coherence to the structural transformations of the American economy that have taken place since the late 1960s, and they were used by academics and management consultants to offer business executives a way to both understand and surmount the challenges created by global competition and financialization. When American managers were desperate to understand why corporate raiders were suddenly able to extort and sometimes take over some of the nation's largest companies, economists and management consultants could tell them it was because those managers were not doing enough for their shareholders. These same arguments were also used by consultants to provide companies that had benefited from years of easy access to global markets that they could dominate in the immediate postwar decades with a response to the challenge coming from nations who had rebuilt themselves after the devastation of the Second World War thanks in part to American trade policies that domestic business managers themselves had lobbied for.[53] Even the institutional investors and populist politicians who railed against rising CEO pay and the excesses of the 1980s relied on shareholder value theory to attempt to address these problems by demanding that companies pay their executives in stock.

The history of the shareholder value revolution can be instructive to contemporary observers who are puzzled by the endurance of an economic regime that seems to have few defenders, even among those who benefit from it the most. As this book has shown, the discrediting of managerialism alone was not enough to clear the way for the rise of shareholder value. By the 1970s and certainly by the early 1980s it was no overstatement to say that managerialism, and postwar corporate social responsibility along with it, had lost some if not most of its defenders in the academy and in popular opinion. But these intellectual and political changes did not cause managers to immediately embrace shareholder value maximization. It was when the financial environment also turned against business managers during the 1980s and 1990s that they became much more receptive to the arguments of people like Jensen or Stern who told them they needed to focus on shareholders in order to regain lost ground. In our present moment, business leaders seem to have sensed the growing intellectual and political discontent with shareholder value maximization, but they have faced hardly any economic or financial downsides to shareholder primacy. The truce between managers and investors in the 1990s that was cemented by stock options and reinforced by a tax system that favors capital and high earners has proven to be a remarkable, and resilient, engine of prosperity for both parties. Those critics of shareholder value maximization who hope to pressure businesses to voluntary abandon it are, in essence, asking business managers and investors to abandon a system that has worked remarkably well for them, often in favor of alternatives that do not match the relative simplicity of shareholder primacy's single-minded focus on stock prices—something the defenders of shareholder value maximization, and some of its critics, have been quick to point out.[54] Political intervention on the order proposed by Senators Bernie Sanders or Elizabeth Warren would certainly be a more straightforward way to break shareholder value maximization's hold on American political economy, but the prospects for political action, at least in the immediate future, seem hazy at best.

Despite their impressive work to date, there is no easy path forward for the opponents of shareholder value maximization. The recent proliferation of books and articles exhorting managers to prioritize stakeholders is a testament to the fact that there is no shortage of ideas about how to reform the corporation, but none of these alternatives have so far seemed to seriously threaten shareholder value maximization's place at the heart of American political economy.[55] This lack of success underlines an inconvenient truth about shareholder value maximization for its critics—namely, that while it does not work for society as a whole, it does work very well for the people who ultimately decide how America's public companies operate. Business managers, investors, and even the millions of Americans who make up the nation's professional class have all won a great deal of wealth from the shareholder value revolution, even if the intense competition and the exposure to risk and debt associated with it have left many of them feeling unsatisfied or burned out. The opponents of the shareholder value revolution have only learned half of its lessons. The shareholder value revolution was not successful because it convinced these millions of people of the importance of agency costs or the need to align incentives within an organization; it was successful because enterprising academics, consultants, and shareholder activists were able to use the ideas associated with shareholder primacy to design a set of corporate practices that allowed executives and investors to create a tremendous amount of wealth for themselves.

At the time of writing, it seems that critics of shareholder value maximization have made significant progress in demonstrating the intellectual and social shortcomings of shareholder primacy. Calls for a transition to "stakeholder capitalism" routinely come out of elite business schools and organizations such as the Business Roundtable, while political leaders as ideologically opposed as Senators Sanders and Warren and Senator Macro Rubio (R-FL), and even Jensen, the intellectual face of the shareholder value revolution, all denounced shareholder primacy.[56] It is important not to overstate the success of critics, however. A recent backlash against twenty-first-century corporate social responsibility—which itself does not seem to meaningfully threaten shareholder primacy—from hardline social conservatives whose anger over corporate statements on issues like LGBTQIA+ rights and environmentalism or the establishment of corporate diversity programs has prompted some conservatives to demand that corporations narrow their focus to shareholder value maximization.[57] This renewed call for shareholder value maximization may indeed jeopardize some of the progress critics of shareholder value maximization have made, but it is too early to say for sure.[58] These most recent debates seem mainly to revolve around corporate stances on social issues, and right-wing critics of corporate behavior have a confused stance on the issue of shareholder value maximization when taken on its own.[59]

Unfortunately for would-be reformers, even if criticisms of shareholder value maximization survive the contemporary back-and-forth over corporate politics, the story of the shareholder value revolution was not simply the story of a battle of ideas, as evidenced by the fact that Jensen's break with the cause barely made an impression. The shareholder value revolution did not end when Harvard or any other university integrated Jensen's theories into their curricula; it ended when executives and directors realized that they could cement a very lucrative alliance between themselves and investors through the use of stock options. This alliance between managers and investors was only possible because of the decades of intellectual work that allowed the champions of shareholder value maximization to make the supposedly scientific case for restructuring programs and paying managers in stock, but once that alliance was formed, shareholder value ideas mattered much less than the fact that executives could make previously unthinkable amounts of money by maximizing the value of their companies' stock prices. Even if reformers were able to convince the heads of America's largest companies that shareholder value maximization was damaging to society (and they may have done so), they would still be stuck in the unenviable position of asking the very people who benefit most from shareholder primacy to unilaterally abandon it in favor of a range of alternatives that would likely make them less money. This challenge would be further exacerbated by the fact that unlike in the 1970s and 1980s, American companies are, overall, quite profitable, which means that corporate leaders have even more to lose now than they did several decades ago and face comparatively fewer economic pressures to change.[60]

While the history of the shareholder value revolution seems to offer few ways forward for the critics of shareholder primacy unless they could somehow make stakeholder capitalism profitable for business leaders, there may still be hope. The specter of political action hung over the entire course of the shareholder value revolution, and political intervention, or even the credible threat of it, may be reformers' last hope for meaningful change. Just as Franklin Roosevelt's New Deal provided the political and legal spine that supported the postwar system of managerial capitalism, the conservative counterattack on the New Deal that carried Ronald Reagan to victory provided a political catalyst for the shareholder value revolution and left the federal government largely unable or unwilling to respond to it. Even when the federal government did respond to the shareholder value revolution, as it did with executive pay reform in the 1990s, lawmakers' acceptance of the idea that stock prices were an accurate representation of corporate performance led them to inadvertently supercharge executive pay, and to further the cause of the shareholder value revolution in the process. To undo the damage of the shareholder value revolution, reformers will have to design a political agenda that moves beyond the still prevalent assumption that the movement of the stock market is the best representation of the health of the American economy. In a nation where only a slim majority of citizens own any stock at all and the wealthiest 10 percent of households own around 87 percent of all stocks, it is hard to argue that an economic system designed around the promotion of shareholder value above all else can possibly serve the best interests of society as a whole.[61] Given the unpredictability of politics, it is hard to forecast what an anti-shareholder value political movement might ultimately look like, though there are certainly plenty of potential models for such a movement, ranging from the Occupy Wall Street movement and the political campaigns of people like Sanders and Warren to an emerging socially conservative, anti-capitalist populism espoused by the so-called "New Right" of American politics.[62] Regardless of what political movement may emerge, any reformist effort is likely to struggle to overcome the hyper-partisanship and institutional dysfunction of American politics. Though history may not provide reformers with a clear path toward success, it does provide inspiration. The ideas behind the shareholder value revolution were crafted by people who were deeply distrustful of democracy and who strove to create a vision of political economy that would protect business and capital from the pressures of popular democracy. It seems only fitting that those same forces of popular democracy should be leaders of the charge for an "economy that serves all Americans"—a revolution in value for everyone else.

Acknowledgments

Writing this book has been a journey through years of graduate school, two career changes, three moves, and one pandemic, among the many other things that have happened since I began this work in 2017. In the seven years that I have worked on this project, I am fortunate to have benefited from the generosity and insight of so many people. No person had a greater hand in shaping both the content of this book and my own development as a scholar than my advisor, Angus Burgin. Over the five and a half years it has been my pleasure to work with him, Angus has been the very model of an ideal teacher, advisor, and mentor. Angus's open-minded approach to scholarship, his seemingly limitless knowledge of any subject I could think of, and his generosity with his time are all inspirations to me and qualities I hope to model in all my future endeavors.

Of course, there have been many more people at Johns Hopkins and beyond to whom I owe my thanks as well. I am grateful to all of my doctoral committee members—François Furstenberg, Louis Galambos, Louis Hyman, and Steven Teles—for not only reading the work that turned into this book, but also offering their support to this project over the years. Many of these chapters were workshopped in the Johns Hopkins Modern America Seminar, and I am grateful to everyone who participated in that seminar for reading my work and offering their insightful feedback and comments. I owe a special thanks to Jessica Levy, Morgan Shahan, Chloe Hawkey, and Jacob Buggerman for coordinating the seminar. I also had the opportunity to present chapters or outlines at the Business History Conference's 2019 Dissertation Colloquium, the International Policy Scholars Consortium's 2018 Minnowbrook Retreat, Duke University's Center for the History of Political Economy, and the annual meetings of the Business History Conference and the Society for US Intellectual History, and I wish to thank all those who attended these events and worked behind the scenes to make them possible. I also wish to thank my fellow graduate students Sam Backer, Allon Brand, Kalina Hadzhikova, Mo Speller, Brooke Lansing, Oriol Sendros, Jana Hoffman, Lauren Feldman, Thera Naiman, Lauren MacDonald, Gregory Smaldone, Jilene Chua, Misha Mintz-Roth, Taylor Stephens, Tarquin Schwartz, Joe Wallace, and Alex Profaci for forming a wonderful community of which I was fortunate to be a part. I also benefited from learning from a wonderful group of teachers at Johns Hopkins, and I am grateful to Sarah Berry, Ken Moss, Phil Morgan, Gabriel Paquette, and Nicolas Jabko for their dedication to teaching. Finally, I wish to thank my students at both Johns Hopkins and the Maryland Institute College of Art—their eagerness to learn about history was an inspiration to me that helped me carry on through the long process of writing this book.

Like every historian, I owe a great deal of thanks to the dedicated archivists and librarians that make our work possible. The staffs of the University of Chicago Hanna Holborn Gray Special Collections Research Center; the University of Rochester River Campus Libraries Rare Books, Special Collections, and Preservation; the Rockefeller Archive Center; the Hagley Museum and Library; and the Harvard Business School Baker Library all went above and beyond (sometimes during a pandemic) to ensure that I was able to find the materials I needed to complete this book. Though not all of that material made its way into these pages and though I was not able to visit all of these archives in person, I have no doubt that the connections I have forged with these dedicated archivists and librarians will inform my work in the future. I also wish to extend a special thanks to the Business History Unit at Harvard Business School and the Hagley Museum and Library for providing me with financial support for my research.

I also owe a great debt of gratitude to my team at the University of Chicago Press, especially my editor, Chad Zimmerman, and Rosemary Frehe. Chad's willingness to take a chance on me is what allowed this book to be born, and his guidance has been essential in helping me turn a lengthy manuscript into a book that readers will hopefully want to pick up. I thank

ACKNOWLEDGMENTS

Stephen Twilley for his diligent work in managing the production of this book and making sure it looks as good as it does. Michaela Luckey has my gratitude for her work to market this book and get it into the hands of reviewers and readers. I am also grateful to David Robertson, for his assistance with creating an index for this book. Finally, I also wish to thank the anonymous reviewers Chicago tapped to read my manuscript for their engagement with my work and the very helpful advice they offered.

This book would not exist were it not for someone at the University of Rochester's Simon Business School taking a chance on admitting me to their MBA program. Even though I did not know the difference between a stock and a bond when I set foot in my first class, the skill of the Simon School's faculty and staff ensured that I left with not only a knowledge of business, finance, and economics but also—unbeknownst to me at the time—a topic for a book. Though I may have come to different conclusions about financial markets and corporate purpose than my former teachers, it was their dedication to management education as a scholarly endeavor that helped inspire me to write this book. I owe everyone at the Simon School, and the University of Rochester as a whole, a debt of gratitude; my attempt to tell the history of these institutions is an attempt to repay some of that debt.

Finally, my deepest thanks belong to my loved ones, whose care and support kept me going through the many years and months it took to get to this point. From my earliest age, my parents have fostered in me a love of learning that I count among my greatest gifts. My parents' support through the ups and downs of my life post-college have literally saved my life, and I would not be here without all they have done for me; this book and everything that comes after is the product of their love and care for me. In the course of writing this book, I have been fortunate to see my brother, Patrick, begin his own journey as a scholar. Paddy, you are a source of incredible pride and inspiration for me, and I can't wait to see what you will do. I also owe a great deal of thanks to my friends Tony Momb, Rick D'Amato, JT Gaskill, Patrick Maxwell, Dan Robinson, Julie Nanvati, and everyone else at St. Ignatius Church in Baltimore and Holy Trinity Church in Georgetown for reminding me that there is more to life than grad school, academia, and writing.

My greatest debt of all belongs to my partner, Alex, and my daughter, Riley. Alex, I am blessed beyond measure to be at your side, and our vision of the life we will build together has been the greatest inspiration for me not only to finish this book but to be the best version of myself. You saw me through countless bouts of writer's block, self-doubt, and every other kind of crisis imaginable. You are a partner in the truest sense of the word. I love you more than words could possibly express. Riley, awaiting your arrival has brought me more joy than I could imagine. Your story is only just beginning, and while I don't think you will have much interest in your dad's book about business history for a while (maybe forever!), I do look forward to sharing with you the love of reading and learning that powered my own journey through this project. I hope you will follow your passions and curiosities to wherever they will lead you, and I will be there to cheer you on every step of the way. Alex and Riley, this book and everything to come is dedicated to you.

Notes

Introduction

1. Business Roundtable, "Business Roundtable Redefines the Purpose of a Corporation." The full statement, with signatures, can be found at https://opportunity.businessroundtable.org/wp-content/uploads/2020/03/BRT-Statement-on-the-Purpose-of-a-Corporation-with-Signatures.pdf.
2. Business Roundtable.
3. MacMillan, Whoriskey, and O'Connell, "America's Biggest Companies Are Flourishing."
4. For CEO pay, see Eavis, "Meager Rewards for Workers"; for the broader divide between investors and working-class Americans, see Donnan, "A Nation's Economy Divided."
5. The twenty-two companies examined in the report were Albertsons, Amazon, Best Buy, Chipotle, Costco, CVS, Dollar General, FedEx, Gap, Hilton, Lowes, Macy's, Marriott, Starbucks, McDonald's, Target, Home Depot, Kroger, Walt Disney Company, UPS, Walgreens, and Walmart. Kinder, Bach, and Stateler, "Profits and the Pandemic."
6. These twelve companies were Albertsons, Amazon, Costco, CVS, Dollar General, FedEx, Home Depot, Kroger, Lowe's, Target, UPS, and Walmart.
7. These six companies were Disney, Gap, Hilton, Macy's, Marriott, and Walgreens.
8. Kinder, Bach, and Stateler, "Profits and the Pandemic," 42.
9. Kinder, Bach, and Stateler, 15–25 The authors' "living wage" calculation was derived from MIT's Living Wage Calculator, which can be found at https://livingwage.mit.edu.
10. For business leaders, see Guerrera, "Welch Condemns Share Price Focus," and Benioff, "A Call for Stakeholder Activists"; for politicians, see Warren, "Companies Shouldn't Be Accountable Only to Shareholders," and Stein, "Bernie Sanders Backs 2 Policies to Dramatically Shift Corporate Power to U.S. Workers"; for

media, see Bower and Paine, "The Error at the Heart of Corporate Leadership," and Yang, "Maximizing Shareholder Value"; for business intellectuals, see Martin, *Fixing the Game*, and Mackey, Sisodia, and George, *Conscious Capitalism*.

11. I am not alone in using the term "shareholder value revolution" to describe the changes that American businesses went through at the end of the twentieth century. For other usages of the term, see Ho, *Liquidated*, chap. 3; Appelbaum and Batt, *Private Equity at Work*, 15.

12. Davis, *Managed by the Markets*, 5. Davis's use of the "Copernican revolution" and his likening of shareholder value's ascent to a scientific revolution is reminiscent of Thomas Kuhn's argument about scientific paradigms and revolutionary change in science. For Kuhn's argument, see Kuhn, *Structure of Scientific Revolutions*.

13. Jensen and Meckling, "Theory of the Firm," 306–7.

14. Davis, *Managed by the Markets*; Khurana, *From Higher Aims to Hired Hands*, 318–24; Fourcade and Khurana, "The Social Trajectory of a Finance Professor"; Heilbron, Jochem, and Quak, "The Origins and Early Diffusion of 'Shareholder Value'"; Dobbin and Zorn, "Corporate Malfeasance and the Myth of Shareholder Value"; Dobbin and Jung, "The Misapplication of Mr. Michael Jensen."

15. Chandler Jr., *Scale and Scope*, 621–27; Eichengreen, *Globalizing Capital*; Arrighi, *Long Twentieth Century*; Krippner, *Capitalizing on Crisis*; Stein, *Pivotal Decade*; Skidelsky, *Money and Government*; Gerstle, *Rise and Fall of the Neoliberal Order*.

16. Cheffins, *Public Company Transformed*, 155–218; Armour and Cheffins, "The Origins of the Market for Corporate Control"; Mizruchi, *Fracturing of the American Corporate Elite*, 180–214; Ho, *Liquidated*, 129–65; Coffee, "Shareholders Versus Managers"; Englander and Kaufman, "The End of Managerial Ideology"; Eichar, *Rise and Fall of Corporate Social Responsibility*, 271–90; Hirsch, "From Ambushes to Golden Parachutes"; Brooks, *Takeover Game*; Teitelman, *Bloodsport*; Madrick, *Age of Greed*.

17. Khurana, *From Higher Aims to Hired Hands*, 317–26.

18. Weil, *Fissured Workplace*, 8.

19. Fourcade and Khurana, "Social Trajectory of a Finance Professor."

20. Business Roundtable, "Statement on Corporate Governance."

21. Frydman and Jenter, "CEO Compensation"; Murphy, "Executive Compensation."

22. Fuller and Jensen, "Just Say No to Wall Street"; Lemann, *Transaction Man*, 127–35.

23. Stewart, "Birth of a New American Aristocracy."

24. Useem, *Executive Defense*, 3.

25. Weil, *Fissured Workplace*, 14–20; Hyman, *Temp*, 12–13.

26. Donnan, "Nation's Economy Divided."

27. For an overview of corporate governance structures and CEO power, see Monks and Minow, *Corporate Governance*.

28. Schleef, *Managing Elites*. In 2018, 66 percent of board seats for Fortune 500

companies were held by White men (Alliance for Board Diversity, "Missing Pieces Report"); in the same year, only three Fortune 500 companies had a Black CEO. Donnelly, "Black History Month."

29. Jackall, *Moral Mazes*.

30. Jackall, 36–38; Hyman, *Temp*, 259–61; Ho, *Liquidated*, 12.

31. Jackall, *Moral Mazes*, 20–25.

32. Khurana, *Searching for a Corporate Savior*, 36; Meindl, Ehrlich, and Dukerich, "Romance of Leadership"; Ungson and Steers, "Motivation and Politics in Executive Compensation"; Davis, *Managed by the Markets*, 96–99.

33. *The Economist*, "What It Takes to Be a CEO"; Malmendier and Tate, "Superstar CEOs"; Cheffins, *Public Company Transformed*, 267–68.

34. Boyer, "From Shareholder Value to CEO Power."

35. Berle and Means, *Modern Corporation and Private Property*. For the importance of *The Modern Corporation and Private Property*, see "Symposium, Corporations and Private Property," *Journal of Law and Economics* 26, no. 2 (1983): 235–496.

36. For Berle and Means's history of "the evolution of control," see Berle and Means, *Modern Corporation and Private Property*, 66–111.

37. For more on this process of corporate transformation, see Chandler, *Visible Hand*; Lamoreaux, *Great Merger Movement in American Business*; Sklar, *Corporate Reconstruction of American Capitalism, 1890–1916*.

38. Berle and Means, *Modern Corporation and Private Property*, 113. In keeping with this definition, I use the term "managers" to refer to the high-ranking executives of a firm who control its day-to-day operations. This usage would include directors, corporate officers, and the high-ranking executives responsible for managing corporate divisions.

39. Berle and Means, 47–65; for more on the expansion of stock holding prior to the Depression, see Ott, *When Wall Street Met Main Street*; for the further expansion of stockholders after the Second World War, see Traflet, *Nation of Small Shareholders*.

40. Berle and Means, *Modern Corporation and Private Property*, 64–65.

41. Berle and Means, 3; Drucker, *Concept of the Corporation*; Christiansen, *Progressive Business*, 91.

42. Abrams, "Management's Responsibilities in a Complex World."

43. Chandler, *Visible Hand*.

44. For the history of corporate social responsibility, see Eichar, *Rise and Fall of Corporate Social Responsibility*.

45. Dodd, "For Whom Are Corporate Managers Trustees?"; for Owen Young, see Sears, *New Place of the Stockholder*, 209; for Swope, see Anthony, "The Swope Plan."

46. Berle and Means, *Modern Corporation and Private Property*, 116.

47. Roosevelt himself articulated these ideas in his speech to the Commonwealth Club of San Francisco in 1932. Though the author of the speech is unidentified,

most historians believe that Berle and his wife almost certainly wrote it. For the text of the speech, see Franklin Roosevelt, "Campaign Address on Progressive Government at the Commonwealth Club in San Francisco, California"; for Berle's authorship, see Bratton and Wachter, "Shareholder Primacy's Corporatist Origins," 110–11; for the connection between the New Deal and the idea of corporate social responsibility, see Bratton and Wachter, 109–22.

48. Phillips-Fein, *Invisible Hands*, 1–25; Delton, *The Industrialists*, 152–55.

49. Jacoby, *Modern Manors*; Eichar, *Rise and Fall of Corporate Social Responsibility*, 133–72.

50. Chandler, *Visible Hand*; Chandler, *Scale and Scope*, 51–233; Davis, *Managed by the Markets*, 67–72; Christiansen, *Progressive Business*, 54–103; Cheffins, *Public Company Transformed*, 39–100.

51. Khurana, *From Higher Aims to Hired Hands*, 198–201; Davis, *Managed by the Markets*, 73.

52. Spector, "'Business Responsibilities in a Divided World'"; Khurana, *From Higher Aims to Hired Hands*, 201.

53. For an overview of the benefits provided, see Wartzman, *End of Loyalty*, 1–127; Weil, *Fissured Workplace*, 28–42.

54. Collins, *More*; Fligstein, *Transformation of Corporate Control*, 18–19; Khurana, *From Higher Aims to Hired Hands*, 207–9.

55. For the rising standard of living until about 1970, see Gordon, *Rise and Fall of American Growth*, 331–521.

56. Cowie, *Great Exception*, 154–68. For a critique from the right, see Schumpeter, *Capitalism, Socialism, and Democracy*; for critiques from the left, see Mills, *Power Elite*, and Mills, *Organization Man*; for more on economic growth, see Collins, *More*.

57. Katznelson, *When Affirmative Action Was White*.

58. Wartzman, *End of Loyalty*, 161–89.

59. Cowie, *Capital Moves*; Hyman, *Temp*.

60. Delton, *The Industrialists*, 210–35.

61. Chandler, *Scale and Scope*, 596–620; Freyer, "Managerial Capitalism Contested," 433–34; Stein, *Pivotal Decade*, 5–12; Delton, *The Industrialists*, 240–44.

62. Collins, *More*, 40–67.

63. Fligstein, *Transformation of Corporate Control*; Chandler, *Scale and Scope*, 621–27.

64. For a journalistic history of this merger wave, see Brooks, *Go-Go Years*.

65. Hyman, *Temp*, 142–60.

Chapter One

1. *Wall Street Journal*, "Litton Industries Says Net Will Fall Sharply"; Brooks, *Go-Go Years*, 180–81.

2. Cheffins, *Public Company Transformed*, 113–14.

3. American business history has been punctuated by periods of intense merger activity commonly referred to as merger waves. The first wave ran from approximately 1897 to 1904, and the second ran from 1916 to 1929. Precise dates for the Third Merger Wave vary considerably, with 1950 being the earliest starting point and 1973 being the latest end point; however, most sources do agree that 1965–1969 was the period of the most intense merger activity. For more on the history of merger waves, see Gaughan, *Mergers, Acquisitions, and Corporate Restructurings*, 41–70.

4. For the size of the Third Merger Wave, see Martynova and Renneboog, "Century of Corporate Takeovers," 2150; Gaughan, *Mergers, Acquisitions, and Corporate Restructurings*, 60.

5. Abele, "Conglomerate Merger Spreads Its Diversified Wings"; Kahn and Kahn, "Conglomerate Companies—What Are They Really?"

6. Fligstein, *Transformation of Corporate Control*, 29; Davis, Diekmann, and Tinsley, "Decline and Fall of the Conglomerate Firm," 552–53; Eichar, *Rise and Fall of Corporate Social Responsibility*, 217.

7. *Wall Street Journal*, "Affluent Companies"; Guthart, "More Companies Are Buying Back Their Stock"; Leontiades, "Use of Capital Markets"; Lazonick, "Innovative Business Models," 638–39.

8. Chandler, *Scale and Scope*, 621–27.

9. Abele, "Conglomerate Merger Spreads Its Diversified Wings."

10. Barber, "Big Government and Big Business."

11. Fox, "Spirit Is Youth."

12. Andrews, "Toward Professionalism in Business Management," 52; Khurana, *From Higher Aims to Hired Hands*, 203–9.

13. Brooks, *Go-Go Years*, 173–74; Cheffins, *Public Company Transformed*, 66.

14. Segal, "Time of the Conglomerates."

15. Hyman, *Temp*, 148–52.

16. For the broader argument about irrational investor behavior during stock market bubbles, see Shiller, *Irrational Exuberance*.

17. Nohria, Dyer, and Dalzell, *Changing Fortunes*, 29; McKenna, *World's Newest Profession*, 75–78; Waterhouse, *Lobbying America*, 99.

18. Fridenson, "Business Failure and the Agenda of Business History."

19. Ho, *Liquidated*, 133.

20. Hyman, "Rethinking the Postwar Corporation," 196–97.

21. For consultants' and investment bankers' prior support of the conglomerate movement, see McKenna, *World's Newest Profession*, 75; Ho, *Liquidated*, 134.

22. Porter, "From Competitive Advantage to Corporate Strategy," 52; Goold and Luchs, "Why Diversify?," 10; Baker and Smith, *New Financial Capitalists*, 10–18; Nohria, Dyer, and Dalzell, *Changing Fortunes*, 29.

23. For a review of different conceptions of financialization, see Van der Zwan, "Making Sense of Financialization."

24. Hyman, *Temp*, 202; Fligstein, *Transformation of Corporate Control*, 293–94; Nelson Espeland and Hirsch, "Ownership Changes, Accounting Practice and the Redefinition of the Corporation."

25. The literature on financialization rarely credits non-financial corporations with driving the process of financialization. Rather, most scholars identify other causes of financialization, including macroeconomic shifts in the global economy during the 1970s, the development of new financial technologies, or central bank policy in the late 1970s and 1980s. For central bank policy, see Krippner, *Capitalizing on Crisis*, 2011; for new financial technologies, see McKenzie, *An Engine, Not a Camera*; for macroeconomic change, see Harvey, *Brief History of Neoliberalism*; Arrighi, *Long Twentieth Century*.

26. Jacoby, "Finance and Labor," 29.

27. Jacoby, 29.

28. Levy and Sarnat, "Diversification, Portfolio Analysis"; Reid, "A Reply to the Weston/Mansinghka Criticisms"; Mason and Goudzwaard, "Performance of Conglomerate Firms"; Amihud and Lev, "Risk Reduction"; Jarrell, "Financial Innovation and Corporate Mergers."

29. Jensen, "Active Investors, LBOs," 36–37.

30. Davis, *Managed by the Markets*.

31. For biographical details on Thornton's life, see *Time*, "Appetite for the Future."

32. The military was relatively late to adopt the kind of statistical control programs that had been developed by American businesses and social science foundations in the previous decades. For more on the history of statistical control and "scientific management" more broadly, see Beniger, *Control Revolution*; Chandler, *Visible Hand*; Hounshell, *From the American System to Mass Production*; Breen, "Foundations, Statistics, and State-Building."

33. *Time*, "Appetite for the Future."

34. For McNamara's recollections of working with Thornton, see Watson and Wolk, "'Whiz Kid.'"

35. For a history of the "whiz kids," see Byrne, *Whiz Kids*.

36. *Time*, "Appetite for the Future."

37. US House of Representatives, Antitrust Subcommittee, *Investigation of Conglomerate Corporations (Part 5)*, Hearing (HRG-1969-HJH-0011; June 4 and 5, 1969; March 4 and 5, 1970), 41.

38. Glen McDaniel, in *Investigation of Conglomerate Corporations (Part 5)*, 46–47.

39. McDaniel, in *Investigation of Conglomerate Corporations (Part 5)*, 42.

40. *Wall Street Journal*, "'Conglomerate' Is a Rock."

41. "'Conglomerate' Is a Rock," 41–42.

42. "'Conglomerate' Is a Rock," 42.

43. Winchester, "Litton Alters Financial Course."

44. Goold and Luchs, "Why Diversify?," 16–17.
45. Ostrow, "Legendary Litton."
46. Charles Thornton, Roy Ash, and Glen McDaniel, in *Investigation of Conglomerate Corporations (Part 5)*, 155.
47. Thornton, Ash, and McDaniel, in *Investigation of Conglomerate Corporations (Part 5)*, 156.
48. *Investigation of Conglomerate Corporations (Part 5)*, 156.
49. Wright, "A Glimpse Behind the Scenes at Litton Industries."
50. Rukeyser, "Litton Down to Earth," 186.
51. Thornton, Ash, and McDaniel, in *Investigation of Conglomerate Corporations (Part 5)*, 155.
52. *Investigation of Conglomerate Corporations (Part 5)*, 157–58.
53. Thornton, Ash, and McDaniel, in *Investigation of Conglomerate Corporations (Part 5)*, 155.
54. CNN Money, "FORTUNE 500: 1969 Archive Full List 1–100."
55. Gray, "The Litton Annual Report."
56. *Forbes*, "Litton's Troubles," 46.
57. Ostrow, "Legendary Litton."
58. Schonberger, "Inside the Market."
59. Rukeyser, "Litton Down to Earth," 140, 184.
60. *Forbes*, "Litton's Shattered Image," 32.
61. *Time*, "U.S. Business: Out at the Ballpark."
62. *New York Times*, "Litton Set to Buy Stouffer Foods."
63. "Convenience Foods System, December 1968 Opportunity Review, Fiscal Review, Fiscal Year 1969," in *Investigation of Conglomerate Companies (Part 5)*, 1207–1333; *Wall Street Journal*, "Litton Division's Hotel Venture."
64. Hartt, "Litton Memo Provides Poverty War Strategy."
65. Sederberg, "Litton Industries Moves into Nation Building."
66. *Time*, "Litton Takes Charge."
67. Ash, "Nation Building," 181–82.
68. Ash, 183.
69. *Wall Street Journal*, "Litton Industries Says Net Will Fall Sharply"; Cheffins, *Public Company Transformed*, 113–14.
70. Rukeyser, "Litton Down to Earth," 139.
71. Hammer, "Litton Says Stock Drop Will Not Slow Down Acquisition Plans."
72. *Time*, "Litton Lesson."
73. Skala, "Conglomerate Trend Fades"; Rukeyser, "Litton Down to Earth," 139.
74. *Forbes*, "Litton's Troubles," 47.
75. Wright, "Glimpse Behind the Scenes."
76. Rukeyser, "Litton Down to Earth," 186.
77. Wright, "Glimpse Behind the Scenes."

78. Nohria, Dyer, and Dalzell, *Changing Fortunes*, 29.
79. Rukeyser, "Litton Down to Earth," 140.
80. *Forbes*, "Litton's Troubles."
81. Glen McDaniel, in *Investigation of Conglomerate Corporations (Part 5)*, 46.
82. Aspin, "Litton Ship Fiasco."
83. Rukeyser, "Litton Down to Earth," 140.
84. "Memorandum from E. B. Gardner to Roy Ash and Seymour Rosenberg, RE: Opportunities," in *Investigation of Conglomerate Corporations (Part 5)*, 998–1014.
85. Rukeyser, "Litton Down to Earth," 140.
86. Aspin, "Litton Ship Fiasco."
87. *Forbes*, "Litton's Troubles"; Rukeyser, "Litton Down to Earth"; *Time*, "Litton Lesson."
88. McLaren, "Excerpts from Assistant Attorney General's Statement on Conglomerate Mergers"; Shanahan, "U.S. Seeks Curb on Conglomerate."
89. Smith, "Litton Acquisitions Questioned."
90. *Washington Post*, "Proxmire Hits Litton 'Payoff.'"
91. *New York Times*, "Greece Ends Litton Deal."
92. *Forbes*, "Litton's Shattered Image."
93. Schonberger, "Inside the Market."
94. For antitrust, see Fligstein, *Transformation of Corporate Control*, 193–94; for the paperwork crisis on Wall Street, see Wells, "Certificates and Computers"; for the onset of the 1969–1970 recession, see *Time*, "Rising Risk of Recession."
95. Goold and Luchs, "Why Diversify?," 10.
96. Salsbury, *No Way to Run a Railroad*.
97. Seeger, "Penn Central"; for railroads' use of diversification strategies, see Shoemaker, "Should Railroads Diversify for Growth and Profits?"
98. Zimmerman, "Penn Central Officials Sold Stock"; Porter, "A Penn Central Director's View"; Belair, "Charges of Fraud at Penn Central."
99. Morris, "Penn Central Debacle Creates Repercussions"; Cheffins, *Public Company Transformed*, 113–14.
100. *New York Times*, "Penn Central Inquest."
101. Abele, "Yesterday's Darling Is Scorned"; McKinsey, "Conglomerate Theory Falters Under Scrutiny"; Metz, "Conglomerates: A Losing Style."
102. *Time*, "America the Inefficient."
103. US House of Representatives, Antitrust Subcommittee, *Investigation of Conglomerate Corporations* (CMP-1971-HJH-0006). Washington, DC: Government Printing Office, 1971.
104. *Wall Street Journal*, "Conglomerates' Efficiency Called Overrated"; Shanahan, "Conglomerates: Data Lack Cited."
105. Farrar and Girton, "Institutional Investors and Concentration of Financial Power."
106. Attiyeh, "Where Next for Conglomerates?"

Chapter Two

1. Graham, *Losing Time*, 13–17; Stein, *Pivotal Decade*, 6–7; Wartzman, *End of Loyalty*, 217–21; Freyer, "Managerial Capitalism Contested," 441.
2. Gordon, *Rise and Fall of American Growth*.
3. Eichengreen, *Globalizing Capital*, 129–42; Hyman, *Debtor Nation*, 220–80.
4. Jacobs, *Panic at the Pump*; Stein, *Pivotal Decade*, 74–100; Sargent, *Superpower Transformed*, 131–61.
5. Blyth, *Great Transformations*, 128–47; Stein, *Pivotal Decade*, 102–23; Krippner, *Capitalizing on Crisis*, 58–73; Fligstein and Shin, "Shareholder Value and the Transformation of American Industries," 8; Dumenil and Levy, *Capital Resurgent*, 14; Wartzman, *End of Loyalty*, 195–98.
6. Harvey, *Condition of Postmodernity*, 141–45; Sargent, *Superpower Transformed*, 100–130. For an earlier history of the politics of inflation, see Jacobs, *Pocketbook Politics*.
7. Jones, *Masters of the Universe*, 211–72; Rodgers, *Age of Fracture*, 47–56.
8. Waterhouse, *Lobbying America*, 36–49; Cheffins, *Public Company Transformed*, 115–19.
9. Stein, *Pivotal Decade*, 102–23.
10. Cowie, *Stayin' Alive*; Windham, *Knocking on Labor's Door*.
11. Bell, *Coming of Post-Industrial Society*, 272.
12. Bell, 270.
13. Bell, 283.
14. Waterhouse, *Lobbying America*, 36–42.
15. Eichar, *Rise and Fall of Corporate Social Responsibility*, 5–9.
16. Jacobs, "Politics of Environmental Regulation," 212–13; Macekura, *Of Limits and Growth*, 176–77; Cowie, *Stayin' Alive*, 138–39.
17. Phillips-Fein, *Fear City*, 207–8; Waterhouse, *Lobbying America*, 63–64; Mizruchi, *Fracturing of the American Corporate Elite*, 6–7.
18. Jacobs, "Politics of Environmental Regulation," 226–27.
19. Nader, Green, and Seligman, "Who Rules the Giant Corporation?"
20. Smith, "Nader Group Urges the Federal Chartering of Big Corporations"; Bradley, "Nader Defends Federal Chartering."
21. Nader, Green, and Seligman, *Taming the Giant Corporation*; Nader and Green, "Corporate Democracy."
22. Benjamin Rosenthal, "Corporate Democracy Act of 1980," Pub. L. No. H.R. 7010 (1980). For more on Nader's lobbying on behalf of the bill, see Waterhouse, "Corporate Mobilization Against Liberal Reform."
23. Ocasio and Joseph, "Cultural Adaptation and Institutional Change," 167.
24. Waterhouse, *Lobbying America*, 36–42; Drutman, *Business of America Is Lobbying*, 55–59.
25. Paluszek, "Business and Society," 25–26.

26. Paluszek, 34.
27. Paluszek, 15.
28. Paluszek, 15.
29. Paluszek, 10.
30. Paluszek, 10.
31. Ellis, *Joe Wilson and the Creation of Xerox*; Tenner, "Mother of All Invention."
32. Brooks, "Xerox, Xerox, Xerox, Xerox," 50.
33. Brooks, 90.
34. Votaw and Sethi, "Do We Need a New Corporate Response?" 10; Ellis, *Joe Wilson and the Creation of Xerox*, 289–300; Greer, "Xerox Comes to Eastman Defense."
35. Ellis, *Joe Wilson and the Creation of Xerox*.
36. Amadae, *Rationalizing Capitalist Democracy*, 168; Amadae and de Mesquita, "Rochester School," 279.
37. Fourcade and Khurana, "Social Trajectory of a Finance Professor," 363–64.
38. Sheehan, "Rich, Risky Life of a University Trustee," 162.
39. Sheehan, 169; Fourcade and Khurana, "Social Trajectory of a Finance Professor," 364.
40. Sheehan, "Rich, Risky Life of a University Trustee," 162.
41. "University-Industrial Relations," address by W. Allen Wallis, President, University of Rochester, Development Council Luncheon, Rochester Chamber of Commerce, May 26, 1964, in W. Allen Wallis Papers, D.261, Rare Books, Special Collections, and Preservation, River Campus Libraries, University of Rochester.
42. Background material on the history of the GSM is drawn from the author's interview of Professor Ronald Hansen, November 10, 2018. Notes are in the author's possession.
43. Fourcade and Khurana, "Social Trajectory of a Finance Professor," 361–63.
44. Interview with Ronald Hansen.
45. Kilpatrick, "1971 End to Draft Is Urged"; Irwin, "Nixon Panel Will Seek Formula to End Draft."
46. Fourcade and Khurana, "Social Trajectory of a Finance Professor," 363.
47. Fourcade and Khurana, 364–66.
48. McKenzie, *An Engine, Not a Camera*, 9–12.
49. Lemann, *Transaction Man*, 105–6.
50. Lemann, 120–30.
51. Lemann, 102–3; Read, *Great Minds in Finance*, chapter 30.
52. Fox, *Myth of the Rational Market*, 89–107.
53. Lemann, *Transaction Man*, 130.
54. Similar efforts associated with public choice theory and political science are detailed in Amadae, *Rationalizing Capitalist Democracy*; MacLean, *Democracy in Chains*. For an earlier example of similar debates, see Purcell, *Crisis of Democratic Theory*.

55. Meckling, "Values and the Choice of the Model."

56. These dismissals of the "general good" all drew from the insights of Kenneth Arrow's "impossibility theorem," which mathematically proved that it was not possible to meaningfully aggregate individuals' preferences. For Arrow's theorem, see Arrow, *Social Choice and Individual Values*. For more on Arrow, especially his skepticism about markets, see Amadae, *Rationalizing Capitalist Democracy*, 83–132.

57. Brunner, "My Quest for Economic Knowledge," 29.

58. Fourcade and Khurana, "Social Trajectory of a Finance Professor," 365.

59. Found in "Graduate School of Management, University of Rochester, 1972–1973 Course Catalogue," personal collection of Ronald Hansen.

60. Brunner, "My Quest for Economic Knowledge," 30.

61. Brunner, "Knowledge, Values and the Choice of Economic Organization."

62. Brunner, 559.

63. Brunner, 560–61.

64. Brunner, 561.

65. Brunner, 560.

66. Brunner, 578.

67. Meckling, "Values and the Choice of the Model," 549.

68. Meckling, 548n4.

69. Meckling, 552.

70. Meckling, 554.

71. Meckling, 554.

72. Though the manuscript was never finished, Jensen did post four unpublished chapters on his SSRN page: : Jensen, "Freedom, Capitalism and Human Behavior Chapter 1. Introduction and Overview"; Jensen and Meckling, "Freedom, Capitalism and Human Behavior Chapter 2"; Jensen, "Freedom, Capitalism and Human Behavior Chapter 3"; Jensen and Meckling, "Freedom, Capitalism and Human Behavior Chapter 4". The unpublished chapters can be found there.

73. Sigler, "Summer of '79," 20.

74. Jensen and Meckling, "Freedom, Capitalism and Human Behavior Chapter 2," 12.

75. Jensen and Meckling, 14–15.

76. Jensen and Meckling, 15.

77. Brunner, "Knowledge, Values and the Choice of Economic Organization*," 560–61.

78. Jensen, "Freedom and the Role of the Government," 3.

79. Jensen and Meckling, "Between Freedom and Democracy," 2.

80. Blyth, *Great Transformations*, 4–6; Cowie, *Stayin' Alive*; Perlstein, *Nixonland: The Rise of a President and the Fracturing of America*; Jones, *Masters of the Universe*, 15. The shared belief in personal responsibility also helps to explain the alliance between free-market advocates and the religious Right in American politics. This relationship is explored in such works as Phillips-Fein, *Invisible Hands*,

221–34; Cooper, *Family Values*; Moreton, *To Serve God and Wal-Mart*; and Kruse, *One Nation Under God*.

81. Buchanan, "Political Economy of the Franchise."
82. Buchanan, 90–91.
83. "Political Entrepreneurship and the Welfare Explosion," 1968, W. Allen Wallis Papers, D.261, Rare Books, Special Collections, and Preservation, River Campus Libraries, University of Rochester.
84. Jensen and Meckling, "Can the Corporation Survive?," 6–7; Jensen and Meckling, "Between Freedom and Democracy," 4–5.
85. Brunner, "Reflections on the Political Economy of Government," 675.
86. Read, *Corporate Financiers*, 191.
87. Stout, *Shareholder Value Myth*, 18; Khurana, *From Higher Aims to Hired Hands*, 317.
88. Friedman, "Friedman Doctrine," 33.
89. Friedman, 33.
90. Friedman, 122.
91. Friedman, 124–26.
92. A similar argument was made in Stigler, "Modern Man and His Corporation."
93. For the Interlaken draft, see Jensen and Meckling, "Theory of the Firm"; Read, *Corporate Financiers*, 192.
94. Jensen and Meckling, "Theory of the Firm," 305.
95. Jensen and Meckling, 306.
96. Jensen and Meckling, 306–7. Though Jensen and Meckling felt like there was not enough work done on the theory of the firm, there were important predecessors to their work, including Coase, "Nature of the Firm"; Alchian and Demsetz, "Production, Information Costs, and Economic Organization."
97. Jensen and Meckling, "Theory of the Firm," 311.
98. Jensen and Meckling, 311.
99. Jensen and Meckling, 311.
100. Berle and Means, *Modern Corporation and Private Property*; Alchian and Demsetz, "Production, Information Costs, and Economic Organization."
101. Jensen and Meckling, "Theory of the Firm," 312–13.
102. Jensen and Meckling, 313.
103. Jensen and Meckling, 308.
104. Jensen and Meckling, "Can the Corporation Survive?" The paper won the 1978 Graham and Dodd Plaque, which was issued by the Certified Financial Analysts Institute to the best manuscript in finance each year. The article was also the cover story of *MBA Magazine* in March 1977, and was widely reprinted and circulated in corporate and academic circles. For more information on the article's publication, see "Jensen Publications," accessed April 18, 2019, http://www.people.hbs.edu/mjensen/pub2.html.
105. Jensen and Meckling, "Can the Corporation Survive?," 13.

106. Jensen and Meckling, 15.
107. Jensen and Meckling, 1.
108. Jensen and Meckling, 17.
109. Jensen and Meckling, 17.
110. Heilbron, Jochem, and Quak, "Origins and Early Diffusion of 'Shareholder Value,'" 9–10.
111. Cheffins, *Public Company Transformed*, 105–6.

Chapter Three

1. Hostile takeovers have a longer history in American business that predates the third merger wave as well. For more on the history of hostile takeovers, see Armour and Cheffins, "Origins of the Market for Corporate Control," 18–27; and Fischel, "Efficient Capital Market Theory," 5–6.
2. Ravenscraft and Scherer, *Mergers, Sell-Offs, and Economic Efficiency*; Fligstein, *Transformation of Corporate Control*; Donaldson, *Corporate Restructuring*, 17–39; Hyman, *Temp*, 161–86.
3. Lemann, *Transaction Man*, 136–50; Teitelman, *Bloodsport*, 63–81; Madrick, *Age of Greed*, 71–85; Madrick, *Taking America*, 1–193.
4. Nippa, Pidun, and Rubner, "Corporate Portfolio Management," 52; Goold and Luchs, "Why Diversify?," 10–13.
5. Cheffins, *Public Company Transformed*, 174–77; Cheffins, "Corporate Governance Since the Managerial Capitalism Era," 729; Madrick, *Age of Greed*, 125–27; Davis, Diekmann, and Tinsley, "The Decline and Fall of the Conglomerate Firm in the 1980s," 554.
6. Heilbron, Jochem, and Quak, "The Origins and Early Diffusion of 'Shareholder Value' in the United States"; Fourcade and Khurana, "The Social Trajectory of a Finance Professor," 369–71.
7. Shleifer and Summers, "Breach of Trust in Hostile Takeovers"; Smith, *Money Wars*; Useem, *Executive Defense*; Donaldson, *Corporate Restructuring*; Davis, Diekmann, and Tinsley, "The Decline and Fall of the Conglomerate Firm in the 1980s"; Baker and Smith, *New Financial Capitalists*; Nohria, Dyer, and Dalzell, *Changing Fortunes*; Kiechel, *Lords of Strategy*, 201–54; Hyman, *Temp*, 210–54; Cheffins, *Public Company Transformed*, 155–218.
8. For a detailed investigation of the back-office crisis, see US House of Representatives, Subcommittee on Commerce and Finance, *Securities Industry Study*, 92nd Congress, 2nd session, 1972, H. Rep. 92–1519.
9. Traflet, *A Nation of Small Shareholders*, 159.
10. Wells, "Certificates and Computers," 215–21.
11. Wells, 223–30.
12. Wells, 232.

13. US House, *Securities Industry Study*, 10; Wells, 200–203.

14. Wells, 233–34.

15. Cheffins, "Corporate Governance Since the Managerial Capitalism Era," 147.

16. For members' lobbying efforts, see *Wall Street Journal*, "Donaldson-Lufkin Moves to Allow"; for the Donaldson, Lufkin, and Jenrette IPO, see *Wall Street Journal*, "Donaldson-Lufkin Shares Due."

17. Robards, "Issue Sold at $28."

18. Wayne, "Going Public on Wall Street"; Cohan, *Why Wall Street Matters*, 74–85.

19. Cheffins, *Public Company Transformed*, 147.

20. Securities and Exchange Commission, *Institutional Investor Study Report of the Securities and Exchange Commission, Summary Volume*, H.R. document 92–64, 92nd Congress, 1st Session (1971), 102, https://www.sechistorical.org/collection/papers/1970/1971_0310_SECInstitutionalInvestor_25.pdf.

21. Lemann, *Transaction Man*, 148–49.

22. For 1970, see US Senate, Subcommittee on Reports, Accounting, and Management, Institutional Investors Common Stock, Holdings and Voting Rights, S. 94–247, 94th Congress, 2nd Session (1976), 4. For 1980, see Edwards and Hubbard, "The Growth of Institutional Stock Ownership," 94.

23. Madrick, *Age of Greed*, 97–99.

24. Jensen, "Risk, the Pricing of Capital Assets"; Skala, "Monthly Report for Investors."

25. Lemann, *Transaction Man*, 139–40; Jacoby, "Finance and Labor," 24–25; Rappaport, "Economics of Short-Term Performance Obsession."

26. Cheffins, *Public Company Transformed*, 79.

27. "INCO Holdings Incorporation Offer to Purchase Any and All Outstanding Shares of Common Stock of ESB Incorporated for Cash at $28.00 Per Share Net," advertisement printed in the *Wall Street Journal*, July 23, 1974.

28. For more on the world of early twentieth-century finance and the Morgan family, see Pak, *Gentlemen Bankers*.

29. Beard, *Blue Blood and Mutiny*, 13–28.

30. Jensen, "The Morgan Stanley Manner."

31. Lemann, *Transaction Man*, 89–95.

32. Beard, *Blue Blood and Mutiny*, 32.

33. McFadden, "Robert H. B. Baldwin."

34. Lemann, *Transaction Man*, 136.

35. Lemann, 138–43.

36. Jensen, "Morgan Stanley Manner."

37. *Time*, "Back to Braces."

38. Lohr, "Mergers," 9.

39. Lemann, *Transaction Man*, 137; Beard, *Blue Blood and Mutiny*, 30.

40. *BusinessWeek*, "Greenhill: A New Takeover Artist."
41. Koshetz, "ESB, Inc., Opposes Purchase Offer."
42. Koshetz, "Inco Sues to Curb ESB's Comments."
43. Koshetz, "United Aircraft Tops INCO ESB Bid."
44. Delugach, "What's Making ESB Inc. Such a Big Deal?"
45. Delugach, "Inco Takes $200 Million Pot."
46. For more on arbs, see Metz, "Takeover Deals"; for the arbs involvement in the ESB takeover, see Madrick, *Age of Greed*, 79.
47. Madrick, *Age of Greed*, 80.
48. Beard, *Blue Blood and Mutiny*, 48.
49. Metz, "Aiding Hostile Takeover Bids"; Chandler, *Scale and Scope*, 621–27.
50. Lohr, "Mergers"; Madrick, *Age of Greed*, 80–81.
51. For more on Rohatyn's work during the New York City bankruptcy crisis, see Phillips-Fein, *Fear City*.
52. For a contemporary account of Flom and Lipton and their work on takeovers, see Brill, "Two Tough Lawyers in the Tender-Offer Game"; for later accounts, see Madrick, *Age of Greed*, 70–85; Teitelman, *Bloodsport*.
53. Arenson, "Takeover Game and Its Outlook." Harold M. Williams, "The Challenges of the New Decade, March 17, 1980," retrieved from Securities and Exchange Commission Historical Society, Virtual Museum and Archive (hereafter SEC-VMA), https://3197d6d14b5f19f2f440-5e13d29c4c016cf96cbbfd197c579b45.ssl.cf1.rackcdn.com/collection/papers/1980/1980_0317_WilliamsChallenges.pdf, 16–7.
54. Ehrbar and Hengstenberg, "Corporate Takeovers Are Here to Stay," 98.
55. Sloan, "Why Is No One Safe?"
56. Salter and Weinhold, "Diversification via Acquisition."
57. Arenson, "Takeover Game and Its Outlook."
58. For Henderson's original presentation of the growth matrix, see Henderson, "Product Portfolio"; for the impact of the growth matrix on the emerging field of corporate strategy, see Bettis and Hall, "Strategic Portfolio Management"; Ghemawat, "Competition and Business Strategy," 46–52; Kiechel, *Lords of Strategy*, 47–73; Hyman, *Temp*, 170–72.
59. Since "dog" is used far more often than "pet" to describe a low growth, low market share business, I will use "dog" for the remainder of this text.
60. Henderson, "Product Portfolio," 2.
61. Ghemawat, "Competition and Business Strategy in Historical Perspective," 49.
62. Haspeslagh, "Portfolio Planning," 59.
63. Eichar, *Rise and Fall of Corporate Social Responsibility*, 259.
64. Salter and Weinhold, "Choosing Compatible Acquisitions"; Hyman, *Temp*, 170–82.
65. Wild, *Management by Compulsion*; Donaldson and Lorsch, *Decision Making at the Top*.

66. Fligstein, *Transformation of Corporate Control*, 256–57.
67. Hirsch, "From Ambushes to Golden Parachutes," 811.
68. Ehrbar and Hengstenberg, "Corporate Takeovers Are Here to Stay," 98.
69. Metz, "Take-over Campaigns Back in Vogue"; Cheffins, *Public Company Transformed*, 210–11.
70. Banks were allowed to be exempted from an acquirer's disclosure of funding sources if those banks provided funding in the form of a "loan made in the ordinary course of business."
71. *Wall Street Journal*, "Tender-Offer Legislation Is Cleared."
72. Metz, "Take-over Campaigns Back in Vogue."
73. Roe, "Takeover Politics," 338–40; Jarrell and Bradley, "Economic Effects of Federal and State Regulations," 405; Cain, McKeon, and Solomon, "Do Takeover Laws Matter?," 34–35.
74. Jarrell and Bradley, "Economic Effects of Federal and State Regulations," 377–79; Cain, McKeon, and Solomon, "Do Takeover Laws Matter?"
75. For the Carter administration's support of antitrust reform, see Shifrin, "Eased Proof of Monopoly Is Urged."
76. US Senate, Subcommittee on Antitrust and Monopoly, *Mergers and Industrial Concentration*, Hearings (HRG-1978-SJS-0019, May 12, July 27–28, September 21, 1978); US House of Representatives, Subcommittee on Antitrust and Restraint of Trade Activities Affecting Small Business, *Conglomerate Mergers— Their Effects on Small Business and Local Communities*, Hearings (HRG-1980-SMB-0024, January 31, February 1, 7–8, 27–28, 1980).
77. Cowan, "Senator Kennedy's Antitrust Bill."
78. For the text of Kennedy's bill, see A Bill to Preserve the Diversity and Independence of American Business, S. 600, 96th Cong. (1979). For hearings on Kennedy's bill, see US Senate, Subcommittee on Antitrust, Monopoly and Business Rights, *Mergers and Economic Concentration, Part 1*, Hearings (HRG-1979-SJS-0033, March 8, 23, April 25, 1979); US Senate, Subcommittee on Antitrust, Monopoly and Business Rights, *Mergers and Economic Concentration, Part 2*, Hearings (HRG-1979-SJS-0034, April 26, May 17, 22, 1979).
79. US Senate, Committee on Banking, Housing and Urban Affairs, *Corporate Takeovers*, Hearings (HRG-1976-BHU-0059 February 16, 1976).
80. Rowe, "Washington's Role in Takeovers Gaining."
81. Harold W. Williams, "Tender Offers and the Corporate Director," address at Seventh Annual Securities Regulation Institute, San Diego, CA, January 17, 1980, SEC-VMA, https://3197d6d14b5f19f2f440-5e13d29c4c016cf96cbbfd197c579b45.ssl.cf1.rackcdn.com/collection/papers/1980/1980_0117_WilliamsTender.pdf. For the reaction to Williams's speech, see Metz, "Unfriendly Tender Studied."
82. Williams, "Tender Offers and the Corporate Director," 3–4; this criticism was echoed in Hayes and Abernathy, "Managing Our Way to Economic Decline."
83. Williams, 4–5.

84. Williams, 5–7.
85. Williams, 9–25.
86. Williams, 7–8.
87. Krippner, *Capitalizing on Crisis*, 116–20.
88. Metz, "Hostile Offers."
89. Metz, "Takeover Candidates."
90. Metz, "Hostile Offers."
91. Cole, "Tight Credit and Takeover."

Chapter Four

1. The term "Deal Decade" is taken from Blair, *Deal Decade*.
2. Ravenscraft and Scherer, *Mergers, Sell-Offs, and Economic Efficiency*.
3. For an overview of academic criticism, see Nippa, Pidun, and Rubner, "Corporate Portfolio Management"; Ghemawat, "Competition and Business Strategy in Historical Perspective," 49–52; for contemporary criticism from management professors, see Salter and Weinhold, "Diversification via Acquisition"; Hayes and Abernathy, "Managing Our Way to Economic Decline"; Porter, "From Competitive Advantage to Corporate Strategy." Financial economists had long opposed diversification strategies. For some of the earliest opposition, see Levy and Sarnat, "Diversification, Portfolio Analysis and the Uneasy Case for Conglomerate Mergers."
4. Davis, Diekmann, and Tinsley, "Decline and Fall of the Conglomerate Firm"; Eichar, *Rise and Fall of Corporate Social Responsibility*, 271.
5. Schneider and Dunbar, "Psychoanalytic Reading of Hostile Takeover Events."
6. Goldstein, "Language of Takeovers"; Schneider and Dunbar, "Psychoanalytic Reading of Hostile Takeover Events."
7. Prokesch, "'People Trauma' in Mergers"; Magnet and Post, "Help! My Company Has Just Been Taken Over"; Hirsch, "From Ambushes to Golden Parachutes."
8. Shleifer and Vishny, "Takeover Wave of the 1980s," 745.
9. Crittenden, "Age of 'Me-First' Management."
10. For the Business Roundtable, see Andrew Seigler, in US House of Representatives, Subcommittee on Telecommunications, Consumer Protection, and Finance, *Corporate Takeovers (Part 2)*, Hearing (HRG-1985-HEC-0089, May 23, June 12, October 24, 1985), 195–211; for the National Association of Manufacturers, see Paul H. Elickler, in *Corporate Takeovers (Part 2)*, Hearing, 212–30; for labor unions, see Henry Schecter, in *Corporate Takeovers (Part 2)*, Hearing, 295–98. For more on the politics of takeovers, see Roe, "Takeover Politics," 321–53.
11. Elickler, in *Corporate Takeovers (Part 2)*, Hearing, 212–14.
12. Andrew Seigler, in *Corporate Takeovers (Part 2)*, Hearing, 195.

13. Henry Schecter, in *Corporate Takeovers (Part 2)*, Hearing, 296.

14. Cheffins, *Public Company Transformed*, 162–67.

15. Hirsch, "From Ambushes to Golden Parachutes," 820–28; Mizruchi, *Fracturing of the American Corporate Elite*, 205–6; Heilbron, Jochem, and Quak, "Origins and Early Diffusion of 'Shareholder Value'"; Fourcade and Khurana, "Social Trajectory of a Finance Professor," 369–71.

16. Coll, "Pickens and the Gospel of Gain."

17. Carley, "Carl Icahn"'s Strategies."

18. Cheffins, "Corporate Governance," 729.

19. For more on Miller, see Crock, "James Miller, FTC Nominee"; De Witt, "Nominee as F.T.C. Head"; for more on Baxter, see Metzenbaum, "Is William Baxter Anti-Antitrust?"

20. For the Chicago School of antitrust, see Bork, *Antitrust Paradox*.

21. For the charge that Reagan abandoned antitrust enforcement, see Fligstein, *Transformation of Corporate Control*, 31; for the reorientation of antitrust policy under Reagan, see Kovacic, "Reagan's Judicial Appointees"; Cheffins, *Public Company Transformed*, 175–76.

22. Vise and Coll, *Eagle on the Street*, 21–24.

23. These recommendations were in keeping with Reagan's broader strategy of filling regulatory agencies with appointees who were ideologically opposed to the mission of the agencies they were appointed to. For more, see Jacobs, "Politics of Environmental Regulation," 226–27; Kruse and Zelizer, *Fault Lines*, 120.

24. SEC Transition Team, "Executive Summary," in "Final Report," December 22, 1980, SEC-VMA, https://3197d6d14b5f19f2f440-5e13d29c4c016cf96cbbfd 197c579b45.ssl.cf1.rackcdn.com/collection/papers/1980/1980_1222_SECTransi tion_6.pdf, 7.5–6.

25. William Proxmire to Ronald Reagan, January 28, 1981, SEC-VMA, https:// 3197d6d14b5f19f2f440-5e13d29c4c016cf96cbbfd197c579b45.ssl.cf1.rackcdn.com /collection/papers/1980/1981_0128_ReaganProxmireT.pdf.

26. US Senate, Committee on Banking, Housing, and Urban Affairs, *Nomination of John S. R. Shad*, Hearing (S. Hrg 97-11, April 6, 1981).

27. Crock, "SEC's Shad Shows Pro-Business Tilt"; Vise and Coll, *Eagle on the Street*, 117.

28. Vise and Coll, *Eagle on the Street*, 100–101.

29. Sloane, "John S. R. Shad Dies at 71."

30. Vise and Coll, *Eagle on the Street*, 27–28.

31. Vise and Coll, 29.

32. Charles Cox oral history interview conducted by Robert Colby in Chicago, Illinois, May 14, 2013, SEC-VMA, https://3197d6d14b5f19f2f440-5e13d29c4c016 cf96cbbfd197c579b45.ssl.cf1.rackcdn.com/collection/oral-histories/20130514_Cox _Charles_T.pdf, 4–11.

33. Vise and Coll, *Eagle on the Street*, 107–8.

34. Details about *Edgar v. MITE* are taken from Edgar v. Mite Corp. Supreme Court Case Files Collection, Box 84, Powell Papers, Lewis F. Powell Jr. Archives, Washington & Lee University School of Law, Lexington, VA, available at https://scholarlycommons.law.wlu.edu/casefiles/270/.

35. Maurer, "Tender Offers."

36. Ingrassa, "Forget Football."

37. "High Noon."

38. Alexander, "Merger Theater of the Absurd"; Salmans, "Tumultuous Takeover Saga Ends"; Cole, "Final Pact for Bendix and Allied."

39. Brooks, *Takeover Game*, 181.

40. Brooks, 179–81.

41. Blustein, "Marietta, Bendix 'Pac-Man' Tactics."

42. Alexander, "Merger Theater of the Absurd"; Blustein, "Marietta, Bendix 'Pac-Man' Tactics"; Hayes, "Undermining of Business Credibility"; Salmans, "Merger Advisers Under Fire."

43. Lowenstein, "Pruning Deadwood in Hostile Takeovers," 250.

44. Salmans, "Merger Advisers Under Fire."

45. Salmans, "Whither Mergers in the Wake of Bendix?"

46. Hudson, "SEC Is Forming Industry Panel"; *New York Times*, "S.E.C. Plans a Review"; Brooks, *Takeover Game*, 261–62.

47. For a full list of the committee's membership, see "Members of the Securities and Exchange Commission Advisory Committee on Tender Offers," attached to "Advisory Committee on Tender Offers Report of Recommendations"; *Wall Street Journal*, "SEC Panel Reunites Veterans"; Ross, "Veterans Chosen."

48. The CVs for Jarrell and Easterbrook can be found at, Forensic Economics, "Gregg A. Jarrell"; Federal Judicial Center, "Easterbrook, Frank Hoover."

49. Securities and Exchange Commission, "Advisory Committee on Tender Offers," xvii.

50. A full list of the committee's recommendations and their explanations for them can be found at Securities and Exchange Commission, "Advisory Committee on Tender Offers," 7–60.

51. The recommendation (#13) that would strengthen disclosure requirements would force anyone who had acquired 5 percent of a company to immediately file paperwork with the SEC identifying themselves and stating their purpose for acquiring shares in the company. The recommendations designed to limit defensive tactics included: mandatory shareholder advisory votes (#37), a ban on "golden parachutes" during a takeover contest (#38), a ban on companies buying back their own shares during a takeover fight (#39), a requirement that shareholders approve any additional stock issues meant to dilute a company's holdings during a takeover fight (#41), and a requirement that shareholders approve any attempt a target company made to purchase back shares from a raider at an inflated price ("greenmail") during a takeover contest (#43).

52. Recommendations 4, 9, 34, and 35.

53. Arthur Goldberg, in Securities and Exchange Commission, "Advisory Committee on Tender Offers," 126.

54. Frank Easterbrook and Gregg Jarrell, in Securities and Exchange Commission, "Advisory Committee on Tender Offers," 70–121.

55. Vise and Coll, *Eagle on the Street*, 174.

56. For Rodino's bill, see "Hostile Takeovers," *Congressional Record* 130 (1984), 5529–30. For Specter's bill, see The Corporate Distribution Tax Reform Act of 1984, S. 2447, and Amendment to the Securities Exchange Act of 1934 Relating to Tender Offers, S. 2448, *Congressional Record* 130 (1984), 5884–89.

57. For more on Wirth, see Tolchin, "Democratic 'Gang of Five' Reflect New Party Priorities"; Dionne, "Greening of Democrats." For more on the "Atari Democrats" and the transformations within the Democratic Party during the 1970s and 1980s, see Stein, *Pivotal Decade*, 270–71; Geismer, *Don't Blame Us*. For letters sent to Wirth's subcommittee, see US House of Representatives, Subcommittee on Telecommunications, Consumer Protection, and Finance, *Takeover Tactics and Public Policy*, Appendix to Hearings (HRG-1984-HEC-0033, March 28, May 23, 1984).

58. Stephen Halpert to William Niskanen, March 23, 1984, Council of Economic Advisors, Memorandum, SEC-VMA, https://3197d6d14b5f19f2f440-5e13d29c4c01 6cf96cbbfd197c579b45.ssl.cf1.rackcdn.com/collection/papers/1980/1984_0323_Ni skanenHalpert.pdf, 1.

59. Tender Offer Reform Act of 1984 (Version 1) H.R. 5693, 98th Cong. (1984), text in: US House of Representatives, Subcommittee on Telecommunications, Consumer Protection, and Finance, *Takeover Tactics and Public Policy*, Hearings (HRG-1984-HEC-0032, March 28, May 23, 1984), 216–221; A Bill to Amend the Securities Exchange Act of 1938 to Prohibit Acquisitions of Corporate Control Except by Means of Tender Offers for All Outstanding Shares (Version 1), H.R. 5964, 98th Cong. (1984), text in: *Takeover Tactics and Public Policy*, Hearings, 222–26; A Bill to Permit Shareholders and the Securities and Exchange Commission to Seek Injunctive Relief from Harmful Defensive Tactics by Management in Corporate Takeover Situations" (Version 1), H.R. 5695, 98th Cong. (1984), text in: *Takeover Tactics and Public Policy*, Hearings, 227–28.

60. Two-tiered offers set two different prices for shares depending on when shareholders sold. The first tier, which offered a higher price, covered all shareholders who sold up to the point when a purchaser obtained control over the company. The second tier covered all the shareholders who sold after a bidder had already obtained control. Two-tiered offers were designed to incentivize shareholders to sell as soon as possible so that they would not lose out on the higher price.

61. Timothy Wirth, in *Takeover Tactics and Public Policy*, Hearings, 201–2.

62. Paul H. Elicker, in *Takeover Tactics and Public Policy*, Hearings, 233–73.

NOTES TO PAGES 91–94   211

63. Charles Munger, in *Takeover Tactics and Public Policy*, Hearings, 295.
64. Felix Rohatyn, in *Takeover Tactics and Public Policy*, Hearings, 314–17.
65. Irwin L. Jacobs, in *Takeover Tactics and Public Policy*, Hearings, 467–79.
66. Anthony J. Celebrezze Jr., in *Takeover Tactics and Public Policy*, Hearings, 435–45.
67. Stephen Brobeck, in *Takeover Tactics and Public Policy*, Hearings, 371–72.
68. *Wall Street Journal*, "Washington Wire."
69. John S. R. Shad, "The Leveraging of America," advance text of address to New York Financial Writers, June 7, 1984, SEC-VMA, https://3197d6d14b5f19f2f440-5e13d29c4c016cf96cbbfd197c579b45.ssl.cf1.rackcdn.com/collection/papers/1980/1984_0607_LeveragingShad.pdf, 1.
70. Vise and Coll, *Eagle on the Street*, 186.
71. Shad, "Leveraging of America," 1.
72. Shad, 4.
73. Shad, 4.
74. Shad, 3.
75. Vise and Coll, *Eagle on the Street*, 188; for an example, see John Shad to James A. Baker III, June 14, 1984, SEC-VMA, https://3197d6d14b5f19f2f440-5e13d29c4c016cf96cbbfd197c579b45.ssl.cf1.rackcdn.com/collection/papers/1980/1984_0614_BakerShadLeveraging.pdf.
76. Vise and Coll, *Eagle on the Street*, 189.
77. For the text of the bill, see "Equity in Foreign and Domestic Credit Act" (Version 2), H.R. 5693, 98th Cong. (1984).
78. Meeting of Cabinet Council on Economic Affairs, June 28, 1984, SEC-VMA, https://3197d6d14b5f19f2f440-5e13d29c4c016cf96cbbfd197c579b45.ssl.cf1.rackcdn.com/collection/papers/1980/1984_0628_MinutesCouncil.pdf.
79. Medvetz, *Think Tanks in America*, 147.
80. Meeting of Cabinet Council on Economic Affairs, July 19, 1984, SEC-VMA, https://3197d6d14b5f19f2f440-5e13d29c4c016cf96cbbfd197c579b45.ssl.cf1.rackcdn.com/collection/papers/1980/1984_0719_MinutesEconomic.pdf.
81. Jarrell's campaign to change Shad's thinking is detailed at length in Vise and Coll, *Eagle on the Street*, 191–206.
82. Vise and Coll, 198.
83. Gregg Jarrell, "The Impact of Targeted Share Repurchases (Greenmail) on Stock Prices," September 11, 1984, SEC-VMA, https://3197d6d14b5f19f2f440-5e13d29c4c016cf96cbbfd197c579b45.ssl.cf1.rackcdn.com/collection/papers/1980/1984_0911_ImpactGreenmailT.pdf; Robert Comment, Gregg Jarrell, Hugh Haworth, and Annette Poulsen, "The Economics of Any-or-All, Partial, or Two-Tier Tender Offers," April 19, 1985, SEC-VMA, https://3197d6d14b5f19f2f440-5e13d29c4c016cf96cbbfd197c579b45.ssl.cf1.rackcdn.com/collection/papers/1980/1985_0419_TwoTierEconomist.pdf; Gregg Jarrell, Ken Lehn, and Wayne Marr, "Institutional Ownership, Tender Offers, and Long-Term Investments," April 19,

1985, SEC-VMA, https://3197d6d14b5f19f2f440-5e13d29c4c016cf96cbbfd197c579 b45.ssl.cf1.rackcdn.com/collection/papers/1980/1985_0419_TenderEconomist.pdf; Office of the Chief Economist, "Adoption of Poison Pills and Impact on Shareholder Wealth," May 17, 1985, SEC-VMA, https://3197d6d14b5f19f2f440-5e13d 29c4c016cf96cbbfd197c579b45.ssl.cf1.rackcdn.com/collection/papers/1980/1985 _0517_PoisonEconomist.pdf.

84. Scheibla, "Greenmail Debate Heats Up."
85. Vise and Coll, *Eagle on the Street*, 184.
86. For a full account of Jarrell's pro-takeover work within the SEC, see Vise and Coll, 191–206.
87. Jensen, "Takeovers: Folklore and Science."
88. Jensen, 112.
89. Jensen, 119.
90. US House, Subcommittee on Telecommunications, Consumer Protection, and Finance, *Corporate Takeovers (Part 1)*, Hearing (HRG-1985-HEC-0088, February 27, March 12, April 23, May 22, 1985), 87.
91. The formula for FCF is as follows: Free Cash Flow = Cash Flow from Operations — Capital Expenditures.
92. Jensen, "Agency Cost of Free Cash Flow."
93. Jensen, "How to Detect a Prime Takeover Target."
94. Jensen, "Free Cash Flow Theory of Takeovers."
95. Committee on Energy and Commerce, Equity in Foreign and Domestic Credit and Tender Offer Reform, H.R. Rep. No. 1028, to accompany H.R. 5693 (1984), including Cost Estimate of the Congressional Budget Office.
96. John Shad to John Dingell, September 7, 1984, in H.R. Rep. 1028 (1984), 33.
97. John Shad to Alphonse D'Amato, September 7, 1984, SEC-VMA, https://3197d6d14b5f19f2f440-5e13d29c4c016cf96cbbfd197c579b45.ssl.cf1 .rackcdn.com/collection/papers/1980/1984_0907_DAmatoShad.pdf.
98. US Senate, Committee on Banking, Housing, and Urban Affairs, *Tender Offer Practices and Corporate Director Responsibilities*, Hearing (S. Hrg. 98–1013, October 2, 1984), 133.
99. Alphonse D'Amato, in *Tender Offer Practices*, 3.
100. Senators Arlen Specter (R-PA), John Chaffee (R-RI), and Howard Metzenbaum (D-OH) all introduced or discussed legislative proposals in this hearing. For Specter's bill, see *Tender Offer Practices*, 143–45; for Chaffee's bill, see *Tender Offer Practices*, 146–47; for Metzenbaum's proposals, see *Tender Offer Practices*, 10–12. For the end of reform efforts in the 98th Congress, see *Wall Street Journal*, "House Won't Take Up Tender-Offer Measure."
101. For more on Milken, see Bruck, *Predators' Ball*.
102. For a summary of the Phillips takeover battles, see DeMott, Griggs, and Ungeheuer, "High Price of Freedom"; Bruck, *Predators' Ball*, 163–69.
103. Ehrbar and Carson, "Have Takeovers Gone Too Far?"

104. Council of Economic Advisors, *Economic Report of the President* (Washington, DC: Government Printing Office, 1985), 212–13.

105. Gramm, *Dear Chairman*, 69–94.

106. Ehrbar and Carson, "Have Takeovers Gone Too Far?"; *Chicago Tribune*, "House Panel to Use Phillips Battle."

107. For the Chamber of Commerce, see Andrew Seigler, US House of Representatives, Subcommittee on Telecommunications, Consumer Protection, and Finance, *Corporate Takeovers (Part 2)*, Hearing (HRG-1985-HEC-0089, May 23, June 12, October 24, 1985), 195–211. For the National Association of Manufacturers, see Paul H. Elickler, in *Corporate Takeovers (Part 2)*, 212–30. For the AFL-CIO, see Wayne E. Glenn, in *Corporate Takeovers (Part 2)*, 295–316. For Warren Buffet, see Brooks, *Takeover Game*, 268. For Felix Rohatyn, see Felix Rohatyn, US Senate, Committee on Banking, Housing, and Urban Affairs, *Impact of Corporate Takeovers*, Hearing (S. Hrg. 99-187, April 3–4, June 6, June 12, 1985), 668–88.

108. *Corporate Takeovers (Part 1)*, 529–90.

109. Brooks, *Takeover Game*, 268–69.

110. Council of Economic Advisors, *Economic Report of the President*, 187–216.

111. Brooks, *Takeover Game*, 226.

112. Council of Economic Advisors, *Economic Report of the President*, 204.

113. For Jensen's prepared statement, see Michael Jensen, in *Corporate Takeovers (Part 1)*, 228–41; for Jensen's comment on the term "raiders," see *Corporate Takeovers (Part 1)*, 273.

114. Jensen, in *Corporate Takeovers (Part 1)*, 274.

115. Timothy Wirth, in *Corporate Takeovers (Part 1)*, 275.

116. Ingersoll, "SEC Won't Propose Major Bill"; *New York Times*, "S.E.C. Refuses to Curb Anti-Takeover Actions."

117. Miller, "Let's Reduce Regulations on Takeovers."

118. Baumgartner et al., *Lobbying and Policy Change*.

119. Pierson and Hacker, *Winner-Take-All Politics*, 43–44.

120. Phillips-Fein, *Invisible Hands*, 185–269; Jacobs, "Politics of Environmental Regulation"; Waterhouse, *Lobbying America*; Drutman, *Business of America Is Lobbying*; Delton, *The Industrialists*, 237–313; Blyth, *Great Transformations*, 152–201; Katz, *Influence Machine*.

121. Fourcade and Khurana, "Social Trajectory of a Finance Professor," 368–74.

122. McCraw and Cruikshank, *Intellectual Venture Capitalist*, 163.

123. Khurana, *From Higher Aims to Hired Hands*, 307–8.

124. McDonald, *Golden Passport*, 365–71.

125. Jensen published a series of four documents related to the CCMO course on his SSRN page. The documents include a detailed history of the course, a series of course notes used to instruct new faculty on how to teach the course, a packet of course slides and class material, and a set of practice questions for students: Jensen et al., "Organizations and Markets: History and Development"; Jensen and

Meckling, "Coordination, Control, and the Management of Organizations: Course Notes"; Wruck and Jensen, "Coordination, Control, and the Management of Organizations: Course Content"; and Jensen et al., "Coordination, Control, and the Management of Organizations: Practice Questions."

126. Jensen et al., "Organizations and Markets: History and Development," 4–5.

127. Jensen et al., 6.

128. Jensen and Meckling, "Coordination, Control, and the Management of Organizations: Course Notes."

129. Jensen et al., "Organizations and Markets: History and Development," 8.

130. Jensen et al., 27.

131. Jensen et al., 14–15; for an example syllabus, see Wruck and Jensen, "Coordination, Control, and the Management of Organizations: Course Content," 3–5.

132. For an example syllabus, see Wruck and Jensen, 6–7.

133. Jensen et al., "Organizations and Markets: History and Development," 13–14; for an example syllabus, see Wruck and Jensen, 8–11.

134. Jensen et al., "Organizations and Markets: History and Development," 8.

135. Jensen et al., 27.

136. Jensen et al., 14–15.

137. Jensen et al., 14–15.

138. Jensen et al., 16.

139. Jensen et al., 5–7.

140. Jensen et al., 11, 27. Jensen began to embrace psychology after he became enamored with EST, a self-help movement started in the 1970s. For more on this, see Fox, *Myth of the Rational Market*, 285. According to Ronald Hansen, Meckling was upset with both Jensen's decision to focus more on outreach than research after moving to Harvard, and his movement away from the EMH. For more, see Fourcade and Khurana, "The Social Trajectory of a Finance Professor," 368–69.

141. Chabrak, "Money Talks," 474–75; Khurana, *From Higher Aims to Hired Hands*, 318–24.

142. Jensen et al., "Organizations and Markets: History and Development," 25.

143. Priem and Rosenstein, "Is Organization Theory Obvious to Practitioners?"

144. Marquis and Tilcsik, "Imprinting," 201.

145. Jung and Shin, "Learning Not to Diversify," 339.

146. Jung and Shin, 355.

147. For more on how theories taught in business school affect managerial behavior, see Ferraro, Pfeffer, and Sutton, "Economics Language and Assumptions"; Ghoshal, "Bad Management Theories Are Destroying Good Management Practices"; Giacalone and Thompson, "Business Ethics and Social Responsibility Education." For how financial theory shapes financial markets, see McKenzie, *An Engine, Not a Camera*; for a psychological explanation of how theoretical knowledge can create ideology, see Schwartz, "Psychology, Idea Technology, and Ideology."

Chapter Five

1. Copeland, Koller, and Murrin, *Valuation*, 96.
2. Little, "How I'm Deconglomerating the Conglomerates."
3. For an overview of this literature, see Cumming, Siegel, and Wright, "Private Equity, Leveraged Buyouts and Governance"; for an academic overview of buyouts in general, see Kaplan and Strömberg, "Leveraged Buyouts and Private Equity"; for a more critical overview of leveraged buyouts, see Appelbaum and Batt, *Private Equity at Work*.
4. Magowan, "Case for LBOs"; Malone, "Characteristics of Smaller Company Leveraged Buyouts"; Baker and Wruck, "Organizational Changes and Value Creation in Leveraged Buyouts"; Lichtenberg and Siegel, "Effects of Leveraged Buyouts"; Zahra, "Corporate Entrepreneurship and Financial Performance"; Baker and Smith, *New Financial Capitalists*; Wright, Hoskisson, and Busenitz, "Firm Rebirth."
5. For a review of these studies, see Cumming, Siegel, and Wright, "Private Equity, Leveraged Buyouts and Governance," 440–51. For examples, see Kaplan, "Effects of Management Buyouts"; Lehn and Poulsen, "Free Cash Flow and Stockholder Gains in Going Private Transactions"; Marais, Schipper, and Smith, "Wealth Effects of Going Private"; Renneboog, Simons, and Wright, "Why Do Public Firms Go Private in the UK?"; Metrick and Yasuda, "Economics of Private Equity Funds"; Braun, Jenkinson, and Stoff, "How Persistent Is Private Equity Performance?"
6. Holland, *When the Machine Stopped*; Burrough and Helyar, *Barbarians at the Gate*; Anders, *Merchants of Debt*; Bartlett, *Money Machine*; Hooke, *Myth of Private Equity*. For more laudatory accounts, see Finkel and Greising, *Masters of Private Equity and Venture Capital*; Carey and Morris, *King of Capital*.
7. Nohria, Dyer, and Dalzell, *Changing Fortunes*, 185; Freyer, "Managerial Capitalism Contested," 442–43; Jacoby, "Finance and Labor," 31; Ho, *Liquidated*, 141–45; Eichar, *Rise and Fall of Corporate Social Responsibility*, 273–74; Cheffins, *Public Company Transformed*, 167–72.
8. Appelbaum and Batt, *Private Equity at Work*, 31–32.
9. Baker and Smith, *New Financial Capitalists*; Anders, *Merchants of Debt*.
10. Baker and Smith, *New Financial Capitalists*, ix–xi.
11. For the authors' defense of KKR, see Baker and Smith, 27–40.
12. The same is true for *Barbarians at the Gate*, the single most famous account of a leveraged buyout fight. Unlike Anders's book, *Barbarians at the Gate* was a reconstruction of one buyout. For the book, see Burrough and Helyar, *Barbarians at the Gate*.
13. Phalon, "Picking Up Cast-Off Companies."
14. For more on conglomerate "cast-offs," see Phalon; Johnson, "To William F. Farley, Firms Nobody Wants Seem Worth Acquiring."
15. The term "The New J. P. Morgans" was used to describe Kravis and Roberts in a *Fortune* magazine "Profile" in 1988. For the profile, see Loomis, "New J. P. Morgans."

16. For details about Kohlberg's early life and career, especially his time in Oregon, see Jerome Kohlberg, interview by Michael O'Rourke, May 19–20, 1999, New York, NY, transcript, Oregon Historical Society, Portland, OR, https://digitalcollections.ohs.org/sr-1229-oral-history-interview-with-jerome-kohlberg-jr-transcript-2.

17. Anders, *Merchants of Debt*, 6; Baker and Smith, *New Financial Capitalists*, 173–74; Ross and Zanders, "How the Champs Do Leveraged Buyouts," 72; Sterngold, "Buyout Pioneer Quitting Fray."

18. Kaufman and Englander, "Kohlberg Kravis Roberts & Co.," 66; Appelbaum and Batt, *Private Equity at Work*, 24.

19. Anders, *Merchants of Debt*, 9–12.

20. Anders, 9–12.

21. For an overview of KKR's business model, see Appelbaum and Batt, *Private Equity at Work*, 23–26; for an in-depth analysis of the general LBO business model, see Appelbaum and Batt, 41–91.

22. Phalon, "Picking Up Cast-Off Companies."

23. Henderson, "Product Portfolio."

24. Baker and Smith, *New Financial Capitalists*, 52–53.

25. Kleinfield, "Kohlberg Collects Companies."

26. Anders, *Merchants of Debt*, 46.

27. Appelbaum and Batt, *Private Equity at Work*, 46.

28. Appelbaum, *Economists' Hour*, 43.

29. Appelbaum and Batt, *Private Equity at Work*, 51–53.

30. For KKR's fees, see Anders, *Merchants of Debt*, 51–52; for industry fees in general, see Appelbaum and Batt, *Private Equity at Work*, 51, 259.

31. Anders, *Merchants of Debt*, 51.

32. Anders, 51; Appelbaum and Batt, *Private Equity at Work*, 52–53.

33. Appelbaum and Batt, 51–53.

34. Anders, *Merchants of Debt*, 73.

35. Metrick and Yasuda, "Economics of Private Equity Funds."

36. Appelbaum and Batt, *Private Equity at Work*, 44–45.

37. For background information on Houdaille, see Holland, "How to Kill a Company."

38. Holland.

39. Metz, "Takeover Hope and Houdaille."

40. *Wall Street Journal*, "Houdaille Announces Financing Cleared."

41. Appelbaum and Batt, *Private Equity at Work*, 25.

42. *Wall Street Journal*, "Houdaille Agrees to Be Purchased."

43. Anders, *Merchants of Debt*, 35.

44. Appelbaum and Batt, *Private Equity at Work*, 73–80.

45. Anders, *Merchants of Debt*, 33–34; Appelbaum and Batt, 25.

46. Appelbaum and Batt, 25.

47. Passell, "How to Defuse the Buyout Bomb"; Easton, "Buyouts"; Reich, "Leveraged Buyouts"; Rosenbaum, "Corporate-Tax Shortfall in Dispute."

48. Holland, "How to Kill a Company." O'Reilly's reorganization of Houdaille into a more focused company was an early example of the broader shift in corporate strategy away from diversified conglomerates and toward smaller companies that focused on their "core competencies." For an articulation of the core competencies strategy, see Prahalad and Hamel, "Core Competence of the Corporation"; for more on core competencies, see Nohria, Dyer, and Dalzell, *Changing Fortunes*, 81; Nippa, Pidun, and Rubner, "Corporate Portfolio Management," 52–53; Cheffins, *Public Company Transformed*, 167–68.

49. For Houdaille's divestiture of its machine tools business, see Risen, "Houdaille to Drop Machine Tools"; for job losses, see Holland, "How to Kill a Company."

50. Holland, "How to Kill a Company."

51. Truell, "TI to Acquire Houdaille from Kohlberg."

52. Holland, "How to Kill a Company"; Anders, *Merchants of Debt*, 197.

53. Appelbaum and Batt, *Private Equity at Work*, 26.

54. Baker and Smith, *New Financial Capitalists*, 22.

55. Anders, *Merchants of Debt*, 35–38.

56. Shorter, "Leveraged Buyouts," 1–2.

57. Shorter, 2.

58. Coffee, "Shareholders Versus Managers," 52–60; Securities Industry Association, "Position Paper, Leveraged Buyouts, May 9, 1989," in US House of Representatives, Subcommittee on Telecommunications and Finance, *Management and Leveraged Buyouts*, Hearings (HRG-1989-HEC-0047, February 22, May 25, 1989), 154–57; Cheffins, *Public Company Transformed*, 167.

59. Davis, Diekmann, and Tinsley, "Decline and Fall of the Conglomerate Firm," 562.

60. Shorter, "Leveraged Buyouts," 2.

61. Cheffins, *Public Company Transformed*, 169.

62. Burrough and Helyar, *Barbarians at the Gate*; for a review of the film, see Rosenberg, "Who Knew Greed Could Be So Fun?"

63. Shleifer and Vishny, "Takeover Wave of the 1980s," 746.

64. Baker and Smith, *New Financial Capitalists*, 26–27; Cheffins, *Public Company Transformed*, 162–72.

65. Kaufman and Englander, "Kohlberg Kravis Roberts & Co."; Appelbaum and Batt, *Private Equity at Work*, 23.

66. For details of the Fred Meyer buyout, see Jerome Kohlberg, interview by Michael O'Rourke, 30–41. For the importance of pension funds in general, see Bartlett, "Gambling with the Big Boys"; Nohria, Dyer, and Dalzell, *Changing Fortunes*, 185.

67. Loomis, "Buyout Kings," 55–56.

68. Hill and Williams, "Leveraged Purchases of Firms Keep Gaining"; for a timeline of major buyout activity in 1983, see *Wall Street Journal*, "Robust Economy and Buyout Boom."

69. For criticism of buyouts, see Thomas, "Free Ride for Management Insiders"; Bleakley, "Surge in Company Takeovers"; Redwood, "Too Much Greed." For a defense of buyouts that concedes the role greed played in motivating them, see Gipson, "Leveraged Buyouts and Greed."

70. For details of Pickens's takeover attempt, see Yemma, "Showdown at Gulf Oil."

71. Williams, "King of the Buyouts."

72. For a recap of the full Gulf story, see Salmans, "Gulf's Defeat and Its Lessons."

73. For an in-depth look at Milken's junk bond operation, see Bruck, *Predators' Ball*.

74. Anders, *Merchants of Debt*, 87–88.

75. Anders, 88–94.

76. Baker and Smith, *New Financial Capitalists*, 83; Kaufman and Englander, "Kohlberg Kravis Roberts & Co.," 65.

77. Anders, *Merchants of Debt*, 135.

78. Anders, 99.

79. Coll, "Henry Kravis Turns Buyouts into Empire Worth Billions."

80. Anders, *Merchants of Debt*, 134–38.

81. Anders, 150–52.

82. Sterngold, "Buyout Pioneer Quitting Fray."

83. Sterngold.

84. Kaplan and Stein, "Evolution of Buyout Pricing and Financial Structure."

85. For the full story of the RJR Nabisco buyout, see Burrough and Helyar, *Barbarians at the Gate*; for the amount KKR contributed to the RJR Nabisco buyout, see Knight, "KKR Using Only $15 Million."

86. Wallace, "All Dressed Up."

87. Wallace.

88. Jensen, "Eclipse of the Public Corporation."

89. For the term "LBO associations," see Jensen, "Active Investors, LBOs"; Baker and Smith, *New Financial Capitalists*, 42–43.

90. Lemann, *Transaction Man*, 117.

91. For the modern private equity industry, see Appelbaum and Batt, *Private Equity at Work*; Witte and Brown, "New Equilibrium"; Protess and Bevacqua, "Primer on Private Equity."

92. Jensen, "Free Cash Flow Theory of Takeovers," 114.

93. Jensen, 115.

94. Jensen, 115.

95. Jensen, 115.

96. Jensen, 121.

97. Jensen, "Active Investors, LBOs"; Jensen, "Eclipse of the Public Corporation."

98. Jensen, "Eclipse of the Public Corporation," 61.

99. Jensen, 63–64.
100. Jensen, 66.
101. Jensen, 68.
102. Jensen, 65.
103. Jensen, 70.
104. Jensen, 71.
105. For the trend of LBO firms taking their acquisitions public again after only a short time, see Anders, "Another Round"; Hector, "Are Shareholders Cheated by LBOs?"
106. Jensen, "Eclipse of the Public Corporation," 72.
107. Lemann, *Transaction Man*, 128.
108. Jensen, "Eclipse of the Public Corporation," 72.
109. Jensen, "Modern Industrial Revolution, Exit."
110. Lemann, *Transaction Man*, 130.
111. For Jensen's bad timing and an overview of why the buyout market crashed, see Cheffins, *Public Company Transformed*, 172–80.
112. Jensen, "Active Investors, LBOs," 43.
113. For Milken's downfall, see Bruck, *Predators' Ball*, 317–59.
114. Hector, "Junk's Bad Times."
115. Smith, "Leveraged Buy-Out Funds."
116. Holusha, "Revco Drugstore Chain in Bankruptcy Filing"; Vise and Mufson, "Defaults Add to Burden of Buyouts"; Taylor, "Crime? Greed? Big Ideas?," 42; Norris, "Win or Lose"; Kaplan and Stein, "Evolution of Buyout Pricing and Financial Structure."
117. Sloan, "KKR and the Big Leveraged Buyout"; Smith and Shapiro, "KKR's Luster Dims."
118. Smith and Shapiro, 195–203.
119. Smith and Shapiro.
120. For similar shifts in strategy by other LBO firms, see Wallace, "Leveraged Buyout Leader Shifts Attention."
121. Reilly, McCurdy, and Chell, "KKR's Course Correction."
122. Eichenwald, "Kohlberg, Kravis Rouses Itself."
123. Mulligan, "KKR to Buy Borden." KKR's acquisition of Borden did not stay friendly for long. A little more than a year after KKR acquired Borden, the firm ousted Borden's CEO, Ervin Shames, because of his initial opposition to the LBO. For Shames's ouster, see Collins, "Kohlberg, Kravis Ousts Borden Chief Executive."
124. Collins, "Kohlberg, Kravis Plans to Divest Remaining Stake."
125. Dow Jones News Service, "Kohlberg Plans Stake in Spalding and Evenflo"; Burko, "Buyout Giant Bets on Day Care"; Bloomberg News, "Kohlberg Kravis Said to Seek Deal"; Steinmetz, "Kohlberg Kravis to Buy Shoppers Drug Mart."
126. Baker and Smith, *New Financial Capitalists*, 194.

127. Appelbaum and Batt, *Private Equity at Work*, 31.

128. For an overview of the private equity industry in the present day, see the *New York Times*'s five-part series, "Bottom Line Nation," which was originally published in 2016. For all parts of the series, see *New York Times*, "Bottom Line Nation."

129. For the IPOs of the three largest private equity firms, see Sorkin, "Blackstone Group Goes Public"; Heath, "Carlyle IPO"; Creswell, "After Years of Anticipation."

130. Appelbaum and Batt, *Private Equity at Work*, 46.

131. Lemann, *Transaction Man*, 128.

132. Loomis, "Buyout Kings."

133. Fromson, "Life After Debt."

134. Reimann, *Managing for Value*; Goold and Luchs, "Why Diversify?," 13–14; Kiechel, *Lords of Strategy*, 212–13.

135. Stewart, *Quest for Value*, xvii–xxiii.

136. Sean Delehanty, telephone interview with G. Bennet Stewart III, March 8, 2021. A recording of the phone interview and interview notes are in the author's possession.

137. The formula for EVA is as follows: EVA = Net Operating Profit After Taxes − (Invested Capital × Weighted Cost of Capital). As noted, EVA was a brand name for the type of economic profit analysis Stern Stewart's consultants performed. In mathematical terms EVA and economic profit are equivalent. This article will use the term EVA due to its wide popularity and frequent appearance in contemporary press accounts.

138. For a conceptual overview of this concept, see Stern, Shiely, and Ross, *EVA Challenge*, 15–26; for an in-depth guide, see Stewart, *Quest for Value*.

139. The cost of equity capital (stocks) is notoriously difficult to estimate; most firms use either a market index or an index of similar firms when making this estimation.

140. Stern, "Let's Abandon Earnings per Share"; Stern, "Earnings per Share Don't Count"; Serwer, "Cashing In on Cash Flow."

141. Jensen, "Eclipse of the Public Corporation," 66.

142. Useem, *Investor Capitalism*; Englander and Kaufman, "End of Managerial Ideology," 427; Cheffins, *Public Company Transformed*, 223–34.

143. Nohria, Dyer, and Dalzell, *Changing Fortunes*, 191–94; Cheffins, *Public Company Transformed*, 242–47.

144. Sean Delehanty, telephone interview with Tim Koller, March 16, 2021. A recording of the phone interview and interview notes are in the author's possession.

145. Ehrbar, *EVA*, 25–26.

146. Sean Delehanty, telephone interview with G. Bennet Stewart III.

147. Briggs & Stratton, *1991 Annual Report* (Wauwatosa, WI: Briggs & Stratton Corporation, 1991), 2.

148. Ehrbar, *EVA*, 30–31. Shiely's mantra was similar to the policy of Jack Welch, the CEO of General Electric, to sell any business that was not either first or second in its market category. For more on Welch, see Wartzman, *End of Loyalty*.

149. For layoffs between 1988 and 1992, see Fauber, "Will the 1990s Be the Decade of Prosperity Without Jobs?"

150. Romell, "Workdays Shortened at Briggs & Stratton"; for more on labor's worries about "focus factories," see Gunn, "Labor Tensions at Briggs Keep Escalating."

151. Fauber, "Briggs Outlines Position on Future of Jobs Here."

152. Sandler, "Much of Engine Work Moving Out of Area."

153. Stern, Shiely, and Ross, *EVA Challenge*, 107–13.

154. Briggs & Stratton, *1995 Annual Report* (Wauwatosa, WI: Briggs & Stratton Corporation, 1995), 32–33.

155. Stern, Shiely, and Ross, *EVA Challenge*; for the work Briggs and Stratton executives did to spread the word about EVA in the Milwaukee area, see Fauber, "EVA."

156. Engel, "Record Briggs Profit Sharing Up 98% to $25.8 Million."

157. Sharma-Jensen, "EVA Means More for All, Briggs President Says."

158. For Briggs and Stratton's position as the region's largest private-sector employer, see Fauber and Gunn, "Who's to Blame?"; for costs to the community, see Sandler, "Much of Engine Work Moving Out of Area"; for displaced workers, see Wirpsa, "Briggs & Stratton Layoffs Tear Family Hopes."

159. Sean Delehanty, telephone interview with Tim Koller.

160. Copeland, Koller, and Murrin, *Valuation*; *The Economist*, "Analyse This."

161. Kiechel, *Lords of Strategy*, 212.

162. Sean Delehanty, telephone interview with G. Bennet Stewart III.

163. Lieber, "Stern Stewart and KPMG Go to War."

Chapter Six

1. Wines, "Bush Collapses at State Dinner with the Japanese."

2. Abramson and Chipello, "High Pay of CEOs Traveling with Bush Touches a Nerve in Asia."

3. Gigot, "Executive Pay—an Embarrassment to Free Marketers."

4. Abramson and Chipello, "High Pay of CEOs Traveling with Bush Touches a Nerve in Asia."

5. Birnbaum, "From Quayle to Clinton, Politicians Are Pouncing."

6. Bennett, "Pay for Performance."

7. Murphy, "Executive Compensation," 72–88; Dorff, *Indispensable and Other Myths*, 81–82.

8. For the history of the tech sector in Silicon Valley, see O'Mara, *Cities of*

Knowledge; O'Mara, *The Code*; Lecuyer, *Making Silicon Valley*; for the history of the Route 128 tech sector, see Geismer, *Don't Blame Us*; for more on the "new economy," see Turner, *From Counterculture to Cyberculture*; Benke, *Risk and Ruin*, 104–6; Thrift, *Knowing Capitalism*, 112–19; Lazonick, "Innovative Business Models and Varieties of Capitalism"; Nohria, Dyer, and Dalzell, *Changing Fortunes*, ix.

9. Hyman, *Temp*, 210–54.
10. Lieberman, "Stock Options—America's Equity Edge."
11. For more on Clinton's alliance with the tech sector, see Cowan, "High Pay in High-Tech Field"; Harlan, "Accounting Proposal Stirs Unusual Uproar"; for more on the rise of suburban liberals in the Democratic Party, see Geismer, *Don't Blame Us*.
12. Porter, "Capital Disadvantage"; Drucker, "Reckoning with the Pension Fund Revolution."
13. Cowan, "The Gadfly C.E.O.s Want to Swat"; Dorff, *Indispensable and Other Myths*, 93; Murphy, "Executive Compensation," 71; for criticisms of Crystal, see Brownstein and Panner, "Who Should Set CEO Pay?"
14. Colvin and Harrington, "Great CEO Pay Heist"; Reuters, "Eisner Pay Is 68% of Profit."
15. McCartney, "Quoth the Maven."
16. Crystal, *In Search of Excess*.
17. McCartney, "Quoth the Maven."
18. Crystal, *In Search of Excess*, 214–40; Williams, "Why Chief Executives' Pay Keeps Rising."
19. Cowan, "Gadfly C.E.O.s Want to Swat."
20. McCartney, "Quoth the Maven."
21. For an example of Crystal's survey, see Crystal, "How Much CEOs Really Make."
22. McCartney, "Quoth the Maven"; Cowan, "Gadfly C.E.O.s Want to Swat."
23. Jensen and Meckling, "Theory of the Firm."
24. Fox, *Myth of the Rational Market*, 274–75.
25. Murphy and Jensen, "Beware the Self-Serving Critics"; Cuff, "Those Well-Paid Executives"; Murphy, "Top Executives Are Worth Every Nickel"; for more on the idea of the "managerial labor market," see Jensen and Ruback, "Market for Corporate Control"; Fama, "Agency Problems."
26. Jensen and Murphy, "CEO Incentives."
27. Fox, *Myth of the Rational Market*, 275.
28. Kiechel, *Lords of Strategy*, 242–43.
29. Jensen and Murphy, "CEO Incentives," 138.
30. Jensen and Murphy, 140.
31. Stern, "Let's Abandon Earnings Per Share"; Rappaport, *Creating Shareholder Value*, 174–81; Stewart, *Quest for Value*, 1–15.
32. Bennett, "Voices of Protest."

33. Jensen and Murphy, "CEO Incentives," 138.

34. Monks and Minow, *Power and Accountability*; Lublin, "Compensation Panels Get More Assertive"; Fuchsberg, "Investors May Seek Vote"; Lublin, "Panel Adopts a Tough Line"; Pulliam, "Paramount Is Targeted"; Useem, *Investor Capitalism*; Cheffins, *Public Company Transformed*, 240–52.

35. Minow, "Executive Pay and Accountability."

36. Malott and Whitworth, "Talking About Pay."

37. Tumulty, "CEO Pay Raises."

38. Frydman and Jenter, "CEO Compensation," 3–5.

39. Crystal, Vincent, and Baig, "Take the Mystery Out of CEO Pay"; Minow, "Executive Pay and Accountability."

40. Wells, "No Man Can Be Worth $1,000,000."

41. Bebchuk and Fried, *Pay Without Performance*, 67.

42. For an example, see Crystal and Gustke, "Seeking the Sense in CEO Pay," 100.

43. Bennett, "Voices of Protest"; Hinden, "Senator Presses for Restrictions."

44. US Senate, Subcommittee on Oversight of Government Management, *SEC and the Issue of Runaway Executive Pay: Hearing Before the Subcommittee on Oversight of Government Management*, S. Hrg. 102–163, 102nd Cong., 1st sess., May 15, 1991.

45. US Senate, *SEC and the Issue of Runaway Executive Pay*, 5.

46. US Senate, *SEC and the Issue of Runaway Executive Pay*, 9–28.

47. US Senate, *SEC and the Issue of Runaway Executive Pay*, 118–20.

48. US Senate, *SEC and the Issue of Runaway Executive Pay*, 44–45.

49. US Senate, *Corporate Pay Responsibility Act*, S. 1198, 102nd Cong., 1st sess., June 4, 1991.

50. US Senate, Subcommittee on Securities, *Shareholder Rights: Hearing Before the Subcommittee on Securities*, 102nd Cong., 1st sess., October 17, 1991.

51. US Senate, *Shareholder Rights*, 62–67.

52. US Senate, *Shareholder Rights*, 87–93.

53. US Senate, *Shareholder Rights*, 98.

54. US Senate, *Shareholder Rights*, 93.

55. Richard C. Breeden, "Draft Press Release: Statement by Richard C. Breeden on Executive Compensation Issues," February 13, 1991, SEC-VMA, https://3197d6d14b5f19f2f440-5e13d29c4c016cf96cbbfd197c579b45.ssl.cf1.rackcdn.com/collection/papers/1990/1992_0213_BreedenCompensationT.pdf; McCartney and Hilzenrath, "SEC to Allow Votes on Executive Pay."

56. Rosenblat, "SEC Orders Disclosure of Executive Pay"; Labaton, "S.E.C. Will Require Fuller Disclosure of Executive Pay."

57. Williams, "Why Chief Executives' Pay Keeps Rising."

58. Colvin and Harrington, "Great CEO Pay Heist"; Dorff, *Indispensable and Other Myths*, 194–96; Cheffins, *Public Company Transformed*, 273; Bank, Cheffins, and Wells, "Executive Pay," 69–71.

59. Ayers, "Clinton Asks Executives"; Siconolfi, "Wall Street Is Upset."
60. Clymer, "Tax Bill Is Passed."
61. Ayers, "Clinton Asks Executives."
62. Siconolfi, "Wall Street Is Upset."
63. Bennett, "Clinton Victory."
64. Lohr, "Avoiding the Clinton Taxman."
65. Lemann, *Transaction Man*, 162.
66. Lewthwaite, "Clinton Targets Business Taxes"; Rosenbaum, "Business Leaders Urged."
67. Wartzman, "Tax Package Gives Holders a Voice."
68. US Congress, Senate, Subcommittee on Taxation, *Executive Compensation: A Hearing Before the Subcommittee on Taxation*, 102nd Cong., Second sess., June 4, 1992, 106–11.
69. Wartzman, "Tax Package Gives Holders a Voice."
70. Bennett, "Voices of Protest."
71. Aigner, "Overtaxing the Executive Stifles Incentive."
72. For the tax law, see 26 U.S.C. §162(m) (1993). For the vote margin on the final bill, see Rosenbaum, "Clinton Wins Approval."
73. Lewthwaite, "Clinton Targets Business Taxes."
74. US House of Representatives, Committee on the Budget, *Omnibus Budget Reconciliation Act of 1993, Report (to Accompany H.R. 2264)*, H. Rep. 103–111, 103rd Cong., 1st sess., 1993, 646.
75. Murphy, "Executive Compensation," 72.
76. Bank, Cheffins, and Wells, "Executive Pay," 70–71; Dorff, *Indispensable and Other Myths*, 82.
77. Harris and Livingstone, "Federal Tax Legislation"; Rose and Wolfram, "Regulating Executive Pay."
78. Murphy, "Executive Compensation," 77–78.
79. Cheffins, *Public Company Transformed*, 225–28.
80. Frydman and Jenter, "CEO Compensation," 5–6; Khurana, *Searching for a Corporate Savior*, 81–82.
81. Murphy, "Executive Compensation," 72.
82. This arrangement is an example of what the historian Brian Balogh has termed the associational state—see Balogh, *Associational State*.
83. SEC Releases, "Statement of Policy on the Establishment and Improving of Accounting Principles and Standards," Accounting Series Release No. 150, December 20, 1973, SEC-VAM (originally, Gerald R. Ford Library), https://3197d6d14b5f19f2f440-5e13d29c4c016cf96cbbfd197c579b45.ssl.cf1.rackcdn.com/collection/papers/1970/1973_1220_SECAccounting.pdf.
84. For an overview of FASB's organizational structure, see "About the FASB."
85. The term "unrestricted" came about as a result of Congress creating, in 1950, a special class of stock options taxed at capital gains rates, which it termed "re-

stricted options." Unless otherwise noted, all the stock options referred to in this chapter are unrestricted options. Bennett, "Executives Will Gain"; Fox, "Next Best Thing to Free Money"; Rappaport, "Economics of Short-Term Performance Obsession," 72–73; Fox, *Myth of the Rational Market*, 279.

86. For a detailed economic case against most executive stock option plans, see Bebchuk and Fried, *Pay Without Performance*; for Crystal's explanation of why he turned against stock options, see Crystal, "At the Top."

87. Stewart and Colodny, "Trouble with Stock Options."

88. For the claim that options did tie pay to performance, see Brindisi, "Why Executive Compensation Programs Go Wrong."

89. Huddart and Lang, "Employee Stock Option Exercises."

90. Ofek and Yermack, "Taking Stock."

91. Ip, "Collars Give Insiders Way."

92. Murphy, "Executive Compensation," 74.

93. Bennett, "Top Dollar"; for more, see Bennett, "A Little Pain and a Lot to Gain."

94. Clifford, *CEO Pay Machine*, 215–20.

95. A good starting point for those interested in the debate over the CEO effect is Lieberson and O'Connor, "Leadership and Organizational Performance."

96. Habib and Ljungqvist, "Firm Value and Managerial Incentives"; Bebchuk and Fried, *Pay Without Performance*, 138.

97. Berenson, *The Number*; Bebchuk and Fried, *Pay Without Performance*, 183–85.

98. Rappaport, "Economics of Short-Term Performance Obsession."

99. Rappaport, 65–66; Fox, *Myth of the Rational Market*, 280.

100. Collingwood, "Earnings Cult."

101. Useem, *Executive Defense*, 1141–44.

102. Cheffins, *Public Company Transformed*, 247–52.

103. For an overview of this history, see US Senate, Subcommittee on the Oversight of Government Management, *Stealth Compensation of Corporate Executives: Federal Treatment of Stock Options, Hearing*, 102nd Cong., 2ond sess., January 31, 1992, 109–20; Murphy, "Executive Compensation," 42–71.

104. *Commissioner v. Smith*, 324 U.S. 177 (1945).

105. US Senate, *Stealth Compensation of Corporate Executives*, 119.

106. Accounting Review Board, "Opinion No. 25: Accounting for Stock Issued to Employees," 1972, https://egrove.olemiss.edu/cgi/viewcontent.cgi?article=1021&context=aicpa_comm.

107. Polsky, "Controlling Executive Compensation Through the Tax Code," 921.

108. Fox, "Amazing Stock Option Sleight of Hand."

109. Bennett, "Hard Times Trim CEO Pay."

110. Black and Scholes, "Pricing of Options and Corporate Liabilities."

111. The creation of Black-Scholes and its influence on financial markets is the subject of McKenzie, *An Engine, Not a Camera*.

112. Serwer, "Payday! Payday!"

113. Miller and Crystal, "Big Bucks for Big Execs"; Fox, *Myth of the Rational Market*, 278–79.
114. Mathews, "Bookkeepers' Billion-Dollar Debate."
115. US Senate, *Stealth Compensation of Corporate Executives*.
116. US Senate, *Stealth Compensation of Corporate Executives*, 42.
117. US Senate, *Stealth Compensation of Corporate Executives*, 45.
118. McCartney, "Accounting Rule Change."
119. Dennis Beresford, interview by James Stocker, April 18, 2011, SEC-VMA, https://3197d6d14b5f19f2f440-5e13d29c4c016cf96cbbfd197c579b45.ssl.cf1.rackcdn.com/collection/oral-histories/20110418_Beresford_Dennis_T.pdf, 41.
120. Grant, "Shareholders Balk at Shift."
121. Stewart and Colodny, "Trouble with Stock Options."
122. McCartney, "Stock Option Windfalls Fuel Debate."
123. US Senate, *Stealth Compensation for Corporate Executives*, 171.
124. John E. Robson, "Remarks by Deputy Secretary of the Treasury John E. Robson," Industrial Biotechnology Association Emerging Company Conference, June 10, 1992, found in J. French Hill, letter to Dennis R. Beresford, June 12, 1992, SEC-VMA, https://3197d6d14b5f19f2f440-5e13d29c4c016cf96cbbfd197c579b45.ssl.cf1.rackcdn.com/collection/papers/1990/1992_0612_HillBeresford.pdf.
125. Baker, "Stock Options"; Akst, "Silicon Valley Fears."
126. Dennis Beresford, "Letter to John Reed," August 28, 1992, SEC-VMA, https://3197d6d14b5f19f2f440-5e13d29c4c016cf96cbbfd197c579b45.ssl.cf1.rackcdn.com/collection/papers/1990/1992_0828_BeresfordReed.pdf.
127. US Senate, *Corporate Executives' Stock Option Accountability Act*, S. 259, 103rd Cong., 1st sess., January 28, 1993.
128. Harlan, "Group Opposes Stock-Option Accounting Plan."
129. "Letter to Dennis R. Beresford," February 17, 1993, SEC-VMA, https://3197d6d14b5f19f2f440-5e13d29c4c016cf96cbbfd197c579b45.ssl.cf1.rackcdn.com/collection/papers/1990/1993_0217_FirmsBeresford.pdf.
130. Harlan, "Group Opposes Stock-Option Accounting Plan."
131. Cowan, "Executives Are Fuming."
132. Lee, "Business Chiefs Try to Derail Proposal"; Cowan, "Methods in Stock Option Madness."
133. For more on CEOs claiming that Black-Scholes was too complicated, see Bennett, "Counting on Options"; for how companies did use Black-Scholes, see Fox, "Amazing Stock Option Sleight of Hand."
134. Harlan, "Accounting Proposal Stirs Unusual Uproar."
135. Ken Hagerty, "Memo to Members and Friends of CAEE," February 1, 1993, SEC-VMA, https://3197d6d14b5f19f2f440-5e13d29c4c016cf96cbbfd197c579b45.ssl.cf1.rackcdn.com/collection/papers/1990/1993_0201_HagertyLevin.pdf.
136. Harlan, "Accounting Proposal Stirs Unusual Uproar."
137. Glassman, "CEOs Unite."

138. *New York Times*, "Stock Options."

139. Cowan, "Stock Option Rule Change."

140. *Equity Expansion Act of 1993*, S. 1175, 103rd Cong., 1st sess., *Congressional Record* 139 pt. 10 14585–91. For the text of the bill, see US Senate, *Equity Expansion Act of 1993*, S. 1175, 103rd Cong., 1st sess., June 29, 1993.

141. Joseph Lieberman, in US Senate, *Equity Expansion Act of 1993*, 14585.

142. Lieberman in US Senate, 14588.

143. Kristof, "Hitting Shareholders Where It Hurts"; Lieberman, "... But They Do Create Good Jobs"; Lee, "Accounting Rule-Making Board's Proposal."

144. Harlan, "Accounting Proposal Stirs Unusual Uproar."

145. Mathews, "Stock Options Rule Fight Escalates."

146. Rowland, "Rare Bird."

147. Fierman and Fefer, "When Will You Get a Raise?"

148. Lieberman, "Options for All Employees."

149. US Senate, Subcommittee on Securities, *Employee Stock Options*, Hearing, 103rd Cong., 1st sess., October 21, 1993.

150. For an example of Beresford using the same defense in the press, see Beresford, "Word from the F.A.S.B. on Stock Options"; Beresford, "In Accounting, Truth Above All."

151. US Senate, *Employee Stock Options*, 62–63.

152. US Senate, *Employee Stock Options*, 66–68.

153. For examples of academic support for FASB, see Johnson, "Stock Options Aren't 'Free' Compensation"; Stangenes, "Accounting Rule Under Fire"; Shiver, "Stock Options for Executives"; Glassman, "CEOs Unite"; Fox, *Myth of the Rational Market*, 279. Academic support was not universal, however; for pro- and anti-FASB sentiments from academics, see Fromson, "Tougher Rule Sought."

154. Stiglitz, "Roaring Nineties," 80.

155. Miller and Crystal, "Big Bucks for Big Execs"; for an expanded version of their argument, see Miller and Crystal, "Case for Expensing Stock Options."

156. Mathews, "Panel Gets an Earful."

157. Fox, "Next Best Thing to Free Money."

158. George Sollman, "Memo to AEA HR Company Contact," March 1, 1994, SEC-VMA, https://3197d6d14b5f19f2f440-5e13d29c4c016cf96cbbfd197c579b45.ssl.cf1.rackcdn.com/collection/papers/1990/1994_0301_SiliconRally.pdf.

159. *San Francisco Chronicle*, "Silicon Valley Workers"; Fox, "Next Best Thing to Free Money."

160. Kaufman, "Area Execs Lash Out."

161. Senator Lieberman (CT), "Amendment No. 1668." *Congressional Record* 140: 51 (May 5, 1994), p. S5028.

162. Lee, "FASB Delays."

163. For Bentsen and Brown, see Harlan, "Accounting Proposal Stirs Unusual Uproar"; for Beese, see Beese, "Rule That Stunts Growth."

164. Cowan, "High Pay in High-Tech Field."

165. Drew Beresford, "Interview with James Stocker," April 18, 2011, SEC-VMA, https://www.sechistorical.org/collection/oral-histories/20110418_Beresford_Dennis_T.pdf, 43; for Levitt's admission of his mistake, see Edmund Jenkins, "Interview with James Stocker," March 16, 2011, SEC-VMA, https://3197d6d14b5f19f2f440-5e13d29c4c016cf96cbbfd197c579b45.ssl.cf1.rackcdn.com/collection/oral-histories/20110316_Jenkins_Edmund_T.pdf, 20.

166. Berton, "Accounting Board to Weigh Softening."

167. Bloomberg Business News, "FASB Pulls Back."

168. Mathews, "Accounting Board Drops Disputed Stock Option Rule."

169. Murphy, "Executive Compensation," 97–100. The decision in 2004 to force companies to expense stock options may be responsible for the rising popularity of restricted stock grants in place of stock options grants. A restricted stock grant provides its holder with shares of a company's stock after a defined vesting period. Restricted stock may be even less tied to performance than stock options since there is no chance that restricted stocks will not have some value upon vesting; for these reasons the economists Lucian Bebchuk and Jesse Fried described restricted stock grants as equivalent to a stock option with an exercise price of $0. For more, see Bebchuk and Fried, *Pay Without Performance*, 171.

170. For an example of this, see US House of Representatives, *A Bill to Amend the Internal Revenue Code of 1986 to Promote the Grant of Incentive Stock Options to Non-Highly Compensated Employees*, H.R. 2788, 105th Cong., 1st sess., October 31, 1997.

171. For continued criticism of executives' pay, see Berger, "CEOs' Wallets Are Well-Stocked"; Yates, "Adding Up Arguments"; for a full-throated defense of high CEO pay, see Kay, "High CEO Pay Helps"; for the change in annual meetings, see Abelson, "Proxy Peace."

172. Boyer, "From Shareholder Value to CEO Power."

173. Holmstrom and Kaplan, "Corporate Governance and Merger Activity," 122.

174. Mathews, "Their Riches Were Your Command."

175. Davis and Wessel, *Prosperity*; Friedman, *The Lexus and the Olive Tree*; for a more measured take on the New Economy, see *The Economist*, "Too Triumphalist by Half."

176. Zuckerman, "Second American Century," 21.

177. For examples of warnings about growing inequality, see Tyson, "Inequality Amid Prosperity"; Aubry, "Income Inequality Still Persists"; Schlessinger, "Americans Feel Rich Get Richer"; Uchitelle, "Surplus Built on Bricks"; for a benign take on inequality, see Kristol, "Income Inequality Without Class Conflict."

178. Business Roundtable, "Statement on Corporate Governance."

179. Coulter, "Managing for Shareholder Value," 68.

180. Hansmann and Kraakman, "End of History for Corporate Law."

181. Hansmann and Kraakman, 440–41.

182. Hansmann and Kraakman, 468.
183. West, "Purpose of the Corporation," 14.
184. Winkler, *We the Corporations*, 247–48.
185. Stout, "On the Rise of Shareholder Primacy," 1178; for similar criticisms, see Gordon, "Rise of Independent Directors," 1529–30; Johnson, "Corporate Law Professors as Gatekeepers."

Conclusion

1. For a historical examination of Enron's rise and fall in the context of the "New Economy" and deregulation, see Benke, *Risk and Ruin*; for a journalistic account of the Enron saga, see McLean and Elkind, *Smartest Guys in the Room*.
2. Benke, *Risk and Ruin*, 138–53.
3. McLean, "Is Enron Overpriced?"
4. Berenson, "Self-Inflicted Wound"; Emshwiller and Smith, "Enron Jolt"; Smith and Emshwiller, "Enron May Issue More Stock."
5. Benke, *Risk and Ruin*, 161.
6. Bragg, "Workers Feel Pain of Layoffs."
7. Zaslow, "How the Former Staff of Arthur Andersen Is Faring."
8. Stein, "World's Most Admired Companies."
9. Healy and Palepu, "Fall of Enron," 13–14.
10. For the full list of Enron's board members, see *The Guardian*, "Enron's Board of Directors"; for the quality and expertise of Enron's board members, see Healy and Palepu, "Fall of Enron," 13.
11. Bratton, "Enron and the Dark Side," 1283–84.
12. Bratton, 1334.
13. Benke, *Risk and Ruin*, 177–90.
14. US Senate, Committee on Governmental Affairs, *Role of the Board of Directors in Enron's Collapse*, S. Prt. 107-70, 107th Cong., 2nd sess. (2002).
15. For a list of corporate "super scandals" in 2001 and 2002, see Cheffins, *Public Company Transformed*, 283–85.
16. Bratton, "Enron and the Dark Side," 1284–85.
17. Romero and Glater, "WorldCom Files for Bankruptcy."
18. Bumiller, "Bush Signs Bill"; Cioffi, *Public Law and Private Power*, 98.
19. Cheffins, *Public Company Transformed*, 290–95.
20. For a detailed treatment of the links between shareholder value maximization and corporate scandals, see Bratton, "Enron and the Dark Side."
21. Jensen and Murphy, "Remuneration," 46; Benke, *Risk and Ruin*, 104–6.
22. Jensen and Murphy, "Remuneration," 47–48; Bratton, "Enron and the Dark Side," 1327–28.
23. Benke, *Risk and Ruin*, 131.

24. Benke, 104.
25. Lemann, *Transaction Man*, 130.
26. Later on, Jensen would be especially disappointed to see major LBO firms such as Blackstone and KKR go public in the later years of the 2000s. Jensen interpreted these firms' decisions to go public as an admission on the part of their leaders that they did not care about agency costs or the separation of ownership and control; instead, they were only interested in making money. For more, see Lemann, 128.
27. Lemann, 128.
28. Fuller and Jensen, "Just Say No to Wall Street."
29. Fuller and Jensen, 42.
30. Jacobs, *Short-Term America*, 37; Rappaport, "CFOs and Strategists," 87; Collingwood, "Earnings Cult"; Rappaport, "Economics of Short-Term Performance Obsession."
31. Jensen and his colleagues who taught the CCMO course at Harvard had already begun to distance themselves from the EMH by 2002. In the 1990s, the group began incorporating elements of behavioral economics into their curricula in an effort to account for "non-rational" behavior. For more, see Jensen et al., "Organizations and Markets: History and Development," 18.
32. Lemann, *Transaction Man*, 123–27.
33. Erhard, Jensen, and Zaffron, "Integrity."
34. Erhard, Jensen, and Zaffron, 16.
35. Erhard, Jensen, and Zaffron, 92.
36. Lemann, *Transaction Man*, 130.
37. McDonald, *Golden Passport*, 378–79; Author's interview with Ronald Hansen on November 10, 2018.
38. US Bureau of Economic Analysis, Corporate Profits After Tax (without IVA and CCAdj) [CP], retrieved from FRED, Federal Reserve Bank of St. Louis; https://fred.stlouisfed.org/series/CP, last accessed December 8, 2024; telephone interview with G. Bennett Stewart III, March 8, 2021.
39. Nohria, Dyer, and Dalzell, *Changing Fortunes*, 196–97.
40. Stewart, "Birth of a New American Aristocracy."
41. Useem, *Executive Defense*, 3.
42. Ilg and Haugen, "Earnings and Employment Trends."
43. Ilg and Haugen, 31.
44. Weil, *Fissured Workplace*; Carnes, "Culture of Work."
45. Tedeschi, "Unemployment Looks Like 2000 Again."
46. Congressional Research Service, "Real Wage Trends." For more on education levels in the American workforce, see "Bachelor's Degree Holders in the Labor Force," National Science Board, Science and Engineering Indicators: State Indicators, accessed July 27, 2020, https://ncses.nsf.gov/indicators/states/indicator/bachelors-degree-holders-in-labor-force.

47. Congressional Research Service, 7–10.

48. Federal Reserve, "Distribution of Household Wealth in the U.S. Since 1989"; for the outsized attention given to the stock market, see Kaissar, "I Ran the Numbers Again"; Phillips, "Repeat After Me."

49. Petrou, "Only the Rich."

50. Hesse, Hofmann, and Weber, "Macroeconomic Effects of Asset Purchases."

51. Petrou, "Only the Rich."

52. Zahn, "Households Plunged into Vicious Cycle."

53. Delton, *The Industrialists*, 15; Stein, *Pivotal Decade*, 6–7.

54. For a defense of shareholder value maximization, see Shinder, "Business Roundtable's Recipe for Confusion"; Bebchuk and Tallarita, "Illusory Promise of Stakeholder Capitalism." For worries about vagueness from critics of contemporary shareholder value maximization, see Winston, "Is the Business Roundtable Statement Just Empty Rhetoric?"; Rappaport, "How CEOs Can Forge a New Kind of Shareholder Value."

55. For a small sample of this literature that was published in the last few years, see Schwab and Vanham, *Stakeholder Capitalism*; Joly and Lambert, *Heart of Business*; Mazzucato, *Mission Economy*; Henderson, *Reimagining Capitalism in a World on Fire*; Marquis, *Better Business*; Benioff and Langley, *Trailblazer*.

56. For business schools, see Goldberg, "Have the Anticapitalists Reached Harvard Business School?"; for Senator Rubio's criticism of shareholder value maximization, see Rubio, "American Investment in the 21st Century."

57. Bykowicz and Au-Yeung, "Conservatives Have a New Rallying Cry."

58. Cutter and Weber, "Companies That Embraced Social Issues"; Bloomberg.com, "ESG Investing Goes Quiet."

59. Rubio is emblematic of the muddled nature of the contemporary debate. Despite his criticisms of shareholder value maximization in 2019, in 2021 he introduced a bill that would allow shareholders to sue managers for promoting socially responsible behavior at the expense of shareholder value. Meyers, "Rubio, Republicans Step Up Attacks."

60. Fox, "Covid Can't Stop Corporate Profits."

61. "Distribution of Household Wealth in the US Since 1989," Board of Governors of the Federal Reserve System, last updated September 20, 2024, https://www.federalreserve.gov/releases/z1/dataviz/dfa/distribute/table/#quarter:126;series:Corporate%20equities%20and%20mutual%20fund%20shares;demographic:networth;population:1,3,5,7;units:shares.

62. For anti-capitalist, pro-redistribution politics on the political right, see Schaffer, "Conservatives Are Having an Epic Argument"; and Tankersly and Duehren, "J. D. Vance Pioneered 'New Right' Economics."

Bibliography

Archives and Collections Consulted

Personal Collection of Ronald Hanson
SEC Virtual Museum and Archive
W. Allen Wallis Papers, University of Rochester River Campus Libraries Rare Books, Special Collections, and Preservation

Oral History Interviews

G. Bennett Stewart III
Tim Kohler
Charles Cox
Ronald Hanson

Periodicals Referenced

Atlantic Monthly
Baltimore Sun
The Banker's Magazine
Barron's
Bloomberg
BusinessWeek
Chicago Tribune
Christian Science Monitor
The Economist
Financial Times
Forbes

Fortune
The Globe and Mail
Harvard Business Review
Institutional Investor
Los Angeles Times
Milwaukee Journal
Milwaukee Journal Sentinel
Milwaukee Sentinel
The Nation
National Catholic Reporter
New Republic
New Yorker
New York Magazine
New York Times
New York Times Magazine
Pensions & Investments
San Francisco Chronicle
San Jose Mercury News
Time
Vital Speeches of the Day
Wall Street Journal
Washington Post

Published Works Referenced

Abele, John J. "Conglomerate Merger Spreads Its Diversified Wings." *New York Times*, May 15, 1967.
Abele, John J. "Yesterday's Darling Is Scorned." *New York Times*, May 31, 1970.
Abelson, Reed. "Proxy Peace." *New York Times*, May 28, 1998.
"About the FASB." Financial Accounting Standards Board. Accessed December 1, 2024. https://www.fasb.org/about-us/about-the-fasb.
Abrams, Frank W. "Management's Responsibilities in a Complex World." *Harvard Business Review* 29, no. 3 (1951): 29–34.
Abramson, Jill, and Christopher Chipello. "High Pay of CEOs Traveling with Bush Touches a Nerve in Asia." *Wall Street Journal*, December 30, 1991.
Aigner, Dennis J. "Overtaxing the Executive Stifles Incentive." *Los Angeles Times*, July 30, 1993.
Akst, Daniel. "Silicon Valley Fears Narrower Pay Options Will Deter Highfliers." *Los Angeles Times*, March 16, 1993.
Alchian, Armen A., and Harold Demsetz. "Production, Information Costs, and Economic Organization." *American Economic Review* 62, no. 5 (1972): 777–95.

Alexander, Charles. "Merger Theater of the Absurd." *Time*, October 4, 1982.
Alliance for Board Diversity. "Missing Pieces Report: The 2018 Board Diversity Census of Women and Minorities on Fortune 500 Boards." Deloitte, 2019. https://www2.deloitte.com/content/dam/Deloitte/us/Documents/center-for-board-effectiveness/us-cbe-missing-pieces-report-2018-board-diversity-census.pdf.
Amadae, S. M. *Rationalizing Capitalist Democracy: The Cold War Origins of Rational Choice Liberalism*. Chicago: University of Chicago Press, 2003.
Amadae, S. M., and Bruce Bueno de Mesquita. "The Rochester School: The Origins of Positive Political Theory." *Annual Review of Political Science* 2 (1999): 269–95.
Amihud, Yakov, and Baruch Lev. "Risk Reduction as a Managerial Motive for Conglomerate Mergers." *Bell Journal of Economics* 12, no. 2 (1981): 605–17.
Anders, George. "Another Round: Many Firms Go Public Within a Few Years of Leveraged Buyout." *Wall Street Journal*, January 2, 1987.
Anders, George. *Merchants of Debt: KKR and the Mortgaging of American Business*. New York: Basic Books, 1992.
Andrews, Kenneth R. "Toward Professionalism in Business Management." *Harvard Business Review* 47, no. 2 (1969): 49–60.
Anthony, Donald. "The Swope Plan." *Social Science* 7, no. 3 (1932): 274–77.
Appelbaum, Binyamin. *The Economists' Hour: False Prophets, Free Markets, and the Fracture of Society*. New York: Little, Brown, 2019.
Appelbaum, Eileen, and Rosemary Batt. *Private Equity at Work: When Wall Street Manages Main Street*. New York: Russell Sage Foundation, 2014.
Arenson, Karen W. "Takeover Game and Its Outlook." *New York Times*, May 17, 1978.
Armour, John, and Brian R. Cheffins. "The Origins of the Market for Corporate Control." Working Paper. ECGI Working Paper Series in Law. Brussels: European Corporate Governance Institute, September 11, 2013.
Arrighi, Giovanni. *The Long Twentieth Century: Money, Power and the Origins of Our Times*. Updated ed. New York: Verso, 2010.
Arrow, Kenneth J. *Social Choice and Individual Values*. New Haven, CT: Yale University Press, 1951.
Ash, Roy L. "Nation Building." *Vital Speeches of the Day* 34, no. 6 (1968).
Aspin, Les. "The Litton Ship Fiasco." *The Nation*, December 11, 1972.
Attiyeh, Robert A. "Where Next for Conglomerates?" *Business Horizons* 12, no. 6 (December 1969): 39.
Aubry, Larry. "Income Inequality Still Persists for Blacks." *Los Angeles Sentinel*, January 30, 1997.
Ayers, B. Drummond, Jr. "Clinton Asks Executives to Accept His Economic Plan." *New York Times*, June 25, 1992, sec. National Report.
Baker, Alisa. "Stock Options—a Perk That Built Silicon Valley." *Wall Street Journal*, June 23, 1992.
Baker, George P., and George David Smith. *The New Financial Capitalists: Kohlberg*

Kravis Roberts and the Creation of Corporate Value. Cambridge: Cambridge University Press, 1998.

Baker, George P., and Karen H. Wruck. "Organizational Changes and Value Creation in Leveraged Buyouts: The Case of the O. M. Scott & Sons Company." *Journal of Financial Economics* 25, no. 2 (December 1989): 163–90.

Balogh, Brian. *The Associational State: American Governance in the Twentieth Century.* Philadelphia: University of Pennsylvania Press, 2015.

Bank, Steven A., Brian Cheffins, and Harwell Wells. "Executive Pay: What Worked?" *Journal of Corporation Law* 42, no. 1 (2016): 59–107.

Barber, Richard J. "Big Government and Big Business." *New Republic*, August 13, 1966.

Bartlett, Sarah. "Gambling with the Big Boys." *New York Times Magazine*, May 5, 1991.

Bartlett, Sarah. *The Money Machine: How KKR Manufactured Power and Profits.* Washington, DC: Beard Books, 2005.

Baumgartner, Frank R., Jeffrey M. Berry, Marie Hojnacki, David C. Kimball, and Beth L. Leech. *Lobbying and Policy Change: Who Wins, Who Loses, and Why.* Chicago: University of Chicago Press, 2009.

Beard, Patricia. *Blue Blood and Mutiny: The Fight for the Soul of Morgan Stanley.* Updated ed. New York: Harper Perennial, 2008.

Bebchuk, Lucian, and Jesse Fried. *Pay Without Performance: The Unfulfilled Promise of Executive Compensation.* Cambridge, MA: Harvard University Press, 2004.

Bebchuk, Lucian, and Roberto Tallarita. "The Illusory Promise of Stakeholder Capitalism." *Cornell Law Review* 106 (2020): 91–178.

Beese, J. Carter. "A Rule That Stunts Growth." *Wall Street Journal*, February 8, 1994.

Belair, Felix, Jr. "Charges of Fraud at Penn Central Are Filed by S.E.C." *New York Times*, May 3, 1974.

Bell, Daniel. *The Coming of Post-Industrial Society.* New York: Basic Books, 1973.

Beniger, James R. *The Control Revolution: Technological and Economic Origins of the Information Society.* Cambridge, MA: Harvard University Press, 1986.

Benioff, Marc. "A Call for Stakeholder Activists." HuffPost, February 2, 2015. https://www.huffpost.com/entry/a-call-for-stakeholder-activists_b_6599000.

Benioff, Marc, and Monica Langley. *Trailblazer: The Power of Business as the Greatest Platform for Change.* New York: Currency, 2019.

Benke, Gavin. *Risk and Ruin: Enron and the Culture of American Capitalism.* Philadelphia: University of Pennsylvania Press, 2018.

Bennett, Amanda. "A Little Pain and a Lot to Gain." *Wall Street Journal*, April 22, 1992.

Bennett, Amanda. "Clinton Victory Wouldn't Slash Top Officer Pay." *Wall Street Journal*, November 3, 1992, sec. Marketplace.

Bennett, Amanda. "Counting on Options." *Wall Street Journal*, April 22, 1992.

Bennett, Amanda. "Executives Will Gain over Time as Lucrative Stock Plans Multiply." *Wall Street Journal*, April 10, 1987.
Bennett, Amanda. "Hard Times Trim CEO Pay." *Wall Street Journal*, April 17, 1991.
Bennett, Amanda. "Pay for Performance." *Wall Street Journal*, April 18, 1990.
Bennett, Amanda. "Top Dollar." *Wall Street Journal*, March 28, 1988.
Bennett, Amanda. "Voices of Protest." *Wall Street Journal*, April 22, 1992, sec. Executive Pay.
Berenson, Alex. "A Self-Inflicted Wound Aggravates Angst over Enron." *New York Times*, September 9, 2001.
Berenson, Alex. *The Number: How the Drive for Quarterly Earnings Corrupted Wall Street and Corporate America*. New York: Random House, 2003.
Beresford, Dennis R. "A Word from the F.A.S.B. on Stock Options." *New York Times*, May 2, 1993.
Beresford, Dennis R. "In Accounting, Truth Above All." *Wall Street Journal*, March 21, 1994.
Berger, Kathy. "CEOs' Wallets Are Well-Stocked: Market Soars, Options' Value Swells; Some Critics Say It's Just Too Much." *Chicago Tribune*, June 2, 1996.
Berle, Adolf A., and Gardiner Means. *The Modern Corporation and Private Property*. 2nd ed. New York: Routledge, 1991.
Berton, Lee. "Accounting Board to Weigh Softening Its Controversial Stock-Option Proposal." *Wall Street Journal*, December 14, 1994.
Berton, Lee. "Accounting Rule-Making Board's Proposal Draws Fire." *Wall Street Journal*, January 5, 1994.
Berton, Lee. "Business Chiefs Try to Derail Proposal on Stock Options." *Wall Street Journal*, February 5, 1993.
Berton, Lee. "FASB Delays for a Year Requirement on Firms Disclosure of Stock Options." *Wall Street Journal*, June 9, 1994.
Bettis, Richard A., and William K. Hall. "Strategic Portfolio Management in the Multibusiness Firm." *California Management Review* 24, no. 1 (1981): 23–38.
Birnbaum, Jeffrey. "From Quayle to Clinton, Politicians Are Pouncing on the Hot Issue of Top Executives' Hefty Salaries." *Wall Street Journal*, January 15, 1992.
Black, Fischer, and Myron Scholes. "The Pricing of Options and Corporate Liabilities." *Journal of Political Economy* 81, no. 3 (1973): 637–54.
Blair, Margaret M., ed. *The Deal Decade: What Takeovers and Leveraged Buyouts Mean for Corporate Governance*. Washington, DC: Brookings Institution Press, 1993.
Bleakley, Fred R. "Surge in Company Takeovers Causes Widespread Concern." *New York Times*, July 3, 1984.
Bloomberg Business News. "FASB Pulls Back Rule on Options." *The Sun*, December 15, 1994.
Bloomberg News. "Kohlberg Kravis Said to Seek Deal for Regal Cinemas Chain." *New York Times*, January 17, 1998.

Bloomberg.com. "ESG Investing Goes Quiet After Blistering Republican Attacks." May 19, 2023. https://www.bloomberg.com/news/articles/2023-05-19/esg-investing-goes-quiet-after-republican-attacks.

Blustein, Paul. "Marietta, Bendix 'Pac-Man' Tactics Cause Concern Among Merger Analysts." *Wall Street Journal*, September 24, 1982.

Blyth, Mark. *Great Transformations: Economic Ideas and Institutional Change in the Twentieth Century*. Cambridge: Cambridge University Press, 2002.

Bork, Robert H. *The Antitrust Paradox: A Policy at War with Itself*. New York: Basic Books, 1978.

Bower, Joseph L., and Lynn S. Paine. "The Error at the Heart of Corporate Leadership." *Harvard Business Review*, May 1, 2017. https://hbr.org/2017/05/the-error-at-the-heart-of-corporate-leadership.

Boyer, Robert. "From Shareholder Value to CEO Power: The Paradox of the 1990s." *Competition and Change* 9, no. 1 (2005): 7–47.

Bradley, Martin. "Nader Defends Federal Chartering." *The Sun* (Baltimore), June 18, 1976.

Bragg, Rick. "Workers Feel Pain of Layoffs and Added Sting of Betrayal." *New York Times*, January 20, 2002.

Bratton, William W. "Enron and the Dark Side of Shareholder Value." *Tulane Law Review* 76 (2002): 1275–1361.

Bratton, William W., and Michael L. Wachter. "Shareholder Primacy's Corporatist Origins: Adolf Berle and the Modern Corporation." *Journal of Corporation Law* 34, no. 1 (2008): 99–152.

Braun, Reiner, Tim Jenkinson, and Ingo Stoff. "How Persistent Is Private Equity Performance? Evidence from Deal-Level Data." *Journal of Financial Economics* 123, no. 2 (2017): 273–91.

Breen, William J. "Foundations, Statistics, and State-Building: Leonard P. Ayres, the Russell Sage Foundation, and U.S. Government Statistics in the First World War." *Business History Review* 68, no. 4 (1994): 451–82.

Brill, Steven. "Two Tough Lawyers in the Tender-Offer Game." *New York Magazine*, June 21, 1976.

Brindisi, Louis, Jr. "Why Executive Compensation Programs Go Wrong." *Wall Street Journal*, June 14, 1982.

Brooks, John. *The Go-Go Years: The Drama and Crashing Finale of Wall Street's Bullish 60s*. New York: Wiley, 1973.

Brooks, John. *The Takeover Game*. New York: Dutton, 1987.

Brooks, John. "Xerox, Xerox, Xerox, Xerox." *New Yorker*, April 1, 1967.

Brownstein, Andrew R., and Morris J. Panner. "Who Should Set CEO Pay? The Press? Congress? Shareholders?" *Harvard Business Review* 70, no. 3 (1992): 28–38.

Bruck, Connie. *The Predators' Ball: The Inside Story of Drexel Burnham and the Rise of the Junk Bond Raiders*. New York: Penguin Books, 1989.

Brunner, Karl. "Knowledge, Values and the Choice of Economic Organization." *Kyklos* 23, no. 3 (1970): 558–80.

Brunner, Karl. "My Quest for Economic Knowledge." In *Economic Analysis and Political Ideology*, vol. 1 of *The Selected Essays of Karl Brunner*, edited by Thomas Lys. Cheltenham, UK: Edward Elgar, 1996.

Brunner, Karl. "Reflections on the Political Economy of Government. The Persistent Growth of Government." *Swiss Journal of Economics and Statistics (SJES)* 114, no. 3 (1978): 649–80.

Buchanan, James M. "The Political Economy of the Franchise in the Welfare State." In *Capitalism and Freedom: Problems and Prospects—Proceedings of a Conference in Honor of Milton Friedman*, edited by Richard T. Selden, 52–91. Charlottesville: University of Virginia Press, 1975.

Bumiller, Elizabeth. "Bush Signs Bill Aimed at Fraud in Corporations." *New York Times*, July 31, 2002.

Burko, Casey. "Buyout Giant Bets on Day Care." *Chicago Tribune*, October 5, 1996.

Burrough, Bryan, and John Helyar. *Barbarians at the Gate: The Fall of RJR Nabisco*. New York: Harper Business, 1990.

Business Roundtable. "Business Roundtable Redefines the Purpose of a Corporation to Promote 'An Economy That Serves All Americans.'" August 19, 2019. https://www.businessroundtable.org/business-roundtable-redefines-the-purpose-of-a-corporation-to-promote-an-economy-that-serves-all-americans.

Business Roundtable. "Statement on Corporate Governance." White paper, September 1997.

BusinessWeek. "Greenhill: A New Takeover Artist." December 14, 1974.

Bykowicz, Julie, and Angel Au-Yeung. "Conservatives Have a New Rallying Cry: Down With ESG." *Wall Street Journal*, February 26, 2023, sec. Markets. https://www.wsj.com/articles/conservatives-have-a-new-rallying-cry-down-with-esg-2ef98725.

Byrne, John A. *The Whiz Kids: The Founding Fathers of American Business—and the Legacy They Left Us*. New York: Doubleday Business, 1993.

Cain, Matthew D., Stephen B. McKeon, and Steven Davidoff Solomon. "Do Takeover Laws Matter? Evidence from Five Decades of Hostile Takeovers." Division of Economic and Risk Analysis Working Paper. Washington, DC: Securities and Exchange Commission, 2014.

Carey, David, and John E. Morris. *King of Capital: The Remarkable Rise, Fall, and Rise Again of Steve Schwarzman and Blackstone*. New York: Currency, 2012.

Carley, William M. "Carl Icahn's Strategies in His Quest for TWA Are a Model for Raiders." *Wall Street Journal*, June 20, 1985.

Carnes, Mark. "The Culture of Work." In *The Columbia History of Post-World War II America*, 106–30. New York: Columbia University Press, 2007.

Chabrak, Nihel. "Money Talks: The Language of the Rochester School." *Accounting, Auditing & Accountability Journal* 25, no. 3 (2012): 452–85.

Chandler, Alfred, Jr. *The Visible Hand: The Managerial Revolution in American Business*. Cambridge, MA: Harvard University Press, 1977.

Chandler, Alfred, Jr. *Scale and Scope: The Dynamics of Industrial Capitalism*. Cambridge, MA: Belknap Press of Harvard University Press, 1994.

Cheffins, Brian R. "Corporate Governance Since the Managerial Capitalism Era." *Business History Review* 89, no. 4 (2015): 717–44.

Cheffins, Brian R. *The Public Company Transformed*. New York: Oxford University Press, 2018.

Chicago Tribune. "House Panel to Use Phillips Battle as Case Study in Probe." February 19, 1985.

Christiansen, Christian. *Progressive Business: An Intellectual History of the Role of Business in American Society*. New York: Oxford University Press, 2015.

Cioffi, John W. *Public Law and Private Power: Corporate Governance Reform in the Age of Finance Capitalism*. Cornell Studies in Political Economy. Ithaca, NY: Cornell University Press, 2010.

Clifford, Steven. *The CEO Pay Machine: How It Trashes America and How to Stop It*. New York: Blue Rider Press, 2017.

Clymer, Adam. "Tax Bill Is Passed by the Democrats and Bush Vetoes It." *New York Times*, March 21, 1992.

CNN Money. "FORTUNE 500: 1969 Archive Full List 1–100." Accessed December 29, 2020. https://money.cnn.com/magazines/fortune/fortune500_archive/full/1969/.

Coase, R. H. "The Nature of the Firm." *Economica* 4, no. 16 (1937): 386–405.

Coffee, John C., Jr. "Shareholders Versus Managers: The Strain in the Corporate Web." *Michigan Law Review* 85, no. 1 (1986): 1–109.

Cohan, William D. *Why Wall Street Matters*. New York: Random House, 2017.

Cole, Robert J. "Final Pact for Bendix and Allied." *New York Times*, September 25, 1982.

Cole, Robert J. "Tight Credit and Takeover." *New York Times*, March 19, 1980.

Coll, Steve. "Henry Kravis Turns Buyouts into Empire Worth Billions." *Washington Post*, December 4, 1988.

Coll, Steve. "Pickens and the Gospel of Gain." *Washington Post*, September 11, 1986.

Collingwood, Harris. "The Earnings Cult." *New York Times Magazine*, June 9, 2002.

Collins, Glenn. "Kohlberg, Kravis Ousts Borden Chief Executive." *New York Times*, January 11, 1995.

Collins, Glenn. "Kohlberg, Kravis Plans to Divest Remaining Stake in RJR Nabisco." *New York Times*, March 16, 1995.

Collins, Robert M. *More: The Politics of Economic Growth in Postwar America*. New York: Oxford University Press, 2002.

Colvin, Geoffrey, and Ann Harrington. "The Great CEO Pay Heist." *Fortune*, June 25, 2001.

Congressional Research Service. "Real Wage Trends, 1979 to 2018." Washington, DC: Congressional Research Service, 2019.
Cooper, Melinda. *Family Values: Between Neoliberalism and the New Social Conservatism*. New York: Zone Books, 2017.
Copeland, Tom, Tim Koller, and Jack Murrin. *Valuation: Measuring and Managing the Value of Companies*. 2nd ed. New York: John Wiley & Sons, 1994.
Coulter, David. "Managing for Shareholder Value at Bank of America." *Journal of Applied Corporate Finance* 10, no. 2 (1997): 68–71.
Cowan, Alison Leigh. "Executives Are Fuming over Data on Their Pay." *New York Times*, August 25, 1992.
Cowan, Alison Leigh. "High Pay in High-Tech Field Poses a Problem for Clinton." *New York Times*, December 23, 1993, sec. Business Day.
Cowan, Alison Leigh. "Methods in Stock Option Madness." *New York Times*, March 26, 1993.
Cowan, Alison Leigh. "Stock Option Rule Change Is Planned." *New York Times*, April 8, 1993, sec. Business Day.
Cowan, Alison Leigh. "The Gadfly C.E.O.'s Want to Swat." *New York Times*, February 2, 1992, sec. Business.
Cowan, Edward. "Senator Kennedy's Antitrust Bill Passed One Obstacle Last Week; Many More Lay Ahead." *New York Times*, May 13, 1979.
Cowie, Jefferson R. *Capital Moves: RCA's Seventy-Year Quest for Cheap Labor*. Ithaca, NY: Cornell University Press, 1999.
Cowie, Jefferson R. *The Great Exception: The New Deal and the Limits of American Politics*. Princeton, NJ: Princeton University Press, 2016.
Cowie, Jefferson R. *Stayin' Alive: The 1970s and the Last Days of the Working Class*. New York: New Press, 2012.
Creswell, Julie. "After Years of Anticipation, a Subdued Public Offering for Kohlberg Kravis." *New York Times*, July 16, 2010.
Crittenden, Ann. "The Age of 'Me-First' Management." *New York Times*, August 19, 1984.
Crock, Stan. "James Miller, FTC Nominee, Seeks Study on Necessity for Two Antitrust Agencies." *Wall Street Journal*, July 27, 1981.
Crock, Stan. "SEC's Shad Shows Pro-Business Tilt but Says He Won't Be a Pushover." *Wall Street Journal*, September 16, 1981.
Crystal, Graef S. "At the Top." *New York Times Magazine*, 1989.
Crystal, Graef S. "How Much CEOs Really Make." *Fortune*, June 17, 1991.
Crystal, Graef S. *In Search of Excess: The Overcompensation of American Executives*. New York: W. W. Norton, 1991.
Crystal, Graef S., and Constance A. Gustke. "Seeking the Sense in CEO Pay." *Fortune*, June 5, 1989.
Crystal, Graef S., Francis T. Vincent Jr., and Edward C. Baig. "Take the Mystery Out of CEO Pay." *Fortune*, April 24, 1989.

Cuff, Daniel F. "Those Well-Paid Executives." *New York Times*, May 2, 1984.
Cumming, Douglas, Donald S. Siegel, and Mike Wright. "Private Equity, Leveraged Buyouts and Governance." *Journal of Corporate Finance* 13, no. 4 (2007): 439–60.
Cutter, Chip, and Lauren Weber. "Companies That Embraced Social Issues Have Second Thoughts." *Wall Street Journal*, June 6, 2023, sec. Business. https://www.wsj.com/articles/companies-new-cause-dodging-the-culture-wars-73e52cf3.
Davis, Bob, and David Wessel. *Prosperity: The Coming Twenty-Year Boom and What It Means to You*. New York: Crown Business, 1998.
Davis, Gerald F. *Managed by the Markets: How Finance Re-Shaped America*. Oxford: Oxford University Press, 2011.
Davis, Gerald F., Kristina A. Diekmann, and Catherine H. Tinsley. "The Decline and Fall of the Conglomerate Firm in the 1980s: The Deinstitutionalization of an Organizational Form." *American Sociological Review* 59, no. 4 (1994): 547–70.
Delton, Jennifer A. *The Industrialists: How the National Association of Manufacturers Shaped American Capitalism*. Princeton, NJ: Princeton University Press, 2020.
Delugach, Al. "Inco Takes $200 Million Pot in Showdown for ESB Control." *Los Angeles Times*, July 30, 1974.
Delugach, Al. "What's Making ESB Inc. Such a Big Deal?" *Los Angeles Times*, July 26, 1974.
DeMott, John S., Lee Griggs, and Frederick Ungeheuer. "The High Price of Freedom." *Time*, March 18, 1985.
De Witt, Karen. "Nominee as F.T.C. Head." *New York Times*, June 27, 1981.
Dionne, E. J. "Greening of Democrats: An 80's Mix of Idealism and Shrewd Politics." *New York Times*, June 14, 1989, sec. US.
Dobbin, Frank, and Jiwook Jung. "The Misapplication of Mr. Michael Jensen: How Agency Theory Brought Down the Economy and Why It Might Happen Again." In *Markets on Trial: The Economic Sociology of the U.S. Financial Crisis*, edited by Michael Lounsbury and Paul M. Hirsch, 29–64. Bingley, UK: Emerald Publishing, 2011.
Dobbin, Frank, and Dirk Zorn. "Corporate Malfeasance and the Myth of Shareholder Value." *Political Power and Social Theory* 17 (2006): 179–98.
Dodd, E. Merrick. "For Whom Are Corporate Managers Trustees?" *Harvard Law Review* 45, no. 7 (1932): 1145–63.
Donaldson, Gordon. *Corporate Restructuring: Managing the Change Process from Within*. Boston: Harvard Business School Press, 1994.
Donaldson, Gordon A., and Jay W. Lorsch. *Decision Making at the Top: The Shaping of Strategic Direction*. New York: Basic Books, 1983.
Donnan, Shawn. "A Nation's Economy Divided: Breadlines vs. Bread Makers." *Bloomberg Businessweek*, December 29, 2020. https://www.bloomberg.com/features/2020-economic-recovery-inequality/.

Donnelly, Grace. "Black History Month: Diversity in CEO Spot Very Low for Blacks." *Fortune*, February 28, 2018. https://fortune.com/2018/02/28/black-history-month-black-ceos-fortune-500/.

Dorff, Michael. *Indispensable and Other Myths: Why the CEO Pay Experiment Failed and How to Fix It.* Berkeley: University of California Press, 2014.

Dow Jones News Service. "Kohlberg Plans Stake in Spalding and Evenflo." *New York Times*, August 16, 1996.

Drucker, Peter F. *Concept of the Corporation*. New York: John Day, 1946.

Drucker, Peter F. "Reckoning with the Pension Fund Revolution." *Harvard Business Review* 69, no. 2 (1991): 106–14.

Drutman, Lee. *The Business of America Is Lobbying: How Corporations Became Politicized and Politics Became More Corporate*. New York: Oxford University Press, 2015.

Dumenil, Gerard, and Dominique Levy. *Capital Resurgent: The Roots of the Neoliberal Revolution*. Translated by Derek Jeffers. Cambridge, MA: Harvard University Press, 2004.

Easton, Thomas. "Buyouts: A Misused Idea?" *Baltimore Sun*, January 1, 1989.

Eavis, Peter. "Meager Rewards for Workers, Exceptionally Rich Pay for C.E.O.s." *New York Times*, June 11, 2021, sec. Business. https://www.nytimes.com/2021/06/11/business/ceo-pay-compensation-stock.html. The Economist. "Analyse This." March 31, 2016. https://www.economist.com/business/2016/03/31/analyse-this.

The Economist. "Too Triumphalist by Half." April 23, 1998.

The Economist. "What It Takes to Be a CEO in the 2020s." February 6, 2020. https://www.economist.com/leaders/2020/02/06/what-it-takes-to-be-a-ceo-in-the-2020s.

Edwards, Franklin R., and R. Glenn Hubbard. "The Growth of Institutional Stock Ownership: A Promise Unfulfilled." *Journal of Applied Corporate Finance* 13, no. 3 (2000): 92–104.

Ehrbar, Aloysius F. "Corporate Takeovers Are Here to Stay." *Fortune*, May 8, 1978.

Ehrbar, Aloysius F. *EVA: The Real Key to Creating Wealth*. New York: John Wiley & Sons, 1998.

Ehrbar, Aloysius F., and Lorraine Carson. "Have Takeovers Gone Too Far?" *Fortune*, May 27, 1985.

Eichar, Douglas M. *The Rise and Fall of Corporate Social Responsibility*. Piscataway, NJ: Transaction Publishers, 2015.

Eichengreen, Barry. *Globalizing Capital: A History of the International Monetary System*. 2nd ed. Princeton, NJ: Princeton University Press, 2008.

Eichenwald, Kurt. "Kohlberg, Kravis Rouses Itself." *New York Times*, April 29, 1991.

Ellis, Charles D. *Joe Wilson and the Creation of Xerox*. Hoboken, NJ: John Wiley & Sons, 2006.

Emshwiller, John R., and Rebecca Smith. "Enron Jolt: Investments, Assets Generate Big Loss." *Wall Street Journal*, October 17, 2001.

Engel, Larry. "Record Briggs Profit Sharing Up 98% to $25.8 Million." *Milwaukee Sentinel*, August 9, 1994.

Englander, Ernie, and Allen Kaufman. "The End of Managerial Ideology: From Corporate Social Responsibility to Corporate Social Indifference." *Enterprise and Society* 5, no. 3 (2004): 404–50.

Erhard, Werner, Michael C. Jensen, and Steve Zaffron. "Integrity: A Positive Model That Incorporates the Normative Phenomena of Morality, Ethics and Legality." SSRN Scholarly Paper. Rochester, NY: Social Science Research Network, March 23, 2009. https://doi.org/10.2139/ssrn.920625.

Fama, Eugene F. "Agency Problems and the Theory of the Firm." *Journal of Political Economy* 88, no. 2 (1980): 288–307.

Farrar, Donald E., and Lance Girton. "Institutional Investors and Concentration of Financial Power: Berle and Means Revisited." *Journal of Finance* 36, no. 2 (1981): 369–81.

Fauber, John. "Briggs Outlines Position on Future of Jobs Here." *Milwaukee Journal*, October 25, 1993.

Fauber, John. "EVA." *Milwaukee Journal*, October 31, 1993.

Fauber, John. "Will the 1990s Be the Decade of Prosperity Without Jobs?" *Milwaukee Journal*, June 13, 1993.

Fauber, John, and Erik Gunn. "Who's to Blame?" *Milwaukee Journal*, May 22, 1994.

Federal Judicial Center. "Easterbrook, Frank Hoover." Federal Judicial Center. Accessed February 11, 2020. https://www.fjc.gov/history/judges/easterbrook-frank-hoover.

Federal Reserve. "Distribution of Household Wealth in the U.S. Since 1989." Board of Governors of the Federal Reserve System. Last updated September 20, 2024, accessed December 1, 2024. https://www.federalreserve.gov/releases/z1/dataviz/dfa/distribute/table/#quarter:126;series:Corporate%20equities%20and%20mutual%20fund%20shares;demographic:networth;population:1,3,5,7;units:shares.

Ferraro, Fabrizio, Jeffrey Pfeffer, and Robert I. Sutton. "Economics Language and Assumptions: How Theories Can Become Self-Fulfilling." *Academy of Management Review* 30, no. 1 (2005): 8–24.

Fierman, Jaclyn, and Mark D. Fefer. "When Will You Get a Raise?" *Fortune*, July 12, 1993.

Finkel, Robert, and David Greising. *The Masters of Private Equity and Venture Capital: Management Lessons from the Pioneers of Private Investing*. New York: McGraw-Hill Education, 2009.

Fischel, Daniel R. "Efficient Capital Market Theory, the Market for Corporate Control, and the Regulation of Cash Tender Offers." *Texas Law Review* 57, no. 1 (1978): 1–46.

Fligstein, Neil. *The Transformation of Corporate Control*. Cambridge, MA: Harvard University Press, 1993.

Fligstein, Neil, and Taekjin Shin. "Shareholder Value and the Transformation of American Industries, 1984–2001." Institute for Research on Labor and Employment, University of California, Berkeley, September 2006. https://sociology.berkeley.edu/sites/default/files/faculty/fligstein/Fligstein%20and%20Shin%20Shareholder%20Value%20and%20Transform%20of%20Am%20Econ.pdf.

Forbes. "Litton's Shattered Image." December 1, 1969.

Forbes. "Litton's Troubles." February 15, 1968.

Forensic Economics. "Gregg A. Jarrell." Accessed February 5, 2020. https://www.forensiceconomics.com/gregg-a-jarrell/.

Fourcade, Marion, and Rakesh Khurana. "The Social Trajectory of a Finance Professor and the Common Sense of Capital." *History of Political Economy* 49, no. 2 (2017): 347–81.

Fox, Justin. "The Amazing Stock Option Sleight of Hand." *Fortune*, June 25, 2001.

Fox, Justin. "Covid Can't Stop Corporate Profits from Climbing to Record Highs." Bloomberg.com, December 6, 2021. https://www.bloomberg.com/news/articles/2021-12-06/stock-market-u-s-corporations-hit-record-profits-in-2021-q3-despite-covid.

Fox, Justin. *The Myth of the Rational Market: A History of Risk, Reward, and Delusion on Wall Street*. New York: Harper Business, 2009.

Fox, Justin. "The Next Best Thing to Free Money." *Fortune*, July 7, 1997.

Fox, Sylvan. "The Spirit Is Youth, the Style Is Money." *New York Times*, January 6, 1969.

Frank, Robert. "The Wealthiest 10% of Americans Own a Record 89% of All U.S. Stocks." CNBC, October 18, 2021. https://www.cnbc.com/2021/10/18/the-wealthiest-10percent-of-americans-own-a-record-89percent-of-all-us-stocks.html.

Freyer, Tony. "Managerial Capitalism Contested: Government Policy, Culture, and Corporate Investment." In *The Columbia History of Post-World War II America*, edited by Mark Carnes, 427–54. New York: Columbia University Press, 2007.

Fridenson, Patrick. "Business Failure and the Agenda of Business History." *Enterprise & Society* 5, no. 4 (2004): 562–82.

Friedman, Milton. "A Friedman Doctrine—the Social Responsibility of Business Is to Increase Its Profits." *New York Times Magazine*, September 13, 1970.

Friedman, Thomas L. *The Lexus and the Olive Tree*. New York: Farrar, Straus and Giroux, 1999.

Fromson, Brett Duval. "Life After Debt: How LBOs Do It." *Fortune*, March 13, 1989.

Fromson, Brett Duval. "Tougher Rule Sought on Stock Option Cost." *Washington Post*, April 8, 1993.

Frydman, Carola, and Dirk Jenter. "CEO Compensation." Working Paper no. 77. Rock Center for Corporate Governance at Stanford University. Last revised November 28, 2010. Available at SSRN, https://ssrn.com/abstract=1582232.

Fuchsberg, Gilbert. "Investors May Seek Vote on Executive Pay Consultants." *Wall Street Journal*, August 27, 1992.

Fuller, Joseph, and Michael C. Jensen. "Just Say No to Wall Street: Putting a Stop to the Earnings Game." *Journal of Applied Corporate Finance* 14, no. 4 (2002): 41–46.

Gallup News. "What Percentage of Americans Owns Stock?" The Short Answer, Gallup News, September 13, 2019. Last updated May 24, 2023. https://news.gallup.com/poll/266807/percentage-americans-owns-stock.aspx.

Gaughan, Patrick A. *Mergers, Acquisitions, and Corporate Restructurings*. 6th ed. Hoboken, NJ: John Wiley & Sons, 2015.

Geismer, Lilly. *Don't Blame Us: Suburban Liberals and the Transformation of the Democratic Party*. Princeton, NJ: Princeton University Press, 2015.

Gerstle, Gary. *The Rise and Fall of the Neoliberal Order: America and the World in the Free Market Era*. Oxford: Oxford University Press, 2022.

Ghemawat, Pankaj. "Competition and Business Strategy in Historical Perspective." *Business History Review* 76, no. 1 (April 15, 2002): 37–74.

Ghoshal, Sumantra. "Bad Management Theories Are Destroying Good Management Practices." *Academy of Management Learning & Education* 4, no. 1 (2005): 75–91.

Giacalone, Robert A., and Kenneth R. Thompson. "Business Ethics and Social Responsibility Education: Shifting the Worldview." *Academy of Management Learning & Education* 5, no. 3 (2006): 266–77.

Gigot, Paul A. "Executive Pay—an Embarrassment to Free Marketers." *Wall Street Journal*, January 10, 1992.

Gipson, James. "Leveraged Buyouts and Greed." *Washington Post*, January 22, 1984.

Glassman, James. "CEOs Unite in a Fight to Keep Running the Options Play." *Washington Post*, June 15, 1994.

Goldberg, Emma. "Have the Anticapitalists Reached Harvard Business School?" *New York Times*, November 28, 2022, sec. Business. https://www.nytimes.com/2022/11/28/business/business-school-social-justice.html.

Goldstein, Tom. "The Language of Takeovers." *New York Times*, December 1, 1978.

Goold, Michael, and Kathleen Sommers Luchs. "Why Diversify? Four Decades of Management Thinking." *Academy of Management Executive* 7, no. 3 (1993): 7–25.

Gordon, Jeffrey N. "The Rise of Independent Directors in the United States, 1950–2005: Of Shareholder Value and Stock Market Prices." *Stanford Law Review* 59, no. 6 (2007): 1465–1568.

Gordon, Robert. *The Rise and Fall of American Growth: The U.S. Standard of Living Since the Civil War*. Princeton, NJ: Princeton University Press, 2016.

Graham, Otis L. *Losing Time: The Industrial Policy Debate*. Cambridge, MA: Harvard University Press, 1992.

Gramm, Jeff. *Dear Chairman: Boardroom Battles and the Rise of Shareholder Activism*. New York: Harper Business, 2016.

Grant, Linda. "Shareholders Balk at Shift in Executive Incentive Plans: Compensation." *Los Angeles Times*, April 12, 1992.

Gray, Harry J. "The Litton Annual Report: Chore or Challenge?" *Journal of Business Communication* 5, no. 3 (1968): 11–18.

Greer, Philip. "Xerox Comes to Eastman Defense in Battle with Militant Group." *Washington Post*, May 21, 1967, sec. Business & Finance.

The Guardian. "Enron's Board of Directors." February 1, 2002. http://www.theguardian.com/business/2002/feb/01/corporatefraud.enron3.

Guerrera, Francesco. "Welch Condemns Share Price Focus." *Financial Times*, March 12, 2009. https://www.ft.com/content/294ff1f2-0f27-11de-ba10-0000779fd2ac.

Gunn, Erik. "Labor Tensions at Briggs Keep Escalating." *Milwaukee Journal*, October 13, 1993.

Guthart, Leo A. "More Companies Are Buying Back Their Stock." *Harvard Business Review* 43, no. 2 (1965): 40–53, 172.

Habib, Michel A., and Alexander Ljungqvist. "Firm Value and Managerial Incentives: A Stochastic Frontier Approach." *Journal of Business* 78, no. 6 (2005): 2053–93.

Hammer, Alexander R. "Litton Says Stock Drop Will Not Slow Down Acquisition Plans." *New York Times*, March 23, 1968.

Hansmann, Henry, and Reinier Kraakman. "The End of History for Corporate Law." *Georgetown Law Journal* 89 (2001): 439–68.

Harlan, Christi. "Accounting Proposal Stirs Unusual Uproar in Executive Suites." *Wall Street Journal*, March 7, 1994.

Harlan, Christi. "Group Opposes Stock-Option Accounting Plan." *Wall Street Journal*, January 14, 1993.

Harris, David G., and Jane R. Livingstone. "Federal Tax Legislation as an Implicit Contracting Cost Benchmark: The Definition of Excessive Executive Compensation." *Accounting Review* 77, no. 4 (October 2002): 997–1018.

Hartt, Julian. "Litton Memo Provides Poverty War Strategy." *Los Angeles Times*, July 23, 1964.

Harvey, David. *A Brief History of Neoliberalism*. Oxford: Oxford University Press, 2005.

Harvey, David. *The Condition of Postmodernity: An Inquiry into the Origins of Cultural Change*. Cambridge, MA: Blackwell, 1990.

Haspeslagh, Philippe. "Portfolio Planning: Uses and Limits." *Harvard Business Review*, February 1, 1982.

Hayes, Robert H. "The Undermining of Business Credibility." *New York Times*, October 10, 1982.

Hayes, Robert H., and William J. Abernathy. "Managing Our Way to Economic Decline." *Harvard Business Review*, July 1980.

Healy, Paul M., and Krishna G. Palepu. "The Fall of Enron." *Journal of Economic Perspectives* 17, no. 2 (June 2003): 3–26.

Heath, Thomas. "Carlyle IPO: Stock Up Slightly in NASDAQ Debut." *Washington Post*, May 3, 2012.

Hector, Gary. "Are Shareholders Cheated by LBOs?" *Fortune*, January 19, 1987.

Hector, Gary. "Junk's Bad Times Are Just Starting." *Fortune*, June 4, 1990.

Heilbron, Johan, Verheul Jochem, and Sander Quak. "The Origins and Early Diffusion of 'Shareholder Value' in the United States." *Theory and Society* 41, no. 1 (2014): 1–22.

Henderson, Bruce. "The Product Portfolio." Perspectives, Boston Consulting Group, January 1, 1970. https://www.bcg.com/publications/1970/strategy-the-product-portfolio.

Henderson, Rebecca. *Reimagining Capitalism in a World on Fire*. New York: PublicAffairs, 2021.

Hesse, Henning, Boris Hofmann, and James Weber. "The Macroeconomic Effects of Asset Purchases Revisited." BIS Working Papers, Bank of International Settlements, Geneva, Switzerland, 2017.

Hill, G. Christian, and John D. Williams. "Leveraged Purchases of Firms Keep Gaining Despite Rising Risks." *Wall Street Journal*, December 29, 1983.

Hinden, Stan. "Senator Presses for Restrictions on Executive Stock Options." *Washington Post*, February 1, 1992.

Hirsch, Paul. "From Ambushes to Golden Parachutes: Corporate Takeovers as an Instance of Cultural Framing and Institutional Integration." *American Journal of Sociology* 91, no. 4 (1986): 800–837.

Ho, Karen. *Liquidated: An Ethnography of Wall Street*. Durham, NC: Duke University Press, 2009.

Holland, Max. "How to Kill a Company: Anatomy of a Leveraged Buyout." *Washington Post*, April 23, 1989.

Holland, Max. *When the Machine Stopped: A Cautionary Tale from Industrial America*. Boston: Harvard Business School Press, 1989.

Holmstrom, Bengt, and Steven Kaplan. "Corporate Governance and Merger Activity in the United States: Making Sense of the 1980s and 1990s." *Journal of Economic Perspectives* 15, no. 2 (2001): 121–44.

Holusha, John. "Revco Drugstore Chain in Bankruptcy Filing." *New York Times*, July 29, 1988.

Hooke, Jeffrey C. *The Myth of Private Equity: An Inside Look at Wall Street's Transformative Investments*. New York: Columbia Business School Publishing, 2021.

Hounshell, David A. *From the American System to Mass Production, 1800–1932: The Development of Manufacturing Technology in the United States*. Baltimore: Johns Hopkins University Press, 1985.

Huddart, Steven, and Mark Lang. "Employee Stock Option Exercises: An Empirical Analysis." *Journal of Accounting and Economics* 21, no. 1 (1996): 5–43.

Hudson, Richard L. "SEC Is Forming Industry Panel to Suggest Changes in Regulation of Tender Offers." *Wall Street Journal*, February 8, 1983.

Hyman, Louis. *Debtor Nation: The History of America in Red Ink*. Princeton, NJ: Princeton University Press, 2011.

Hyman, Louis. "Rethinking the Postwar Corporation: Management, Monopolies, and the Market." In *What's Good for Business: Business and American Politics*

Since World War II, edited by Kim Phillips-Fein and Julian E. Zelizer, 195–211. New York: Oxford University Press, 2012.

Hyman, Louis. *Temp: How American Work, American Business, and the American Dream Became Temporary*. New York: Viking, 2018.

Ilg, Randy E., and Steven E. Haugen. "Earnings and Employment Trends in the 1990s." *Monthly Labor Review*, March 2000, 21–33.

Ingersoll, Bruce. "SEC Won't Propose Major Bill in 1985 to Curb Takeovers." *Wall Street Journal*, May 21, 1985.

Ingrassa, Paul. "Forget Football. We Have Bendix and U. Tech." *Wall Street Journal*, September 24, 1982.

Ip, Greg. "Collars Give Insiders Way to Cut Risk." *Wall Street Journal*, September 17, 1997.

Irwin, Don. "Nixon Panel Will Seek Formula to End Draft: Committee to Submit Recommendations in November on Switch to Volunteer Army." *Los Angeles Times*, March 28, 1969.

Jackall, Robert. *Moral Mazes: The World of Corporate Managers*. Updated edition. New York: Oxford University Press, 2009.

Jacobs, Meg. *Panic at the Pump: The Energy Crisis and the Transformation of American Politics in the 1970s*. New York: Hill & Wang, 2016.

Jacobs, Meg. *Pocketbook Politics: Economic Citizenship in Twentieth-Century America*. Princeton, NJ: Princeton University Press, 2005.

Jacobs, Meg. "The Politics of Environmental Regulation: Business-Government Relations in the 1970s and Beyond." In *What's Good for Business: Business and American Politics Since World War II*, edited by Kim Phillips-Fein and Julian E. Zelizer, 212–32. New York: Oxford University Press, 2012.

Jacobs, Michael T. *Short-Term America: The Causes and Cures of Our Business Myopia*. Boston: Harvard Business School Press, 1991.

Jacoby, Sanford M. "Finance and Labor: Perspectives on Risk, Inequality, and Democracy." *Comparative Labor Law & Policy Journal* 30, no. 1 (2008): 17–65.

Jacoby, Sanford M. *Modern Manors: Welfare Capitalism Since the New Deal*. Princeton, NJ: Princeton University Press, 1997.

Jarrell, Gregg A. "Financial Innovation and Corporate Mergers." Conference Series (Proceedings), Federal Reserve Bank of Boston, vol. 31 (1987): 58–77.

Jarrell, Gregg A., and Michael Bradley. "The Economic Effects of Federal and State Regulations of Cash Tender Offers." *Journal of Law & Economics* 23, no. 2 (1980): 371–407.

Jensen, Michael C. "Active Investors, LBOs, and the Privatization of Bankruptcy." *Journal of Applied Corporate Finance* 2, no. 1 (1989): 35–44.

Jensen, Michael C. "Agency Cost of Free Cash Flow, Corporate Finance, and Takeovers." *American Economic Review* 76, no. 2 (1986): 323–29.

Jensen, Michael. "Eclipse of the Public Corporation." *Harvard Business Review*, September–October (1989). Revised 1997.

Jensen, Michael C. "The Free Cash Flow Theory of Takeovers: A Financial Perspective on Mergers and Acquisitions and the Economy." In *The Merger Boom: Proceedings of a Conference Sponsored by the Federal Reserve Bank of Boston*, 102–37. Boston: Federal Reserve Bank of Boston, 1987.

Jensen, Michael C. "Freedom and the Role of the Government." SSRN Scholarly Paper, Social Science Research Network, November 30, 2003. https://papers.ssrn.com/abstract=391221.

Jensen, Michael C. "Freedom, Capitalism and Human Behavior Chapter 1. Introduction and Overview." SSRN Scholarly Paper, Social Science Research Network, 1999. https://papers.ssrn.com/abstract=638702.

Jensen, Michael C. "Freedom, Capitalism and Human Behavior Chapter 3: Applications of the Jensen Meckling Concept of Freedom." SSRN Scholarly Paper, Social Science Research Network, June 30, 1999. https://papers.ssrn.com/abstract=638801.

Jensen, Michael C. "How to Detect a Prime Takeover Target." *New York Times*, March 9, 1986.

Jensen, Michael C. "The Modern Industrial Revolution, Exit, and the Failure of Internal Control Systems." *Journal of Finance* 48, no. 3 (1993): 831–80.

Jensen, Michael C. "The Morgan Stanley Manner." *New York Times*, May 25, 1975.

Jensen, Michael C. "Risk, the Pricing of Capital Assets, and the Evaluation of Investment Portfolios." *Journal of Business* 42, no. 2 (1969): 167–247.

Jensen, Michael C. "Takeovers: Folklore and Science." *Harvard Business Review* 62, no. 2 (1984): 109–21.

Jensen, Michael C., George P. Baker, Carliss Y. Baldwin, and Karen H. Wruck. "Organizations and Markets: History and Development of the CCMO Course and the Field (1st of 4 CCMO Documents)." SSRN Scholarly Paper, Social Science Research Network, December 10, 1997. https://papers.ssrn.com/abstract=78009.

Jensen, Michael C., and William H. Meckling. "Between Freedom and Democracy." SSRN Scholarly Paper, Social Science Research Network, October 30, 1977. https://papers.ssrn.com/abstract=391200.

Jensen, Michael C., and William H. Meckling. "Can the Corporation Survive?" SSRN Scholarly Paper, Social Science Research Network, January 30, 1978. https://papers.ssrn.com/abstract=244155.

Jensen, Michael C., and William H. Meckling. "Coordination, Control, and the Management of Organizations: Course Notes (2nd of 4 CCMO Documents)." SSRN Scholarly Paper, Social Science Research Network, October 17, 1999. https://papers.ssrn.com/abstract=78008.

Jensen, Michael C., and William H. Meckling. "Freedom, Capitalism and Human Behavior Chapter 2: Human Rights and the Meaning of Freedom." SSRN Scholarly Paper, Social Science Research Network, June 30, 1999. https://papers.ssrn.com/abstract=638703.

Jensen, Michael C., and William H. Meckling. "Freedom, Capitalism and Human Behavior Chapter 4: Capitalism." SSRN Scholarly Paper, Social Science Research Network, June 30, 1999. https://papers.ssrn.com/abstract=638802.
Jensen, Michael C., and William Meckling. "Theory of the Firm: Managerial Behavior, Agency Costs and Ownership Structure." *Journal of Financial Economics* 3 (1976): 305–60.
Jensen, Michael C., William H. Meckling, George P. Baker, and Karen H. Wruck. "Coordination, Control, and the Management of Organizations: Practice Questions (4th of 4 CCMO Documents)." SSRN Scholarly Paper, Social Science Research Network, April 20, 1998. https://papers.ssrn.com/abstract=78010.
Jensen, Michael C., and Kevin J. Murphy. "CEO Incentives—It's Not How Much You Pay, but How." *Harvard Business Review* 68, no. 3 (1990): 138–49.
Jensen, Michael C., and Kevin J. Murphy. "Remuneration: Where We've Been, How We Got to Here, What Are the Problems, and How to Fix Them." ECGI Working Paper, European Corporate Governance Institute, Brussels, Belgium, 2004.
Jensen, Michael C., and Richard Ruback. "The Market for Corporate Control: The Scientific Evidence." *Journal of Financial Economics* 11 (1983): 5–50.
Johnson, Calvin H. "Stock Options Aren't 'Free' Compensation." *Los Angeles Times*, April 8, 1994.
Johnson, Lyman P. Q. "Corporate Law Professors as Gatekeepers." *University of St. Thomas Law Journal* 6, no. 2 (2009): 447–53.
Johnson, Robert. "To William F. Farley, Firms Nobody Wants Seem Worth Acquiring." *Wall Street Journal*, December 21, 1983.
Joly, Hubert, and Caroline Lambert. *The Heart of Business: Leadership Principles for the Next Era of Capitalism*. Boston: Harvard Business Review Press, 2021.
Jones, Daniel Stedman. *Masters of the Universe: Hayek, Friedman, and the Birth of Neoliberal Politics*. Updated edition. Princeton, NJ: Princeton University Press, 2014.
Jordan, Glenn, dir. *Barbarians at the Gate*. Los Angeles: HBO Films, Columbia Pictures Television, Rastar Pictures, 1993. DVD, 107 min.
Jung, Jiwook, and Taekjin Shin. "Learning Not to Diversify: The Transformation of Graduate Business Education and the Decline of Diversifying Acquisitions." *Administrative Science Quarterly* 64, no. 2 (2019): 337–69.
Kahn, Irving, and Alan R. Kahn. "Conglomerate Companies—What Are They Really?" *Financial Analysts Journal* 24, no. 2 (1968): 197–98.
Kaissar, Nir. "I Ran the Numbers Again. Stocks Are Not the Economy." Bloomberg.com, October 27, 2020. https://www.bloomberg.com/opinion/articles/2020-10-27/stock-market-is-not-the-economy-by-any-yardstick.
Kaplan, Steven N. "The Effects of Management Buyouts on Operating Performance and Value." *Journal of Financial Economics* 24, no. 2 (1989): 217–54.

Kaplan, Steven N., and Per Strömberg. "Leveraged Buyouts and Private Equity." *Journal of Economic Perspectives* 23, no. 1 (2009): 121–46.

Kaplan, Steven N., and Jeremy C. Stein. "The Evolution of Buyout Pricing and Financial Structure in the 1980s." *Quarterly Journal of Economics* 108, no. 2 (1993): 313–57.

Katz, Alyssa. *The Influence Machine: The U.S. Chamber of Commerce and the Corporate Capture of American Life.* New York: Random House, 2015.

Katznelson, Ira. *When Affirmative Action Was White: An Untold History of Racial Inequality in Twentieth-Century America.* New York: W. W. Norton, 2006.

Kaufman, Allen, and Ernest Englander. "Kohlberg Kravis Roberts & Co. and the Restructuring of American Capitalism." *Business History Review* 67, no. 1 (1993): 58–97.

Kaufman, Steve. "Area Execs Lash Out at FASB." *San Jose Mercury News*, March 26, 1994.

Kay, Ira T. "High CEO Pay Helps the U.S. Economy Thrive." *Wall Street Journal*, February 23, 1998.

Khurana, Rakesh. *Searching for a Corporate Savior: The Irrational Quest for Charismatic CEOs.* Princeton, NJ: Princeton University Press, 2002.

Khurana, Rakesh. *From Higher Aims to Hired Hands: The Social Transformation of Business Schools and the Unfulfilled Promise of Management as a Profession.* Princeton, NJ: Princeton University Press, 2007.

Kiechel, Walter, III. *The Lords of Strategy: The Secret Intellectual History of the New Corporate World.* Cambridge, MA: Harvard Business Review Press, 2010.

Kilpatrick, Carroll. "1971 End to Draft Is Urged: All-Volunteer Force Backed by Nixon Unit." *Washington Post, Times Herald*, February 22, 1970, sec. General.

Kinder, Molly, Katie Bach, and Laura Stateler. "Profits and the Pandemic: As Shareholder Wealth Soared, Workers Were Left Behind." Research, the Brookings Institution, April 21, 2022. https://www.brookings.edu/research/profits-and-the-pandemic-as-shareholder-wealth-soared-workers-were-left-behind/.

Kleinfield, N. R. "Kohlberg Collects Companies." *New York Times*, December 12, 1983.

Knight, Jerry. "KKR Using Only $15 Million of Its Own in Nabisco Buyout." *Washington Post*, December 2, 1988.

Koshetz, Herbert. "ESB, Inc., Opposes Purchase Offer." *New York Times*, July 20, 1974.

Koshetz, Herbert. "Inco Sues to Curb ESB's Comments on Stock Bid." *New York Times*, July 23, 1974.

Koshetz, Herbert. "United Aircraft Tops INCO ESB Bid." *New York Times*, July 27, 1974.

Kovacic, William E. "Reagan's Judicial Appointees and Antitrust in the 1990s." *Fordham Law Review* 60, no. 1 (1991): 78.

Krippner, Greta. *Capitalizing on Crisis: The Political Origins of the Rise of Finance.* Cambridge, MA: Harvard University Press, 2011.

Kristof, Kathy. "Hitting Shareholders Where It Hurts." *Chicago Tribune*, April 20, 1993.

Kristol, Irving. "Income Inequality Without Class Conflict." *Wall Street Journal*, December 18, 1997.

Kruse, Kevin M. *One Nation Under God: How Corporate America Invented Christian America*. New York: Basic Books, 2016.

Kruse, Kevin M., and Julian E. Zelizer. *Fault Lines: A History of the United States Since 1974*. New York: W. W. Norton, 2019.

Kuhn, Thomas S. *The Structure of Scientific Revolutions*. Chicago: University of Chicago Press, 1962.

Labaton, Stephen. "S.E.C. Will Require Fuller Disclosure of Executive Pay." *New York Times*, October 15, 1992.

Lamoreaux, Naomi R. *The Great Merger Movement in American Business, 1895–1904*. Cambridge: Cambridge University Press, 1988.

Lazonick, William. "Innovative Business Models and Varieties of Capitalism: Financialization of the U.S. Corporation." *Business History Review* 84, no. 4 (2010): 675–702.

Lecuyer, Christophe. *Making Silicon Valley: Innovation and the Growth of High Tech, 1930–1970*. Cambridge, MA: MIT Press, 2007.

Lehn, Kenneth, and Annette Poulsen. "Free Cash Flow and Stockholder Gains in Going Private Transactions." *Journal of Finance* 44, no. 3 (1989): 771–87.

Lemann, Nicholas. *Transaction Man: The Rise of the Deal and the Decline of the American Dream*. New York: Farrar, Straus and Giroux, 2019.

Leontiades, Milton. "Use of Capital Markets by Large Manufacturing Corporations." *Financial Analysts Journal* 23, no. 2 (1967): 19–23.

Levy, Haim, and Marshall Sarnat. "Diversification, Portfolio Analysis and the Uneasy Case for Conglomerate Mergers." *Journal of Finance* 25, no. 4 (1970): 795–802.

Lewthwaite, Gilbert A. "Clinton Targets Business Taxes, Executives' Pay." *Baltimore Sun*, February 12, 1993.

Lichtenberg, Frank R., and Donald Siegel. "The Effects of Leveraged Buyouts on Productivity and Related Aspects of Firm Behavior." *Journal of Financial Economics* 27, no. 1 (1990): 165–94.

Lieber, Ronald B. "Stern Stewart and KPMG Go to War." *Fortune*, February 2, 1998.

Lieberman, Joseph I. "Options for All Employees." *Washington Post*, April 15, 1994.

Lieberman, Joseph I. ". . . But They Do Create Good Jobs." *Los Angeles Times*, April 8, 1994.

Lieberman, Joseph I. "Stock Options—America's Equity Edge." *NACD Directorship* 19, no. 6 (June 1994): 3.

Lieberson, Stanley, and James F. O'Connor. "Leadership and Organizational Performance: A Study of Large Corporations." *American Sociological Review* 37, no. 2 (1972): 117–30.

Little, Royal. "How I'm Deconglomerating the Conglomerates." *Fortune*, July 16, 1979.
Lohr, Steve. "Avoiding the Clinton Taxman." *New York Times*, December 2, 1992, sec. Business Day.
Lohr, Steve. "Mergers: The Billion-Dollar Game." *Atlantic Monthly*, July 1979.
Loomis, Carol J. "Buyout Kings." *Fortune*, July 4, 1988.
Loomis, Carol J. "The New J. P. Morgans." *Fortune*, January 1, 1988.
Lowenstein, Louis. "Pruning Deadwood in Hostile Takeovers: A Proposal for Legislation." *Columbia Law Review*, no. 2 (1983): 249–334.
Lublin, JoAnn. "Compensation Panels Get More Assertive, Hiring Consultants and Sparking Clashes." *Wall Street Journal*, July 15, 1992, sec. Marketplace.
Lublin, JoAnn. "Panel Adopts a Tough Line on CEO Pay." *Wall Street Journal*, February 10, 1993.
Macekura, Stephen. *Of Limits and Growth: The Rise of Global Sustainable Development in the Twentieth Century*. New York: Cambridge University Press, 2015.
Mackey, John, Rajendra Sisodia, and Bill George. *Conscious Capitalism: Liberating the Heroic Spirit of Business*. Boston: Harvard Business Review Press, 2013.
MacLean, Nancy. *Democracy in Chains: The Deep History of the Radical Right's Secret Plan for America*. New York: Viking, 2017.
MacMillan, Douglass, Peter Whoriskey, and Jonathan O'Connell. "America's Biggest Companies Are Flourishing During the Pandemic and Putting Thousands of People Out of Work." *Washington Post*, December 16, 2020. https://www.washingtonpost.com/graphics/2020/business/50-biggest-companies-coronavirus-layoffs/.
Madrick, Jeff. *Age of Greed: The Triumph of Finance and the Decline of America, 1970 to the Present*. New York: Vintage, 2011.
Madrick, Jeff. *Taking America: How We Got from the First Hostile Takeover to Megamergers, Corporate Raiding, and Scandal*. Toronto: Bantam Books, 1987.
Magnet, Myron, and Tom Post. "Help! My Company Has Just Been Taken Over." *Fortune*, July 9, 1984.
Magowan, Peter A. "The Case for LBOs: The Safeway Experience." *California Management Review* 32, no. 1 (1989): 9–18.
Malmendier, Ulrike, and Geoffrey Tate. "Superstar CEOs." *Quarterly Journal of Economics* 124, no. 4 (2009): 1593–1638.
Malone, Stewart C. "Characteristics of Smaller Company Leveraged Buyouts." *Journal of Business Venturing* 4, no. 5 (1989): 349–59.
Malott, Robert, and Ralph Whitworth. "Talking About Pay." *Wall Street Journal*, April 21, 1993, sec. Executive Pay.
Marais, Laurentius, Katherine Schipper, and Abbie Smith. "Wealth Effects of Going Private for Senior Securities." *Journal of Financial Economics* 23, no. 1 (1989): 155–91.
Marquis, Christopher. *Better Business: How the B Corp Movement Is Remaking Capitalism*. New Haven, CT: Yale University Press, 2020.

Marquis, Christopher, and András Tilcsik. "Imprinting: Toward a Multilevel Theory." *Academy of Management Annals* 7, no. 1 (2013): 195–245.

Martin, Roger L. *Fixing the Game: Bubbles, Crashes, and What Capitalism Can Learn from the NFL*. Boston: Harvard Business Review Press, 2011.

Martynova, Marina, and Luc Renneboog. "A Century of Corporate Takeovers: What Have We Learned and Where Do We Stand?" *Journal of Banking & Finance* 32, no. 10 (2008): 2148–77.

Mason, R. Hal, and Maurice B. Goudzwaard. "Performance of Conglomerate Firms: A Portfolio Approach." *Journal of Finance* 31, no. 1 (1976): 39–48.

Mathews, Jay. "Accounting Board Drops Disputed Stock Option Rule." *Washington Post*, December 15, 1994.

Mathews, Jay. "The Bookkeepers' Billion-Dollar Debate." *Washington Post*, March 28, 1993.

Mathews, Jay. "Panel Gets an Earful on Stock Options Rule." *Washington Post*, March 8, 1994.

Mathews, Jay. "Stock Options Rule Fight Escalates." *Washington Post*, September 1, 1994.

Mathews, Jay. "Their Riches Were Your Command: Demands That Executive Pay Be Tied to Performance Are What Led to Downsizers' Bonuses." *Washington Post*, March 24, 1996. https://search.proquest.com/docview/1030757147/abstract/3DD8B6C454984607PQ/66.

Maurer, Charles J., III. "Tender Offers—Edgar v. Mite Corp. and State Tender Offer Regulation." *Journal of Corporation Law* 9, no. 1 (1983): 95–112.

Mazzucato, Mariana. *Mission Economy: A Moonshot Guide to Changing Capitalism*. New York: Harper Business, 2021.

McCartney, Robert. "Accounting Rule Change Takes Aim at Employee Stock Option Plans." *Washington Post*, May 15, 1992.

McCartney, Robert. "Quoth the Maven, Cut Some More." *Washington Post*, January 29, 1992.

McCartney, Robert. "Stock Option Windfalls Fuel Debate on Corporate Pay." *Washington Post*, January 31, 1992.

McCartney, Robert, and David Hilzenrath. "SEC to Allow Votes on Executive Pay." *Washington Post*, February 14, 1992.

McCraw, Thomas K., and Jeffrey L. Cruikshank, eds. *The Intellectual Venture Capitalist: John H. McArthur and the Work of the Harvard Business School, 1980–1995*. Boston: Harvard Business Review Press, 1999.

McDonald, Duff. *The Golden Passport: Harvard Business School, the Limits of Capitalism, and the Moral Failure of the MBA Elite*. New York: Harper Business, 2017.

McFadden, Robert D. "Robert H. B. Baldwin, Transformer of Morgan Stanley, Dies at 95." *New York Times*, January 6, 2016.

McKenna, Christopher D. *The World's Newest Profession: Management Consulting in the Twentieth Century*. Cambridge: Cambridge University Press, 2010.

McKenzie, Donald. *An Engine, Not a Camera: How Financial Models Shape Markets*. Cambridge, MA: MIT Press, 2006.

McKinsey, Philip W. "Conglomerate Theory Falters Under Scrutiny." *Christian Science Monitor*, September 15, 1971.

McLaren, Richard W. "Excerpts from Assistant Attorney General's Statement on Conglomerate Mergers." *New York Times*, March 13, 1969.

McLean, Bethany. "Is Enron Overpriced?" *Fortune*, March 5, 2001.

McLean, Bethany, and Peter Elkind. *Smartest Guys in the Room: The Amazing Rise and Scandalous Fall of Enron*. New York: Portfolio, 2003.

Meckling, William. "Values and the Choice of the Model of the Individual in the Social Sciences." *Swiss Journal of Economics and Statistics* 112, no. 4 (1976): 545–60.

Medvetz, Thomas. *Think Tanks in America*. Chicago: University of Chicago Press, 2014.

Meindl, James R., Sanford B. Ehrlich, and Janet M. Dukerich. "The Romance of Leadership." *Administrative Science Quarterly* 30, no. 1 (1985): 78–102.

Metrick, Andrew, and Ayako Yasuda. "The Economics of Private Equity Funds." *Review of Financial Studies* 23, no. 6 (2010): 2303–41.

Metz, Robert. "Aiding Hostile Takeover Bids." *New York Times*, December 28, 1981.

Metz, Robert. "Conglomerates: A Losing Style." *New York Times*, June 21, 1972.

Metz, Robert. "Hostile Offers: The Outlook." *New York Times*, May 2, 1980.

Metz, Robert. "Take-over Campaigns Back in Vogue." *New York Times*, December 27, 1975.

Metz, Robert. "The Takeover Candidates." *New York Times*, July 29, 1980.

Metz, Robert. "Takeover Deals: How to Invest." *New York Times*, May 17, 1979.

Metz, Robert. "Takeover Hope and Houdaille." *New York Times*, July 7, 1978.

Metz, Robert. "The Unfriendly Tender Studied." *New York Times*, February 6, 1980.

Metzenbaum, Howard M. "Is William Baxter Anti-Antitrust?" *New York Times*, October 18, 1981.

Meyers, Ellen. "Rubio, Republicans Step Up Attacks on Corporate Embrace of ESG." Roll Call, September 30, 2021. https://www.rollcall.com/2021/09/30/rubio-republicans-step-up-attacks-on-corporate-embrace-of-esg/.

Miller, James C. "Let's Reduce Regulations on Takeovers." *New York Times*, July 1, 1985.

Miller, Merton H., and Graef S. Crystal. "Big Bucks for Big Execs: Who Pays for the Golden Egg?" *Washington Post*, March 20, 1994.

Miller, Merton H., and Graef S. Crystal. "The Case for Expensing Stock Options Against Earnings." *Journal of Applied Corporate Finance* 7, no. 2 (1994): 88–90.

Mills, C. Wright. *The Organization Man*. New York: Simon & Schuster, 1956.

Mills, C. Wright. *The Power Elite*. New York: Oxford University Press, 1956.

Minow, Nell. "Executive Pay and Accountability." *Chicago Tribune*, May 28, 1991, sec. 1.
Mizruchi, Mark S. *The Fracturing of the American Corporate Elite*. Cambridge, MA: Harvard University Press, 2013.
Monks, Robert A. G., and Nell Minow. *Corporate Governance*. 5th ed. Chichester, UK: John Wiley & Sons, 2011.
Monks, Robert A. G., and Nell Minow. *Power and Accountability*. New York: Harper Business, 1991.
Moreton, Bethany. *To Serve God and Wal-Mart: The Making of Christian Free Enterprise*. Cambridge, MA: Harvard University Press, 2009.
Morris, Jack H. "Penn Central Debacle Creates Repercussions in Much of Philadelphia." *Wall Street Journal*, July 10, 1970.
Mulligan, Thomas S. "KKR to Buy Borden in $2-Billion Deal." *Los Angeles Times*, September 13, 1994.
Murphy, Kevin J. "Executive Compensation: Where We Are, and How We Got There." SSRN Scholarly Paper, Social Science Research Network, 2012.
Murphy, Kevin J. "Top Executives Are Worth Every Nickel They Get." *Harvard Business Review* 64, no. 2 (1986): 125–32.
Murphy, Kevin J., and Michael C. Jensen. "Beware the Self-Serving Critics." *New York Times*, May 20, 1984.
Nader, Ralph, and Mark Green. "Corporate Democracy." *New York Times*, December 28, 1979, sec. Archives. https://www.nytimes.com/1979/12/28/archives/corporate-democracy.html.
Nader, Ralph, Mark Green, and Joel Seligman. *Taming the Giant Corporation: How the Largest Corporations Control Our Lives*. New York: W. W. Norton, 1976.
Nader, Ralph, Mark Green, and Joel Seligman. "Who Rules the Giant Corporation?" *Business & Society Review* 18 (1976): 40.
Nelson Espeland, Wendy, and Paul M. Hirsch. "Ownership Changes, Accounting Practice and the Redefinition of the Corporation." *Accounting, Organizations and Society* 15, no. 1 (1990): 77–96. https://doi.org/10.1016/0361-3682(90)90015-M.
New York Times. "Bottom Line Nation." Article series, 2016. https://www.nytimes.com/series/private-equity-bottom-line-nation.
New York Times. "Greece Ends Litton Deal." October 15, 1969.
New York Times. "Litton Set to Buy Stouffer Foods." April 3, 1967.
New York Times. "The Penn Central Inquest." January 17, 1972.
New York Times. "S.E.C. Plans a Review of Tender Offer Tactics." March 1, 1983.
New York Times. "S.E.C. Refuses to Curb Anti-Takeover Actions." May 21, 1985.
New York Times. "Stock Options: Bentsen's View." April 6, 1993.
Nippa, Michael, Ulrich Pidun, and Harald Rubner. "Corporate Portfolio Management: Appraising Four Decades of Academic Research." *Academy of Management Perspectives* 25, no. 4 (2011): 50–66.

Nohria, Nitin, Davis Dyer, and Frederick Dalzell. *Changing Fortunes: Remaking the Industrial Corporation*. New York: Wiley, 2002.

Norris, Floyd. "Win or Lose, Buyouts Do It Big." *New York Times*, January 28, 1992.

Ocasio, William, and John Joseph. "Cultural Adaptation and Institutional Change: The Evolution of Vocabularies of Corporate Governance, 1972–2003." *Poetics* 33 (2005): 163–78.

Ofek, Eli, and David Yermack. "Taking Stock: Equity-Based Compensation and the Evolution of Managerial Ownership." *Journal of Finance* 55, no. 3 (2000): 1367–84.

O'Mara, Margaret Pugh. *Cities of Knowledge: Cold War Science and the Search for the Next Silicon Valley*. Princeton, NJ: Princeton University Press, 2015.

O'Mara, Margaret Pugh. *The Code: Silicon Valley and the Remaking of America*. New York: Penguin Press, 2019.

Ostrow, Ronald J. "Legendary Litton: A Case for Entrepreneurs." *Los Angeles Times*, December 1, 1963.

Ott, Julia C. *When Wall Street Met Main Street: The Quest for an Investors' Democracy*. Cambridge, MA: Harvard University Press, 2011.

Pak, Susie J. *Gentlemen Bankers: The World of J. P. Morgan*. Cambridge, MA: Harvard University Press, 2013.

Paluszek, John L. "Business and Society: 1976–2000." AMA Survey Report, American Management Association, New York, 1976.

Passell, Peter. "How to Defuse the Buyout Bomb." *New York Times*, December 7, 1988.

Perlstein, Rick. *Nixonland: The Rise of a President and the Fracturing of America*. London: Scribner, 2009.

Petrou, Karen. "Only the Rich Could Love This Economic Recovery." *New York Times*, July 12, 2021, sec. Opinion. https://www.nytimes.com/interactive/2021/07/12/opinion/covid-fed-qe-inequality.html.

Phalon, Richard. "Picking Up Cast-Off Companies." *New York Times*, August 1, 1976.

Phillips, Matt. "Repeat After Me: The Markets Are Not the Economy." *New York Times*, May 10, 2020. https://www.nytimes.com/2020/05/10/business/stock-market-economy-coronavirus.html.

Phillips-Fein, Kim. *Fear City: New York's Fiscal Crisis and the Rise of Austerity Politics*. New York: Metropolitan Books, 2017.

Phillips-Fein, Kim. *Invisible Hands: The Businessmen's Crusade Against the New Deal*. New York: W. W. Norton, 2010.

Pierson, Paul, and Jacob S. Hacker. *Winner-Take-All Politics: How Washington Made the Rich Richer—and Turned Its Back on the Middle Class*. New York: Simon & Schuster, 2010.

Polsky, Gregg D. "Controlling Executive Compensation Through the Tax Code." *Washington & Lee Law Review* 64, no. 3 (2007): 877–926.

Porter, Frank C. "A Penn Central Director's View: '. . . Poor and Inept Management.'" *Washington Post*, June 26, 1970.

Porter, Michael E. "Capital Disadvantage: America's Failing Capital Investment System." *Harvard Business Review* 70, no. 5 (1992): 65–82.

Porter, Michael E. "From Competitive Advantage to Corporate Strategy." *Harvard Business Review* 65, no. 3 (1987): 43.

Prahalad, C. K., and Gary Hamel. "The Core Competence of the Corporation." *Harvard Business Review* 68, no. 3 (1990): 79–91.

Priem, Richard L., and Joseph Rosenstein. "Is Organization Theory Obvious to Practitioners? A Test of One Established Theory." *Organization Science* 11, no. 5 (2000): 509–24.

Prokesch, Steven E. "'People Trauma' in Mergers." *New York Times*, November 19, 1985.

Protess, Ben, and Ari Isaacman Bevacqua. "A Primer on Private Equity." *New York Times*, June 25, 2016, sec. Business. https://www.nytimes.com/2016/06/26/business/dealbook/what-is-private-equity.html.

Pulliam, Susan. "Paramount Is Targeted by Pension Fund Due to Weak Stock Price, Executive Pay." *Wall Street Journal*, March 4, 1993.

Purcell, Edward. *The Crisis of Democratic Theory: Scientific Naturalism and the Problem of Value.* Lexington: University Press of Kentucky, 1973.

Rappaport, Alfred. "CFOs and Strategists: Forging a Common Framework." *Harvard Business Review* 70, no. 3 (1992): 84–91.

Rappaport, Alfred. *Creating Shareholder Value: A Guide for Managers and Investors.* New York: Free Press, 1986.

Rappaport, Alfred. "The Economics of Short-Term Performance Obsession." *Financial Analysts Journal* 61, no. 3 (2005): 65–79.

Rappaport, Alfred. "How CEOs Can Forge a New Kind of Shareholder Value." Bloomberg.com, September 4, 2019. https://www.bloomberg.com/opinion/articles/2019-09-04/business-roundtable-statement-of-purpose-fails-on-specifics.

Ravenscraft, David J., and F. M. Scherer. *Mergers, Sell-Offs, and Economic Efficiency.* Washington, DC: Brookings Institution Press, 1987.

Read, Colin. *The Corporate Financiers: Williams, Modigliani, Miller, Coase, Williamson, Alchian, Demsetz, Jensen, Meckling.* Great Minds in Finance 5. Basingstoke, UK: Palgrave Macmillan, 2014.

Redwood, John. "Too Much Greed." *Baltimore Sun*, May 17, 1985.

Reich, Robert B. "Leveraged Buyouts: America Pays the Price." *New York Times Magazine*, January 29, 1989.

Reid, Samuel R. "A Reply to the Weston/Mansinghka Criticisms Dealing with Conglomerate Mergers." *Journal of Finance* 26, no. 4 (1971): 937–46.

Reilly, William, Charles McCurdy, and Beverly Chell. "KKR's Course Correction." *Fortune*, April 20, 1992.

Reimann, Bernard C. *Managing for Value: A Guide to Value-Based Strategic Management.* Oxford: Basil Blackwell, 1987.

Renneboog, Luc, Tomas Simons, and Mike Wright. "Why Do Public Firms Go Private in the UK? The Impact of Private Equity Investors, Incentive Realignment and Undervaluation." In "Private Equity, Leveraged Buyouts and Corporate Governance," special issue, ed. D. Cumming, M. C. Jensen, D. Siegel, and M. Wright, *Journal of Corporate Finance* 13, no. 4 (2007): 591–628.

Reuters. "Eisner Pay Is 68% of Profit." *New York Times*, April 16, 1994.
Risen, James. "Houdaille to Drop Machine Tools." *Los Angeles Times*, October 1, 1985.
Robards, Terry. "Issue Sold at $28 by Merrill Lynch." *New York Times*, June 24, 1971.
Rodgers, Daniel. *Age of Fracture*. Cambridge, MA: Harvard University Press, 2011.
Roe, Mark J. "Takeover Politics." In *The Deal Decade: What Takeovers and Leveraged Buyouts Mean for Corporate Governance*, edited by Margaret M. Blair, 321–53. Washington, DC: Brookings Institution Press, 1993.
Romell, Rick. "Workdays Shortened at Briggs & Stratton." *Milwaukee Sentinel*, September 17, 1993.
Romero, Simon, and Jonathan D. Glater. "WorldCom Files for Bankruptcy; Largest U.S. Case." *New York Times*, July 22, 2002.
Roosevelt, Franklin D. "Campaign Address on Progressive Government at the Commonwealth Club in San Francisco, California," September 23, 1932. Online by Gerhard Peters and John T. Woolley. The American Presidency Project. Accessed February 4, 2021. https://www.presidency.ucsb.edu/documents/campaign-address-progressive-government-the-commonwealth-club-san-francisco-california.
Rose, Nancy L., and Catherine Wolfram. "Regulating Executive Pay: Using the Tax Code to Influence Chief Executive Officer Compensation." *Journal of Labor Economics* 20, no. 2 (2002): 138–75.
Rosenbaum, David E. "Business Leaders Urged by Clinton to Back Tax Plan." *New York Times*, February 12, 1993.
Rosenbaum, David E. "Clinton Wins Approval of His Budget Plan as Gore Votes to Break Senate Deadlock." *New York Times*, August 7, 1993.
Rosenbaum, David E. "Corporate-Tax Shortfall in Dispute." *New York Times*, May 4, 1990.
Rosenberg, Howard. "Who Knew Greed Could Be So Fun?" *Los Angeles Times*, March 19, 1993.
Rosenblat, Robert A. "SEC Orders Disclosure of Executive Pay." *Los Angeles Times*, October 16, 1992.
Ross, Irwin. "How the Champs Do Leveraged Buyouts." *Fortune*, January 23, 1984.
Ross, Nancy L. "Veterans Chosen to Study SEC Merger Rules." *Washington Post*, March 1, 1983.
Rowe, James L. "Washington's Role in Takeovers Gaining." *Washington Post*, March 15, 1979.
Rowland, Mary. "Rare Bird: Stock Options for Many." *New York Times*, August 1, 1991.
Rubio, Marco. "American Investment in the 21st Century." Project for Strong Labor Markets and National Development, United States Senate, 2019. https://www.rubio.senate.gov/public/_cache/files/9f25139a-6039-465a-9cf1-feb5567ae

bb7/4526E9620A9A7DB74267ABEA5881022F.5.15.2019.-final-project-report-american-investment.pdf.

Rukeyser, William S. "Litton Down to Earth." *Fortune*, April 1968.

Salmans, Sandra. "Gulf's Defeat and Its Lessons." *New York Times*, March 10, 1984.

Salmans, Sandra. "Merger Advisers Under Fire: Wall St. Views Bendix Battle." *New York Times*, October 4, 1982.

Salmans, Sandra. "Tumultuous Takeover Saga Ends: Allied and Bendix Agree to Merge." *New York Times*, September 25, 1982.

Salmans, Sandra. "Whither Mergers in the Wake of Bendix?" *New York Times*, October 10, 1982.

Salsbury, Stephen. *No Way to Run a Railroad: The Untold Story of the Penn Central Crisis*. New York: McGraw-Hill, 1981.

Salter, Malcolm S., and Wolf A. Weinhold. "Choosing Compatible Acquisitions." *Harvard Business Review* 59, no. 1 (1981): 117–27.

Salter, Malcolm S., and Wolf A. Weinhold. "Diversification Via Acquisition: Creating Value." *Harvard Business Review* 56, no. 4 (1978): 166–76.

Sandler, Larry. "Much of Engine Work Moving Out of Area." *Milwaukee Sentinel*, May 18, 1994.

San Francisco Chronicle. "Silicon Valley Workers Protest Stock Options Ruling." March 26, 1994.

Sargent, Daniel J. *A Superpower Transformed: The Remaking of American Foreign Relations in the 1970s*. New York: Oxford University Press, 2017.

Schaffer, Michael. "Conservatives Are Having an Epic Argument About Capitalism. Too Bad the Campaigns Are Ignoring It." *Politico*, July 28, 2023. https://www.politico.com/news/magazine/2023/07/28/conservatives-capitalism-campaigns-00108594.

Scheibla, Shirley Hobbs. "Greenmail Debate Heats Up Behind the Scenes." *Barron's National Business and Financial Weekly*, September 3, 1984.

Schleef, Debra. *Managing Elites: Socialization in Law and Business Schools*. Lanham, MD: Rowman & Littlefield, 2005.

Schlessinger, Jacob M. "Americans Feel Rich Get Richer, New Poll Finds." *Wall Street Journal*, October 21, 1998.

Schneider, Susan C., and Roger L. M. Dunbar. "A Psychoanalytic Reading of Hostile Takeover Events." *Academy of Management Review* 17, no. 3 (1992): 537–67.

Schonberger, Ernest A. "Inside the Market: Can Litton Industries Recapture Old Magic?" *Los Angeles Times*, December 21, 1969.

Schumpeter, Joseph A. *Capitalism, Socialism, and Democracy*. 3rd ed. New York: Harper, 1950.

Schwab, Klaus, and Peter Vanham. *Stakeholder Capitalism: A Global Economy That Works for Progress, People and Planet*. Hoboken, NJ: Wiley, 2021.

Schwartz, Barry. "Psychology, Idea Technology, and Ideology." *Psychological Science* 8, no. 1 (1997): 21–27.

Sears, John Harold. *The New Place of the Stockholder.* New York: Harper & Brothers, 1929.
Securities and Exchange Commission. "Advisory Committee on Tender Offers Report of Recommendations." Washington, DC: Securities and Exchange Commission, July 8, 1983. https://www.sechistorical.org/collection/papers/1980/1983_0708_TenderRecommendations.pdf.
Sederberg, Arelo. "Litton Industries Moves into Nation Building." *Washington Post,* June 25, 1967.
Seeger, Murray. "Penn Central: Anatomy of an Ailing Railroad." *Los Angeles Times,* June 15, 1970.
Segal, Harvey H. "The Time of the Conglomerates." *New York Times Magazine,* October 27, 1968.
Serwer, Andrew Evan. "Payday! Payday! What CEOs Make." *Fortune,* June 14, 1993.
Serwer, Andrew Evan. "Cashing In on Cash Flow." *Fortune,* May 23, 1988.
Shanahan, Eileen. "Conglomerates: Data Lack Cited." *New York Times,* January 4, 1973.
Shanahan, Eileen. "U.S. Seeks Curb on Conglomerate in Antitrust Test." *New York Times,* March 24, 1969.
Sharma-Jensen, Geeta. "EVA Means More for All, Briggs President Says." *Milwaukee Journal Sentinel,* June 24, 1996.
Sheehan, Robert. "The Rich, Risky Life of a University Trustee." *Fortune,* January 1967.
Shifrin, Carole. "Eased Proof of Monopoly Is Urged." *Washington Post,* December 19, 1978.
Shiller, Robert J. *Irrational Exuberance.* 3rd ed. Princeton, NJ: Princeton University Press, 2016.
Shinder, Richard J. "The Business Roundtable's Recipe for Confusion." *Wall Street Journal,* September 17, 2019, sec. Opinion. https://www.wsj.com/articles/the-business-roundtables-recipe-for-confusion-11568760132.
Shiver, Jube, Jr. "Stock Options for Executives Threatened by Panel's Action." *Los Angeles Times,* April 8, 1993.
Shleifer, Andrei, and Lawrence H. Summers. "Breach of Trust in Hostile Takeovers." In *Corporate Takeovers: Causes and Consequences,* 33–67. Chicago: University of Chicago Press, 1988.
Shleifer, Andrei, and Robert W. Vishny. "The Takeover Wave of the 1980s." *Science* 249, no. 4970 (1990): 745–49.
Shoemaker, Perry M. "Should Railroads Diversify for Growth and Profits?" *Transportation Journal* (American Society of Transportation & Logistics, Inc.) 9, no. 1 (1969): 5–16.
Shorter, Gary W. "Leveraged Buyouts: Recent Trends." Washington, DC: Congressional Research Service, 1989.

Siconolfi, Michael. "Wall Street Is Upset by Clinton's Support on Ending Tax Break for 'Excessive' Pay." *Wall Street Journal*, October 21, 1992, sec. Money & Investing.

Sigler, Elaine. "Summer of '79." *Rochester Review*, 1979.

Skala, Martin. "Conglomerate Trend Fades." *Christian Science Monitor*, February 14, 1968.

Skala, Martin. "Monthly Report for Investors to Measure Fund Volatility." *Christian Science Monitor*, January 29, 1972.

Skidelsky, Robert. *Money and Government: The Past and Future of Economics*. New Haven, CT: Yale University Press, 2018.

Sklar, Martin J. *The Corporate Reconstruction of American Capitalism, 1890–1916*. Cambridge: Cambridge University Press, 1988.

Sloan, Allan. "KKR and the Big Leveraged Buyout: End of an Age." *Washington Post*, June 19, 1990.

Sloan, Allan. "Why Is No One Safe?," *Forbes*, March 11, 1985.

Sloane, Leonard. "John S. R. Shad Dies at 71; S.E.C. Chairman in the 80's." *New York Times*, July 9, 1994.

Smith, Randall. "Leveraged Buy-Out Funds Are High-Fliers No Longer." *Wall Street Journal*, May 24, 1990.

Smith, Randall, and Eben Shapiro. "KKR's Luster Dims as Fall in RJR Stock Hurts Investors' Take." *Wall Street Journal*, April 26, 1993.

Smith, Rebecca, and John R. Emshwiller. "Enron May Issue More Stock to Cover Obligations." *Wall Street Journal*, October 24, 2001.

Smith, Robert M. "Nader Group Urges the Federal Chartering of Big Corporations: Five Years in Preparation." *New York Times*, January 25, 1976.

Smith, Roy. *The Money Wars: The Rise and Fall of the Great Buyout Boom of the 1980s*. New York: Truman Talley Books, 1990.

Smith, William D. "Litton Acquisitions Questioned." *New York Times*, April 10, 1969.

Sorkin, Andrew Ross. "Blackstone Group Goes Public." *New York Times*, June 23, 2007.

Spector, Bert. "'Business Responsibilities in a Divided World': The Cold War Roots of the Corporate Social Responsibility Movement." *Enterprise and Society* 9, no. 2 (2008): 314–26.

Stangenes, Sharon. "Accounting Rule Under Fire." *Chicago Tribune*, April 14, 1993.

Stein, Jeff. "Bernie Sanders Backs 2 Policies to Dramatically Shift Corporate Power to U.S. Workers." *Washington Post*, May 28, 2019. https://www.washingtonpost.com/us-policy/2019/05/28/bernie-sanders-backs-policies-dramatically-shift-corporate-power-us-workers/.

Stein, Judith. *Pivotal Decade: How the United States Traded Factories for Finance in the Seventies*. New Haven, CT: Yale University Press, 2010.

Stein, Nicholas. "The World's Most Admired Companies." *Fortune*, October 2, 2000.

Steinmetz, Greg. "Kohlberg Kravis to Buy Shoppers Drug Mart for $1.74 Billion." *Wall Street Journal*, November 19, 1999.

Stern, Joel M. "Earnings Per Share Don't Count." *Financial Analysts Journal* 30, no. 4 (1974): 39–43, 67–75.

Stern, Joel M. "Let's Abandon Earnings per Share." *Wall Street Journal*, December 18, 1972.

Stern, Joel M., John S. Shiely, and Irwin Ross. *The EVA Challenge: Implementing Value-Added Change in an Organization*. New York: John Wiley & Sons, 2001.

Sterngold, James. "Buyout Pioneer Quitting Fray." *New York Times*, June 19, 1987.

Stewart, G. Bennett, III. *The Quest for Value: A Guide for Senior Managers*. New York: Harper Business, 1991.

Stewart, Matthew. "The Birth of a New American Aristocracy." *Atlantic Monthly*, June 2018.

Stewart, Thomas A., and Mark M. Colodny. "The Trouble with Stock Options." *Fortune*, January 1, 1990.

Stigler, George. "Modern Man and His Corporation." DeKalb AgResearch Business Lecture, Northern Illinois University, December 9, 1970.

Stiglitz, Joseph. "The Roaring Nineties." *Atlantic Monthly*, October 2002.

Stout, Lynn A. *The Shareholder Value Myth: How Putting Shareholders First Harms Investors, Corporations, and the Public*. San Francisco: Berrett-Koehler, 2012.

Stout, Lynn A. "On the Rise of Shareholder Primacy, Signs of Its Fall, and the Return of Managerialism (in the Closet)." *Seattle University Law Review* 36, no. 2 (2013): 1169–85.

Tankersley, Jim, and Andrew Duehren. "J. D. Vance Pioneered 'New Right' Economics. Trump May Not Embrace It." *New York Times*, August 2, 2024.

Taylor, William. "Crime? Greed? Big Ideas? What Were the '80s About?" *Harvard Business Review*, February 1, 1992.

Tedeschi, Ernie. "Unemployment Looks Like 2000 Again. But Wage Growth Doesn't." *New York Times*, October 22, 2018. https://www.nytimes.com/2018/10/22/upshot/mystery-slow-wage-growth-econony.html.

Teitelman, Robert. *Bloodsport: When Ruthless Dealmakers, Shrewd Ideologues, and Brawling Lawyers Toppled the Corporate Establishment*. New York: PublicAffairs, 2016.

Tenner, Edward. "The Mother of All Invention." *The Atlantic*, June 8, 2010. https://www.theatlantic.com/magazine/archive/2010/07/the-mother-of-all-invention/308123/.

Thomas, Michael M. "A Free Ride for Management Insiders." *New York Times*, January 22, 1984.

Thrift, Nigel. *Knowing Capitalism*. London: Sage Publications, 2008.

Time. "America the Inefficient." March 23, 1970.

Time. "An Appetite for the Future." October 4, 1963.

Time. "Back to Braces." July 18, 1983.

Time. "High Noon." September 20, 1982.
Time. "Litton Lesson." March 1, 1968.
Time. "Litton Takes Charge." June 23, 1967.
Time. "The Rising Risk of Recession." December 19, 1969.
Time. "U.S. Business: Out at the Ballpark." April 21, 1967.
Tolchin, Martin. "Democratic 'Gang of Five' Reflect New Party Priorities." *New York Times*, June 1, 1980.
Traflet, Janice M. *A Nation of Small Shareholders: Marketing Wall Street After World War II*. Baltimore: Johns Hopkins University Press, 2013.
Truell, Peter. "TI to Acquire Houdaille from Kohlberg." *Wall Street Journal*, August 26, 1987.
Tumulty, Karen. "CEO Pay Raises Rise to Level of Campaign Issue." *Los Angeles Times*, December 31, 1991.
Turner, Fred. *From Counterculture to Cyberculture: Stewart Brand, the Whole Earth Network, and the Rise of Digital Utopianism*. Chicago: University of Chicago Press, 2006.
Tyson, Laura D'Andrea. "Inequality Amid Prosperity." *Washington Post*, July 9, 1997.
Uchitelle, Louis. "A Surplus Built on Bricks of Income Inequality." *New York Times*, February 28, 1999.
Ungson, Gerardo Rivera, and Richard M. Steers. "Motivation and Politics in Executive Compensation." *Academy of Management Review* 9, no. 2 (1984): 313–23.
Useem, Michael. *Executive Defense: Shareholder Power and Corporate Reorganization*. Cambridge, MA: Harvard University Press, 1993.
Useem, Michael. *Investor Capitalism: How Money Managers Are Changing the Face of Corporate America*. New York: Basic Books, 1996.
Van der Zwan, Natasha. "Making Sense of Financialization." *Socio-Economic Review* 12 (2014): 99–129.
Vise, David A., and Steve Coll. *Eagle on the Street*. New York: Collier Books, 1992.
Vise, David A., and Steven Mufson. "Defaults Add to Burden of Buyouts." *Washington Post*, August 21, 1989.
Votaw, Dow, and S. Prakash Sethi. "Do We Need a New Corporate Response to a Changing Social Environment? Part I." *California Management Review* 12, no. 1 (Fall 1969): 3–16. https://doi.org/10.2307/41164199.
Wallace, Anise C. "All Dressed Up and 'No Place to Go?'" *New York Times*, August 7, 1988.
Wallace, Anise C. "Leveraged Buyout Leader Shifts Attention." *New York Times*, November 3, 1989.
Wall Street Journal. "Affluent Companies: Build-Up of Cash Makes Firms Less Dependent on Banks, Stock Issues." September 9, 1963.
Wall Street Journal. "'Conglomerate' Is a Rock, Say Men Who Dislike Word." July 25, 1968.

Wall Street Journal. "Conglomerates' Efficiency Called Overrated, But FTC Staff Finds Few Antitrust Signs." January 4, 1973.
Wall Street Journal. "Donaldson-Lufkin Moves to Allow Big Board Houses to Go Public, Plans to Sell 800,000 Common Shares." May 23, 1969.
Wall Street Journal. "Donaldson-Lufkin Shares Due for a Good Reception." April 9, 1970.
Wall Street Journal. "Houdaille Agrees to Be Purchased For $338.5 Million." March 7, 1979.
Wall Street Journal. "Houdaille Announces Financing Cleared in Planned Takeover." April 3, 1979.
Wall Street Journal. "House Won't Take Up Tender-Offer Measure." October 2, 1984.
Wall Street Journal. "Litton Division's Hotel Venture." July 24, 1972.
Wall Street Journal. "Litton Industries Says Net Will Fall Sharply in 2nd Fiscal Period." January 23, 1968.
Wall Street Journal. "Robust Economy and Buyout Boom Highlighted 1983." January 3, 1984.
Wall Street Journal. "SEC Panel Reunites Veterans of Bendix, Allied Takeover Fight." March 1, 1983.
Wall Street Journal. "Tender-Offer Legislation Is Cleared by House Panel." July 15, 1968.
Wall Street Journal "Washington Wire." Capital Bureau. June 22, 1984.
Warren, Elizabeth. "Companies Shouldn't Be Accountable Only to Shareholders." *Wall Street Journal*, August 14, 2018. https://www.wsj.com/articles/companies-shouldnt-be-accountable-only-to-shareholders-1534287687.
Wartzman, Rick. *End of Loyalty: The Rise and Fall of Good Jobs in America.* New York: PublicAffairs, 2017.
Wartzman, Rick. "Tax Package Gives Holders a Voice on Executive Pay." *Wall Street Journal*, April 9, 1993.
Washington Post. "Proxmire Hits Litton 'Payoff.'" May 4, 1969.
Waterhouse, Benjamin C. "The Corporate Mobilization Against Liberal Reform: Big Business Day, 1980." In *What's Good for Business: Business and American Politics Since World War II*, edited by Kim Phillips-Fein and Julian E. Zelizer, 233–48. New York: Oxford University Press, 2012.
Waterhouse, Benjamin C. *Lobbying America: The Politics of Business from Nixon to NAFTA.* Princeton, NJ: Princeton University Press, 2013.
Watson, George M., and Herman S. Wolk. "'Whiz Kid': Robert S. McNamara's World War II Service." *Air Power History* 50, no. 4 (2003): 4–15.
Wayne, Leslie. "Going Public on Wall Street." *New York Times*, January 27, 1986.
Weil, David. *The Fissured Workplace: Why Work Became So Bad for So Many and What Can Be Done to Improve It.* Cambridge, MA: Harvard University Press, 2014.

Wells, Harwell. "No Man Can Be Worth $1,000,000 a Year: The Fight over Executive Compensation in 1930s America." *University of Richmond Law Review* 44, no. 2 (2010): 689–770.

Wells, Wyatt. "Certificates and Computers: The Remaking of Wall Street, 1967 to 1971." *Business History Review* 74, no. 2 (2000): 193–235.

West, Darrell M. "The Purpose of the Corporation in Business and Law School Curricula." Governance Studies at Brookings. Brookings Institution, 2011. https://www.brookings.edu/research/the-purpose-of-the-corporation-in-business-and-law-school-curricula/.

Wild, Rolf H. *Management by Compulsion: The Corporate Urge to Grow*. Boston: Houghton Mifflin, 1978.

Williams, John D. "King of the Buyouts, Kohlberg Kravis Helps Alter Corporate U.S." *Wall Street Journal*, April 11, 1986.

Williams, Monci Jo. "Why Chief Executives' Pay Keeps Rising." *Fortune*, April 1, 1985.

Winchester, James H. "Litton Alters Financial Course." *Christian Science Monitor*, September 19, 1964.

Windham, Lane. *Knocking on Labor's Door: Union Organizing in the 1970s and the Roots of a New Economic Divide*. Chapel Hill: University of North Carolina Press, 2017.

Wines, Michael. "Bush Collapses at State Dinner with the Japanese." *New York Times*, January 9, 1992.

Winkler, Adam. *We the Corporations: How American Businesses Won Their Civil Rights*. New York: Liveright, 2018.

Winston, Andrew. "Is the Business Roundtable Statement Just Empty Rhetoric?" *Harvard Business Review*, August 30, 2019. https://hbr.org/2019/08/is-the-business-roundtable-statement-just-empty-rhetoric.

Wirpsa, Leslie. "Briggs & Stratton Layoffs Tear Family Hopes." *National Catholic Reporter*, December 2, 1994.

Witte, Pete, and Greg Brown. "A New Equilibrium: Private Equity's Growing Role in Capital Formation and the Critical Implications for Investors." Ernst and Young, October 2019. https://assets.ey.com/content/dam/ey-sites/ey-com/en_gl/topics/private-equity/private-equity-pdfs/ey-a-new-equilibrium-report.pdf?download.

Wright, Mike, Robert E. Hoskisson, and Lowell W. Busenitz. "Firm Rebirth: Buyouts as Facilitators of Strategic Growth and Entrepreneurship." *Academy of Management Executive* 15, no. 1 (2001): 111–25.

Wright, Robert A. "A Glimpse Behind the Scenes at Litton Industries." *New York Times*, March 22, 1968.

Wruck, Karen H., and Michael C. Jensen. "Coordination, Control, and the Management of Organizations: Course Content and Materials (3rd of 4 CCMO Documents)." SSRN Scholarly Paper. Social Science Research Network, April 20, 1998. https://papers.ssrn.com/abstract=77969.

Yang, Jia Lynn. "Maximizing Shareholder Value: The Goal That Changed Corporate America." *Washington Post*, August 26, 2013. https://www.washingtonpost.com/business/economy/maximizing-shareholder-value-the-goal-that-changed-corporate-america/2013/08/26/26e9ca8e-ed74-11e2-9008-61e94a7ea20d_story.html.

Yates, Ronald E. "Adding Up Arguments on CEO Pay." *Chicago Tribune*, March 3, 1996.

Yemma, John. "A Showdown at Gulf Oil over T. Boone Pickens's Breakup Plan." *Christian Science Monitor*, December 2, 1983.

Zahn, Max. "Households Plunged into Vicious Cycle of Debt as Interest Rates Soar." ABC News, February 3, 2023. https://abcnews.go.com/Business/households-plunge-debt-amid-inflation-high-interest-rates/story?id=96848731.

Zahra, Shaker A. "Corporate Entrepreneurship and Financial Performance: The Case of Management Leveraged Buyouts." *Journal of Business Venturing* 10, no. 3 (1995): 225–47.

Zaslow, Jeffrey. "How the Former Staff of Arthur Andersen Is Faring Two Years After Its Collapse." *Wall Street Journal*, April 8, 2004.

Zerofsky, Elisabeth. "How the American Right Fell in Love with Hungary." *New York Times Magazine*, October 19, 2021. https://www.nytimes.com/2021/10/19/magazine/viktor-orban-rod-dreher.html.

Zimmerman, Fred L. "Penn Central Officials Sold Stock as Carrier Was Nearing Disaster." *Wall Street Journal*, July 14, 1970.

Zuckerman, Mortimer B. "A Second American Century." *Foreign Affairs*, June 5, 1998.

Index

Page numbers in italics refer to figures.

Accounting Review Board (ARB), 155
accounting scandals, 154
affirmative action, 55, 60
AFL-CIO, 83, 97. *See also* labor unions
African Americans, 45; enfranchisement of, 55
Agee, William, 88
agency theory, 84, 94, 98, 101, 105, 175, 178
Aigner, Dennis, 149
Alchian, Armen, 58
American dream, 3; of economic opportunity and social mobility, 16
American Electronics Association (AEA), 163–65
American Express, 77–78
anti-capitalism: pro-redistribution politics on the political right as, 231n62; socially conservative populism as, 185. *See also* capitalism
antidiscrimination, 41, 55
antitrust laws, 12, 71; "Chicago School" of, 85, 93; congressional advocates of, 63, 77, 85; enforcement of, 35–36, 77, 85
Ash, Roy, 24–28, 31–32
Atwater, Bruce, 146

Baker, George P., *The New Financial Capitalists*, 108
Baldwin, Robert H. B., 69
Bank of America, 24, 169
Bank of International Settlements, 181
Barbarians at the Gate (book and made-for-TV movie), 118

Barth, Mary, 163
Baxter, William, 85
Bear Sterns, 109–10
Beatrice Companies, 120–21
behavioral economics, 104
Bell, Daniel, *The Coming of Post-Industrial Society*, 40
Bendix Corporation, 88
Bennet, Amanda, 153
Bentsen, Lloyd, 148, 161
Beresford, Dennis, 157–59, 163
Berkshire Hathaway, 158
Berle, Adolph, *The Modern Corporation and Private Property*, 11–13, 58, 123, 193n36
Besse, J. Carter, Jr., 165
Black, Fischer, 156
Black-Scholes model, 156–57, 160, 163–64, 225n111, 226n133
Boesky, Ivan, 86
Bork, Robert, 85
Boston Consulting Group, 136
Boxer, Barbara (senator), 162–63
Bradley, Bill (senator), 163
Bratton, William, 173
Breeden, Richard, 146–47
Bretton Woods system, 39
Briggs and Stratton, 133–36
brokerages: back-office crisis of the late 1960s for, 64–65; competition on price to attract investors' business among, 66; need for capital and consolidation of the industry of, 65–66; paperwork crisis

brokerages (cont.)
  on Wall Street that crippled the nation's leading, 36; as publicly traded companies, 65–66; stock, 85. See also Smith Barney
Brooks, John, 45, 98
Brown, Kathleen, 165
Brown, Ronald, 165
Brunner, Karl, 47, 53–58, 102–3; "Knowledge, Values, and the Choice of Economic Organization," 50–51
Buchanan, James, 54–55
Buchanan, Pat, 138
Buffet, Warren, 91, 97, 158
bull markets, 2, 16, 65, 81, 153. See also Wall Street
Bush, George H. W. (president), 137–38, 143, 147
Bush, George W. (president), 174
Business Roundtable, 1, 4, 16, 82–83, 97, 99, 139, 144, 146, 151, 159, 169, 183
buyouts: buyout market crash, 123, 127–28, 219n111; contradictory legacies of, 117–22; and corporate managers, 125–26, 130, 136; defense of, 218n69; divestiture, 117–18; emerging industry in, 107–8; "going private," 118, 124; hostile, 118, 121, 123, 128, 130; leveraged takeovers and, 92, 123; as major force in reshaping American capitalism, 109; "overheated" demand for, 122; profits from successful, 113–15; and publicly traded private equity firms, 129. See also leveraged buyouts (LBOs)

California, 151; Enron's manipulation of energy markets of, 171
capital, 27; and the consolidation of the brokerage industry, 65–66; corporate capital structure, 57, 64–65, 116; corporate cost of, 131–32, 134; corporate managers on cash flow and the cost of, 107, 134; corporate reliance on financial markets to obtain, 124–25, 131; corporate waste on financial transactions of, 78–79; cost for stocks of, 131–32; cost of debt, 132; cost of equity, 132, 220n139; equity funds and, 111–12; expenditures of, 72, 95; modern theory of, 98; pressures of popular democracy and protection of business and, 185; profit calculations and cost of, 132;

and raising economic productivity, 32; small companies lacking resources of management and, 26; and takeover practitioners, 81, 89; tax system that favors, 182; venture, 111, 151, 161, 165; Volcker on productive uses of, 79. See also capitalism; opportunity cost
capitalism: buyouts as major force in reshaping American, 109, 122; corporate commitments to a more inclusive, 2; and democracy, 41, 44, 61, 171; FASB's plan as the end of, 161; freedom, human behavior, and, 49–55; ideas about the corporation transforming American, 16; ills in the 1970s of, 57; managerial, 13–16, 18, 122, 185; shareholder value revolution as a transformational event in the history of American, 3–4, 8; social responsibility and, 13; stakeholder, 183, 185; stock options as a way to tie executive compensation to corporate performance as a foundation of American, 151–52; welfare, 12. See also anti-capitalism; capital; venture capitalists
Carter, Jimmy (president), 77, 206n75
Catholicism, 51
Cato Institute, 90
Celebrezze, Anthony, Jr., 91
Celler-Kefauver Act (1950), 18
CEO pay, 2, 137–53, 166; Clinton tax plan on, 147–50; concealment by firms of, 145; disclosure mandates for, 144–47; imposition of market discipline on, 138; incentive, 150; investors' opposition to high, 145, 159, 182; Japanese, 137; as major campaign issue, 144, 147; and managerial unaccountability, 146; as matching what other firms are paying their executives, 147; median grant-date compensation for CEOs in S&P 500 firms (1992–2001), 167; and performance, 142–45, 153; as set by an efficient managerial labor market, 142; stock options and, 150–54, 156–57; tax penalties for high, 144. See also executive compensation; executives
Chandler, Alfred, 18
Chicago Mercantile Exchange, 156
Chicago School, 40–41, 48, 85, 87, 91–93
Chrysler, 137
Cisco, 177

INDEX

Clinton, Bill (governor and president), 138–39, 141, 147–49, 165–66, 222n11
Coalition for American Equity Expansion (CAEE), 160–63
Cold War, 13, 41–42
Collingwood, Harris, 154
Columbia University, 46
conglomerates, 17–38, 71, 73, 125, 195n21; and cash cow businesses, 111; corporate raiders and, 82–96; downfall in the 1970s of, 40, 62, 109; LBOs as the preferred tool of investors and managers looking to break up, 106–7, 117–18, 128; mania in the 1960s of, 64, 75, 109, 118; recessions in the early 1980s and, 81; smaller businesses being spun off from large, 117, 168, 217n48; stock options and, 168; troubled, 114–17; widespread criticism of, 81–82. *See also* corporations
Congress, 25, 44, 66, 76–79, 82–85, 89–91, 97–99, 139, 141, 145, 149, 157, 166–67, 174; antitrust advocates in, 63; House Antitrust Subcommittee, 37; House Committee on Energy and Commerce, 96; House Ways and Means Committee, 149; lobbying of, 82, 160–61; restricted stock options as a special class of options created by, 155, 224n85. *See also* Democrats; Republicans
consumer rights, 41
corporate diversification. *See* conglomerates
corporate governance, 169, 173, 192n27; disputes regarding, 143; failures of, 173–74; pre–New Deal, 125; politics of, 146; purpose of, 146; reform of, 147. *See also* corporations
Corporate Pay Responsibility Act (1991), 146
corporate social responsibility (CSR), 31, 40–45, 84, 231n59; debate over, 42–45; defenders of, 58; expanded conception of, 42; Friedman on, 56–58; history of, 41, 61; managerial, 12–13, 31, 41; opponents of, 41; public's desire for, 59–60. *See also* corporations
corporations: "agency problem" in organization of, 58; capital structure of, 57, 64–65, 116; cost of capital for, 131–32, 134; eclipse of public, 106–36; and financial markets, 78–79, 124–25, 131; managers of, 154. *See also* conglomerates; corporate governance; corporate social responsibility (CSR); hostile takeovers
Coulter, David, 169
Council of Economic Advisors (CEA), 90, 164
Council of Institutional Investors, 146, 158–59, 163, 165
COVID-19 pandemic, 3, 181
Cox, Charles, 87, 90, 92, 94
Crystal, Graef, 140–41, 145, 151; "The Crystal Report" (newsletter), 141; *In Search of Excess* (book), 141
Cuomo, Mario (governor), 138

D'Amato, Alfonse (senator), 96–97
Davis, Gerald, 4, 192n12
deficit reduction, 149
democracy, 3; capitalistic, 44; criticisms of, 49, 59, 185; freedom and, 53–54; and market capitalism, 49; political project of protecting capitalism from, 61
Democrats, 39, 79, 96, 98, 143–47, 162, 165. *See also* Congress
Demsetz, Harold, 58
deregulation, 40, 90, 93, 98–99, 126, 171, 173, 229n1
derivatives market, 151, 156
Dimon, Jamie, 1
Dingell, John (representative), 96
Dodd, Christopher (senator), 146, 163
Dodd-Frank Act (2010), 108
dot-com bubble, 171–72
Drexel Burnham Lambert, 97, 119–20

earnings cult, 154, 177
Easterbrook, Frank, 89–90
Eastman Kodak, 46
economic growth, 14; lifetime employment as reliant on predictable and endless, 15; rush of technological advance and, 25; stock market and, 60, 181; stock options as responsible for, 151, 163; unlimited potential of globalization and technological innovation to deliver, 168. *See also* employment
Efficient Markets Hypothesis (EMH), 48, 95, 98, 156, 164, 177, 214n140, 230n31
Eicher, Douglas, 41
Eisner, Michael, 140, 148

Electro Dynamics Corporation, 25
employment: Democratic Party and Republican Party prioritizing fighting inflation over boosting, 39; economic features of the New Deal order such as lifetime, 15; growth in the nation's rate of, 179; public goods such as, 12; stock options and flexible practices of, 168. *See also* economic growth; unemployment
energy: corporate profits and the quadrupling of prices of, 39; Enron's manipulation of California's markets of, 171; high-tech financial trading and, 171; institutional investors in, 179
Enron scandal, 166, 171–77, 229n1, 229n10
environmentalism, 41, 55, 57, 60, 184
Environmental Protection Agency (EPA), 42–43, 55
EPS growth, 154
Equal Employment Opportunity Commission, 55
Equity Expansion Act (1993), 161–62
Erhard, Werner, 177–78
Erhard Seminars Training (EST), 177
ESB Inc., 68
executive compensation: Clinton tax plan including an exemption tied to corporate performance that targets, 148–49; political fight over, 44; reform regarding, 44, 144–47. *See also* CEO pay; executives; stock options
executives, 6, 9–11, 19–20; denunciation of shareholder primacy as a threat to the "American dream" by, 3; restructuring programs of the 1980s and 1990s as redefining success for, 7; and social responsibility programs, 44; in stock market bubbles, 20; as "value maximizing entrepreneurs," 143. *See also* CEO pay; executive compensation

Fama, Eugene, 48, 57
Federal Communications Commission, 78
Federal Reserve Board, 66, 79, 81, 180–81
Federal Trade Commission (FTC), 35, 37, 78
Feinstein, Diane (senator), 162
Financial Accounting Foundation, 150
Financial Accounting Standards Board (FASB), 139, 150–51, 155, 160–66

financial economics, 5–6, 16, 20–21, 38, 75, 84, 100, 105–7, 122, 125, 138, 164, 179, 207n3
Fligstein, Neil, 20
Flom, Joseph, 72
Ford, Henry, II, 24
Ford Motor Company, 24, 137
Fourcade, Marion, 47
fourth merger wave, 62–83, 107, 109, 118, 127
fraud: conglomerates' waste and, 16; Enron's elaborate, 172–76; large grants of stock options and managerial, 154; Litton's billing of the Pentagon as, 35; Milken's indictment on ninety-eight counts of racketeering and, 127; Penn Central's insider trading and, 37; shareholder value maximization and, 175–79; WorldCom's large-scale accounting, 174
Fred Meyer, Inc., 119, 217n66
Free Cash Flow (FCF), 95–96, 132, 212n91
freedom: the democratic process and the elimination of market, 42, 49; expansion of government and erosion of, 55–56; inefficient restrictions on, 55; Jensen and Meckling definition of, 53; property rights and the supposed violence of redistribution as basis for a theory of, 55
Friedman, Milton, 40–41; *Capitalism and Freedom*, 54; "The Social Responsibility of Business Is to Increase Its Profits," 56–58
Friedman, Steven, 72, 80
Fukuyama, Francis, *The End of History and the Last Man*, 171
Fuller, Joseph, "Just Say No to Wall Street: Putting a Stop to the Earnings Game," 176–77
fund managers, 66–67, 69, 175

Galbraith, John Kenneth, 53–54
Geismer, Lilly, 139
gender discrimination, 15, 40, 87
General Cable Corporation, 77
General Dynamics, 34
General Mills, 146
General Motors, 19, 68, 137
Gigot, Paul, 137–38
Ginsburg, Douglass, 93
Glass-Steagall Act (1935), 68
Goldberg, Arthur (Supreme Court justice), 89

INDEX

Goldman Sachs, 71–72, 80, 115, 148, 156
Gramm, Phil (senator), 163, 166
Graziano, Joseph, 165
Great Depression, 13, 62, 193n39
Green, Mark, 43; *Taming the Giant Corporation*, 43
Greenhill, Robert, 70–73
greenmail, 83, 94, 97, 209n51
growth-share matrix, 74–75, 74, 109, 205n58
Gulf Oil, 119–20

Hacker, Jacob, 99
Hagerty, Ken, 160–62, 166; "Why We Need Stock Option Reform," 160–61
Halpert, Stephen, 90
Hansen, Ronald, 47, 214n140
Hansmann, Henry, "The End of History for Corporate Law," 169, 171
Harris, David, 150
Harris Corporation, 146
Hartley, John, 146
Harvard Business School, 7, 24, 61, 70, 88, 100–105, 108, 142, 163, 184, 214n140; CCMO enrollment at, *102*, 230n31
Henderson, Bruce, 74–75, 205n58
Holmstrom, Bengt, 168
Holtzman, Elizabeth, 158
hostile takeovers, 29, 68, 70–72, 105; boom in, 61–64, 79–96, 106; defenses of, 84, 95, 98; return of, 75–80. *See also* corporations; leveraged buyouts (LBOs); takeover reform
Houdaille Industries, 114–18, 217n48
Huddart, Steven, 152
Hudson, Tom, 115
Hughes, Howard, 24
Hughes Aircraft, 24
Hyman, Louis, 20

Icahn, Carl, 6, 82, 84, 97, 118
inflation: erosion of wage gains by, 3; and fiscal relief (2020–21), 181; high rates of, 3, 39, 66, 72; merger markets dormant and the nation's economy in the grips of recession and, 37; Volcker's raising of interest rates and, 6, 79, 81. *See also* stagflation
institutional investors, 38, 66–69, 92, 97–99, 132–33, 138–40, 146–54, 173, 179, 182. *See also* Wall Street

273

Institutional Shareholder Partners, 145
Institutional Shareholder Services, 143, 162
integrity, 110, 178
Intel, 165
International Nickel Company of Canada (INCO), 68, 70–71
investment banks, 20, 24–25, 97, 109–10, 115, 148. *See also* Wall Street

Jackall, Robert, 10
Jacobs, Irwin, 91, 114
James, William, 103
Jameson, Hugh, 24–25
Jarrell, Gregg, 89–94, 98, 100, 105, 211n81, 212n86
Jensen, Michael, 48–49, 62, 67, 84, 98–109, 122–27, 133, 141–42, 149, 152–53, 214n140; "Between Freedom and Democracy," 54; "Can the Corporation Survive?," 59–61; "CEO Incentives—It's Not How Much You Pay, but How," 142–43; "Coordination, Control, and the Management of Organizations" (CCMO) (elective course), 101, 103–5; "The Eclipse of the Public Corporation," 124; *Freedom, Capitalism, and Human Behavior*, 52–53; "Just Say No to Wall Street: Putting a Stop to the Earnings Game," 176–77; "Takeovers: Folklore and Science," 94–95; "Theory of the Firm," 41–42, 56, 58–59, 141–42
Job Corps, 31–32
John Birch Society, 45
John Crane (company), 116
Johnson, Lyndon (president), 15; Job Corps of, 31–32; War on Poverty of, 31
J. P. Morgan & Co., 1, 68, 125, 204n28
Jung, Jiwook, 104–5
junk bond financing, 119–22, 218n73; crash in, 127; hyperactive market for, 97, 122. *See also* Milken, Michael

Kaplan, Robert, 168
Kaplan, Steven, 122
Kennedy, Edward (senator), 77
Kennedy, John F. (president), 15
Keynesian economics, 14, 39–40
Khurana, Rakesh, 47
Kochin, Lecis, 54
Kohlberg, Jerome, 109–11, 114, 121–22, 128–30, 133, 216n16

INDEX

Kohlberg, Kravis, Roberts (KKR), 108–23, 128–30, 216n21, 218n85, 219n123, 230n26
Koller, Tim, *Valuation: Measuring and Managing the Value of Companies*, 136
Kraakman, Reinier, "The End of History for Corporate Law," 169, 171
Kravis, Henry, 110

labor unions, 13, 82–83, 90. *See also* AFL-CIO
Lang, Mark, 152
law: antitrust, 77, 85; equal employment, 55; executive pay reform, 145–47; redistributive, 54; state anti-takeover, 79, 82–83, 91, 98–99; tax and regulatory treatment of stock options improvement, 160–61
Lazard Freres, 72, 148
Lazarus, Charles, 165
Lehman Brothers, 24–25
Leisenring, James, 157, 163
Lemann, Nicholas, 176
leveraged buyouts (LBOs), 106–14, 117–30, 134, 138, 176, 219n105, 219n123, 230n26. *See also* buyouts; hostile takeovers
Levin, Carl (senator), 145–46, 151, 163, 165–66
Levitt, Arthur, 161, 166
liberalization: deregulation and economic, 40, 99; economic, 99, 173; global capital flows and, 6
Lieberman, Joseph (senator), 162–63, 165–66
Lipton, Martin, 72, 76, 90–92, 205n52
Litton, Charles, 25
Litton Industries, 17, 19, 21–37, 176
Livingstone, Jane, 150
Lovett, Robert, 23–24

Mack, Connie (senator), 162–63
management consultants, 4–8, 16, 20, 131–38, 181–83; and corporate takeovers, 61, 84; reform-minded, 20; shareholder value, 142, 154
Marcus, Bernie, 164
Marquis, Christopher, 104
Martin Marietta (company), 88
Marxism, 51
McGraw-Hill, 77
McKinsey & Co., 136
McLain, Bethany, "Is Enron Overpriced?," 172

McLaren, Richard, 35
McNamara, Robert, 24, 196n34
Means, Gardiner, *The Modern Corporation and Private Property*, 11–13, 58, 123, 193n36
Meckling, William H., 47, 54, 62, 102–3, 214n140; "Between Freedom and Democracy," 54; "Can the Corporation Survive?," 59–61; "Coordination, Control, and the Management of Organizations" (CCMO) (elective course), 101, 103; *Freedom, Capitalism, and Human Behavior*, 52–53; "Theory of the Firm," 41–42, 56, 58–59, 141–42
media, 3, 5, 10, 53; commentators in the, 16, 19, 22, 32, 35, 42, 84; critics and admirers of corporate raiders and shareholder value theorists in the, 63, 82, 87–88; discussions on executive pay in the, 141–42; investigations of companies' financial statements in the, 171, 174
Merrill Lynch, 65
Metrick, Andrew, 113
Microdot Incorporated, 77
Milken, Michael, 86, 97, 119–22, 127, 218n73. *See also* junk bond financing
Miller, James, 85, 99
Miller, Merton, 164
Minnow, Neil, 143, 145
Miyazawa, Kiichi (prime minister), 137
Monitor Group, 176
Monks, Robert A. G., 145
Moore, Gordon, 165
Morgan, James, 165
Morgan Stanley, 68–71
Munger, Charles, 91
Murphy, Kevin, 141–42, 149, 153; "CEO Incentives—It's Not How Much You Pay, but How," 142–43

Nader, Ralph, 41–43, 199n22; *Taming the Giant Corporation*, 43
National Association of Manufacturers (NAM), 82–83, 91, 97, 99, 146–47, 149, 163
National Economic Council, 148
National Venture Capital Association, 159, 163, 165
New Deal, 13–16, 62; conservative counterattack on the, 185

INDEX

New Left, 51
New York Stock Exchange (NYSE), 64–65, 97
Niskanen, William, 90, 93, 98
Nixon, Richard (president), 35, 39, 47
Nortel, 177

Occupational Safety and Health Administration (OSHA), 42–43, 60
Occupy Wall Street movement, 185. *See also* political movements
Ofek, Eli, 152
OPEC oil embargo (1973), 39
opportunity cost, 111, 131–32, 156. *See also* capital
O'Reilly, Anthony J. F., 141, 217n48

Penn Central Railroad, 36–37, 176
Perella, Joseph, 72
Perelman, Ronald, 82
Performance Share Agreements (PSAs), 161–62
Performance Share Options (PSOs), 162
personal responsibility, 49, 53–54, 201n80
Phillips Petroleum, 97, 212n102
Pickens, T. Boone, 6–7, 82, 84, 88, 94–97, 106, 109, 118–20, 133
Pierson, Paul, 99
political movements: anti-shareholder value, 185; conservative backlash to rights-oriented, 54. *See also* Occupy Wall Street movement
Poole, William, 98
populism, 84, 133, 143, 162, 182; and high CEO pay, 138; socially conservative anticapitalist, 185
poverty: and international development, 31; reduction of, 57; as social problem beyond the business sector, 22; sociological understanding of mankind and, 53
private equity industry, 107, 110, 113, 123, 129, 220n128, 220n129
productivity, 28, 32, 95, 102, 126, 137–38, 161, 178
Proxmire, William (senator), 35, 77
Prudential Insurance, 119

quantitative easing (QE), 180–81
Quayle, Dan (vice president), 138, 141
Quinn, Linda, 145–46

racial discrimination, 40, 180; gender discrimination and, 15, 87; in mortgage lending, 55
Raychem, 161
Reagan, Ronald (president), 6, 63, 84–86, 89–92, 98–99, 185, 208n21
Reagan Revolution, 81–105
recapitalization, 116–17
recession, 16, 36, 67, 79, 81, 92, 116, 168; and buyout financing, 127; high CEO pay and, 137–38; inflation and, 37; job creation and, 147; OPEC oil embargo and, 39
Regan, Donald, 65, 93
Reich, Robert, 148
REMM (Resourceful, Evaluating, Maximizing Man), 49, 51–52, 56, 58, 102–4, 178
rent control, 60, 103
Republicans, 39, 85, 97–98, 144. *See also* Congress
Reuss, Henry (representative), 77–78
Roberts, George, 108, 110, 121, 128–30
Robson, John, 158–59
Rodino, Peter (representative), 90
Rohatyn, Felix, 72, 80, 91, 97
Roosevelt, Franklin (president), 11, 13, 174, 185, 193n47
Rubel, John, 31
Rubin, Robert, 148
Rubio, Marco (senator), 183, 231n56, 231n59
Russian invasion of Ukraine, 181

Sanders, Bernie (senator), 183, 185
Sarbanes-Oxley Act (2002), 174
Scholes, Myron, 156
Schwab, Charles, 130
scientific economics, 49, 51
Second World War, 24, 39–40, 46, 66–67, 182, 193n39
Securities Act (1934), 144
Securities and Exchange Commission (SEC), 66, 76, 78, 85–98, 108, 127, 145–47, 150
Seligman, Joel, 43; *Taming the Giant Corporation*, 43
Shad, John S. R., 85–94, 96, 99, 121, 211n81
shareholder primacy, 1, 3, 105, 183–84. *See also* shareholder value maximization
shareholder value maximization, 9–10, 99, 146, 178, 181–84; critics of, 3–4, 170; in MBA curricula, 105; opponents of, 183; as sole purpose of corporate management,

shareholder value maximization (*cont.*) 21; triumph of, 169. *See also* shareholder primacy
shareholder value revolution, 4, 10–11, 16–17, 105, 123, 176–80, 184–85
shareholder value theory, 5–6, 63–64, 105, 144, 154, 169, 182
Shiely, John, 134; *The EVA Challenge*, 135
Shin, Taekjin, 104–5
Siegel, Martin, 72
Silicon Valley: entrepreneurial culture of, 165; history of the tech sector in, 221n8; "new economy" firms of, 139; showdown in, 157–66. *See also* technology
Smith, George David, *The New Financial Capitalists*, 108
Smith Barney, 119. *See also* brokerages
socialism, 56–57
Sommer, A. A., 92
Soviet Union, 13
Special Purpose Entities (SPEs), 172
Specter, Arlen (senator), 90, 212n100
stagflation, 6, 39; effects of the conglomerate crash and, 62, 114. *See also* inflation
Standard Oil, 120
statistical control, 23–24, 27–28
Stein, Jeremy, 122
Stern, Joel, 6; *The EVA Challenge*, 135
Stiglitz, Joseph, 163
stock market. *See* stocks
stock options: as capital gains transaction, 155; as CEO pay, 150–54, 156–57; complexity of, 151; expensing of, 151, 155, 228n169; governmental endorsement of, 150; "intrinsic value" of, 155; minimal holding period of, 151; money for CEOs and shareholders in the form of, 143; SEC requiring firms to report the value in their proxy statements of executives', 147; trouble with, 150–57; unindexed, 156; unrestricted, 155–56, 224n85. *See also* executive compensation; stocks
stocks: cost of capital for, 131–32; prices of, 143, 181; restricted grants of, 228n169; wealth generated by rising prices of, 180. *See also* stock options
Stouffer Foods, 30–31
Stout, Lynn, 170
Supreme Court, 81, 87, 127, 155
Svenska Dataregistrar, 26

Swope, Gerald, 12
synergy, 27, 30

takeover reform, 84–96. *See also* hostile takeovers
tax: capital gains, 113; Clinton's compensation, 147–50; and regulatory treatment of stock options improvement, 160–61; special class of stock options at capital gains rates of, 224n85
technology: economic sector of, 144, 151, 222n11; unlimited potential of globalization and innovation in, 168. *See also* Silicon Valley
tender offer reform, 96–100
third merger wave, 17–18, 36–37, 62, 76
Thomson Financial / First Call, 154
Thornton, Charles "Tex", 23–28, 30, 196n31
TI Group, 116
Tilcsik, András, 104
trade deficit, 39
Trump, Donald, 121

unemployment: social problems beyond the business sector such as, 22; "weapons system" approach to the problem of, 31. *See also* employment
United Aircraft, 71
United Nations, 45
United Shareholders Association, 143, 146
University of Rochester, 45–61, 89, 101, 103–4, 142

venture capitalists, 111, 151, 161, 165. *See also* capitalism
Volcker, Paul, 6, 79

Wallis, Allen, 46–47, 54–55
Wall Street, 6, 8, 25, 36, 62–72, 86, 91, 110, 117–19, 125, 148, 151–56, 164, 172, 177, 179. *See also* bull markets; institutional investors; investment banks
Wall Street Rule, 67
War on Poverty, 31
Warren, Elizabeth (senator), 183, 185
Wasserstein, Bruce, 72, 79
Watts, Ross, 47
Whitworth, Ralph, 143, 145
Williams, Harold, 78–79, 85–86
Williams Act (1968), 76, 78, 87–88

Wilson, Joseph C., 45–46
Wirth, Timothy (representative), 90–93, 96–99
working classes, 10, 64, 149, 168, 179–80, 191n4
WorldCom, 174
World War II. *See* Second World War

Xerox, 45–46

Yasuda, Ayako, 113
Yermack, David, 152
Young, Owen, 12

Zuckerman, Mortimer, 168

www.ingramcontent.com/pod-product-compliance
Ingram Content Group UK Ltd.
Pitfield, Milton Keynes, MK11 3LW, UK
UKHW041037200925
463070UK00001B/5/J